MW01043039

Womanist and Mujerista Psychologies

PSYCHOLOGY OF WOMEN BOOK SERIES

Bringing Cultural Diversity to Feminist Psychology: Theory, Research, and Practice
Edited by Hope Landrine

The New Civil War: The Psychology, Culture, and Politics of Abortion
Edited by Linda J. Beckman and S. Marie Harvey

Shaping the Future of Feminist Psychology: Education, Research, and Practice
Edited by Judith Worell and Norine G. Johnson

Sexuality, Society, and Feminism
Edited by Cheryl Brown Travis and Jacquelyn W. White

Practicing Feminist Ethics in Psychology
Edited by Mary M. Brabeck

Relationships Among Asian American Women
Edited by Jean Lau Chin

Feminist Family Therapy: Empowerment in Social Context
Edited by Louise B. Silverstein and Thelma Jean Goodrich

Featuring Females: Feminist Analyses of Media
Edited by Ellen Cole and Jessica Henderson Daniel

Psychology and Economic Injustice: Personal, Professional, and Political Intersections
Bernice Lott and Heather E. Bullock

Listening to Battered Women: A Survivor-Centered Approach to Advocacy, Mental Health, and Justice
Lisa A. Goodman and Deborah Epstein

The Glass Ceiling in the 21st Century: Understanding Barriers to Gender Equality
Edited by Manuela Barreto, Michelle K. Ryan, and Michael T. Schmitt

Talking About Sexual Assault: Society's Response to Survivors
Sarah E. Ullman

Psychological Practice With Women: Guidelines, Diversity, Empowerment
Edited by Carolyn Zerbe Enns, Joy K. Rice, and Roberta L. Nutt

Womanist and Mujerista Psychologies: Voices of Fire, Acts of Courage
Edited by Thema Bryant-Davis and Lillian Comas-Díaz

Womanist and Mujerista Psychologies

VOICES OF FIRE, ACTS OF COURAGE

Edited by
Thema Bryant-Davis and
Lillian Comas-Díaz

American Psychological Association
Washington, DC

Published by
American Psychological Association
750 First Street, NE
Washington, DC 20002
www.apa.org

To order
APA Order Department
P.O. Box 92984
Washington, DC 20090-2984
Tel: (800) 374-2721; Direct: (202) 336-5510
Fax: (202) 336-5502; TDD/TTY: (202) 336-6123
Online: www.apa.org/pubs/books
E-mail: order@apa.org

In the U.K., Europe, Africa, and the Middle East, copies may be ordered from
American Psychological Association
3 Henrietta Street
Covent Garden, London
WC2E 8LU England

Typeset in Goudy by Circle Graphics, Inc., Columbia, MD

Printer: United Book Press, Inc., Baltimore, MD
Cover Designer: Minker Design, Sarasota, FL

Library of Congress Cataloging-in-Publication Data

Names: Bryant-Davis, Thema, editor. | Comas-Díaz, Lillian, editor.
Title: Womanist and mujerista psychologies : voices of fire, acts of courage / edited by Thema Bryant-Davis and Lillian Comas-Díaz.
Description: Washington, DC : American Psychological Association, [2016] | Series: Psychology of women | Includes bibliographical references and index.
Identifiers: LCCN 2015046302 | ISBN 9781433822117 | ISBN 1433822113
Subjects: LCSH: Feminist psychology. | Minority women—Psychology. | Women—Psychology.
Classification: LCC BF201.4 .W646 2016 | DDC 155.3/33—dc23 LC record available at http://lccn.loc.gov/2015046302

British Library Cataloguing-in-Publication Data
A CIP record is available from the British Library.

Printed in the United States of America
First Edition

http://dx.doi.org/10.1037/14937-000

I would like to dedicate this book to the person who introduced me to womanism, my mother Rev. Cecelia Williams Bryant. I am reminded of her words and work as a womanist theologian, particularly when she stated, "God is speaking. My life is God's vocabulary."

I also dedicate this book to my daughter Ife Davis, an emerging womanist artist and scholar who at the age of 10 inspires me daily.

—*Thema Bryant-Davis*

I dedicate this book to Antonia Morales Díaz and to María Emperatriz Díaz Comas, two mujeristas who shaped my life, and to my goddaughters Antonia Comas-Soares, and Isabel Comas-Soares, who have enriched it.

—*Lillian Comas-Díaz*

CONTENTS

CONTRIBUTORS

Tyonna Adams, MA, Psychology Division, Pepperdine University, Los Angeles, CA

Darcy Alcántara, MA, Psychology Department, University of Massachusetts Boston

Martha E. Banks, PhD, ABackans DCP, Inc., Akron, OH

Linda J. Beckman, PhD, California School of Professional Psychology, Alliant International University, Alhambra

Thema Bryant-Davis, PhD, Graduate School of Education and Psychology, Pepperdine University, Los Angeles, CA

Carrie L. Castañeda-Sound, PhD, Graduate School of Education and Psychology, Pepperdine University, Los Angeles, CA

Jeanett Castellanos, PhD, School of Social Sciences, University of California, Irvine

Lillian Comas-Díaz, PhD, Transcultural Mental Health Institute, Washington, DC, and Department of Psychiatry and Behavioral Sciences, George Washington University, Washington, DC

Danielle Drake-Burnette, MA, School of Psychology, Fielding Graduate University, Santa Barbara, CA

Josefina E. Durán, BS, Counterparts, Inc., Phoenix, AZ
BraVada Garrett-Akinsanya, PhD, LP, private practice, Brakins Consulting & Psychological Services, LLC, Golden Valley, MN
Alberta M. Gloria, PhD, Department of Counseling Psychology, University of Wisconsin–Madison
Stephanie Lee, MDiv, MACE, Christ United Methodist Church, Alliance, OH
Susana Martinez, PsyD, Counseling Services, University of Texas at San Antonio
Ana Paulina Moreno, MEd, Department of Education, University of California, Santa Cruz
Kysa Nygreen, PhD, Teacher Education and Curriculum Studies, College of Education, University of Massachusetts Amherst
Mariella Saba, BA, Departments of Literature, Creative Writing, and Theater Arts, University of California, Santa Cruz
Janis V. Sanchez-Hucles, PhD, Professor Emerita, Department of Psychology, Old Dominion University, Norfolk, VA
Ester Shapiro, PhD, Psychology Department, University of Massachusetts Boston
Melba J. T. Vasquez, PhD, ABPP, independent practice, Austin, TX
Karen Fraser Wyche, PhD, School of Nursing, George Washington University, Washington, DC

SERIES FOREWORD

Contemporary women continue to face oppressions and challenges, such as poverty, racism, violence and abuse, physical and mental health disparities, ageism, and of course sexism, to name just a few. By applying multiple alternative feminist lenses to these issues, researchers can better understand them. More important, they can identify and promote interventions and solutions that improve women's status in society and advance social justice. The Society for the Psychology of Women (Division 35) book series of the American Psychological Association is dedicated to supporting and disseminating feminist scholarship on education, research, and practice that can contribute to advocacy and social activism on behalf of women and other disempowered groups. This mission reflects a primary principle of feminist psychology: the application of knowledge through action.

Whereas feminism and the psychology of women began with emphasis on White, middle-class women, this book series examines the diversity of women's experiences. It recognizes that women have multiple intersecting identities that include race, ethnicity, gender, sexual orientation, nationality, socioeconomic status, religion, ability, and age. The series highlights not only demographic trends in the United States but also the interplay between national and global concerns. Specific objectives are to synthesize, integrate, and apply empirical knowledge and clinical perspectives for underrepresented women, women who have been previously ignored in research and clinical application. We seek to extend psychological theory on women and gender so that it includes *all* groups of women.

This book on womanist and mujerista psychologies epitomizes the values and major objectives of the book series. Its editors have skillfully interwoven the different, yet often overlapping viewpoints of womanist African American psychologists and mujerista Latina psychologists. Both psychologies owe much to other disciplines, such as theology, cultural studies, and sociology. However, the book takes a decidedly psychological approach, examining the cognitions, affect, behavior, learning, and development of African American and Latina women and girls, as well as the risks and trauma they very frequently experience and the cultural strengths that can help them gain fulfillment and empowerment. Particularly emphasized are the roles of spirituality, resistance, inclusivity, intersectionality of social identities, social activism, and the art of healing. It is noteworthy that the editors and authors are themselves African American womanists and Latina mujeristas whose writing is based on both the scholarly literature (including what is known about the lived experiences of women of color) and their personal lived experiences. Their lived experiences have influenced the questions that they ask and the methods they use to attempt to answer these questions.

All of the book's sections except the last consist of two chapters on the same topic (e.g., research) from the overlapping perspectives of the two psychologies. This juxtaposition is both fascinating and synergetic. Although the differing approaches of chapters may in part be attributed to the unique backgrounds and characteristics of the individual authors, they also reflect differences in the two psychologies, including differences in theoretical perspectives, historical roots of activism, therapeutic approaches, and so on. Both psychologies differ from dominant "White" feminism in their emphasis on the centrality of spirituality, creativity, and a collective approach to family, community, and global connections.

This groundbreaking book is the first to my knowledge to consolidate multiple aspects of the psychologies of both Latina and African American women, including theory, research, and practice. It not only extends the field of feminist psychology but also promotes new paradigms for psychology that incorporate the global diversity of thought and culture. I hope that these new psychologies, with their inherent activist bases, can enhance diverse individuals' ability to overcome oppression and to live satisfying, empowered lives.

—Linda J. Beckman
Division 35 Book Series Editor

ACKNOWLEDGMENTS

There are many persons who have been a gift to this project. We are grateful for all of those who have come to walk alongside us with full hearts to the completed book you are now holding. We would like to particularly extend gratitude to the following people:

Linda Beckman, the series editor for Division 35 books, and Susan Reynolds, senior acquisitions editor of APA Books, both of whom were strong supporters of our topic and vision from the beginning.

The contributors, who brought to this project their knowledge, hearts, and experiences which together have enriched their chapters with great depth and spirit.

Our reviewers, Shelly Harrell and Linda Beckman, who gave us an in-depth read and thoughtful revisions that assisted us in bringing greater clarity and cohesion to this expansive project.

Beth Hatch, development editor, APA Books, who worked tirelessly and patiently to assist us in the development process.

The full team of APA Books who worked with us, namely, Joseph Attanasio and Ron Teeter, who were generous with their time and consideration.

We would like to acknowledge our womanist and mujerista academic foremothers who laid the groundwork for this project. Specifically we celebrate the life and legacy of Alice Walker, who coined the term womanist, and Ada M. Isai-Díaz, who coined the term mujerista.

I (Thema Bryant-Davis) would also like to publicly acknowledge my coeditor, Lillian Comas-Díaz, who had the idea for this great project. I am honored that she invited me to take this journey with her and am so glad to count her not only as an esteemed colleague but as a sister.

I (Lillian Comas-Díaz) would like to acknowledge my inspiring coeditor, Thema Bryant-Davis, my *hermana del alma*, for accompanying me in this wondrous journey.

Womanist and Mujerista Psychologies

INTRODUCTION: WOMANIST AND MUJERISTA PSYCHOLOGIES

THEMA BRYANT-DAVIS AND LILLIAN COMAS-DÍAZ

You may trod me in the very dirt, but still, like dust, I'll rise.
—Maya Angelou (African American poet)

They tried to bury us. They didn't know we were seeds.
—Mexican Proverb

The psychology of African American women and Latinas is rich and complex, encompassing self-expression, creativity, nuanced gender roles, spirituality, community and family orientation, resistance, and resilience. We are women who bring healing, wholeness, and restoration to ourselves and our communities. The growing literature on our experiences, affect, cognitions, and agency includes narratives of survival, struggle, and soaring. Although we live with great risk economically, psychologically, socially, and politically, we also employ noteworthy ways of coping, growing, and thriving. As opposed to much general psychology literature that pathologizes or marginalizes our experiences, this work centralizes our psyches and unpacks the underexplored areas of our historical and contemporary ways of knowing and approaches to living. The value of the cultural and gender identity of African American women and Latinas must not be narrowly viewed from a deficit perspective but instead as an asset and contributor to meaning, identity, and strengths.

http://dx.doi.org/10.1037/14937-001
Womanist and Mujerista Psychologies: Voices of Fire, Acts of Courage, T. Bryant-Davis and L. Comas-Díaz (Editors)

Psychologists, personally and through their professionally directed efforts of advocacy, counseling, teaching, research, and consultation, are in a unique position to promote equity and social justice (Comas-Díaz, 2000). The American Psychological Association (APA) has promoted a number of key priorities that have assisted in laying the groundwork for this work. APA's *Guidelines on Multicultural Education, Training, Research, Practice and Organization* (American Psychological Association, 2002) state that race and ethnicity must be understood in concert with other identity markers, such as gender, socioeconomic status, sexual orientation, migration status, disability, and spirituality/religious identity. In the APA (2010) *Ethical Principles of Psychologists and Code of Conduct*, the organization noted,

> Where scientific or professional knowledge in the discipline of psychology establishes that an understanding of factors associated with age, gender, gender identity, race, ethnicity, culture, national origin, religion, sexual orientation, disability, language or socioeconomic status is essential for effective implementation of their services or research, psychologists have or obtain the training, experience, consultation or supervision necessary to ensure the competence of their services, or they make appropriate referrals. (p. 4)

This underscores the need for education regarding the psychology of African American women and Latinas. It is unethical to ignore these factors, and doing so can be clinically damaging. The Ethics Code states clearly that psychologists are to take steps to avoid doing harm to their clients. Specifically,

> Psychologists do not knowingly engage in behavior that is harassing or demeaning to persons with whom they interact in their work based on factors such as those persons' age, gender, gender identity, race, ethnicity, culture, national origin, religion, sexual orientation, disability, language or socioeconomic status. (p. 5)

APA (2001) also adopted a resolution to counter the prevalence and consequences of racism, oppression, discrimination, religious intolerance, and xenophobia, including the specific manifestations of these violations on women. These guidelines and resolutions clearly articulate the mandate for the field of psychology to be open to the multiple, layered, complex, intersecting identities of all peoples.

AIM AND AUDIENCE

The aim of this book is to provide an overview of two emerging and intersecting psychological frameworks: womanist psychology and *mujerista* psychology. As with the sociological study of womanism and *mujerismo*, it is important to note that although in name these theories may be early in development, in praxis they are long-standing, often overlooked realities of numerous racially and ethnically marginalized women. This text explores the interdisciplinary foundations of these psychologies, the state of the current literature on each, and the needs for future development. We, the editors of this volume, hope that this work provokes new thought in these areas that will result in innovative, nuanced, and life-enhancing theories and interventions. The intended audience is primarily psychologists and psychology students of diverse backgrounds who are committed to developing an inclusive, ethical, and culturally congruent approach to their understanding and application of psychology. The second and equally important audience is ethnically diverse women, African American and Latina women nonpsychologists in particular, who are interested in this work for either personal edification or scholarship in fields outside of psychology.

This book is the first psychology text to centralize the psychology of African American women and Latinas from theory to practice. We chose to examine womanist and mujerista psychologies together for three primary reasons: (a) They have similar priorities and overlapping focus areas; (b) they face common comparable intersections of oppression while having a history of adopting cultural strengths to navigate and resist those oppressive forces; and (c) the joint scholarly effort undertaken to produce this book mirrors the value of collaboration and sisterhood that are critical aspects of both psychologies. In approaching this work, we adopted the perspective of womanism and mujerismo, which are defined more fully below. Womanism and mujerismo branched out of theology and cultural studies to reach psychology's bastion. This volume articulates the womanist and mujerista psychologies by first grounding the reader in an understanding of womanist and mujerista sociological thought, then expanding that thought to psychological science and practice.

It is important to note that the identity of the editors and authors are African-descendant womanists and Latina mujeristas. Although all scholars can contribute to the study of African American women and Latinas, scholars writing from both the basis of the literature as well as their lived experience are valuable. Recognizing the value of lived experience counters the false notion of objectivity and instead embraces the reality that the scholar both influences and is influenced by his or her scholarship.

DEFINITION OF WOMANISM

The term *womanist* was coined by Walker (1983): "a Black feminist or feminist of color committed to the survival and wholeness of entire people, male and female. Not a separatist, except periodically for health" (p. xi). In other words, in addition to centralizing survival and wholeness of women and men, a womanist does not create a hierarchy between the fights against racism and sexism but sees both of these fights as necessary and central. Womanism is a sociopolitical framework that centralizes race, gender, class, and sexuality as central markers of women's lived experiences (Brown-Douglas, 1993). It moves beyond the compartmentalizing of Black women's experience as is often seen in feminism and multiculturalism and moves toward an integrated perspective and analysis. The womanist perspective maintains that addressing racism, ethnocentrism, and poverty is equally important as addressing gender issues, such as sexism (Henley, Meng, O'Brien, McCarthy, & Sockloskie, 1998). Similar to Black theology, central aspects of womanism are liberation, self-determination, and the humanity of all people with special attention to those who have been dehumanized. Similar to feminism, womanism honors women's multiple ways of knowing, including the valuing of spirit and the unspoken. Womanism is holistic in its recognition and celebration of the various aspects of black female identity.

According to Walker (1983), womanist identity has multiple aspects; one aspect is that the affect and behavior of a womanist demonstrate empowerment, love, spirituality, and strength. *Womanist agency* was described by Walker as courageous, audacious, and willful. Womanists love themselves and other women, sexually or nonsexually, and this love transcends boundaries to reach all of humanity, desiring that all people would survive and thrive. Walker further noted that womanists celebrate life fully, through the arts, such as music and dance, as well as through the spirit. Despite the realities of oppression, a womanist recognizes her divine identity as a living reflection of powerful good on the earth. Womanists are also collectivistic and community oriented in that the focus of womanism moves beyond individual well-being to encompass the well-being of entire peoples and communities and then to humanity overall. To counter the notion that womanism is merely a subset of feminism, Walker described a womanist as purple in contrast to the lavender of feminism. In other words, womanism represents strength that is not a dilution or lesser construct than feminism or Black identity. Harrell, Coleman, and Adams (2014) noted that womanism is "a way of understanding the struggle for wholeness among women of African descent who refuse to collude with the invisibility of their womanhood or Blackness demanded by gender and racial oppression" (p. 75). Womanism is grounded in notions of possibility, hope, and change that enhance optimal living that transcends from survival to thriving (Westfield, 2007). Walker gave a psychological rationale for the use of the word *womanism* in her 1984 *New York Times* interview (Bradley, 1984) when she stated that a new word must be created when the old word (*feminism*) fails to capture the behavior and change that one is seeking to identify.

It is important to take note of the criticism that has arisen regarding the term *womanism*. Although Walker (1983) explicitly included same-gender-loving women in her original definition of the term, Coleman (2013) described the tendency of many womanist theologians to exclude lesbian and bisexual women of faith from their scholarship and ministry. Their application of the term to only apply to the experiences of heterosexual Christian women has led to some lesbians of color rejection of the label *womanist*. Given its original inclusive intent as well as the presence of womanist theologians who are also inclusive in their use of the word, we find it valuable to claim the construct for this discourse of holistic psychology, which attends to life at the intersection of multiple identities, including but not limited to race, gender, socioeconomic status, and sexuality. Additionally, we note that some have championed the terms *Africana womanist* or *African womanist* to refer to a more Black nationalist political view, which is also less inclusive than the original construct proposed by Walker. Given its original meaning and the phrasing "Africana womanist," which can distinguish the two constructs, we choose to embrace the term *womanist* as attending to and centralizing issues of race and culture while still holding on to the aims of creating communities that build bridges cross racial lines.

An additional debate has centered on who can adopt the label *womanist*, with some arguing that the term describes African-descent women, others broadening the term to include all ethnically marginalized women, and still others including all people who endorse the sociopolitical priorities of womanism. Concern has been raised about persons with White privilege coming into womanist scholarship and erasing Black women's power and voice through appropriation. Another concern is that those who personally and/or politically are not committed to combating anti-Blackness and anti-womanhood will enter womanist circles and dilute the focus resulting in the repeated marginalization of African-descendant women. For the purposes of womanist and mujerista psychologies, we contend that ethnically marginalized women and men can contribute to womanist and mujerista psychologies through teaching, counseling, and research. Other persons who would like to practice, teach, or research womanist and mujerista psychologies should do so with particular self-reflection, awareness, and ownership of their privilege, respect for self-definition, and a focused active commitment to combating racialized gender oppression, as well as all intersecting forms of oppression. Additionally, we recommend that persons who identify as feminists or liberation psychologists engage actively in immersing those fields in combating oppression that particularly targets African American and Latina women.

DEFINITION OF MUJERISMO

As a construct, mujerismo (from the Spanish word *mujer*, meaning woman) emerged when Latina feminist theologians baptized themselves as mujeristas (Isasi-Díaz, 1994). Mujerismo is a Latina womanism (Comas-Díaz,

2008; Mejia et al., 2013; Ojeda, 2014). Indeed, the conceptual and political translation of womanist into Spanish is mujerista (see http://centrodeartigo.com/articulos-informativos/article_79325.html).

Like womanists, mujeristas embrace an interdisciplinary perspective. They endorse inclusion as an essential ingredient for the movement's continual development. In this way, diverse voices are not only welcomed but also sought after.

The term *mujerismo* was initially used during the 1970s when Peruvian women used it to dissociate themselves from feminist movements (Vuola, 2002). Due to this historical antecedent, the translation of *womanism* into *mujerista* has had negative connotations in the Latin American context. For instance, Lily (2013) argued that the term *mujerismo* has been historically associated with female gender without considering class, race, location, and their interaction. Moreover, some Latin American women theologians have criticized mujerismo, accusing it of lacking a sociopolitical component (Aquino, 2002). To illustrate, Lamas (as quoted in Aquino, 2002) accused mujeristas of glorifying differences, assuming a homogenous identity, subscribing to a unitarian ideology, and producing oppositions that weaken the political impact of feminism. However, these accusations appear to be decontextualized. Such concerns emanate from a Latin American location where feminists may be oppressed because of their gender but not necessarily because of their gendered-coded ethnicity and race. In other words, compared with Latinas in the United States, numerous Latin American feminists are not an ethnic minority in a Latin American context. This perspective ignores the diversity and the multiple oppressions among Latinas in the United States, who as women of color, are exposed to intersecting oppressions including gender, race/ethnicity, class, location, xenophobia, and language. Chapter 6 of this volume, "Mujerista Psychospirituality," provides an extended discussion of mujerismo.

WOMANIST AND MUJERISTA PSYCHOLOGIES

Womanist and mujerista psychologies centralize the need to focus on the self-definition and art of healing of Black women and Latinas as they strive to survive, grow, and thrive in the face of multiple, intersecting forms of oppression. Recognizing that the word *psyche* has its roots in the Greek word for soul or spirit, we find it noteworthy that a foundational aspect of African and Latina-descendant women's psychology has been a study of their spirituality and theology. Womanist and mujerista psychologies are holistic in nature, understanding the necessity of interdisciplinary scholarship that honors the role of psychology, as well as theology, cultural studies, gender studies, sociology, and cultural anthropology. Womanist and mujerista psychologies focus on emotional healing from a psychospiritual perspective that connects with transpersonal thought; an understanding and respect for their framework is critical for the provision of culturally congruent treatment and ethical multicultural research (Holiday, 2010). In keeping with this recognition, although this volume is based in a psychological worldview, it integrates the literature and conceptualizations of multiple disciplines.

Womanist and mujerista psychologies maintain that three of the tasks central for wholeness and well-being are self-definition, self-empowerment, and critical awareness (Sears-Louder, 2008). These tasks become building blocks for a holistic life that encompasses connection and spirituality (Bryant-Davis, 2013). According to Sears-Louder (2008), the aim of health from the perspective of womanist and mujerista psychologies is liberation, which has such indicators as destiny, joy, freedom, and well-being. The spiritual quest and liberation aims of womanist and mujerista psychologies lead not only to whole, empowered individuals but also to transformed societies in which all people have access to well-being, freedom, and liberation (Sears-Louder, 2008).

Although feminism held broad appeal for women from different racial and ethnic communities, it took different forms according to the ideological, sociopolitical, and cultural contexts of the movements from which they emerged (Baumgardner & Richards, 2000). Womanism and mujerismo emerged in the midst of White-dominant feminism's initial failure to address women of color's multiple intersecting oppressions and realities and multiculturalism's initial neglect of ethnically marginalized women's racial and gender concerns. Womanist and mujerista psychologies call for the centralizing of intersectional identities and the wholeness of African- and Latina-descendant women globally, as well as all of humanity. Consequently, priorities that separated womanists and mujeristas from White feminists include racism, culture, immigration, class, unemployment, poverty, colonization, and domestic violence (Ojeda, 2014). Being aware of their compounded oppressions, women of color enact resistance from multiple forms of opposition. According to Sandoval (1998), this awareness fosters women of color's development of a differential consciousness (for a fuller discussion on this issue, see Chapter 6, this volume). Moreover, other significant differences between womanist/mujeristas and dominant feminists included womanist/mujeristas' attention to decolonization, antiracism, xenophobia, and collective liberation. In particular, mujeristas differ from dominant feminism as in their focus on location, biculturarism/transculturation, *transfrontera*/borderlands, and transnational issues. Even more, womanists and mujeristas subscribe to a global vision.

Womanism and mujerismo represent alternative kinds of feminism. They constitute oppositional expressions to dominant feminism. Within this perspective, womanism and mujerismo expand feminist psychology by focusing on the centrality of community, mutual caring, and global solidarity; while aiming towards collective liberation and transformation.

These feminisms of color are part of U.S. third-world feminism. According to Sandoval (1991), U.S. third-world feminism represents a new form of historical consciousness whose structure remains outside the dominant feminism. As members of the U.S. third-world feminism, womanists and mujeristas engage in social justice actions and ally themselves in solidarity with other oppressed groups across the world.

A central defining factor among womanists and mujeristas is their commitment to spirit (Isasi-Diaz, 1994; Walker, 1983). Indeed, spirituality permeates the lives of both womanists and mujeristas. Such an everyday spiritual orientation relates to womanist/mujerista's aspiration of pursuing knowledge, meaning, transcendence, hope, connectedness, and compassion (C. B. Williams & Wiggins, 2010). Spirit and spirituality are womanists' coping mechanisms against oppression, and vehicles of transformation. Within this context, the term *womanism* has both religious and secular uses. However, neither womanism nor mujerismo are religious in the sense of adhering to an organization, doctrine, or set of rituals (C. B. Williams & Wiggins, 2010). Rather, both womanism and mujerismo involve theoretical, methodological, healing, and developmental processes. They both recognize the nuanced and intersecting realities of spirituality and religiosity and their bidirectional relationship with well-being (Bryant-Davis & Wong, 2013).

Drawing on the current literature, we propose that womanist and mujerista psychologies focus on self-definition, agency, community or social support, survival strategies, coping strategies, resistance strategies, growth, healing, resilience, and thriving. These defining aspects take place in the context of a relational priority that seeks to create, nurture, and maintain a range of healthy relationships, including connections between women or sisterhood (Bryant-Davis, 2013). From a cognitive perspective, these psychologies unpack the ways women come to know themselves despite an often toxic society that devalues them with racism and sexism, as well as other forms of oppression, such as classism, heterosexism, religious intolerance, ageism, and able-bodyism. From a behavioral perspective, womanist and mujerista psychologies explore the agency and motivating factors that influence the actions of womanist and mujerista women and girls. In keeping with a learning and development perspective, racial and gender socialization is examined in ways that lend insight into the social messages that African American and Latina girls and women are given and the impact of these messages. Considering the trauma lens, womanist and mujerista psychologies explore the factors that create risk for Black women and Latinas, as well as the protective factors that prevent trauma and those factors that aid in women's survival, healing, coping, and thriving, not only in the aftermath of trauma but also in the reality of ongoing trauma. Finally from a strengths-based approach, womanist and mujerista psychology underscores the cultural strengths of Black women and Latinas and the ways these strengths are taught, developed, and maintained. Next, we present womanist and mujerista psychologies' theory, method, practice, and social action.

Theory

Womanism and mujerismo are anchored in a metatheory, with an interdisciplinary approach (Coleman, 2013; Harvey, Johnson, & Heath, 2013; Maparyan, 2011; Phillips, 2011; Thomas, 1998, 2009; C. B. Williams & Wiggins, 2010; D. D. Williams, 2012). As such, this metatheory comprises spirituality/religion, cultural studies, history, education, indigenous and non-Western healing traditions, art, politics, psychology, anthropology, sociology, queer studies, and mythology—among others. Moreover, it challenges hierarchies, such as rational ways of knowing versus other ways of knowing.

Womanist theory, as outlined by Harrell et al. (2014), has significant connections to African psychology and positive psychology. It is not a mere subset of feminism but has independent cultural roots. Womanist theory is culturally based and strengths-based in that its focus goes beyond pathology and oppression to the development of optimal psychological and collective well-being of African-descended women and all of humanity, across race and gender lines (Harrell et al., 2014). Womanist psychological theory is a liberation-based approach that is based in the idea that difference does not equal deviance (Brown-Collins, 1988). Recently, Harrell et al. proposed a positive womanist psychospirituality framework that emphasizes thriving and optimal functioning from a culturally contextualized view of human behavior that aims to highlight and support the strengths and agency of women of African descent. Six positive womanist life principles are proposed on the basis of womanist theory: (a) extended ways of knowing, (b) spirited and inspired living, (c) interconnected love, (d) balance and flexibility, (e) liberation and inclusion, and (f) empowered authenticity (Harrell et al., 2014).

Both womanism and mujerismo provide integrated analyses of gender, race, class, and sexual orientation to avoid essentialism (C. B. Williams & Wiggins, 2010). As such, a womanist/mujerista theory subverts hierarchies of race, gender, class, place, and sexuality. The source of womanist and mujerista metatheory is the lived experience of women of color. Indeed, women of color's experiences differ from those of White women. A womanist theory articulates how women of color can rescue and preserve their history and improve their traditions. Certainly, a womanist/mujerista theory entails an affirmation of women of color's voice; a critical analysis of their place in the world; and an examination of the sociopolitical construction of their realities within the intersecting contexts of race, ethnicity, gender, culture, class, sexuality, and other diversity variables (Paz, 2006).

Using a womanist psychological lens, women of color revise dominant feminist psychological theories of identity development and view women of color's negative self-images as the result of their historical, contemporary, and internalized oppression. Therefore, they have developed gendered and racialized theories of identity development. In this manner, they address women of color's realities, including identity development, challenges, and strengths. Indeed, womanist identity development models and feminist models differ in that womanist theories are able to capture women of color's experience of identity growth (Boisnier, 2003).

Ossana, Helms, and Leonard (1992) proposed a model of womanist identity development and a scale to measure it. The stages Helms adopts are pre-encounter, encounter, immersion–emersion, and internalization. These stages represent the stages of lack of awareness of the realities of gender oppression and the impact it has on one's self-definition as a woman, the conscious encountering of oppressive forces, the immersion into exploring one's gender and the quest for sisterhood, to an internalized, grounded, secure sense of a self that is aware of oppression but not defined by it. Helms argued that to develop a healthy identity, Black women must move from an externally and societally based definition of womanhood to an internal definition within which women define their values, beliefs, and abilities for themselves (Ossana et al., 1992). Helms's model ends at the point of self-definition instead of the mandate for social action, as she sees self-definition and acceptance as primary. Hoffman (2006) found a positive correlation between gender self-definition and achieved racial identity. In other words, gender identity development does not conflict with positive racial and ethnic identity development but can be developed and nurtured together.

Many mujeristas endorse a transfronteriza/borderland identity development model. Anzaldúa (1987) advanced a transfronteriza/borderlands theory of identity development, one that affirms national, ethnic, racial, linguistic, psychological, and spiritual aspects of Latina identity. The transfronteriza/borderlands theory offers the new *Mestiza* (a Latina with mixed indigenous and European ancestry) as well as the new *Mulata* (a Latina with mixed African, European and indigenous ancestry) a multiplicity of aspects of identity without negating or canceling out the diverse parts of the self.

Womanist and mujerista psychologies are the daughters of the marriage between psychology and spirituality. However, they are dissident daughters, giving birth to a feminist psychospirituality. To illustrate, womanists and mujeristas acknowledge spirit as a driving force in their life. Spirituality helps women to cope with oppression, positively reframe their situation, become resilient, and act in an affirming way. Spirituality infuses women's development with values such as compassion, tending, and care. For instance, among many African American women, care is a form of activism (Ramsey, 2012). Moreover, spirituality affirms women of color's values of connectedness, and interrelatedness. It ignites women's personal growth and ability to commit to their community's and larger society's well-being. Within this perspective, womanism is a positive psychological principle that predicates the oneness with nature principle, strengthens emotional wholeness and resilience, and affirms solidarity among oppressed individuals. To sustain these goals womanist and mujeristas use participatory, healing, and liberating methods. Additionally, as women empower and strengthen themselves, they share their knowledge and wisdom with others, creating what Castillo (1994) called a "collective state of being." Womanists and mujeristas use gender- and culturally specific methods to oppose oppression and foster personal and collective liberation.

Method

The womanist psychological methodology entails a participatory, inclusive, and liberating orientation. It aims to help women restory and reauthor their lives, engage in liberating expressions, and commit to social justice. Informed by the realities of women of color, womanist methods aim to give voice to the voiceless; foment critical consciousness; affirm women's gender, racial, and ethnocultural strengths; and engage in transformative social action. As a result, these methods help women to work towards the cocreation of a socially just society. To work toward these goals, womanists oppose inequality and oppression. They engage in social actions aimed at the democratization of power.

Woman-centered liberation scholarship requires the perpetual seeking and maintaining of survival strategies to address intersecting forms of oppression that confront the scholar and manifests in a range of cognitive dissonance challenges related to lack of mentorship, isolation, and demanding expectations (Cannon, Gise Johnson, & Sims, 2005). Our methodology is aimed at unearthing our untold stories, raising awareness of the realities of our oppression, developing our survival pathways, maintaining spiritual well-being, and nurturing relational connections across the diaspora (Cannon et al., 2005). These aims require that we develop methods of translating our mother language experiences into academic, official scholarly language (Cannon et al., 2005)

Women with a coalitional consciousness and a collective state of being endorse a global solidarity with all oppressed people. To contribute to the creation of a better society, most womanists and mujeristas favor what Sandoval (2000) called the *methodology of the oppressed*. In other words, women of color engage in strategies of resistance to promote the development of a coalitional consciousness (Sandoval, 2000). Some of the methods of the oppressed include storytelling, womanist/mujerista research (qualitative and interpretative methods) and *artivism*—art for the purpose of empowerment and social change.

Storytelling

Storytelling is a way a relating among many people of color. Within a womanist and mujerista context, telling a story—either in spoken or written words—is a way to counter women of color's traditions of silence (Lockhart, 2006–2007). Story telling can take the form of testimony—whether political (*testimonio*) and or spiritual. *Autohistoria*—woman of color self-history using diverse media such as narratives, art, spoken word, and others—is a self-inquiry method favored by many mujeristas. *I, Rigoberta Menchú: An Indian Woman in Guatemala* (Menchú, 2010) is an example of both testimonio and autohistoria. Yet, another narrative method, storytelling circles, enables women of color to tell their own story and learn from other women's stories. These empowering narrative methods are a collaborative, noncompetitive tool to enhance womanist's self-confidence, cultural consciousness, and agency.

Womanist/Mujerista Research

Womanist and mujerista research focuses on the lived experiences of women of color. Womanist research requires rediscovering previously neglected and rejected womanist repositories of knowledge, as womanist scholars perpetually seek to balance the multiple explicit and implicit priorities of womanists, including but not limited to maintaining pro-Black and pro-woman analytic frameworks (Cannon et al., 2005). As such these methods allow women to rethink the hierarchies of power with the aim at democratizing society. Womanist research methods involve qualitative, quantitative, interpretative, and mixed approaches. However, womanists prefer self-inquiry methods as opposed to only quantitative approaches to highlight subjectivity (J. Williams & Lykes, 2003). Therefore, a womanist method integrates multiple psychological approaches including psychodynamic, cognitive behavior, Jungian, humanistic, positive psychology; and others. To illustrate, participatory action research (PAR) is an inquiry method that emphasizes community participation and social action (Smith, Rosenweig, & Schmidt, 2010). This engaged inquiry is grounded in sociopolitical history to address issues of concern for community members who participate as co-researchers (McIntyre, 2008). Womanist scholarship has as an ending point the creation of womanist-works-in-action that manifest themselves as community relationships and transformative projects embedded in the communities where women "live, work, and worship" (Cannon et al., 2005). The teaching of womanist scholarship and methodology requires a radical commitment to inclusivity and a positioning of the students as co-learners, as well as creative learning projects such as the use of student journal entries, mind mapping, multimedia engagement, and student-led discussions (Cannon et al., 2005). Freire's (1970) work, particularly the pedagogy of the oppressed, inspired the development of PAR. An interdisciplinary research approach, PAR is a knowledge-making research method that promotes social change. Chapter 2, on mujerista research, in this volume provides an example of the application of a PAR method.

Photovoice

Photovoice, another womanist/mujerista method, combines photography with grassroots social action. Based on Freire's (1970) critical consciousness, photovoice, also known as *participatory photography*, was originally developed to empower marginalized women in China. Participants in photovoice take photographs that represent their points of view regarding their communities. Afterward, a group of participants analyze the photos and develop narratives to understand the community and take action (Wang & Burris, 1997). Examples of these actions are outreach programs designed to improve community health, education, and empowerment. A community consultation, photovoice helps participants to author the representation of their communities.

Artivism

Many women of color create their own art to express their life experiences, oppose oppression, foster empowerment, and advance liberation. Artivism (art created to promote critical consciousness and social change) helps womanists and mujeristas to author their lives and represent their communities, as well as to promote transformative action. As artivists, womanists/mujeristas use their creative expressions to struggle against oppression and injustice. Sandoval and Latorre (2008) identified spoken word, street art, indigenous murals, protesting, altar making, and others creative forms as Chicana/Latina examples of artivism. A powerful illustration of artivism is Ester Hernandez's image *Wanted: Terrorist La Virgen de Guadalupe—Should Be Considered Powerful and Dangerous* (Román-Odio, 2013). You can see the image at http://collections.museumca.org/?q=collection-item/2010941 and http://www.garlandgrey.com/

Womanist and mujerista psychology includes cultural traditions, such as music and dance, as a way of accessing and expressing their spirituality. Womanist and mujerista psychologists adopt a holistic view highlighting the intersection of mind, body, and spirit and the interconnection of people, spirit, ancestors, and nature. For these psychological lenses, the central aim of combating racism, sexism, and classism, as well as other forms of oppression, is crucial (Hill Collins, 1998; Townes, 1995). With this in mind, the art of womanists and mujeristas seeks to tell the truth about oppression and to eradicate it through the vehicle of the arts, including textiles, crafts, spoken word, music, dance, theater, and filmmaking.

In this volume, the chapters "Womanism, Creativity, and Resistance: Making A Way Out of 'No Way'" (Chapter 7) and "Mujerista Creativity: Latin@ Sacred Arts as Life-Course Developmental Resources" (Chapter 8) offer examples of artivism.

Practice

Unlike many Western models of counseling, womanist and mujerista practice centralizes race, gender, and spirituality, honoring the active role of spirituality in the lives of everyday Black and Latina women (Comas-Díaz & Greene, 2013). Womanist and mujerista practice centralizes the therapeutic survival, healing, and resistance strategies of self-determination, social support, and activism (Hill Collins, 1990). Womanist and mujerista psychologies in practice honor ethnically marginalized women's culture, strength, and emotional flexibility to empower women and men to survive and thrive (Nabors & Pettee, 2003). Womanist therapy in particular focuses on incorporating family, religion/spirituality, community life, and the intersection of oppression (Nabors & Pettee, 2003). Similar to feminist practice, womanist and mujerista psychological practice is cognizant of power dynamics in the therapeutic relationship and honors women's wisdom and perspective about themselves (Nabors & Pettee, 2003). Depending on the centrality of gendered cultural identity for a client, an awareness of womanist and mujerista psychologies can enhance the rapport in interracial therapeutic dyads between African American women or Latinas and clinicians of other ethnic backgrounds (Mitchell, 2003). Although clients are likely unfamiliar with the terminology of "womanist and mujerista psychologies," the defining variables, priorities, and aims are likely to resonate with many African-descendant and Latina women. Womanist and mujerista psychologies in practice address the multiple roles of women and the intersection of their identities, and aim to make the invisible visible and the unspoken spoken. In addressing oppression therapeutically, womanist and mujersita psychologies recognize the need to address the themes of acknowledgment, sharing, shame and internalized oppression, grief, safety and self-care, anger, coping strategies, and resistance strategies (Bryant-Davis & Ocampo, 2006).

Based on the Kantian constructivist perspective, which argues that people create reality, they do not merely discover it, womanist practice uses the stories women tell their therapists to begin the process of cocreating a new story that is empowering, authentic, and rewarding (C. B. Williams & Frame, 1999).

Womanist and muerista practitioners must engage in self-reflection and be aware of their values, biases, and assumptions. They must be open to the reality of oppression in their clients' lives and approach the work from the perspective of holistic care and egalitarianism (C. B. Williams & Frame, 1999).

C. B. Williams and Frame (1999) advocated the adoption of cultural resources within therapy for the purposes of promoting survival, growth, and resilience. One of the approaches used in these therapeutic frames is narrative therapy, in which the therapist assists in the empowerment of clients' so they can cocreate life stories that serve their well-being. Another approach is bibliotherapy, which gives the woman the direct access to knowledge that can help transform their lives (C. B. Williams & Frame, 1999). Self-help books are beneficial, of course, but so are books that highlight the voices and experiences of Black women. Related to bibliotherapy is the use of storytelling within session. For religious and/or spiritual clients, the use of faith stories, such as biblical stories, can get them to reflect on a deeper level regarding their experiences and aims. Given collectivistic cultures, with confidentiality in mind, group counseling and the building of informal social support networks can also be quite beneficial. Finally, the womanist and mujerista practitioner connects her or his clients with community resources. Major cities often have numerous culturally affirming events, agencies, and services that may aid in the survival and growth of Black women and Latinas. These strategies, within a holistic therapeutic stance that integrates identity markers (e.g., race, gender) can assist in promoting the self-definition and agency of Black women and Latinas (Moradi & Subich, 2002). In the practice section of this volume (Part II), Sanchez-Hucles' chapter (Chapter 3) "Womanist Therapy With Black Women" and Gloria and Castellanos's chapter (Chapter 4) "Latinas Poderosas: Shaping Mujerismo to Manifest Sacred Spaces for Healing and Transformation" more fully describe the therapeutic process from a womanist and mujerista psychological perspective.

Social Action

Womanist and mujerista psychologies are twofold in that they both (a) celebrate and affirm African-descendant and Latina women and simultaneously (b) combat oppressive forces that threaten to drain and destroy communities, such as racism, sexism, and classism (C. B. Williams & Frame, 1999). To celebrate the identity of African-descendant and Latina women, womanists and mujeristas recognize and use cultural healing practices, such as community, emotional expressiveness, ritual, humor, music and dance, and folk wisdom (Williams & Frame, 1999). To combat various forms of oppression, womanists and mujeristas use community support, spirituality, activism, and the arts (Bryant-Davis, 2005; Hill Collins, 1990). Womanism and mujerismo incorporate the arts of healing and agency, and define Black women and Latinas in ways the counter racism, sexism, and classism (Heath, 2006).

The psychology of womanist and mujerista activism is bidirectional, aimed at simultaneously empowering the African American and Latino community and transforming systems of oppression and discrimination (Hill Collins, 1998). The work directed at the community is intended to produce empowerment, value, dignity, and self-esteem, including racial and gender identity. This internal work highlights the fact that the individual and collective validation of the oppressed is in and of itself a revolutionary act. To dare to believe one is worthy of respect in the midst of systemic disrespect is an act of courageous resistance. Ramsey (2012) argued that tending to the hearts, minds, and spirits of community members reveals a unique approach to activism: caring activism. Tending to and caring for the marginalized are acts of caring activism. Caring activism not only seeks to prevent future violations but also provides care, provision, and healing for those who have already been wounded. Caring for the marginalized is the motivation for one's social activism and advocacy (Beauboeuf-Lafontant, 2002, 2005). As one womanist activist, Crosby (1993), declared, "We are loving warriors!" Womanist and mujerista activists are observed in multiple domains protesting and working to create just change. These sites of protests have included government agencies, corporations, schools, and the public streets.

In the activism section of this volume, Bryant-Davis and Adams' chapter (Chapter 9) "A Psychocultural Exploration of Womanism, Activism, and Social Justice" and Castañeda-Sound, Duran, and Martinez's chapter (Chapter 10) "Mujeristas and Social Justice: *La Lucha es la Vida*" describe the psychology of womanist and mujerista activism. Recognizing the need to continue to teach and socialize individuals in the paradigms of womanist and mujeristas psychologies, Vasquez provides a challenging chapter (Chapter 11) on generativity and development womanist and mujerista leadership development.

Gaps and Limitations

There is minimal theoretical literature and empirical research on womanist and mujerista psychologies. As a result, much of the scholarship in this initial text is a result of building bridges between the sociological literature that names womanism and mujerismo and the psychological literature that often does not name these constructs directly. Further theoretical development of these psychologies are needed, as well as empirical exploration of their construction and application. Issues that remain about womanist and mujerista psychologies include which aspects are most salient, to whom these constructs are most applicable, the relationship between their defining variables and mental health outcomes, and the clinical effectiveness of treatment models that emerge from these psychologies. Many of these issues are explored in this book, but we caution the reader that these psychologies are yet emerging and require ongoing attention, investigation, and critique. We also note that this text is missing an exploration of teaching womanist and mujerista psychologies, which is critical to the development and growth of the field. We must also acknowledge that, as with all edited volumes, there is some variation in the chapters regarding allocation of time devoted to an exploration of the interdisciplinary nature of these constructs, summary and critique of the current psychological literature, proposal of new conceptualizations, and personal experience. These variations serve to remind the reader of the realities of womanist and mujerista psychologies, which honor both multiple ways of knowing and the necessity of self-reflection within honest scholarship. As womanist and mujerista psychologies develop, sustained and respectful attention to intersectionality and the diverse experiences and ideologies of African-descendant and Latina women is needed. On that note, we must acknowledge that African American and Latina women who do not identify with womanist and mujerista priorities and values would likely not fit into frameworks of womanist and mujerista research, practice, and leadership development. However, some aspects within each subdiscipline may connect with nonaffiliated women. The priority of self-definition makes this reality both accepted and expected. Spiritual practices or artistic expression will not resonate at all with some African American and Latina women. Despite this fact, a woman may connect with other components within each psychology.

ROAD MAP

The contributors to this historic text discuss the interdisciplinary perspectives on their topic and then examine it from a womanist or mujerista vantage point. The chapter authors review and analyze the state of the field on the basis of psychological theory, empirical analyses, practice, and reflections on personal experience. The text starts the journey with two of the pillars of traditional psychology, research and practice. Wyche (Chapter 1) and Nygreen, Saba, and Moreno (Chapter 2) provide insight into womanist and mujerista research, respectively. After providing a sense of womanist and mujerista scholarship, the book turns to practice in Chapters 3 and 4. Sanchez-Hucles discusses the perspective of womanist healing and Gloria and Castellanos examine, from the viewpoint of mujerista sacred spaces, approaches to healing and well-being. Having addressed these core traditional tenets of psychology, the book then shifts to a psychological construct that is more unique to womanism and mujerismo: spirituality. Spirituality, which is considered foundational to both psychologies is specifically spirituality in Chapters 5 and 6. In Chapter 5, Banks and Lee provide insight into womanist theology as it intersects with womanist psychology, and in Chapter 6, Comas-Díaz examines Latinas' sacred rituals, beliefs, and experiences. Next, the expressive arts, which highlight the value of self-definition, self-expression, and creativity in both psychologies, are investigated by Drake-Barnett, Garrett-Akinsanya, and Bryant-Davis (Chapter 7) and by Shapiro and Alcantara (Chapter 8). Finally and of great importance is the shift to social justice in Chapters 9 and 10, which is an ideal of both psychologies in the sense of the interconnection of all people and the necessity of an awareness of one's capacity to improve not only one's immediate circumstanced but the life of humanity more globally. Bryant-Davis and Adams (Chapter 9) explore the intersection of social justice activism and the well-being of African-descendant women, and Castañeda-Sound, Duran, and Martinez (Chapter 10) analyze the role of social justice in mujerista psychology. Finally this volume centers on the generativity of womanist and mujerista psychologies as demonstrated through leadership development and engagement as explored by Vasquez in Chapter 11. The editors then conclude the book with some reflections on the significance of this work, as well as the areas that need continued development for womanist and mujerista psychologies to best enhance the psychosocial status of African-descendant and Latina women across the lifespan.

CONCLUSION

> I know that, like every woman of the people, I have more strength than I appear to have.
>
> —Evita Perón

> When we speak we are afraid our words will not be heard or welcomed. But when we are silent, we are still afraid. So it is better to speak.
>
> —Audre Lorde

Without progression, all movements come to an end. Womanist and mujerista psychologies must be taught and new leaders must perpetually be developed so that these psychologies can be promoted and preserved. The aim of this volume is both to define womanist and mujerista psychologies and to present them in such a way that the reader can adopt them, adapt them, and build onto them new ways of understanding and enhancing women and all people to live empowered lives. We as African-descended and Latina women are so much more than the stereotypes and stigmas that have been used to bind us, so we must know and speak who we are. We speak it to ourselves, speak to our daughters, and speak it to the world. In the knowing and the speaking, we are made whole.

REFERENCES

American Psychological Association. (2001). *Resolution against racism and in support of the goals of the 2001 UN World Conference Against Racism, Racial Discrimination, Xenophobia, and Related Intolerance*. Retrieved from http://www.apa.org/about/policy/racism.aspx

American Psychological Association. (2002). *APA guidelines on multicultural education, training, research, practice and organizational change for psychologists*. Retrieved from http://www.apa.org/pi/oema/resources/policy/multicultural-guidelines.aspx

American Psychological Association. (2010). *Ethical principles of psychologists and code of conduct (2002, Amended June 1, 2010)*. Retrieved from http://www.apa.org/ethics/code/index.aspx

Anzaldúa, G. (1987). *Borderlands/la frontera: The new Mestiza*. San Francisco, CA: Spinster/Aunt Lute.

Aquino, M. P. (2002). Latina feminist theology: Central features. In M. P. Aquino, D. L. Machado, & L. Rodriguez (Eds.), *A reader in Latina feminist theology* (pp. 133–160). Austin, TX: University of Texas Press.

Baumgardner, J., & Richards, A. (2000). *Manifesta: Young women, feminism, and the future*. New York, NY: Farrar, Straus, and Giroux.

Beauboeuf-Lafontant, T. (2002). A womanist experience of caring: Understanding the pedagogy of exemplary Black women teachers. *The Urban Review, 34*, 71–86. http://dx.doi.org/10.1023/A:1014497228517

Beauboeuf-Lafontant, T. (2005). Womanist lessons for reinventing teaching. *Journal of Teaching Education, 56*, 436–445. http://dx.doi.org/10.1177/0022487105282576

Boisnier, A. (2003). Race and women's identity development: Distinguishing between feminism and womanism among Black and White women. *Sex Roles, 49*, 211–218. http://dx.doi.org/10.1023/A:1024696022407

Bradley, D. (1984, January 8). Novelist Alice Walker telling the Black woman's story. *The New York Times*. Retrieved from https://www.nytimes.com/books/98/10/04/specials/walker-story.html

Brown-Collins, A. (1988). Integrating third world womanism into the psychology of women course. In P. A. Bronstein, K. Quina, P. A. Bronstein, & K. Quina (Eds.), *Teaching a psychology of people: Resources for gender and sociocultural awareness* (pp. 102–111). Washington, DC: American Psychological Association. http://dx.doi.org/10.1037/10066-012

Brown-Douglas, K. (1993). *The Black Christ*. Maryknoll, NY: Orbis Books.

Bryant-Davis, T. (2005). Coping strategies of African American adult survivors of childhood violence. *Professional Psychology: Research And Practice, 36*, 409–414. http://dx.doi.org/10.1037/0735-7028.36.4.409

Bryant-Davis, T. (2013). Sister friends: A reflection and analysis of the therapeutic role of sisterhood in African American women's lives. *Women & Therapy, 36*, 110–120. http://dx.doi.org/10.1080/02703149.2012.720906

Bryant-Davis, T., & Ocampo, C. (2006). A therapeutic approach to the treatment of racist-incident-based trauma. *Journal of Emotional Abuse*, 6, 1–22. http://dx.doi.org/10.1300/J135v06n04_01

Bryant-Davis, T., & Wong, E. C. (2013). Faith to move mountains: Religious coping, spirituality, and interpersonal trauma recovery. *American Psychologist*, 68, 675–684. http://dx.doi.org/10.1037/a0034380

Cannon, K. G., Gise Johnson, A. P., & Sims, A. D. (2005). Womanist works in word. *Journal of Feminist Studies in Religion*, *21*, 135–146. http://dx.doi.org/10.2979/FSR.2005.21.2.135

Castillo, A. (1994). *Massacre of the dreamers: Essays on Xicanisma*. New York, NY: Penguin.

Coleman, M. (2013). *Ain't I a woman too? Third wave womanist religious thought*. Minneapolis: Fortress Press.

Comas-Díaz, L. (2000). An ethnopolitical approach to working with people of color. *American Psychologist*, *55*, 1319–1325. http://dx.doi.org/10.1037/0003-066X.55.11.1319

Comas-Díaz, L. (2008). Spirita: Reclaiming womanist sacredness in feminism. *Psychology of Women Quarterly*, *32*, 13–21. http://dx.doi.org/10.1111/j.1471-6402.2007.00403.x

Comas-Díaz, L., & Greene, B. (Eds.). (2013). *Psychological health of women of Color: Intersections, challenges, and opportunities*. Santa Barbara, CA: Preager/Greenwood.

Crosby, K. (1993, June 9). *Interview by Sonya Ramsey* [Audiotape recording]. Durham, NC: Special Collections of the Duke University Library.

Freire, P. (1970). *Pedagogy of the oppressed*. New York, NY: Seabury Press.

Harrell, S., Coleman, A., & Adams, T. (2014). Toward a positive womanist psychospirituality: Strengths, gifts, and optimal well-being among women of African descent. In T. Bryant-Davis, A. Austria, D. Kawahara, & D. Willis (Eds.), *Religion and spirituality for diverse women: Foundations of strength and resilience* (pp. 49–70). Santa Barbara, CA: Praeger.

Harvey, I., Johnson, L., & Heath, C. (2013). Womanism, spirituality, and self health management behaviors of African American women. *Women, Gender, and Families of Color*, *1*, 59–84. http://dx.doi.org/10.5406/womgenfamcol.1.1.005

Heath, C. (2006). A womanist approach to understanding and assessing the relationship between spirituality and mental health. *Mental Health, Religion & Culture*, 9, 155–170.

Henley, N. M., Meng, K., O'Brien, D., McCarthy, W. J., & Sockloskie, R. J. (1998). Developing a scale to measure the diversity of feminist attitudes. *Psychology of Women Quarterly*, *22*, 317–348. http://dx.doi.org/10.1111/j.1471-6402.1998.tb00158.x

Hill Collins, P. (1990). *Black feminist thought*. New York, NY: Routledge.

Hill Collins, P. (1998). *Fighting words: Black women and the search for justice*. Minneapolis: University of Minnesota Press.

Hoffman, R. M. (2006). Gender self-definition and gender self-acceptance in women: Intersections with feminist, womanist, and ethnic identities. *Journal of Counseling & Development, 84*, 358–372. http://dx.doi.org/10.1002/j.1556-6678.2006.tb00415.x

Holiday, J. M. (2010). The word, the body, and the kinfolk: The intersection of transpersonal thought with womanist approaches to psychology. *International Journal of Transpersonal Studies, 29*, 103–120.

Isasi-Díaz, A. M. (1994). Mujeristas: A name of our own. In N. B. Lewis (Ed.), *Sisters struggling in the spirit: A women of color theological anthology* (pp. 126–38). Louisville, KY: Women's Ministries Program, Presbyterian Church (USA).

Lily, S. (2013, July 14). *Mujerismo no es feminismo, ni hembrismo* [Mujerism is not feminism nor hembrismo] [web log post]. Retrieved from http://blogs.publico.es/shangaylily/2013/07/14/mujerismo-no-es-feminismo-ni-hembrismo/

Lockhart, T. (Fall 2006–Spring 2007). Writing the self: Gloria Anazaldúa, textual for, and feminist epistemology. *Michigan Feminist Studies, 20*. Retrieved from http://quod.lib.umich.edu/cgi/t/text/text-idx?cc=mfsfront;c=mfs;c=mfsfront;idno=ark5583.0020.002;rgn=main;view=text;xc=1;g=mfsg

Maparyan, L. (2011). *The womanist idea*. New York, NY: Routledge.

McIntyre, A. (2008). *Participatory action research*. Thousand Oaks, CA: Sage.

Mejia, A. P., Quiroz, O., Morales, Y., Ponce, R., Limon Chavez, G., & Olivera y Torre, E. (2013). From *madres* to *mujeristas*: Latinas making change with Photovoice. *Action Research, 11*, 301–321. http://dx.doi.org/10.1177/1476750313502553

Menchú, R. (2010). *I, Rigoberta Menchú: An Indian Woman in Guatemala* (E. Burgos-Debray, Ed., & A. Wright, Trans.). London, England: Verso Books.

Mitchell, K. N. (2003). Cultural knowing: A means to therapeutic alliance between White and African-American women. *Dissertation Abstracts International: Humanities and Social Science, 64A*, 1699.

Moradi, B., & Subich, L. M. (2002). Perceived sexist events and feminist identity development attitudes: Links to women's psychological distress. *Counseling Psychologist, 30*, 44–65. http://dx.doi.org/10.1177/0011000002301003

Nabors, N. A., & Pettee, M. F. (2003). Womanist therapy with African American women with disabilities. *Women & Therapy, 26*, 331–341. http://dx.doi.org/10.1300/J015v26n03_10

Ojeda, O. (2014, June 22). Latinas in the American patriarchy: The struggles Latinas face in their pursuit of the American dream [web log post]. Retrieved from http://feminismandmujerismo.weebly.com/

Ossana, S. M., Helms, J. E., & Leonard, M. M. (1992). Do "womanist" identity attitudes influence college women's self-esteem and perceptions of environmental bias? *Journal of Counseling & Development, 70*, 402–408. http://dx.doi.org/10.1002/j.1556-6676.1992.tb01624.x

Paz, K. M. (2006). Womanist archetypical psychology: A model of counseling for Black women and couples based on Yoruba mythology. In L. Phyllis (Ed.), *The womanist reader* (pp. 235–246). New York, NY: Routledge.

Phillips, N. R. (2011). Death unto life: The power of incarnation. *Pastoral Psychology, 60*, 339–354.

Ramsey, S. (2012). Caring is activism: Black Southern womanist teachers theorizing and the careers of Kathleen Crosby and Bertha Maxwell-Roddey, 1946–1986. *Educational Studies: Journal of the American Educational Studies Association, 48*, 244–265. http://dx.doi.org/10.1080/00131946.2012.660667

Román-Odio, C. (2013). *Sacred iconographies in Chicana cultural productions*. New York, NY: Palgrave/Macmillan. http://dx.doi.org/10.1057/9781137077714

Sandoval, C. (1991). U.S. third world women feminism. The theory and method of oppositional consciousness in the post-modern world. *Genders, 10*, 1–24.

Sandoval, C. (1998). Mestizaje as method: Feminists-of-color challenge the canon. In C. Trujillo (Ed.), *Living Chicana theory* (pp. 352–370). Berkeley: Third Woman Press.

Sandoval, C. (2000). *Methodology of the oppressed*. Minneapolis: University of Minnesota Press.

Sandoval, C., & Latorre, G. (2008). Chicana/o artivism: Judy Baca's digital work with youth of color. In A. Everett (Ed.), *Learning race and ethnicity: Youth and digital media*. Cambridge, MA: MIT Press.

Sears-Louder, S. M. (2008). Spiritual quest and crisis in African American liberative writing: Seeking complementarity, generative power, and constructive agency through a womanist psychology and religion framework. *Dissertation Abstracts International Section A, 69*, 1400.

Smith, L., Rosenweig, L., & Schmidt, M. (2010). Best practices in the reporting of participatory action research: Embracing both the forest and the tress, *The Counseling Psychologist, 38*, 1115–1138.

Thomas, L. E. (1998). Womanist theology, epistemology, and a new anthropological paradigm. *Cross Currents, 48*. Retrieved from http://www.crosscurrents.org/thomas.htm

Thomas, L. E. (2009). Womanist theology and epistemology in the postmodern U.S. context. In D. N. Hopkins & M. Lewis (Eds.), *Another world is possible: Spiritualities and religions of global darker peoples* (pp. 307–312). Sheffield, England: Equinox.

Townes, E. M. (1995). *In a blaze of glory: Womanist spirituality as social witness*. Nashville, TN: Abingdon Press.

Vuola, E. (2002). *Limits of liberation: Feminist theology and the ethics of poverty and reproduction*. New York, NY: Sheffield Academic Press.

Walker, A. (1983). *In search of our mothers' gardens: Womanist prose*. New York, NY: Harcourt.

Wang, C., & Burris, M. A. (1997). Photovoice: Concept, methodology, and use for participatory needs assessment. *Health Education & Behavior, 24*, 369–387. http://dx.doi.org/10.1177/109019819702400309

Westfield, N. L. (2007). *Dear sisters: A womanist practice of hospitality*. Bohemia, NY: Pilgrim Press.

Williams, C. B., & Frame, M. W. (1999). Constructing new realities: Integrating womanist traditions in pastoral counseling with African-American women. *Pastoral Psychology*, *47*, 303–314. http://dx.doi.org/10.1023/A:1021303513046

Williams, C. B., & Wiggins, M. I. (2010). Womanist spirituality as a response to the racism-sexism double bind in African American women. *Counseling and Values*, *54*, 175–186. http://dx.doi.org/10.1002/j.2161-007X.2010.tb00015.x

Williams, D. D. (2012). Black theology and womanist theology. In D. N. Hopkins & E. Antonio (Eds.), *The Cambridge companion to Black theology* (pp. 58–72). New York, NY: Cambridge University.

Williams, J., & Lykes, M. B. (2003). Bridging theory and practice: Using reflexive cycles in feminist participatory action research. *Feminism & Psychology*, *13*, 287–294. http://dx.doi.org/10.1177/0959353503013003002

I

RESEARCH

1

WOMANIST RESEARCH

KAREN FRASER WYCHE

Researchers tell a story. Feminist researchers tell stories that give voice to the women they study—that is, women's narratives of gender, race, ethnicity, and other intersecting identities that shape their lives and influence their responses to research questions. Feminist researchers may embrace different methodological approaches, as well as theoretical or conceptual frameworks to guide their research inquiry. One such conceptual framework is a womanist approach. As a conceptual model, a *womanist* research framework enables exploration of the intersectionality between concepts related to women's social locations, identities, and multiple oppressions based on gender, race, and ethnicity. In this chapter, I discuss these concepts and explore what a womanist orientation is within feminist research approaches, offer examples of womanist studies, and consider the role of the researcher.

http://dx.doi.org/10.1037/14937-002
Womanist and Mujerista Psychologies: Voices of Fire, Acts of Courage, T. Bryant-Davis and L. Comas-Díaz (Editors)

WHAT IS A WOMANIST ORIENTATION?

Womanism as a concept can be traced to the writings of feminist social scientists and novelists. Sociologist Patricia Hill Collins and novelist Alice Walker in the 1980s and 1990s were instrumental in articulating womanism as a concept (Wells-Wilbon & Simpson, 2009). Each of these scholars emphasized specific phenomena of Black women's lives. Collins discussed womanism as part of Black feminism and characterized by Black women's knowledge based on life experience and expressed through narratives. Some argue that such knowledge, as an informational concept, should be distinguished from wisdom, which involves applying the knowledge (Banks-Wallace, 2000). In addition, womanism encompasses an ethic of both caring and personal responsibility (Taylor, Mackin, & Oldenburg, 2008). Walker used the term *womanism* to discuss the ways Black women's identity is shaped by developmental processes characterized by moving from external and societal definitions of womanhood to an awareness of the intersectionality of multiple marginalized identities (Moradi, 2005). Hudson-Weems (2004) used the term *Africana womanism* to describe the power of giving voice to and naming oppression related to gender, race, and social class (Wells-Wilbon & Simpson, 2009). Although these concepts are used interchangeably today, they signify an identity category and a telling of stories/narratives from life experiences.

Contemporary scholars view the term *womanism* as complementary, and not in opposition, to the term *feminism* (Miguda, 2010). Additionally, womanism and Black feminist thought are characterized by a focus on issues related to social injustices and oppressions within the historical context of oppression (Taylor, 2005). For African American women, it is the collective and historical group knowledge that helps to focus on change that is influenced by the simultaneous intersections of race, class, and gender as experienced by self, family, and community (Taylor, 2005). These experiences are expressed in thoughts and behaviors. It is an "ethic of caring" for the family and community. This ethic of caring involves emotions, expressiveness, and empathy (Banks-Wallace, 2000). The concept of womanism applies not only to African American women but also to women of color, whose life experiences can differ from those of White women (DeBlaere & Bertsch, 2013). Thus, gender, race, and ethnicity are experienced synergistically within the social environment and not as separate from each other (Reid, Lewis, & Wyche, 2014). The conceptualization of womanism was broadened by Comas-Díaz (2008), who urged a focus on women of color across the world and the incorporation of their spirituality (*Spirita*). Spirita, together with cultural values and behaviors, shapes a woman's identity to fight oppression and create social justice.

As researchers using a womanist conceptual framework, we want to know how women struggle, define, and analyze critically their experiences.

We ask questions about the workings of race and racism as experienced in the social contexts of a woman's life. We want to know their story.

THE MANY FACES OF GENDER-FOCUSED RESEARCH

Gender-Focused Research Using Traditional Methodologies

Research on women's experiences across the lifespan is no longer marginal within psychology. Much information has been gained from the collective and robust scholarship that appears in women-focused journals (e.g., *Sex Roles*, *Psychology of Women Quarterly*, *Feminism and Psychology*, *Gender and Society*). Readers of these journals will recognize that although the published studies help one understand the lived experience of women for certain topics, the studies are frequently on college-age women, rather than community-based samples, and are predominately quantitative studies. Fewer qualitative studies are published in these journals. Although research about women continues to gain publication outlets, as producers and consumers of research, we need to continue to ask meaningful questions about women's lives. That is, what questions need investigating to better understand the complexities of women's lives and/or how to improve women's well-being? All of the above-mentioned journals try to address these questions in some fashion in their scope and aims. Only readers can evaluate whether the resulting studies fill the gap in our understanding of the multiple issues intersecting in women's lives and offer ways to address these issues so that suffering and social problems are alleviated.

It is unfortunate that the field of psychology is constrained by the intransigence of research traditions, making it difficult for some to embrace feminist research. For example, Abrams (2014) lamented that the use of experimental research designs and power analyses to detect statistical differences is the gold standard in research. Psychologists report results that show differences between participants, rather than the ones that show no statistical differences between participants. Additionally, the field of psychology is especially enamored by investigating deficit behaviors rather than the strengths of participants who live in difficult life situations and communities. Emphasized and rewarded is evidence-based practice, which as Fine (2012) questioned, is evidence for whom? Although research to improve and understand social issues that affect populations is needed, we as psychologists manipulate the variables we think are important and use statistical control to make dissimilar populations more similar. Hence, we rely often on student participants to study real-world problems or questions. Of course, there are exceptions, but the culture of psychology still predominately values experimental designs or randomized controlled trials over less rigorous methodologies to answer real-world questions. For the most part, we train students to emulate the logical positive model of empiricism to gain scientific knowledge (Beckman, 2014). The resulting studies are published in high-impact journals (Fine, 2012), the gold standard in academia—just ask any untenured academic psychologist whether this is still true. I am not arguing that we do not want rigor. Rather, if we want to answer questions about matters that impact the lives of women, and especially women of color, we need flexible research paradigms and theoretical concepts to guide inquiry. This type of research is not easy to conduct or to publish, but it does address real-world questions.

Feminist Approaches to Research

Participatory Action Research

Feminist researchers seek to move beyond the traditional research methodology described here to find more contextually sensitive ways to study women's lives. Participatory action research (PAR) and its expansions are viewed as useful methodological approaches to study women within a community and social action context. Feminist researchers embrace PAR because knowledge gained with community participation and on behalf of the community can promote both the well-being of the community and the lives of women who live there (Gatenby & Humphries, 2000; Smith & Romero, 2010). The PAR experience has six principles that are foundational to feminist, multicultural, and social justice practice: practicing ongoing self-examination, sharing power, giving voice, facilitating consciousness raising, building on strengths, and giving people tools for social change (Fine, 2007). The PAR methodological approach has been expanded and also includes community-based participatory research (CBPR), a method for examining women's diversity around specific community issues (White, Yuan, Cook, & Abbey, 2013). For example, to understand and to combat intimate partner violence (IPV) in any community, culturally informed quantitative instruments (the typical way this topic is studied) are needed to measure that experience (White et al., 2013). White et al. (2013) discussed how CBPR methodology is a way to develop measures that can be flexible in assessing forms of IPV and noted that it has unique features to capture the problem of IPV within specific cultural groups. In this approach, the women and community are involved in developing the measures in collaboration with the researchers. Such collaboration can target prevention and treatment outcomes to help women.

Another PAR approach is feminist participatory action research (FPAR), which focuses on research questions and interventions related to engagement, empowerment, self-efficacy, self-esteem, and structural inequalities to achieve social change (Fine, 2007; Krumer-Nevo, 2009). An example of FPAR among

Latin American feminists is the recognition of a geopolitical emphasis as important in a participatory approach to emphasize women's collective organizing in social movements, such as labor and politics (Cornwall & Sardenberg, 2014).

Womanist Research

How does a womanist approach to research fit into the well-developed area of PAR types of feminist research? I argue that a womanist framework complements a PAR framework to incorporate the microlevel factors of a woman's life. Taylor (2005) described a womanist framework, applied to African American women, as emphasizing personal narratives of self awareness and understanding in response to the intersectionality of race, social class, and gender. However, a womanist-framed research inquiry is not only about African American women but also applies to all women of color to explore their understanding of race consciousness, the social context of race and racism in their personal lives, and their critical analysis of this experience. As a result, qualitative methods are common because they enable the development of the woman's story in her own words. Being able to tell the story is critical. What you know or do not know, and your struggles and honesty in appraising situations, are valued. An ethic of caring and of personal accountability/knowledge (Taylor et al., 2008) and the spiritual aspects of self (Comas-Díaz, 2008; see also Chapter 2, this volume) are other components of the woman's narrative. The inner self is explored, and the outcomes are experienced both by self and within the community. The critical appraisal of the intersectionality of gender, race, social class, and spirituality is a foundational aspect of the experiences that help move the woman to function in her community. Hence, although social action is not emphasized directly as in the PAR approaches, it is how the woman's behavior is exhibited in the community and in service to the community based on her lived experience.

Examples of Womanist Research Studies

Not many published research studies use a womanist conceptual framework. For those that have been published, it is not surprising that education and pedagogy is a common topic of study, as teaching continues to be an "acceptable" profession for African American women and other women of color. Furthermore, when a woman chooses to become an educator, she has made the choice to give back to others and to her community. Womanist research studies often use qualitative methods as a culturally sensitive research tool. The study participants are usually African American women. Studies are framed from a strengths, rather than a deficits, perspective. This paradigm guides the types of questions asked. For example, in exploring strength and resilience in the lives of HIV-infected mothers, I asked them what caused stress in their lives and how they handled the identified stress (Wyche, 1998).

Posing the question in this way enabled the women to develop their own list of life stressors that did not parallel those hypothesized by me. In this study, it was not the chronic illness of HIV that caused stress, but their concerns about their children.

Studies of teachers using a womanist analysis framework have examined historical events and the ways in which African American teachers have responded. For example, Ntiri (2014) discussed the adult literacy schools (Citizenship Schools) established by Bernice Robinson in South Carolina in the 1950s. The womanist analysis explores how Robinson used the model of adult literacy education as a social change agent to address the oppressive experiences of race, class, gender, and inequality. Ntiri argued that Robinson is a womanist because she addressed oppression in her community in both the classroom and in her life, and Ntiri contrasted this to a feminist approach that would have emphasized sexism and women's experiences. African American elementary teachers' reasons for becoming educators were studied by Dixson and Dingus (2008), who interviewed both novice and experienced teachers, as well as these teachers' colleagues, principals, and parents of students. Weekly classroom observations over 10 months were conducted; teacher participants provided written reflections on their teaching; and documents were collected that included e-mail correspondence, newsletters, and print articles featuring the participants. Three convergent themes emerged that represent the teachers' views of why they and other Black women become teachers: Becoming a teacher continued the intergenerational encouragement for and legacy of teaching as a profession by their mothers and/or "other mothers" who were inspirational role models; teaching was community work for and a connection with the Black community; and teaching was spiritual and provided them a moral and humanistic way to use themselves and their pedagogical approaches help the community. In analyzing African American teachers' pedagogical practices and philosophies from a womanist framework, Beauboeuf-Lafontant (2002) reported that teachers combined race, social class, gender, and spirituality in their teaching for and social activism. Their goal was to help themselves, their students, and their communities deal with oppression.

Using oral histories, Patterson, Mickelson, Hester, and Wyrick (2011) asked participants to remember back 50 years to when they were students, and to evaluate their teachers working in segregated schools. Transcript analysis detailed the womanist tradition of caring among the teachers. Teachers were described as proactively dealing with the social injustice experiences of their students by engaging in "other mothering" and pedagogical strategies (e.g., collective responsibility, interdependence) to help students achieve academically, thus defying the social stereotypes of Black students as poor learners. Students discussed feeling nurtured and protected by their teachers as they faced racial discrimination. In Chapter 2 of this volume, Nygreen, Saba, and Moreno expand on this area of inquiry in their study of Latina womanist pedagogy (*mujerista*). They describe an ethnographic study of young adult educators working in a community-based education program. Emphasized is the collaborative method of pedagogy (mujerista) ethics and the womanist value of knowing that is collective and not individual.

A smaller womanist literature explores the role of spirituality in a womanist framework as related to mental health (Comas-Díaz, 2008; Heath, 2006). Spirituality is viewed therein as health promotion and using cultural traditions to cope with oppression. Heath (2006) argued that womanist research frameworks are needed to explore how to address mental health issues in women of color. Borum (2012) followed up on this suggestion with a focus groups study of African American women's perceptions of depression and suicide risk protection. Analyzed from a womanist framework, the results showed that women emphasized their faith, spirituality, culture, and the collectivist nature of the community as protective factors against suicide. Borum discussed these findings as the intersectionality of self-knowledge, cultural pride, and community concern. Cummings and Latta (2010) explored the role of spirituality within a womanist conceptualization through a qualitative study of ordained African American women that sought to understand how they experienced the "call" to preach. The results showed that these women shared a commonality of womanist spirituality in shaping their identity and viewed themselves as agents of culture and community.

THE WOMANIST RESEARCHER

Does doing research change you in any way? Cornwall and Sardenberg (2014) discussed how doing empowerment research with women in Salvador, Brazil, became an empowering experience for the researchers. Muhanna (2014) described her ethnographic study in the Gaza strip, where similarities of personalities between herself and the women in the study shaped her experience as a researcher in that she also became a subject of the research.

How do the researcher's race and social position of education, as well as the role of researcher itself, influence the power dynamics with the participants? What happens when the researcher who espouses a womanist research conceptualization feels a kinship to the women in her study? I gained insight into these questions while conducting one of my studies (Wyche, 1998). As an African American woman, I felt a common bond with African American HIV-infected women who lived in the community in which I was reared. I interviewed them in a facility that was known to me from my childhood, and I recognized the landmarks they described and the schools they attended. However, I realized that these women saw me as an outsider, a college professor, a "sister" who made it. They did not know my story. I wanted to know their story, but in being the "researcher," I maintained my outsider status.

Good researchers need to engage in self-reflection and self-examination about their biases and stereotypes. Family studies scholars emphasize that feminist perspectives in research challenge researchers to portray sensitively the intersectionality of the lives of the women they study. These scholars argue that researchers should become attuned to the ways each component of women's identity intersects in subjective ways so they can understand behaviors and life trajectories (Lloyd, Few, & Allen, 2007). Researchers should ask themselves the question, Does my choice of the story to tell confirm my hypotheses, while those that disconfirm my hypotheses are not told? We as researchers hold the power as we decide which stories to make public in a publication and which stories are not (Gatenby & Humphries, 2000). Further, researchers should ask themselves, Once the story is told—that is, published—has the authority and primacy of the women's words been maintained (Taylor, 2005)? Womanist researchers strive to communicate accurately the woman's voice, as that is a fundamental value of a womanist conceptualization.

Do you have to be a woman of color to be a womanist researcher? The answer is: no. Because more researchers are White than are people of color, Tillman (2002) argued that the researcher needs cultural knowledge to accurately interpret and validate the experiences of the women of color within the context of the phenomenon under study. This can be a slippery slope, for how the researcher interprets results makes a difference. For example, in studying women of color living in stressful life circumstances, are findings reported that confirm a strengths perspective or only those that indicate pathological ways of handling environmental stressors? I would like to believe that researchers who are not members of the groups they study will worry about the accuracy of the conclusions they draw, seek consultation from members of the group they are studying, and have their participants look at the study results and give feedback. However, I am less optimistic. I can think of two well-known, well-funded women research psychologists who told me that they understand African American people and other people of color well enough and that they are comfortable in their studies' conclusions. When asked how they could be sure, they said they have read enough to understand what is going on. These researchers will never embrace a womanist conceptual framework. However, for those of you who are open to exploring the intersectionality between the concepts related to women's social locations, identities, and multiple oppressions based on gender, race, and ethnicity, a womanist research framework may be the way to achieve this understanding.

REFERENCES

Abrams, D. (2014, June). Reality check: Rigor, relevance, and the value of social psychological research. *Newsletter: Society for the Psychological Study of Social Issues, 251*, 3–6.

Banks-Wallace, J. (2000). Womanist ways of knowing: Theoretical considerations for research with African American women. *Advances in Nursing Science, 22*, 33–45. http://dx.doi.org/10.1097/00012272-200003000-00004

Beauboeuf-Lafontant, T. (2002). A womanist experience of caring: Understanding the pedagogy of exemplary Black women teachers. *The Urban Review, 34*, 71–86. http://dx.doi.org/10.1023/A:1014497228517

Beckman, L. (2014). Training in feminist research methodology: Doing research on the margins. *Women & Therapy, 37*, 164–177. http://dx.doi.org/10.1080/02703149

Borum, V. (2012). African American women's perceptions of depression and suicide risk and protection: A womanist exploration. *Affilia: Journal of Women and Social Work, 27*, 316–327. http://dx.doi.org/10.1177/0886109912452401

Comas-Díaz, L. (2008). 2007 Carolyn Sherif Award address: *Spirita*: Reclaiming womanist sacredness into feminism. *Psychology of Women Quarterly, 32*, 13–21. http://dx.doi.org/10.1111/j.1471-6402.2007.00403.x

Cornwall, A., & Sardenberg, C. (2014). Participatory pathways: Researching women's empowerment in Salvador, Brazil. *Women's Studies International Forum, 45*, 72–80. http://dx.doi.org/10.1016/j.wsif.2014.01.006

Cummings, M., & Latta, J. (2010). When they honor the voice: Centering African American women's call stories. *Journal of Black Studies, 40*, 666–682. http://dx.doi.org/10.1177/0021934708318666

DeBlaere, C., & Bertsch, K. (2013). Perceived sexist events and psychological distress of sexual minority women of color: The moderating role of womanism. *Psychology of Women Quarterly, 37*, 167–178. http://dx.doi.org/10.1177/0361684312470436

Dixson, A., & Dingus, G. (2008). In search of our mothers' gardens: Black women teachers and professional socialization. *Teachers College Record, 110*, 805–837.

Fine, M. (2007). Feminist designs for difference. In S. Hesse-Biber (Ed.), *Handbook of feminist research: Theory and praxis* (2nd ed., pp. 613–620). Thousand Oaks, CA: Sage.

Fine, M. (2012). Troubling calls for evidence: A critical race, class, and gender analysis of whose evidence counts. *Feminism & Psychology, 22*, 3–19. http://dx.doi.org/10.1177/0959353511435475

Gatenby, B., & Humphries, M. (2000). Feminist participatory action research: Methodological and ethical issues. *Women's Studies International Forum, 23*, 89–105. http://dx.doi.org/10.1016/S0277-5395(99)00095-3

Heath, C. (2006). A womanist approach to understanding and assessing the relationship between spirituality and mental health. *Mental Health, Religion & Culture*, 9, 155–170. http://dx.doi.org/10.1080/13694670500116938

Hudson-Weems, C. (2004). *Africana womanist literary theory*. Trenton, NJ: Africa World Press.

Krumer-Nevo, M. (2009). From voice to knowledge: Participatory action research, inclusive debate and feminism. *International Journal of Qualitative Studies in Education, 22*, 279–295. http://dx.doi.org/10.1080/09518390902835462

Lloyd, S., Few, A., & Allen, R. (2007). Feminist theory, methods, and praxis in family studies. *Journal of Family Issues, 28*, 447–451.

Miguda, E. (2010). A view from womanism: A comment on Hester Eisenstein's "feminism seduced" employing Chilla Bulbeck's re-orienting Western feminisms. *Australian Feminist Studies, 25*, 453–458. http://dx.doi.org/10.1080/08164649.2010.520683

Moradi, B. (2005). Advancing womanist identity development: Where we are and where we need to go. *Counseling Psychologist, 33*, 225–253. http://dx.doi.org/10.1177/0011000004265676

Muhanna, A. (2014). When the researcher becomes a subject of ethnographic research: Studying "myself" and "others" in Gaza. *Women's Studies International Forum, 45*, 112–118. http://dx.doi.org/10.1016/j.wsif2013.11.010

Ntiri, D. W. (2014). Adult literacy reform through a womanist lens: Unpacking the radical pedagogy of Civil Rights Era educator, Bernice V. Robinson. *Journal of Black Studies, 45*, 125–142. http://dx.doi.org/10.1177/0021934714522264

Patterson, J. A., Mickelson, K. A., Hester, M. L., & Wyrick, J. (2011). Remembering teachers in a segregated school: Narratives of womanist pedagogy. *Urban Education, 46*, 267–291. http://dx.doi.org/10.1177/0042085910377511

Reid, P. T., Lewis, L. J., & Wyche, K. F. (2014). An intersectional framework for a multicultural analysis of gender. In F. Leong (Ed.), *APA handbook of multicultural psychology* (Vol. 1, pp. 379–394). Washington, DC: American Psychological Association. http://dx.doi.org/10.1037/14189-020

Smith, L., & Romero, L. (2010). Psychological interventions in the context of poverty: participatory action research as practice. *American Journal of Orthopsychiatry, 80*, 12–25. http://dx.doi.org/10.1111/j.1939-0025.2010.01003.x

Taylor, J. Y. (2005). No resting place: African American women at the crossroads of violence. *Violence Against Women, 11*, 1473–1489. http://dx.doi.org/10.1177/1077801205280275

Taylor, J. Y., Mackin, M. A., & Oldenburg, A. M. (2008). Engaging racial autoethnography as a teaching tool for womanist inquiry. *Advances in Nursing Science, 31*, 342–355. http://dx.doi.org/10.1097/01.ANS.0000341414.03963.fa

Tillman, L. (2002). Culturally sensitive research approaches: An African-American perspective. *Educational Researcher, 31*, 3–12. http://dx.doi.org/10.3102/0013189X031009003

Wells-Wilbon, R., & Simpson, G. (2009). Transitioning the caregiving role for the next generation: An African-centered, womanist perspective. *Black Women, Gender, and Families*, 3, 87–105. http://dx.doi.org/10.1353/bwg.0.0010

White, J., Yuan, N., Cook, S., & Abbey, A. (2013). Ethnic minority women's experiences with intimate partner violence: Using community-based participatory research to ask the right questions. *Sex Roles*, 69, 226–236. http://dx.doi.org/10.1007/s11199-012-0237-0

Wyche, K. F. (1998). Let me suffer so my kids won't: African American mothers living with HIV/AIDS. In C. Garcia Coll, J. Surrey, & K. Weingarten (Eds.), *Mothering against the odds: Diverse voices of contemporary mothers* (pp. 173–189). New York, NY: Guilford Press.

2

MUJERISTA RESEARCH: INTEGRATING BODY, EMOTION, SPIRIT, AND COMMUNITY

KYSA NYGREEN, MARIELLA SABA, AND ANA PAULINA MORENO

This chapter reports on findings from a *mujerista* research study of young adult educators (ages 18–24) working in a community-based popular education program.[1] The program, *Aprendamos*, is part of the popular education-based community organization Instituto de Educacion Popular del Sur de California/Popular Education Institute of Southern California. It has incorporated popular education methodology (Freire, 1999) to empower Latino immigrant families to identify, analyze, and take collective action against

[1]Following the confidentiality procedures approved by our institutional review board (IRB) prior to initiating this research project, we use pseudonyms in this chapter for all individual participants except those who are named as coauthors. As outlined in our IRB documents, collaborating coresearchers from Aprendamos are permitted to coauthor, coproduce, and disseminate results of the collaborative research; as authors, they may choose whether to reveal their own identities (or to write with a pseudonym). All participants at the Aprendamos staff retreat were informed about this chapter, invited to coauthor, and to read and comment on drafts. Those who are listed as coauthors are only those who committed to substantial writing and/or editing of the chapter.

http://dx.doi.org/10.1037/14937-003
Womanist and Mujerista Psychologies: Voices of Fire, Acts of Courage, T. Bryant-Davis and L. Comas-Díaz (Editors)

problems and injustices in their communities. The authors of this chapter are the current program director of Aprendamos (Mariella Saba), a university-based researcher (Kysa Nygreen), and a doctoral student research assistant (Ana Paulina Moreno) who worked together on a collaborative community-based ethnography of Aprendamos between 2009 and 2011. In this chapter, we use *mujerismo*, or Latina womanism (Galván, 2006), as a theoretical lens for describing our collaborative research methodology and analyzing the work of Aprendamos. We outline key aspects of the mujerista worldview, especially its underlying epistemological assumptions, and show how mujerismo can inspire, inform, and guide both research and pedagogy for humanization, wholeness, and healing. We offer our collaborative ethnographic study as an example of mujerista research and analyze an ethnographic vignette from our research as an illustrative example of mujerista pedagogy in action.

In the following sections, we first define the terms *mujerismo* and *mujerista research* as we have come to understand them in the context of our collaboration. We discuss differences and similarities between mujerista and feminist research methodologies, and we offer three illustrative examples of mujerista research from the literature. Second, we describe the research context of Aprendamos and our own collaborative, engaged ethnographic study as another example of mujerista research. Last, we analyze an ethnographic vignette from our research that illustrates mujerista pedagogy in action. Throughout, we attempt to show how mujerista research and pedagogy nourish wholeness, support personal healing, and contribute to liberation. Reflecting our mujerista perspective, the format of this chapter differs from conventional scholarly writing in that it contains a multiplicity of voices. These include the scholarly voice of academic theory and our personal, emotional, spiritual, and self-reflective voices. Writing in this way enables us to bring our whole selves to the analysis—including the bodily, emotional, spiritual, personal, and political parts of ourselves, as we also draw from relevant academic theory. As such, in this chapter, we periodically insert our own personal self-reflections.

WHAT IS *MUJERISMO*?

We define *mujerismo* as a system of thought, or worldview, that centers on Latina women's concrete experiences, sources of knowledge, and survival strategies (Dyrness, 2008, 2011; Galván, 2006; Villenas, Godinez, Delgado Bernal, & Elenes, 2006). Mujerismo shares some common themes with other worldviews that can be grouped under the category of multicultural feminism (Shohat, 2001) or women-of-color feminism (Hong, 2006; e.g., Black feminism, Chicana feminism, decolonial feminism, U.S. Third World feminism, womanism).[2] All of these racially conscious strands of feminism center on the unique experiences and perspectives of women of color, while promoting liberation, self-definition, and self-determination for all women. They all articulate intersectional analyses of oppression, recognizing how socially constructed categories of race, class, gender, sexuality, and nationality overlap and intersect with each other, shaping women's (and men's) experiences and opportunities in ways that position them multiply as both oppressed and privileged. They all assume that institutionalized racism works in gender-specific ways and that institutionalized sexism works in race-specific (and class-specific) ways. They all explore how various levels of oppression interact with and reinforce each other—on the micro level of face-to-face sexism (acts of prejudice, insults, microaggressions, harassment, violence against women); together with the larger institutional structures of gender oppression; and finally in the cultural realm of beliefs, assumptions, and ideologies that promote or legitimize women's subordinate social status. Last, racially conscious feminisms assert that women of color possess a unique perspective based on their social location at the intersection of racism and sexism. This social location provides women of color with a privileged epistemological standpoint from which to discern how oppression and dominance operate.

As we use the term, *mujerismo* (or Latina womanism) shares these broad overarching assumptions and goals with other racially conscious strands of feminism. What distinguishes mujerismo from Chicana or Latina feminism (in our view) is not so much a difference in substance but a difference in emphasis. Although the term *feminism* is generally associated with a political movement for women's rights and with public action to promote those rights, *mujerismo* is associated with the realm of the private, intimate, everyday spaces of women's lives (Villenas et al., 2006). As Villenas et al. (2006) explained,

> *Feminista* refers to a Latin American and/or Greater Mexican/Chicana feminist movement, while *mujerista* refers to a Latina-oriented "womanist" sensibility or approach to power, knowledge, and relationships rooted in convictions for community uplift. Often we use the former to signify the mobilized and historical base for Chicana feminist thought. We use the latter to call attention to a sensibility and orientation to everyday Latina communal relationships and issues—especially because *el feminismo* as a concept often does not have meaning for ordinary women as they go about their everyday lives. (p. 7)

[2]All of these are contested terms that have been used, promoted, (re)defined, and critiqued by many scholars. Exemplary works that have used or popularized these terms include Collins (1998) for Black feminism, Hurtado (1996, 2003) for Chicana feminism, Pérez (1999) for decolonial feminism, Sandoval (2000) for U.S. third world feminism, and Walker (1983) for womanism. This paragraph's description of common themes from across the different strands of women of color feminisms is our own synthesis of this literature and based on our own analysis. See also Kim (2007) for a useful, and more thorough, review.

Another subtle difference between the concepts of feminismo (feminism) and mujerismo (womanism) is the relative emphasis placed on race versus gender as categories of analysis. Despite the important work that women-of-color feminists have done to emphasize the significance of racial oppression in structuring women's experiences, Collins (1996) observed that many Black women continued to associate the concept of feminism with White women, seeing it as a movement that aimed to forge solidarity between White women and women of color. On the other hand, she notes, the concept of womanism grew out of an Afrocentric tradition and has been positioned as a movement aimed primarily at forging solidarity between Black women and Black men. These distinctions may not accurately reflect the perspectives of all who claim a feminist (*feminista*) or womanist (mujerista) perspective, but they do reflect the terms' different histories of use.

In our view, the concepts of feminismo (feminism) and mujerismo (Latina womanism) are not in conflict with each other, but they signal a different center of gravity in terms of where they draw our attention. Following Villenas et al. (2006), Galván (2006), and Dyrness (2008, 2011), we understand mujerismo as a worldview that begins from, and honors, Latina women's everyday lived experiences. A mujerista perspective draws attention to the strategies that Latina women have developed to survive at the intersections of racism, classism, sexism, heterosexism, xenophobia, linguistic prejudice, and neo/internal colonialism. It is grounded in a deep respect for these survival strategies, for the knowledge they produce and represent, and the wisdom held in community among Latina women. As Galván (2006) articulated,

> A *mujerista* or Latina womanist vision . . . aims to uncover, share, and validate the diverse knowledge and experiences of Latinas in the United States and abroad. It takes a holistic approach to self that includes spirit and emotion, and recognizes our individual/communal struggles and efforts to name ourselves, record our history, and choose our own destiny. (p. 172)

Mujerismo expands on feminist epistemologies by drawing attention to the body and the spirit as valid sources of knowledge (Cruz, 2001, 2006; Galván, 2006). A mujerista epistemology recognizes how knowledge is produced in, and accessed through, bodies, emotions, spiritualities, relationships with others, and relationships with self. It draws attention to the intimate spaces of the home, of mother–daughter relationships, friendships, love, and the spiritual world as sources of knowledge (Galván, 2006; Dyrness, 2008, 2011; Villenas, 2006). Finally, mujerismo emphasizes wholeness and the need to nourish all parts of the self—the spiritual, emotional, corporal, relational, and intellectual dimensions of self—as an essential step in healing the wounds inflicted by oppression, including one's own internalized oppression (Dyrness, 2008, 2011). Mujerismo is about rehumanizing oneself and reclaiming one's wholeness in the face of dehumanizing institutions that break one apart into pieces. This emphasis on nourishing the whole self—and specifically the spiritual, emotional, and corporal dimensions of self—is what distinguishes mujerismo, in our view, as a distinctive worldview within the broader category of multicultural feminisms.

WHAT IS MUJERISTA RESEARCH?

We define *research* as any deliberate, systematic attempt to produce new knowledge. We define *mujerista research* as an approach to research that begins from, and is guided by, mujerista epistemology and ethics. In this research, a mujerista worldview shapes what questions are asked, how they are framed, how relationships between researcher(s) and "subjects" are defined and negotiated, how data are collected and analyzed, how results are interpreted and disseminated and for what purpose, and who is in control of the process. Although examples of mujerista research exist in the literature, we know of only one example of academic scholarship that explicitly uses this term to describe a research methodology (Dyrness, 2008). We believe the concept of mujerismo adds an important new dimension to the robust literature on feminist research methodologies. Below, we outline the key components of mujerista research, offer three examples of mujerista research from the literature, and describe our own research project at Aprendamos as another example.

The first aspect of mujerista research is its epistemological framework, which is based on four key claims: (a) There are multiple ways of knowing; (b) knowledge is socially constructed, socially located, and contested; (c) social positionality shapes what and how people know; and (d) knowledge is produced, held, and accessed through one's bodies, emotions, spiritualities, and relationships (including relationships with others and relationships with self).[3] These four assumptions are consistent with a broad range of feminist epistemologies (see Hesse-Biber, 2007, for an overview). Like feminist standpoint epistemology (e.g., Hesse-Biber, 2007; Smith, 1987), mujerista epistemology recognizes the unique standpoint of Latinas/Chicanas in the United States and transnationally—living at the intersections of racism, sexism, heterosexism, neo/internal colonialism, xenophobia, and linguistic prejudice. What distinguishes mujerista epistemology from other feminist

[3]These four claims are a synthesis based on our review and analysis of scholarship that uses a mujerista theoretical lens. Key sources include Villenas et al. (2006), Galván (2006), Villenas (2006), Delgado Bernal (2006), and Dyrness (2008, 2011).

epistemologies (as discussed previously) is not so much their substance but their emphasis: Mujerista epistemology uniquely emphasizes the corporal, emotional, and spiritual dimensions of self as valid sources of knowledge.

Mujerista epistemology (similar to other feminist epistemologies) counters the dominant epistemological paradigm of social science research, often referred to as *logical positivist empiricism* (Beckman, 2014). Where mujerismo emphasizes the holistic and interconnected nature of the self, logical positivism assumes the division of self into mind and body. Whereas mujerismo recognizes the bodily, emotional, relational, and spiritual dimensions of self as valuable sources of knowledge, logical positivism positions the intellectual realm as the sole source of knowledge while dismissing other dimensions as mere superstition, distortions, or distractions from the pursuit of true knowledge. Mujerismo encourages viewing knowledge in the context of relationships, communities and structures of oppression, whereas logical positivism frames knowledge as individualized, abstract, and value free. Mujerismo recognizes knowledge as situated, contextualized, and power laden, whereas logical positivism frames knowledge as neutral, decontextualized, and therefore independent of power relations.

In addition to its epistemological foundations, mujerista research embodies mujerista values, such as wholeness, humanization, and liberation. Mujerista research strives to nourish the wholeness of its participants and capture a holistic understanding of the phenomena of study. A holistic understanding recognizes complexity, nuance, history, emotion, and the body; it does not seek to compartmentalize, categorize, hierarchize, or isolate dimensions of reality. Mujerista research assumes, and draws attention to, the multiple dimensions of women's selves and experiences. Mujerista research recognizes how systems of oppression structure the human experience; therefore, research questions and analytical procedures are designed with the intention of illuminating these processes, and interpreting human stories through an intersectional lens. Mujerista research is power conscious, meaning participants are aware of how power shapes the research process and are sensitive to power asymmetries between researchers and "subjects." As such, mujerista researchers enter into research relationships with care and from a stance of solidarity. Mujerista research centers the unique experience/perspective of Latina women. It does not seek to understand Latina women's experience in relation to Latino men and/or White women; rather, it seeks to understand the Latina women's experience on its own terms (without glossing over important differences based on class, sexuality, gender expression, dis/ability, ethnicity, skin color, language, immigration status, etc.) Mujerista research illuminates the wisdom, resilience, and survival strategies (*sobrevivencia*) present within Latina communities.

Finally, as Dyrness (2008) explained, mujerista research redefines the purpose of research, and specifically, the relationship between research and social change. Feminist research has long promoted research for social change. Feminist scholars have embraced research that lends itself to advocacy, organizing, and activism for feminist goals, such as eliminating sexism. However, in her discussion of mujerista research, Dyrness (2008) challenged the limited ways in which activist scholars have conceptualized the relationship between research and social change. In the activist or advocacy-based research tradition, scholars aim to conduct research that benefits a marginalized community. Often, scholars working in this tradition align themselves with an organized social movement and produce research that lends support for specific policy objectives. Without discounting the contributions of such research, Dyrness (2008) pointed out that it continues to position academic researchers as the sole source of knowledge. She noted, even within an activist research paradigm, "It is the researcher's knowledge production that is key to the change process, not that of community members" (p. 25). In contrast, she offered the lens of mujerismo, which enables one to see a more diverse set of possibilities for how research may contribute to social change: "A Latina feminist or mujerista lens calls attention to the means of achieving change, and highlights the need for a research process that supports womanist ways of being in community, based on wholeness and *confianza* (trust)" (p. 27). Dyrness (2008) combined the methodology of participatory action research (e.g., Fals-Borda & Rahman, 1991; Maguire, 1987) with mujerismo to develop an approach she called "mujerista participatory research." She differentiated this approach from others in the activist research tradition as follows: "While policy-oriented activist research depends on the researcher to sensitively represent and defend the interests of marginalized groups, mujerista participatory research illuminates and strengthens Latinas' own capacity for social critique and transformative resistance" (Dyrness, 2008, pp. 40–41).

In other words, mujerista research takes seriously the epistemological claim that Latina women's intimate daily lives are sources of valuable knowledge. Rather than relying on academic scholars to produce knowledge on their behalf, mujerista research empowers Latina women to become their own agents of change. It is the research process, not just the product, that becomes the site of social change. This change is nurtured through a research process that is "humanizing" and "based on wholeness and confianza" (Dyrness, 2008, p. 40). Dyrness (2008) explained: "Valuing wholeness means acknowledging the need for personal healing and for relationships that support our emotional, spiritual, and mental well-being as prerequisites for collective action" (p. 40). A characteristic of mujerista research, then, is a careful attention to the research process and the construction of a process that fosters wholeness, humanization, and healing.

EXAMPLES OF MUJERISTA RESEARCH

Although numerous scholars have used mujerismo as a theoretical lens in writing and analyzing research data, Dyrness (2008) offered the only example we know of that specifically uses this term in describing a research methodology. Dyrness's work is based on an ethnographic and participatory action research study of Latina immigrant mothers who participated in a school reform initiative in Oakland, California. Dyrness used ethnography and participatory action research methods to study how a group of Latina immigrant mothers exercised agency and reclaimed a sense of wholeness. From the early conceptualization of her study, the framing of research questions and negotiating of research relationships, Dyrness positioned herself in solidarity with the Latina immigrant women she worked with and had already come to know. In writing about her methods, she situated herself as both an insider and an outsider, and acknowledged power asymmetries. She positioned the women as knowledge producers rather than data sources and actualizes this perspective through a participatory action research project. Dyrness's analysis draws attention to the intimate, everyday spaces of women's lives, illuminates the multiple dimensions of self, and exemplifies the mujerista emphasis on wholeness. She writes eloquently about how the research process provided a space for *confianza* and *testimonio*, allowing the women to reclaim a sense of wholeness and healing. It was a space where experiences of shame were transformed into acts of resistance (p. 35), where anger was affirmed "as a healthy alternative to the self-blame and hurt" (p. 35), and where they enacted a "seamless relationship between research and action" (p. 36; see also Dyrness, 2011, for a book-length illustration of these issues).

In addition to Dyrness's (2008, 2011) research, we offer two illustrative examples of studies that meet our definition of mujerista research. Both scholars use mujerismo as a theoretical lens to interpret research data, although they do not apply this term to describe their methodology. First, Villenas's (2006) ethnographic study of Latina mothers focuses on what she called "*mujer*-oriented pedagogies," or ways of teaching and learning between mothers and daughters that occurred in "everyday" spaces of the home. For this study, Villenas worked with Latina immigrant women in North Carolina. She approached her research "subjects" from a stance of solidarity, recognizing her dual positionality as both an insider and outsider in their community. Her research questions led her to focus on the hidden, private spaces of Latina women's lives (the home and the mother–daughter relationship) and explore the wisdom and survival strategies present in those spaces. In writing up her findings, she names her own social location as a Latina woman. But rather than proceeding on to a (disembodied) scholarly analysis, she continues to weave her personal story and self-reflections through her analysis of the ethnographic findings. The researcher's own life story thus enters into dialogue with her ethnographic data. All the parts of herself—as a Latina woman, daughter, mother, and researcher—are brought to bear in her interpretation of her findings. These distinct parts of the self are not filtered out, nor does she attempt to "minimize" their impact on the analysis. Instead, her whole self is present in the collection, analysis, and presentation of her research findings. Likewise, the immigrant mothers of study are presented as complex, contextualized, embodied whole selves.

The second example is work by Galván (2006), who used a mujerista framework to analyze the narratives of Latina women. Galván worked with women in Mexican rural communities in nongovernmental organizations focused on popular literacy and organizing. She positioned herself in solidarity with these women and worked alongside them, rather than positioning herself as a "neutral" observer. Her study focused on the practices of teaching and learning that occurred in "everyday" (nonformal) spaces of the women's lives, as well as the organized spaces of the nongovernmental organization. In analyzing her data, she paid attention to the role of spirituality in the women's lives, or what she called "*campesina* spiritual epistemologies—their way of knowing and being in the world and the source of their strength and *sobrevivencia*" (p. 163). In naming spirituality as an *epistemology* (rather than a cultural trait to be analyzed), Galván validated it as a "way of knowing." She also went a step further by reflecting on her own spirituality and how it shapes her understanding of her research data. Like Villenas, her self-reflections do more than simply "locate" herself as a researcher, they enter into dialogue with her research data and integrate seamlessly into her scholarly analysis. She wrote the following:

> I situate my story directly alongside that of the women I spent time with as part of a research study so as to demonstrate my own spiritual inclinations—hence, the epistemologies from which I describe and interpret *campesina* (rural or peasant women's) spirituality. It is important to expose from the outset the lens that informs my understanding of spirituality and what I perceive to be spiritual about what *campesinas* believe and hold precious, as well as how they interact, live, learn, and teach each other. (p. 162)

As such, Galván recognized the spiritual dimension of self in reflecting on her own identity, as well as that of the women in her study. She brought this dimension of herself to the collection, analysis and presentation of her research findings.

In reflecting on our work together at Aprendamos, we have come to understand it as an example of mujerista research. In the following section, we describe the Aprendamos program and its local community to provide the context of our work. We then describe how our research collaboration came about, what we accomplished, and why we characterize it as an example of mujerista research.

APRENDAMOS: A MUJERISTA RESEARCH STUDY

The context of our collaborative study is the family literacy program Aprendamos, located in a densely populated, high-poverty neighborhood in Los Angeles. The neighborhood is home to a large number of newly arrived Latino immigrant families. Although its population includes individuals and families from many Latin American countries, the neighborhood is known locally as a destination for migrants from Central America and Mexico. Many of these residents migrated from indigenous communities in rural areas and speak indigenous languages. It is estimated that many of its residents are undocumented. The neighborhood also contains some of the highest poverty census tracts and lowest performing public schools in the state, and it has historically been a center of gang activity. The Aprendamos family education program offers a range of different services for children and their families in the neighborhood, including summer and after-school programs for children, parent education, and parent-organizing workshops. These programs all emphasize the importance of multilingualism and multiliteracy (literacy in multiple languages). Furthermore, they use critical, culturally relevant pedagogical practices that honor and make use of the knowledge that is already present in the community, while challenging children and adults to critically question the root causes of injustice.

A common thread across all of Aprendamos's programming is the use of what its leaders call *popular education methodology*. Popular education is both a theory and practice of education for liberation. It has roots in Latin American popular social movements, and many of its core ideas and pedagogical practices were popularized by the work of Freire (1999). Although definitions vary, *popular education* is typically understood as a democratic, nonhierarchical, dialogical practice of teaching and learning, undertaken with members of oppressed communities, for the purpose of generating critical consciousness of oppression and collective action for liberation (Arnold & Burke, 1983; Fink, 1992; Freire, 1999; Hamilton & Cunningham, 1989; Kollins & Hansman, 2005; Torres & Fischman, 1994). Core values of popular education include participatory democracy; egalitarianism; dialogue; a critique of oppression; a bottom–up theory of change; and an epistemology that values popular, subjugated, experiential knowledge (Arnold & Burke, 1983; Fink, 1992; Freire, 1999; Hamilton & Cunningham, 1989; Kollins & Hansman, 2005; Torres & Fischman, 1994). The goal of popular education is to empower oppressed people to become their own leaders in liberation struggles by first developing a critical consciousness of oppression. This type of critical consciousness—which sees oppression as unjust, unnatural, socially constructed, and ultimately changeable—is what Freire referred to as *conscientização* (translated in English as *conscientization*; in Spanish, *concientización*). For Freire, liberation for the oppressed requires an ongoing process of reflection and action for social change. This reflection–action–reflection process is what he referred to as *praxis*.

This model of popular education is central to Aprendamos's mission. Its leaders refer to themselves as "popular educators" and note the work of Freire (e.g., 1999) as a foundational influence. Staff and volunteer members attend quarterly popular education trainings, and they work to operationalize the principles and values of popular education in all of their work, as well as in their operating procedures, for example, by adopting a deliberately nonhierarchical organizational structure. Some of the founders and leaders of Aprendamos's parent organization are Latino/a transnationals who brought firsthand experience with popular education movements in Latin America. As such, the Latin American tradition of popular education provides Aprendamos's staff and volunteers with a shared language, values, and theoretical analysis of oppression that guide their work across a variety of programs.

Our research project focused on the Aprendamos family education program that served children in Grades K–5. This program was unique in that it was led and staffed by young adults between the ages of 18 and 24 (the program director at the time, Lidia, was 21 years old). These young adult educators were, with only a few exceptions, 1.5-generationor second-generation Latina/o immigrants and first-generation college students or recent college graduates.[4] By and large, these politicized young adults came to work with Aprendamos as an expression of their commitments to social justice, immigrant rights, and the Latino immigrant community. Most were active in political organizing work, most commonly in movements for immigrant rights or labor rights for immigrant workers. The young adult educators in Aprendamos saw their political organizing work and their educational work with children as inextricably linked: Both were fundamentally geared toward liberation for Latino immigrant families and communities.

The director of the Aprendamos family education program, Lidia, put popular education methodology into practice with children, their parents,

[4]A *1.5-generation immigrant* is someone who migrated to the United States as a young child (Rumbaut, 2004).

and program staff. As we show in this chapter, Lidia also deepened popular education methodology in ways that reflect mujerista ethics and epistemology. Our collaborative mujerista research project was initially conceived through a conversation between Lidia and Kysa (this chapter's first author). Kysa recalls the origins of our study this way:

> I met Lidia when I was a postdoctoral researcher at the University of California, Santa Cruz (UC Santa Cruz). In our first meeting, I was up front about why I had reached out to her: I wanted to do research "on" her and the student activist group she had started for undocumented students. I had a research interest in youth activism and popular education. I had studied Paulo Freire's work and thought I was an expert on it. Now I was looking for some youth activists to do research on, so I could advance my career as an aspiring university professor. I was honest and unashamed about my agenda. She was honest in return. She turned down my invitation to be a research "subject" but invited me to collaborate with her student group as an ally and co-researcher. "Wow!" I thought. "That is one sophisticated 18-year-old!" I was humbled and intrigued. I accepted her invitation and worked with the student group Students Informing Now (SIN) as an ally and coauthor on two articles documenting their work (The S.I.N. Collective, 2007).
>
> Two years later, I got my "dream job" as a tenure-track assistant professor at UC Santa Cruz. The students in SIN—who called themselves SINistas—continued to be part of my life. Whenever I could, I attended SIN events, gatherings, demonstrations, and protests. Some SINistas occasionally dropped by to hang out in my office, and sometimes I dropped by to visit them at the SIN House, a large off-campus house where about 10 SINistas lived together.
>
> Lidia graduated early and moved home to become the director of the Aprendamos family education program. In December 2008, she came to visit Santa Cruz, and I went to the SIN house to say hello. I remember she was cooking dinner at the stove when she started telling me about her work at Aprendamos. She talked about the program, how they practiced popular education methodology with children and their parents, and about her vision for a popular education–based public school. We talked for a couple of hours, and the next thing I knew I was writing up an IRB and grant proposal for a collaborative, community-based engaged ethnographic study of Aprendamos. It may have appeared impulsive from the outside, but it felt so right—so natural and easy. I never even hesitated before jumping into it fully and with all my heart.

We described our collaboration as a "participatory documentation" project, designed to document Aprendamos's work for the broader community while also providing a tool for critical self-reflection on the work. From March 2009, Kysa participated with Aprendamos as an ally and volunteer, and helped recruit and mentor the undergraduate students who served as volunteer popular educators during the summer of 2009. At that time, Mariella graduated from UC Santa Cruz, where she had been an active SINista, and joined the Aprendamos staff as a popular educator working with fifth graders. Paulina Moreno joined the project as Kysa's doctoral student research assistant in the summer of 2009. Paulina recalls her experience joining the collaborative research project:

> I was both excited and nervous to join my advisor and the group of student activists she had been working with. I knew most of them had been her former students and had worked together through SIN, a student organization at UC Santa Cruz. I became aware of their work through an article Kysa and the students coauthored about 540 students' educational experiences and political organizing (Dominguez et al., 2009). As a first-generation, undocumented student attending college I knew firsthand the struggles and challenges of matriculating to an institution of higher education, *sin papeles*. I could recall the anger and frustration I felt after learning the reason why many of the universities I had applied to for undergraduate studies denied me admission. The administration in many of these universities made a systemic decision to exclude me from their incoming class on the basis of my immigration status. Though I had lived in California since I was 5 years old, my nonresident status prevented me from receiving any federal or state financial aid to help me pay for college.
>
> To some degree, I felt that our shared experiences as first-generation, undocumented/documented, immigrant students working toward social change provided us with a common ground, and while nervous, I was equally excited and motivated to join the group whose values of collective action for social justice and educational equity, I deeply shared.

Between March 2009 and March 2011, Kysa and Paulina conducted systematic, ethnographic participation-observations in a variety of spaces: the Aprendamos education program for children, weekly staff meetings, leadership team meetings, parent workshops and parent-organizing events, fundraisers, staff workshops, and retreats. We wrote detailed ethnographic field notes during and/or immediately after every observation. We made audio transcripts of Aprendamos group meetings, including staff meetings, leadership team meetings, parent meetings, and parent workshops. We conducted audiorecorded, semistructured interviews with 12 members of the Aprendamos staff and volunteer educator team. This formal data collection supplemented the informal interactions and relationships we developed as we engaged in the full range of activities that other Aprendamos staff and volunteers undertook. These included the many unglamorous tasks of keeping an underfunded program running—scrubbing a moldy refrigerator at the end of the summer, running out to buy ice packs and Band-Aids for injured children, stepping in to substitute for a sick teacher, moving heavy furniture in preparation for a fundraising event, stacking and unstacking chairs before and after meetings, sweeping and cleaning up the educational spaces and the communal kitchen every day. We were fully engaged in the work of Aprendamos even as we carried out our defined role as collectors of ethnographic data. Paulina reflects back on the ethnographic research this way:

> I was interested in developing a relationship based on solidarity and reciprocity with the participants of Aprendamos. I consciously wanted to reject the role of "spectator" and instead engaged in the role of "witness" and even at times "active participant." Engaged ethnography provided me with an orientation to this process of solidarity and trust building and enabled me to gain access to the experiences and perspectives of Aprendamos participants. Ethnography also facilitated my access to a rich and complex picture of the local and micro processes of resistance that parents and organizers engaged in.

In emphasizing collaboration from a stance of solidarity, our research project recognized the unique and equally valuable knowledge that all participants brought to the process. It aimed to validate and build from the distinct knowledge base of all participants, while recognizing the ways in which our identities and positionalities (e.g., race, class, gender, sexuality, language, immigration status, educational credentials) shape our ways of knowing. In our collaboration, the university-based researcher (Kysa Nygreen) is a university professor and a White, native-born U.S. citizen; these positionalities granted her greater access to power and voice than the young adult educators in Aprendamos. Looking back, she reflects on her identity and positionality in relation to Aprendamos with these words:

> Sometimes I felt like an imposter at Aprendamos, wondering why everyone was so kind and welcoming to me. I felt a deep sense of belonging and comfort in this group of young adult activists . . . but why? Why did they welcome me so warmly? I was an outsider in so many ways . . . by generation, race, ethnicity, national origin, language, social class, social status, educational credentials, social position, and sometimes legal status. All my differences were highly visible—my blond hair, pale skin, and blue eyes standing out in stark contrast within this group of young people of color. And all of my differences conferred power. I am a White, native-born U.S. citizen of Scandanavian descent; a college professor in my 30s; the third generation in my family to obtain a PhD. I was born with every imaginable unearned privilege, especially White privilege and class privilege and U.S. citizenship privilege. I learned to speak Spanish in Spain, in a college study abroad program. I graduated from a private liberal arts college but never carried any student debt. I was an outsider at

> Aprendamos on so many dimensions, but I was always made to feel welcome. And when I got pregnant with my son, the young adult activists in Aprendamos were the first (and only) people outside my immediate family to throw me a baby shower.

We did not deny that such power inequalities existed. Rather, we committed to a consistent dialogue and consciousness on these issues. We recognized that, to cocreate a relationship of solidarity, reciprocity, and trust, we had to acknowledge the existence of power and privilege and the ways in which these play out in the research process. We also recognized the importance of bringing our whole selves to the process. As such, we committed time to nurturing our relationships with each other rather than simply getting down to business in our meetings. The collaborative nature of our research enabled us to share power in articulating relevant questions, interpreting our findings, and sharing our results. The ethnographic methods, as well as the personal relationships we shared, allowed us to focus attention on the private, everyday spaces of knowledge production—such as conversations at Lidia's kitchen table or in sleeping bags on her living room floor, on the subway or in the car, at the *taqueria* or otherwise outside the official spaces of data collection.

In the following section, we offer an extended ethnographic vignette from our research. The setting is a day-long staff retreat that occurred at the end of the Aprendamos summer program for children in 2009. Present at the retreat were 13 paid and volunteer popular educators who had taught more than 100 children between the ages of 5 and 10 in an 8-week summer program, plus two university-based researchers (Kysa Nygreen, Ana Paulina Moreno). The retreat participants ranged in age from 18 to 22, with the exception of one volunteer (14 years old), Kysa (33 years old), and Paulina (28 years old). The purposes of the retreat were to reflect on and evaluate the summer program and to construct a vision for Aprendamos's future. It also aimed to provide closure on what had been an intense 8 weeks for many of the young adult educators.

In writing this chapter, each of us analyzed the written transcript from this staff retreat (107 single-spaced pages of text), together with Kysa's and Paulina's detailed ethnographic field notes from the event. The transcript was a particularly rich and insightful source of data because it captures the organic, back-and-forth conversations and interactions of the participants. In this retreat, the young adult educators reflected on successes and challenges, attempted to solve problems, wrestled together with difficult decisions, and planned actions and activities. Furthermore, they engaged in side conversations and interacted in ways that both revealed and nurtured relationships in the group. The transcript captures all of this dialogue—the planned as well as the impromptu conversations, digressions, personal stories, humor, laughter, and tears. As such, it offers a rich data source for analyzing relational interactions and group processes within Aprendamos. Our participation in the Aprendamos program, and recollections from the retreat itself, provided a lens through which we interpreted and analyzed the transcript. Furthermore, ongoing conversations among ourselves about the program and the retreat served to deepen our analysis and provide further insights. In the following section, we offer an ethnographic picture of the retreat's opening activity, *el altar*. We present this event as an example of mujerista pedagogy in action, that is, a practice of teaching/learning that embodies mujerista epistemology and ethics by engaging the whole self—body, emotions, relationships and spirit.

El Altar: Engaging the Body, Emotions, Relationships, and Spirit

> I am grateful for the transcription/documentation of this moment in our lives at the end of our 2009 summer program. Every word comes back to life as I read it, I remember the experience, the emotions, the colors, the space.
>
> —Mariella Saba

On a hot afternoon in late August, the 13 young adult educators of Aprendamos and two university-based researchers gathered in the living room of a small ground-floor apartment that Lidia, the program director at the time, shared with a roommate. We formed a circle in the room—sitting crossed-legged on the floor, side-by-side on the couch, or on three chairs brought from the kitchen table. The atmosphere was warm and relaxed as everyone talked, joked, laughed, and reminisced. Lorena played her guitar as a few others looked on, sometimes singing or humming along to familiar melodies. Lidia had written an agenda on butcher paper and taped it up over the window. It included a range of activities in this sequence: ground rules, objectives of the meeting, *dinámica*, breathing, el altar, reflection (small groups), reflection (whole group), art, movie.

The written transcript of the meeting begins with Lidia calling everyone's attention and reviewing the agenda. This is how Lidia introduced the meeting:

> I was going to do ground rules, but then I figured we'll just follow all the rules that we've been just doing the whole time that we've been at Aprendamos. But the one thing that I do want to remind you is, two things—This is a safe space and whatever you feel or want to share, this is the space that we definitely need to do that to improve for next years to come and things like that. And two, to respect each other's opinion, too, but not to just be passive about it too. If you have questions and if somebody said something that you don't necessarily agree, make sure you put your opinion forward, but not in disagreement or trying to minimize the other person's opinion, but just as another, serving another opinion.

Lidia's introduction captures some of the core values that we experienced in Aprendamos. First, it is a safe space. In Aprendamos, the notion of "safe space" was not just an empty concept but something that was taken seriously and continuously recreated. It implied a deep notion of safety, meaning the safety to bring one's whole self, in all its complexity, and have all parts of ourselves recognized and validated. It meant the safety to examine and share emotions as well as doubts, fears, uncertainties, and shame. It meant safety to laugh, play, move our bodies, sing, and act silly. And it meant the safety to make mistakes, to not know, to express oneself, and to disagree with each other at times. This is what Lidia's second ground rule speaks to—her request for participants to "make sure you put your opinion forward" and "not just be passive." This statement shows how Lidia is setting a tone of welcoming all voices and encouraging deep dialogue. It also shows her consciousness of how power relations in a group setting can inadvertently function to silence or invalidate certain voices and experiences. Ensuring a safe space means paying attention to power imbalances and taking an explicit welcoming stance on issues like gender identity and expression, sexual identity, dis/ability, immigration status, language, race and ethnicity. As we show in this chapter, the activity of el altar provides evidence that this deep sense of safety was achieved in Aprendamos.

The first activity on the agenda was a dinámica: a fun, light activity (icebreaker) that gets everyone moving, talking, and loosened up in the group. *Dinámicas* are an important part of popular education methodology used in Aprendamos. In addition to their icebreaker function, dinámicas can facilitate deeper reflection. Because they often involve moving or working with our bodies, they invite participants to access the knowledge that exists in our bodies and our emotions. Dinámicas facilitate community building by getting participants to interact together in new and sometimes unfamiliar (even uncomfortable) ways. The first dinámica in the staff retreat was called *las canciones*. Participants picked a piece of paper from a basket with a song name on it. Lidia instructed us to "look around this room and grab anything that will help you and, your paper, or like any instrument or thing that will make a noise. Grab it, go!" The object of the game was to perform a song without using any words, while the group tried to guess the title of the song. Lidia's instruction to move around the room and choose instruments or objects that made noise ensured that everyone got up and walked around, and engaged our bodies in the activity rather than just standing and humming the melody of our song. The dinámica served as a true icebreaker in that everyone was engaged, with much laughter at certain points that some of us were contorting our bodies and rolling on the floor to contain ourselves.

As she moved from the dinámica to the breathing exercise, Lidia explained, "I wanted to do some breathing, just for all of us for like 10 minutes, just to relax . . . to kind of get in that moment of reflection." It would be a 10-minute silent meditation, during which she asked us to focus on our breath and notice what emotions came up for us as we thought about the summer, "your roles, how you felt about it, moments of happiness, stress, emotions, et cetera." She instructed us to close our eyes if we felt comfortable doing so, or to rest our eyes softly on the floor or the wall if we preferred that. The room fell completely silent and still for 10 minutes. Lidia used a quiet chime to bring us out of the meditation, and the room remained silent. In a gentle voice, she asked us to "find an object that represents the feeling that came to you during the meditation. We're going to create an altar with all of those objects." At one end of the room, she had placed a colorful tapestry on a table with incense, dried corn, and cotton. That was the foundation on which we would build our altar. Lidia lighted the incense as she welcomed us out of the meditation.

We all followed Lidia's instruction to find an object in the house. She had not instructed us to remain silent, but everyone did. It was a peaceful, sacred silence rather than an awkward one—a drastic change from the rambunctious laughter we had experienced just moments earlier during the dinámica. Everyone took the activity seriously. Respect for Lidia and for the process we were engaged in was evident. When everyone returned to the circle with our objects, Lidia introduced the altar activity with these words:

> In a lot of different, a lot of different indigenous cultures and spiritual circles, creating altars or altares is something very symbolic. The things that we remember from our past and when we envision something, things that represent also the future. And so, for example in Mexican culture, you know *Dia de Muertos*, you put an altar in representation of people that passed away, right? And to remember them. But other, like ceremonies, like sweat lodges or peyote ceremonies, you create altars with different things to represent the past and the future, right? For future generations.
>
> And I think a lot of the things we did this summer is not necessarily for us, right? Because we're not kids anymore. But we were once and some of us will have kids in the future. So it's very symbolic and very spiritual and, you know, spirituality is different from religion. . . . I definitely wanted to take this one thing to bring us together in that way, the deeper way, because what we did has really left a huge mark in that community, and I wanted to recognize it as such.
>
> So who would like to start talking about their object and then placing it on the altar? I started off just with the incense because fire represents passion and we definitely have to have a lot of passion for what we did this summer, and so it's there already for us to enjoy. And then the cotton and the corn are crops from our, from my ancestors, and from our ancestors, but also corn is very representative of productivity and growth and life. So that's already there as a foundation and then we'll add on to those.

Participants shared, one by one, the objects they had chosen. Each spoke when he or she felt inspired to do so, rather than going in order. Each person spoke in a frank, honest tone. We were not made to feel as if there was a right or wrong way to do it, and nobody seemed tempted into saying something clever or trite for the sake of performance. The responses, instead, conveyed authenticity and vulnerability. They also spoke to the interconnectedness of the personal, political, spiritual, and historical dimensions of participants' identities. For example, Gustavo had selected a poster that he himself had designed for an immigrant rights rally: "It symbolizes my passion, organizing, and also just being involved in the arts." The poster is a holistic representation of Gustavo as a complex human being with multiple parts of self—political commitments to immigrant rights, experience with political organizing movements, a passion and a talent for artistic expression, and an identity as an immigrant himself. He is all of these at once and they cannot be separated, just as these dimensions cannot be separated out of the poster.

Migration, immigrant identity, and family history were salient themes for many of the participants. Izel, who lived in the apartment with Lidia, had taken a framed photo of herself as a child with her grandmother. She explained that the photo had been taken in Mexico, the last time she saw her grandmother before migrating to the United States. "We're always migrating, right?" she reflected, "No matter if we're migrating to different countries, different cities. And our students, they come from migrating families too." With this statement, Izel is recognizing her connection to the children of Aprendamos on the basis of shared transnational migrant identities, and conveying the significance of her own migration history to her sense of self. She went on: "The word *lak'ech*, how we are each other, I see you, you see me, you are me, you know?" Here, Izel connected her identity to a deeper history, drawing from indigenous language and culture to express the unity of all beings—"you are me," she said. She explained further:

> Even though we may be a different generation, they [the children in Aprendamos] look up to us and we also look up to them, and how we really learn from them. And so this is my grandmother, on my mom's side, and this is me. And it just reminded me of that. It's just like this movement, this circle, learning from each other. That's what I saw at Aprendamos a lot, teachers with students, students with teachers.

Izel's image of the circle, and the interconnectedness of beings and generations, is connected to her migrant identity, her transnational identity, and her sense of self rooted in a family history. For Izel, as with other Aprendamos educators, her familial, historical, spiritual, cultural, and immigrant identities were a framework and source of inspiration for her work at Aprendamos. These aspects of the self could not be untangled or separated out, but together made up the complex whole of her being.

Izel's words reflect a mujerista way of knowing because they honor multiple parts of self and embody a historicized and politicized way of understanding the self. Mujerista theory reminds us that everyone is socially located at the intersection of multiple intersecting oppressions and histories. These histories, and these structures of oppression in which our histories unfold, are parts of the self and they inform our selves. We cannot conceive of our identities without acknowledging the role of history, and of oppression, in shaping our experiences and our selves. Like Izel, other young adult educators in Aprendamos consistently articulated this holistic awareness and understanding of self in relation to history, power, and oppression. This mujerista understanding of self was encouraged and nurtured through the popular education methodology used in Aprendamos.

The altar activity also enabled the young adult educators to express vulnerability and creativity. For example, Lorena chose a tampon for the altar, "because I felt *tapada* [covered/stuck] this summer." She went on, "I would stop myself and I would try to let something out and I would stop myself." Her words convey a level of self-reflection as well as trust in the group as a safe space for expressing vulnerability. As she continued to talk about her object, she said,

> I'm so passionate about education and I became more passionate about it working with them [children in Aprendamos] because it's such a challenge but it was . . . it was sacred. And that's how I was referring to it, the interactions that we have with these individuals and people is very sacred.

Here, Lorena chose the word *sacred* to talk about her experience of teaching, and the relationships and interactions that she had with children, parents, and other staff members during the summer. The altar activity enabled participants to access this part of ourselves—the dimension of the sacred and spiritual—and to reflect on how these dimensions of self connect to the work of educating children. As Lorena placed the tampon on the altar, the group laughed a little and Lorena commented, "It represents moodiness, too, because there was a lot of moodiness. And there's a lot of women."

The presence of emotional safety was also evident when Alex shared a bottle with a white label with three black Xs on it:

> I picked this up because it's black and white and so am I. It has a lot of polarities, and I think I'm like that. I'm a lot of both things, both opposites. Like I'm a lot of adult but I'm definitely a lot of kid.

This statement conveys various dimensions of Alex's personal identity as someone who was a young adult (a mix of adult and child), and also identified as biracial and genderqueer—"a lot of both things, both opposites"—a person whose experience both contains and challenges binaries. Alex continued,

> And I think that I picked it up because it said "germs," and I'm so used to being the one person or the one, being in a room that people can't stand, or that they don't want to be around because I'm different.

Alex showed a feeling of safety to be vulnerable here, bringing in the personal experience of feeling shamed or ostracized, (like "germs") for being "different." Alex went on:

> And you asked us to think about this whole summer, and a lot of stuff with my family came up in my head, about how they just don't want me to be there. . . . I think that I found a lot more family with Aprendamos than I did with my own family this period of time that I was here.

Here, Alex brought in aspects of family life and connects those to the work of Aprendamos, while also conveying the sense that Aprendamos has become like a family—a truly welcoming and safe space. This experience of emotional safety in Aprendamos carried a special significance for Alex, as she went on to suggest:

> I was so scared of what the kids would say to me, or like what they would ask me, and I was so scared about the parents and how it was going to be just looking so different from what is the norm. And I was afraid that they weren't going to like me. But they did.

Interpreting El Altar

We offer this description of el altar as an example of mujerista pedagogy. This pedagogy engages the whole self; integrates the corporal, emotional, spiritual, and relational dimensions of self; and honors multiple ways of knowing. It is a pedagogy that recognizes and invites the sacred, emotional, raw, honest, and vulnerable parts of self to be fully present. It acknowledges that all parts of the self are sources of knowledge, and that each person is a complex integrated human being that cannot be divided or compartmentalized. It is grounded in a mujerista epistemology: the belief that knowledge is accessed through one's body, emotions, and connection to the spiritual world and to community. This pedagogy creates a safe space and nurtures a sense of belonging.

The altar activity was but one in a day-long staff retreat that included agenda items to engage multiple parts of the self. Although the retreat included some standard meeting items that one would expect to find at a professional staff retreat—such as the mix of small-group and whole-group discussions—it also included items such as meditation, the creation of an altar, and opportunities for artistic expression and for spontaneous fun and play. These activities invite participants to access their whole selves, and they strengthen and nurture relationships that are the core of Aprendamos's work. It is impressive that Lidia, only 21 at the time, was able to incorporate an activity such as this with young adults who were not joined together in an organized spiritual community. Lidia commanded their respect and full investment in el altar, an activity that could lead young adults in other contexts to resist, roll eyes, giggle, or dismiss (Cannon, 2014). For more than an hour, as the 15 young adults took turns placing objects on the altar and explaining why we chose them, the mood in the room remained solemn and focused. The space was vulnerable and intimate, with many tears and hugs along the way. It felt like a family in the best sense of the term. These outcomes are evidence of Lidia's extraordinary leadership abilities, as well as the power and potential of mujerista pedagogy.

Nourishing the Whole Self

> When I look back upon my time at Aprendamos, I remember feeling at ease, welcomed, and accepted. I remember feeling intellectually and politically challenged, but in a deeply loving, nurturing, and non-judgmental way . . . I had never experienced anything quite like it. When I was hanging around at Aprendamos, I felt valued, seen and heard, and fully accepted for who I am. For once, I wasn't posturing or posing or performing. I was just allowed to be myself—nothing to prove, nothing to hide, no one to be. And that was a strange feeling for me, because it's not the way I was used to living my life. The mujerista pedagogy I witnessed and experienced in Aprendamos touched me inside, opened my heart, grew my compassion, and propelled my own personal journey of healing. In a certain sense, it saved my life . . . because I had been living a false life, a fabricated life that concealed layers upon layers of guilt, shame and self-hate. It saved my life by setting me on a journey toward self-love.
>
> —Kysa

Looking back on this intimate moment in our lives as youth colearners and coeducators, we recognize our contribution to a continued story, a legacy, a practice, a movement that works to nourish the whole self. Looking back, we are happy to notice that we are more whole today than we were then, because we have continued this path and practice of *nourishing*—unlearning, healing, growing, loving the whole self, as in me, you, us, the big picture we all shape. Each of us was touched in personal ways by our experience with Aprendamos, and by the mujerista pedagogy we participated in. We are happy to say that the Aprendamos program continues on to this day, under Ana Mariella Moreno's leadership, continuing the legacy of mujerista popular education pedagogy with children, their parents, and a new generation of young adult activist staff.

Popular education methodology strives for critical consciousness and liberation from oppression. But we, as mujerista popular educators, know true liberation can only be achieved when we first attend to our personal healing. We must heal our selves from the pain inflicted by trauma, violence, criminalization, institutionalized oppression and internalized oppression. We must facilitate education, a daily life practice, to nourish the whole self. When we say *self*, we mean an entire community—*self* as collective identity. We say *whole* because we recognize that we find ourselves in pieces—broken, injured, segregated, divided, standardized, incarcerated, dehumanized—within systems that control our lives including our education. Although our minds, bodies, spirit, families, and communities have been historically and systemically broken, we are still whole people. We must attend to our whole selves, and nurture our relationships with self, spirit, and each other. Critical consciousness, liberation, and personal healing are profoundly connected and must be approached in an integrated fashion. The concept of mujerismo helps us to recognize these connections, and guides us toward research processes, pedagogies, and clinical practices that nourish the whole self. These practices integrate the cognitive with the emotional, corporal, spiritual, and relational dimensions of self to promote personal healing and true liberation.

REFERENCES

Arnold, R., & Burke, B. (1983). *A popular education handbook: An educational experience taken from Central America and adapted to the Canadian context*. Toronto, Ontario, Canada: CUSO Development Education. Retrieved from http://files.eric.ed.gov/fulltext/ED289024.pdf

Beckman, L. J. (2014). Training in feminist research methodology: Doing research on the margins. *Women & Therapy, 37*, 164–177. http://dx.doi.org/10.1080/02703149.2014.850347

Cannon, J. (2014). *Toward an embodied liberatory pedagogy: Mindfulness, student resistance, and the limits of fast-track teacher prep* (Unpublished doctoral dissertation). University of Massachusetts Amherst, Amherst, MA.

Collins, P. H. (1996). What's in a name? Womanism, Black feminism, and beyond. *The Black Scholar, 26*, 9–17.

Collins, P. H. (1998). *Fighting words: Black women and the search for justice*. Minneapolis, MN: University of Minnesota Press.

Cruz, C. (2001). Toward an epistemology of a brown body. *International Journal of Qualitative Studies in Education, 14*, 657–669. http://dx.doi.org/10.1080/09518390110059874

Cruz, C. (2006). *Testimonial narratives of queer street youth: Toward an epistemology of a brown body* (Unpublished doctoral dissertation). University of California, Los Angeles.

Delgado Bernal, D. (2006). Learning and living pedagogies of the home: The Mestiza consciousness of Chicana students. In D. Delgado Bernal, C. A. Elenes, F. E. Godinez, & S. Villenas (Eds.), *Chicana/Latina education in everyday life: Feminista perspectives on pedagogy and epistemology* (pp. 113–132). Albany: State University of New York Press.

Dominguez, N., Duarte, Y., Espinosa, P. J., Martinez, L., Nygreen, K., Perez, R., . . . Saba, M. (2009). Constructing a counternarrative: Students Informing Now (S.I.N.) reframes immigration and education in the United States. *Journal of Adolescent & Adult Literacy, 52*, 439–442. http://dx.doi.org/10.1598/JAAL.52.5.8

Dyrness, A. (2008). Research for change versus research as change: Lessons from a *Mujerista* participatory research team. *Anthropology and Education Quarterly, 39*, 23–44.

Dyrness, A. (2011). *Mothers united: An immigrant struggle for socially just education*. Minneapolis: University of Minnesota Press.

Fals-Borda, O., & Rahman, M. A. (1991). *Action and knowledge: breaking the monopoly with participatory action-research*. New York, NY: Apex Press.

Fink, M. (1992). Women and popular education in Latin America. In N. P. Stromquist (Ed.), *Women and education in Latin America: Knowledge, power, and change* (pp. 174–194). Boulder, CO: Lynne Rienner.

Freire, P. (1999). *Pedagogy of the oppressed*. New York, NY: Continuum.

Galván, R. T. (2006). *Campesina* epistemologies and pedagogies of the spirit: Examining women's *sobrevivencia*. In D. Delgado Bernal, C. A. Elenes, F. E. Godinez, & S. Villenas (Eds.), *Chicana/Latina education in everyday life: Feminista perspectives on pedagogy and epistemology* (pp. 161–179). Albany: State University of New York Press.

Hamilton, E., & Cunningham, P. (1989). Community-based adult education. In S. B. Merriam & P. M. Cunningham (Eds.), *Handbook of adult and continuing education* (pp. 439–450). San Francisco, CA: Jossey Bass.

Hesse-Biber, S. N. (2007). Feminist research: Exploring the interconnections of epistemology, methodology, and method. In S. N. Hesse-Biber (Ed.), *Handbook of feminist research: Theory and praxis* (pp. 1–26). Thousand Oaks, CA: Sage.

Hong, G. K. (2006). *The ruptures of American capita: Women of color feminism and the culture of immigrant labor*. Minneapolis, MN: University of Minnesota Press.

Hurtado, A. (1996). *The color of privilege: Three blasphemies on race and feminism*. Ann Arbor: University of Michigan.

Hurtado, A. (2003). *Voicing Chicana feminisms: Young women speak out on sexuality and identity*. New York, NY: New York University Press.

Kim, H. S. (2007). The politics of border crossings: Black, postcolonial, and transnational feminist perspectives. In S. N. Hesse-Biber (Ed.), *Handbook of feminist research: Theory and praxis* (pp. 107–122). Thousand Oaks, CA: Sage.

Kollins, J. M., & Hansman, C. A. (2005). The role of women in popular education in Bolivia: A case study of the Oficina Juridica Para La Mujer. *Adult Basic education: An Interdisciplinary Journal for Adult Literacy Educational Planning, 15*, 3–20.

Maguire, P. (1987). *Doing participatory research: A feminist approach*. Amherst: Center for International Education, School of Education, University of Massachusetts.

Pérez, E. (1999). *The decolonial imaginary: Writing Chicanas into history*. Bloomington: Indiana University Press.

Rumbaut, R. G. (2004). Ages, life states, and generational cohorts: Decomposing the immigrant first and second generations in the United States. *International Migration Review, 38*, 1160–1205. Retrieved from http://papers.ssrn.com/sol3/papers.cfm?abstract_id=1887924

Sandoval, C. (2000). *Methodology of the oppressed*. Minneapolis: University of Minnesota Press.

Shohat, E. (2001). Introduction. In E. Shohat (Ed.), *Talking visions: Multicultural feminism in a transnational age*. Cambridge, MA: MIT Press.

Smith, D. (1987). *The everyday world as problematic: A feminist sociology*. Boston, MA: Northeastern University Press.

The Students Informing Now Collective. (2007). Students Informing Now (SIN) challenge the racial state in California without shame . . . SIN verguenza. *Educational Foundations, 21*, 71–90.

Torres, C. A., & Fischman, G. (1994). Popular education: Building from experience. *New Directions for Adult and Continuing Education, 63*, 81–92. http://dx.doi.org/10.1002/ace.36719946309

Villenas, S. (2006). Pedagogical moments in the borderlands: Latina mothers and daughters teaching and learning. In D. Delgado Bernal, C. A. Elenes, F. Godinez, & S. Villenas (Eds.), *Chicana/Latina education in everyday life: Feminista perspectives on pedagogy and epistemology* (pp. 147–159). Albany, NY: State University of New York Press.

Villenas, S., Godinez, F. E., Delgado Bernal, D., & Elenes, C. A. (2006). Chicanas/Latinas building bridges: An introduction. In D. Delgado Bernal, C. A. Elenes, F. E. Godinez, & S. Villenas (Eds.), *Chicana/Latina education in everyday life: Feminista perspectives on pedagogy and epistemology* (pp. 1–10). Albany, NY: State University of New York Press.

Walker, A. (1983). *In search of our mothers' gardens: Womanist prose*. San Diego, CA: Harcourt Brace Jovanovich.

[illegible] (20[illegible]). [illegible] women in [illegible] in Bolivia [illegible] North Africa [illegible]

[illegible] (19[illegible]). [illegible] Education, School of Education [illegible]

[illegible] (20[illegible]). [illegible] University Press.

[illegible] (20[illegible]). [illegible] the United States [illegible]

[illegible] (20[illegible]). [illegible]

[illegible] (20[illegible]). [illegible] Cambridge, MA: MIT Press.

[illegible] Alternative [illegible]

The [illegible] (20[illegible]). [illegible]

[illegible] (20[illegible]). [illegible] Education [illegible]

[illegible] (20[illegible]). [illegible]

[illegible] (20[illegible]). [illegible] New York [illegible]

[illegible]

II

CLINICAL PRACTICE

3

WOMANIST THERAPY WITH BLACK WOMEN

JANIS V. SANCHEZ-HUCLES

Effective psychotherapy with Black women requires vigilant attention to both race and gender, but within psychology, the issues of race and gender have been compartmentalized (Williams, 2005). Afrocentric models have emphasized spirituality, communalism, fluid time, emotional expressiveness, harmony with nature, interdependence, and allegiance to African cultural ideals to protect against the vicissitudes of racism (Mbiti, 1990; Nobles, 1991; White, 1984). Concomitantly, feminist models of therapy have emphasized affectional relatedness, empathy, and nurturance as vehicles for women's ways of being, knowing, caring, and deciding as sources of emotional strength (Alcoff, 1988; Belenky, Clinchy, Goldberger, & Tarule, 1986; Chodorow, 1978; Gilligan, 1982; Jordan, Kaplan, Miller, Stiver, & Surrey, 1991; Miller, 1986; C. B. Williams & Wiggins, 2010). But neither the Afrocentric nor feminist models have fully incorporated the diversity of Black women (C. B. Williams & Wiggins, 2010).

http://dx.doi.org/10.1037/14937-004
Womanist and Mujerista Psychologies: Voices of Fire, Acts of Courage, T. Bryant-Davis and L. Comas-Díaz (Editors)

These Afrocentric and feminist concepts tend to marginalize Black women, as their beliefs about who they were do not fully fit in accord with either model (Williams, 2005; C. B. Williams & Wiggins, 2010). Afrocentric theories concentrate on race and the experiences of Black men (Asante, 1987, 1992; Nobles, 1991; White, 1984). Feminist theories focus on highly educated White women with different characteristics from many Black women (Barnett & Rivers, 2004; Bohan, 1993; Comas-Díaz & Greene, 1994; Landrine, 1995; Pollitt, 1992; Reid, 1993; West & Zimmerman, 1991).

Black women live in a world that still stigmatizes race and gender, as well as sexual orientation, class, age, disability, economic status, and other social distinctions. They have developed womanist therapy to encompass Black women who embody multiple cultural identities. Womanist therapy offers strategies that integrate multiple cultural variables into a coherent sense of self (C. B. Williams & Wiggins, 2010).

In this chapter, I highlight important features of womanist therapy, noting the problems with feminist theories for Black women, discussing the defining features of womanist therapy, and concluding with case vignettes of womanist therapy with three Black women. I have worked with clients for more than 40 years and regularly receive referrals to work with Black women in my private practice.

As a Black woman who has personally and professionally examined multiple and intersecting identities with ancestors from Virginia, New York, and Cuba, I enjoy the challenge of working with clients who also have multiple identities. As noted by L. S. Brown (1994), effective therapy cannot stem from a theory that would require someone to choose which aspect of her identity is to be liberated while others are silenced, unattended, or rendered marginal. Therapy needs to be multicultural in its core (Enns & Byars-Winston, 2010). I therefore describe womanist therapy in this chapter in the belief that with determined effort, womanism can be used to incorporate the full experiences of women of color (WOC).

WOMANIST THEORIES

Historically, what was missing from the literature was a multicultural feminist therapy for Black women that fully embraced all aspects of their being. Hence, Black women have developed the concept of womanism. This idea addresses the concomitant and interactive forces of racism, sexism, and classism that Black women face and is built on the strengths of African American female culture, with its commitment to survival and emotional strength (C. B. Williams & Wiggins, 2010). The term *womanist* was coined by Alice Walker (1983):

> A woman who loves another woman, sexually and/or nonsexually. She appreciates and prefers women's culture, women's emotional flexibility . . . she is committed to the survival and wholeness of an entire people, male and female. Not a separatist, except periodically for health . . . loves the spirit . . . loves struggle. Loves herself. Regardless. (p. xi)

Ogunyemi (1985) contended that the womanist vision is to answer the ultimate question of how to equitably share power among the races and between the sexes. Another definition of womanism comes from Phillips (2006), who asserted that the basic tenets of womanism include a strong, self-authored spirit of activism. In addition, a key component of a womanist discourse is the role that spirituality and ethics has in ending the interlocking oppression of race, gender, and class that circumscribes the lives of African American women (Comas-Díaz, 2008; C. B. Williams, 2008). The strong focus on spirituality is a key element of womanism and is a holdover from the Afrocentric philosophy (A. C. Jones, 1993).

Many therapists bring their unique cultural experiences to the form of womanism that they practice. For instance, Boyd-Franklin (2003) emphasized womanist therapy from a family therapy approach. Bryant-Davis used the wholeness, stress, and resilience of womanist therapy to discuss childhood violence (Bryant-Davis, 2005a), trauma (Bryant-Davis, 2005b), and the importance of sisterhood in the lives of African American women (Bryant-Davis, 2013). Comas-Díaz (2008) introduced the concept of *Spirita*, a womanist and mujerista spirituality. Spirita is a universal way of knowing and being that increases collective healing, international solidarity, and global social justice and helps move the experiences of WOC from the margins to the center of feminist thought (Comas-Díaz, 2008). Evans, Kincade, Marbley, and Seem (2005) are counseling psychologists and use womanist approaches to illustrate that the personal is political and are interested in not only women but also uplifting an entire culture through therapy with individual women. Greene and Sanchez-Hucles (1998) articulated a framework for using a more womanist therapy in their work to expand feminist theory and clinical practice. Moodley (2005) is one of the few men of color to discuss therapy with WOC and does so in the context of suggesting the use of gender to talk about unwanted and split-off feelings by bestowing upon race a special set of vocabularies, epistemologies, and linguistic resonance that offers client and therapist a "good-enough" holding environment to explore complex interpersonal issues through the gendering of race. Nabors and Pettee (2003) used womanism in a therapeutic context for working with African American women with disabilities. They stress the importance of family roles for these women, as well as how such patient roles were rendered invisible by the health system (Matlin, 2000). Nabors and Pettee highlight the need to discard "superwoman" expectations and the importance of not replicating any experiences of invisibility but, instead, of empowering clients to express their needs and to identify what they wish to address. C. B. Williams has written extensively on the use of womanism with Black women (C. B. Williams, 2005, 2008), and with Wiggins (C. B. Williams & Wiggins, 2010). C. B. Williams (2005) noted that successful work with Black women requires an understanding and devotion to cultural context to address their oppressions and to offer strategies (e.g., contextualizing problems, drawing on the legacy of social justice activism, creating networks of support and connection) to counteract attempts to minimize and marginalize their identities. She further noted (C. B. Williams, 2008) that *womanism* is a therapeutic term that transcends the universalizing, hierarchical, and dualistic limitations of Afrocentric and feminist psychology and, based on the folk culture of Black women, offers a model that is committed to survival and wholeness and addresses all of the oppressions experienced by them. C. B. Williams and Wiggins (2010) avered that womanism is not religious with respect to being aligned with a specific organization, polity, doctrine, or set of rituals but is focused on issues of empowerment and life enhancement for Black women who embrace gender, race, and cultural and spiritual strengths to confront the vicissitudes of life. Womanism is still a new and evolving therapy that has some features in common across therapists as well as some areas of difference. The womanism that I use draws on many elements from the womanist authors noted above and in Exhibit 3.1, and in the case studies at the end of this chapter.

My therapeutic work with Black women is similar to that of these womanist therapists. Each of us brings our own individual training to the womanist arena. My therapy with WOC uses elements of all of these therapists with different clients and establishes women as equal to men in stature, in speech, and thought. It acknowledges and discards the notion that WOC are somehow less than men, despite living in a culture that often values men of color over WOC. It recognizes that WOC have a ritual of life that is inherently different from White women with respect to how they relate to partners, children, family members, and work because of the forces of gender, sexism, race, and culture. This womanism acknowledges that WOC seek equality with all women and men, and fights for justice for all across race, gender, and class. It recognizes that WOC are different from White women in subtle ways as well. If one witnesses a gathering of women, WOC do not emulate the social/nervous laughter of some White women, nor do they feel the need to apologize, smile in the absence of stimuli, or laugh at jokes that

EXHIBIT 3.1
The Defining Principles of Womanism

1. Women of color (WOC) are equal to all other women and men in status, speech, and thinking.
2. Their ritual of life is unique with respect to partners, children, family members, and work.
3. Their lives are shaped by the interaction of gender, race, sexism, racism, sexual orientation, culture, class, and ability.
4. WOC are inspired and strengthened by other women and men (including ancestors), spirituality, and a belief in themselves as strengthened by each other.
5. WOC come from an amalgam of cultures that is unique, and they have a deep sense of what is important and should be valued.
6. WOC have their own sense of humor; they do not always laugh when others do and can tear up easily or resist showing emotions. They can be flexible and spontaneous in their emotional expression.
7. This idea of womanism accepts clients where they are and works to help free clients from oppressive heterosexist, racist, and class-bound strictures of society.
8. WOC adhere to and value womanist culture, womanist stories, and their race and ethnicity as they actively work to share power among the races and sexes
9. WOC have the belief that all people are connected, even if people must work to view and comprehend our connection.

are not funny in the ways that some White women might. At times, the Black women in the group might be stoic and, at others times, voluble and expressive. WOC come from a different culture, perhaps with a different sense of what is important and valued. They are inspired and strengthened by other men and women, ancestors, spirituality, and a belief in themselves as reinforced by each other. They have a unique culture and set of values, a distinct sense of humor, and a flexible and spontaneous expression of emotions. A womanist therapist accepts clients where they are and works to help free clients from oppressive heterosexist, racist, and class-bound strictures of society. WOC value their womanist culture, race, and ethnicity as they strive to share power across race and sex. Many WOC believe that people are all connected, even if they must work to view and comprehend those connections.

Borrowing from Walker's (1983) ideas, I use an understanding of womanism as appreciating and adhering to a woman's culture and a commitment to one's own race. Further, this womanism adhere to activism and use spirituality and ethics to break the interlocking oppressions of race, gender, and class (Phillips, 2006). The principles of Exhibit 3.1 offer common ground for womanist therapists, and Exhibit 3.2 lists the multiple intersecting identities that womanism addresses and honors—intersecting identities that have often been overlooked in feminist therapy but that are important to the health and well-being of Black women.

EXHIBIT 3.2
Intersecting Identities Addressed by Womanism

1. Gender
2. Ethnicity
3. Race
4. Class
5. Sexual orientation
6. Spirituality
7. Culture
8. Ability status
9. Occupation
10. Balancing multiple roles
11. Caring for family and extended family members
12. Involvement in church and community
13. Contending with sexism and stereotyping
14. Relationships with fictive kin
15. Transmitting their values to others by life examples

PROBLEMS WITH FEMINIST THEORIES FOR BLACK WOMEN

Feminist psychology was developed to correct and counteract the prevailing masculine views of women that have historically framed women in opposition to men and found them lacking. Feminist theories have long focused primarily on middle-class White women (Collins, 1991; Comas-Díaz, 1991; Walker, 1995) and have examined gender issues, career options, and political involvement (M. K. Williams, McCandies, & Dunlap, 2002).

However, the issues most relevant to WOC were initially overlooked in feminism and feminist therapy. Missing from the dialogue were careful examinations of race, class, gender, sexual orientation, spirituality, culture, ethnicity, physical disability, their intersection, multiple identities, and oppressions. Fine (1985, 1997) has consistently noted that feminist psychology has been nonrepresentative of the full diversity of the female experience and has often overlooked ethnic minority, working-class, poor, and sexual minority women.

Ethnic minority theorists underlined several areas that were different for WOC versus White women. A primary distinction is the use of an all-inclusive definition for *woman*: A shared biological and social bond that produces some common experiences and gender oppression and does not outweigh, overshadow, or minimize the diverse individual and group differences that WOC bring (di Stefano, 1990). Collins (1991) noted that the "universal woman" of feminist psychology was in fact White and middle class. Further, although White women experience sexism, they concomitantly are privileged by virtue of their Whiteness (McIntosh, 1992).

Another essential difference is that historically, feminism advocated that gender is the most important aspect for all women, whereas WOC have asserted that gender is mediated by other identities to produce different valences, resulting in different understandings of what it is to be a woman in different ethnic groups (Collins, 1991; Espin & Gawelek, 1992; Greene, 1994). For White women, the central model of inquiry has been the study of the mother–daughter relationship; the historical expectation to remain at home to raise children and not work; and the resultant effects on identity, self-esteem, and ability to form and maintain interactions with others (Golden, 1996; Miller, 1991).

In contrast, WOC have a longer history of working both within and outside of the home, of balancing multiple roles within their families while caring for extended family members, of being extensively involved in church and community activities, and of contending with varying degrees of stereotyping (Al-Mateen, Christian, Mishra, Cofield, & Tildon, 2002). WOC often have close relationships with their mothers, and many WOC have pseudomothers—aunts, grandmothers, godmothers, and nonfamilial relationships with "fictive kin" (Boyd-Franklin, 1989).

Because ethnic communities are generally more collectivistic, they have diverse models of socialization across ethnic women that create unique identities. Constantine, Greer, and Kindaichi (2003) indicated that given the collectivistic orientation of WOC, it is important to use holistic approaches that include family, friends, spirituality, and community resources rather than focusing more narrowly on individualistic and introspective approaches to understand them theoretically and clinically. Whereas feminism for White women has focused on gender, a feminist approach with WOC must include both ethnic- and gender-specific approaches (Comas-Díaz, 2013).

Reid and Kelly (1994) empirically demonstrated the biases inherent in research on WOC. Many studies lack generalizability to all women, because of limited sampling of WOC, a lack of specificity with respect to analyses by ethnicity, and a concentration on what are deemed to be specific problem areas for WOC: poverty and teen pregnancy. Thus, WOC are often overlooked in the theoretical and clinical research currently conducted on women.

A final charge against feminism is that the literature has not been able to come up with a term that fully incorporates the unique experiences of individual WOC and the overall study of poverty, racism, and ethnocentrism. Further, it has not viewed all of these oppressive forces as being on par with sexism and equally in need of further study (Henley, Meng, O'Brien, McCarthy, & Sockloskie, 1998).

WOMANIST THERAPY VIGNETTES

Case Study 1: Madeline

Madeline was a single, heterosexual, 32-year-old Black woman from Hampton Roads, Virginia. She was the eldest in a family of five children and two parents. Her parents were deceased. When they were living, they appeared to have a good relationship. The father had worked full time as a janitor, and her mother had done part-time work as a seamstress. Growing up, Madeline often had the responsibility of assisting her mother and father in babysitting and parenting her siblings. Following the death of both her parents, when she was 22, she began raising her two youngest siblings, two sisters who were 12 and 14 (and are now 22 and 24). She has had several unsuccessful love affairs in her past.

Madeline: Well, I guess I came in today because it seems that I am carrying loads of stress that are just coming out in ways that I can't predict or control.

Therapist: Can you give me an example?

Madeline: Yes, I can. I am a flight attendant, and on a recent trip I had a passenger that kept making demands. The pilot instructed the flight attendants to be seated, but this woman rang the bell to ask for more juice. I was so over her litany of requests. I leaned over her, looked her in the eyes and told her to sit still and shut up! The woman was shocked. She paled, cowered, and complied. I went back to my seat and sat down. I realized that I had broken so many rules on proper decorum for flight attendants, and I realized that if she complained, I could lose my job. But right then, all I could feel was good for finally telling someone to leave me alone.

Therapist: So you initially felt good about your response?

Madeline: Yes, very much so. I felt a sense of freedom in telling that woman to just back off! I thought of how many times people had made demands on me and I always had to smile and politely comply.

Therapist: I am sure that you felt good for giving her a piece of your mind. It sounds as though you also felt some conflict for endangering your job.

Madeline: Yes. I had never lost it like that before. Most of me is pretty amazed that I said what I did. I don't recall ever feeling so angry and out of control. I am typically a model of decorum.

Soul Wounds

This segment shows Madeline acting in a wildly divergent way from her typical patterns of interaction. When she stated that she had never lost control of her actions before, I immediately thought of Duran's (2006) work on soul wounds and also of the functioning of unconscious motivation. WOC often have deep soul wounds stemming from cultural trauma that incorporates ungrieved losses, learned helplessness, and internalized oppression (Duran, 2006). As we talked over the course of sessions, Madeline spoke about all of the times that she had to force back a biting response to a person in authority who had belittled her in some way. She had been taught by her parents to be polite and respectful to others, but this behavior caused "soul wounds" to her psyche when she let attacks go unchallenged.

Madeline was adhering to a standard that many Black women have been taught (Jack & Ali, 2010). She learned from her family that she should be stoic and silent about environmental pressures and the attendant pain and distress (Sue & Sue, 2008; T. M. Williams, 2008). These pressures and pain build up and can lead to unpremeditated outbursts. Most frequently, Madeline felt that insensitive comments had come from White individuals. Eventually however, she also shared a story about an older relative who had tried to take sexual advantage of her when she was growing up. Although Madeline had been able to escape from further assault, she had been subjected to the fondling of this relative. She immediately became concerned with protecting her younger siblings from this abuse, so she spoke to her sisters to warn them of this danger. Madeline's feelings of protectiveness toward her younger sisters were quite evident. We spoke of how frequently Black women have been violated and named authors who shared stories of rapes in their own lives and in their literature (Bryant-Davis, 2005a, 2005b).

Self-Care

A primary focus early in therapy was to help Madeline recognize that as supportive as she was to her younger sisters, she herself needed more love and attention. I stressed how important it was for her to take care of herself and that we uplift others eventually by effective self-care first (Evans et al., 2005). I challenged her to make a list of things that she liked to do and how frequently she did them. I prescribed three easy activities to do per day, one special event per week, two special events per month, and something significantly special to look forward to every 6 months. Gradually, Madeline incorporated long baths with candles and tea, sit-down dinners, chocolate chip cookies, weekly church visits and meeting with girlfriends, monthly visits to a salon for pedicures and manicures, and occasional trips to visit with friends.

Cultural Strengths and Shifting

We spoke of the myriad of emotions that she had felt from White individuals growing up and from customers on flights, as well as the long-buried and ignored interaction with her abusive relative. I agreed with Madeline that Black women had long suffered from this type of treatment, but I asserted that she did not have to bury her feelings of anger and insult to have them reemerge without her conscious control. In the safety of the therapy room, we experimented with responses that she could make to people that she felt were treating her with disrespect (Nabors & Pettee, 2003). I advocated that she draw on cultural strengths from her mother, aunts, and grandmother to overcome the emotions that threatened to control her. The process we were using is referred to as *shifting* (C. Jones & Shorter-Gooden, 2003): Madeline drawing strength from her ancestors to bolster her self-image. We talked about how she could have handled some of her past challenges. We also role-played what she could have said to her abusive relative, with the understanding that she could not control what had already happened and that it was in no way her fault, but that she could control how she processed that event.

Depression

We also probed the deep-seated depression that she felt because of her experiences. Although African American women are less prone to depression than White women, the depression that they experience is severe and persistent (Duckworth, 2009). This depression was worsened by posttraumatic stress from the abuse of her relative. We discussed the fact that repressed feelings eventually will come to the surface and the importance of overcoming the silencing of her feelings. We spent several sessions processing the events that led to Madeline's depression: her perception of her mother as overburdened; her parents' death; feelings of overresponsibility for her siblings; work stress; and anxiety about finding a partner that she could love, marry, and be happy with. We talked about these issues and developed statements that she could use to counter the anxiety and depression she felt when she thought about them. I suggested to Madeline that she take two 5-minute periods during the day to write down issues that were upsetting her and then reading the action statement she could use to mitigate her uncomfortable feelings.

Empowerment

I reminded Madeline that she was in control of her actions and that she had the freedom to choose each moment who she would be. We both believed that the personal is political and that she could transform her world into a place where she could be comfortable (S. L. Brown & May, 2009; Evans et al., 2005). We acknowledged the stress of her juggling multiple roles that had consequences for her emotionally, spiritually, and mentally (Tang & Tang, 2001). Our goal for her treatment involved *empowerment*: "achieving reasonable control over one's destiny, learning to cope constructively with debilitating forces in society, and acquiring the competence to initiate change at the individual and system level" (Pinderhughes, 1995, p. 136). We both believed that she was on the road to empowerment when we concluded her therapy.

Case Study 2: Rosa

Rosa was a single, lesbian, 48-year-old Black woman who was raised in the Hampton Roads area and is employed in the information technology field. She was an only child, born to older parents, and her father is deceased but her mother is still living. She has had several long-term relationships. Her last relationship had been with a woman, Denise, who had been married previously and had two children. Rosa and Denise had met at a local gay gathering spot, dated, and then moved in together. They ended up being together for 8 years. During that period, I saw Rosa and her partner for more than 2 years, when they were enduring many problems in the relationship. Subsequently, the relationship ended, and Denise decided to initiate a relationship with a man. Several years later, Rosa came to see me again.

Rosa: Hey, Doc, I am surprised to be back in. Denise and I started having problems again after we last saw you. It seemed as though things were going well for about a year, but then I picked up on clues that she was seeing someone else. I confronted her one evening and she admitted that she was interested in a guy that she met at a work conference. We talked over several weeks and finally she decided to move out.

Therapist: I am sorry to hear of the breakup. You two had been together for quite a while and you had strong relationships with her daughters.

Rosa: Yes, it was very hard, but I still stay in touch with her daughters. We get together for lunch or dinner so that I can stay up with what is happening in their lives. But I wanted to talk to you today about a new love interest. I met her at a club downtown. We clicked pretty quickly and we are talking about her moving in with me.

Therapist: I hear a "but."

Rosa: I guess so. I am just not sure about this relationship.

Therapist: It sounds as though you have some reservations.

Rosa: Yes, sort of. She had just broken up with her partner when I met her. She was very depressed, had missed a lot of work and had been fired. I lent her some cash to help her with her bills and she is currently looking for a new job. She has spent several nights at my place and indicated that she is ready to move in, but I find myself feeling unsure about the move.

Therapist: What else are you unsure about?

Rosa: I don't know. Hmm. Maybe I am actually unsure of what the future holds for us.

Therapist: What do you mean?

Rosa: Well, we have great talks, I feel as though we understand each other, and the sex is really good. But somehow I am not ready to take that next step and invite her to move in.

Therapist: It sounds as though you have some unanswered questions about her and the relationship. Is she still depressed? Did she seek assistance when she broke up with her last partner?

Rosa: I guess I am unsure of her emotional stability, although she generally seems okay. She never sought help after her last breakup. She is about 15 years younger than me, and at times her youth is evident. I am not sure that she is really launched on a career path. She seems to have a lot of debt and she has had credit cards cancelled on her.

Therapist: Okay, so she is a good communicator and you are sexually compatible but you have questions about her emotional and financial stability and her maturity. Also, what was her last relationship like? Is she looking to move in with you because she loves you or because she is trying to get away from her mother or her last partner?

Rosa: I don't know. I guess those are some of the questions I have.

Therapist: Given some of your questions and concerns, are you sure that you are ready to have her move in?

Rosa: No, I guess not. Now that you have raised some of my concerns and hesitations, I am not sure.

Support Systems

I felt that Rosa had a strong support system. Our community, like many others, has several places, occasions, and activities where gay, lesbian, bisexual, and transgendered individuals are welcome (Appleby, Colon, & Hamilton,

2001). Rosa has been active in the Interdenominational Metropolitan Community Church, and several bars in the downtown area are great spots to talk to or meet others and have been where Rosa has met her former and current partners. She feels that she has known that she was gay all of her life, identifies as being "butch," has travelled on several Olivia cruises that cater to lesbian clients exclusively, and is comfortable in her lifestyle. We talked about and reinforced these strengths that Rosa saw in herself and her very solid support system, including her mother, extended family members, and friends.

Conscientização or Conscientization

In listening to Rosa, I had the impression that she had skimmed over the ending of her previous relationship and had quickly found a new partner. I wondered whether she had given herself enough time to grieve the ending of her past relationship. The notion of *conscientização* (conscientization) arose, a process of culling a critical sense of one's social reality through reflection and action that changes reality (Freire, 1970). In this process, people acquire social myths, which have a dominating effect so that learning is a process depending on uncovering real problems and actual needs (Freire, 1970). I did not think that Rosa had used conscientization to become aware of the ways that she had applied dominant culture rules to her life (Enns & Byars-Winston, 2010). After her breakup with Denise, she seemed to feel that she needed to be partnered and became involved with a woman without asking what were typically important questions for her in the areas of mental, emotional, financial, and spiritual functioning.

As therapy progressed, I asked Rosa if she had really processed her breakup with Denise. As we talked about their relationship, it became clear that Rosa still had a variety of strong emotions about it. She remembered an accident that had hurt her knees and her sense that Denise had not been sensitive or concerned. Rosa also felt that she had taken on most of the household and child-care duties and had allowed Denise latitude because her job was so demanding.

Empowerment

We did some consciousness raising in the process of Rosa identifying and venting her anger. As we processed these negative emotions, I reminded Rosa that there had to have been some positives in the relationship. With time, she remembered the caring surprises that Denise would engineer, their trips together, Denise's frequent displays of love and affection, and the fun that they had with both sets of family. As we talked about areas of balance in the relationship, Rosa showed better posture, more smiles, and a greater sense of self-worth. She was able to gradually release her relationship with Denise, and she was able to talk about her new relationship. Rosa eventually ended her new relationship on a positive note when she shared with her partner that it was too soon for both of them to start a new relationship. I was pleased that she had developed new strategies and ways of looking at herself that empowered her and changed some of her painful and uncomfortable experiences (Comas-Díaz & Greene, 1994; C. B. Williams, 2005, 2008).

Case Study 3: Kathy

Kathy was a Black, 63-year-old, heterosexual woman from a large family. Her father died 30 years ago, and her mother had just died recently. Kathy was in the middle of her family of six children and had three sisters and two brothers. She currently works for a large corporation in the Hampton Roads area. Kathy had been previously married and had two children, who are now married adults. She divorced her husband after her children became adults, and she has no idea what has become of him. She has been married to her current husband, Gerry, for 6 years. At first the relationship seemed idyllic, but she now has serious concerns about her husband and the marriage.

Kathy: I guess I am a bit more nervous than I realized.

Therapist: No problem. You said on the phone that you were worried about your relationship with your husband. What are you concerned about? Has he threatened or harmed you?

Kathy: No, no. He has never hit me or threatened me. But he has changed so much since we married 6 years ago. At first he was just perfect. This is the second marriage for both of us, but he treated me like a newlywed at first. He was a great listener; he bought me gifts for my birthday, anniversary, and Christmas; and he just seemed like such a joy to me.

Therapist: How long did this "newlywed" stage last?

Kathy: I have to say for the first 4 or 5 years. He retired from his full-time job and just took another retirement job with a new company about 4 years ago. That's when I first noticed a change in his behavior.

Therapist: What is he doing differently that concerns you?

Kathy: In addition to his not being attentive, he is spending huge sums of money for different types of dental work. I finally decided to look at the desk where he stores all of his paperwork, and I saw that he had forged my name on several documents. I was so upset that I decided to file my income taxes separately this year, but I do not want him to know that I have been looking at his papers.

Therapist: That is alarming! Has he done anything else that is unusual?

Kathy: He seems to be extremely forgetful. He comes downstairs and has forgotten what he is looking for; he commented that he has paid several bills twice; and he does not seem to remember important social events that we have agreed to attend.

Therapist: How old is your husband?

Kathy: He just turned 66 in December.

Therapist: Could he be suffering from some type of dementia?

Kathy: I don't know. All I know is that his behavior is inconsistent He is angry at me now because I refuse to sleep with him. But I will not put up with all of his lying, deceptions, and inattentiveness. I will not stay married to him. I went through too much in my first marriage to let Gerry ruin my credit and trample my spirit. I just don't know what to do because he is spending money from his retirement savings, he is forging my name for loans, he is often angry and aggressive, and he is not the man that I married.

I next asked Kathy for more information on her husband. She replied that he had always been respectful, hardworking, and in the past, sensitive to her needs. He definitely did not fulfill stereotyped depictions of alarming behaviors, such as hypersexuality, disloyalty to family, and aggressive and violent activity (Cervantes, 2012). She noted that Gerry had complained about depression when he retired and she had encouraged him to see his doctor for treatment. He was given an antidepressant from his internist. She reported that he did not smoke and drank only occasionally.

Support Systems

It was clear that Kathy was upset and deeply confused by her husband's actions. I first asked Kathy about her support system. She replied that she had just lost her mother the year before and that this was a huge loss, as her mother had been her primary confidante. Kathy reported that she was close to her sisters and that, similar to many African American women, she had good support from her minister and several church friends (Boyd-Franklin, 1989; Bryant-Davis, Ellis, & Perez, 2013; Chatters, Taylor, Jackson, & Lincoln, 2008). She had children and grandchildren from her first marriage, and Gerry had a daughter from his first marriage, but all of their children were struggling themselves with relationships and finances. Kathy was deeply concerned about her husband's spending because she was married to a husband with some financial resources and she had a good steady job and savings as well, unlike many WOC who are nearing retirement (U.S. Census Bureau, 2010).

Financial and Emotional Security

Kathy wanted financial and emotional protection from her husband. To handle the former issue, I suggested that she speak to an attorney. We talked about how important it was to protect herself emotionally and financially (Evans et al., 2005; Nabors & Pettee, 2003). Because her husband sometimes lashed out in anger toward her, I suggested that she keep her comments to him noncommittal and that she focus more on listening to what he had to say. As Kathy became less assertive, she told me that her husband was changing also. He confessed to being confused and disoriented and thanked her for her help and understanding. This confirmed for me that Gerry was experiencing some type of dementia. As we talked about this possible development, Kathy agreed that she needed to make an appointment to speak to Gerry's doctor by accompanying him on his next visit. The possibility that Gerry might have dementia led to a dissipation of Kathy's anger.

Empowerment

Kathy, like other Black women, has experienced cultural trauma; she handled current stress adaptively by using coping flexibility (Lykes, 1983) to handle the problems in her first marriage and the stress of her children and job. She had long relied on her relationship with her mother, her rock, to give her strength. When her mother died, she felt adrift for the first time. Kathy had stood on her mother's shoulders for years and was unaware of her own strength and resiliency. In therapy, I reminded Kathy of her strength and fortitude in accepting her mother's death and moving forward in handling life's challenges. I reminded her that she was still a strong advocate for her children and grandchildren, and I delineated how they benefitted from her involvement. I also applauded Kathy for her initiative in seeking therapy when she felt that she could no longer cope alone with her problems. I viewed Kathy as a strong, competent, and empowered woman, and I told her so. We worked on promoting a higher level of liberation for Kathy by affirming her strength to speak to a lawyer to request information on protecting her finances and by speaking with Gerry's physician to share information about her concerns and to hear what the doctor thought was occurring (Comas-Díaz, 2013). Finally, I supported Kathy's involvement with her family and church as a means for her to be supported spiritually as she coped with the pressures of home (Boyd-Franklin, 1989; Bryant-Davis, 2013).

KEY ELEMENTS OF WOMANIST THERAPY

In discussing these three cases, key elements of womanist therapy appear: These women were supported and affirmed within the unique culture of Black women, and all employed multiple roles as daughter, partner, mother or mother figure, and worker inside and outside of the home. I initially used the honorific "Ms." or "Mrs." and their last names in addressing them, and after several sessions I asked and was granted permission to use their first names. I communicated my respect for their individual arrangements across their individual decisions regarding their partners, children, other family members, and work.

In therapy, the women discussed challenges arising from issues in part due to how their lives have been shaped by the interaction of gender, race, sexism, sexual orientation, culture, class, and ability. Madeline's outburst during a flight was triggered by working as a Black female flight attendant with the challenge of serving customers in a culture that often expects Black women to conform to its expectations and demands. Rosa was trying to come to terms with society's and her own expectation that she be partnered. As a lesbian, she felt pressure to be in a relationship before she had fully resolved her feelings of grief and loss for her former partner. Kathy felt caught in a bind to be dutiful and respectful to her husband and fully realized that she had been fortunate to be able to marry again, given the high rates of single, never-married, or divorced Black women. But she could no longer tolerate her husband's aberrant and confusing behaviors.

Madeline was grieving her loss of dignity and self-respect that she felt her job demanded; Rosa was grieving the loss of her prior partner; and Kathy was grieving the new loss of her mother and the dissipating loss of the person she believed her husband to be. All three experienced deep soul wounds, and all needed more love and attention focused on themselves.

All three of these women had strong support systems, consisting of family, friends, and church members and leaders. I encouraged all of them to use the resources that they had in their lives by talking to friends and family and by continuing or becoming active in their worship traditions. I also encouraged consulting with a lawyer and a physician, in the case of Kathy, to find out how she could legally protect herself and to ensure that her husband's physician had all the necessary information to offer his diagnosis of her husband's behavior.

On some occasions, these women shared stories of friends and relatives with similar problems who "made it through" by faith, prayer, help from friends and family, and believing in themselves. I encouraged my clients to follow these role models. We discussed how these role models were unique, what they stood for, and what they valued. This helped shape clients' roads to recovery.

In all of these cases, we drew on the cultural strengths of Black women. I affirmed the real suffering that these women had endured, and we used the process of shifting and embodying the strengths of others for support to build a stronger self. We used tools of empowerment, cognitive behavior exercises, and consciousness-raising to dissipate depression and anxiety.

A final element of womanist therapy in these psychotherapeutic relationships is that of the client–therapist dyad itself. My work as a womanist therapist is informed by years of interactions with Black women in therapy and learning from them what is important and valued. Despite the fact that there is a culture of Black women, I must always be alert to the possibility that a client may not adhere to a stereotype. As I work with Black women from a womanist perspective, I am aware that clients at times view me as a role model. They often guess that I am married, because of my hyphenated name, and they ask if I have children. I acknowledge that I am married and that I have adult children, but I maintain the focus on clients. Occasionally, I will smile and nod in an "I've been there also" manner, but I do not offer any solutions to their problems on the basis of what I have experienced. I believe that my work with clients illustrates that Black women can achieve their educational and professional goals and be seen as effective change agents in their respective fields.

The nature of my work with clients is problem-and-solution-focused, with treatment typically lasting across the course of several months and, rarely, across the course of years. Therefore, transference reactions are typically mild. Countertransference issues sometimes arise for me with certain clients. For instance, when one client's father had died unexpectedly and she cried when telling me of his sudden death, I felt tears prickling because of the unexpected death of my father at the time. I believe that the client saw me as sympathetic and empathic, and meanwhile, I recognized the need to better vent my unresolved feelings to a professional therapist. Typically, I feel a strong sense of shared purpose and values as I conduct womanist therapy with clients. I can relate to the myriad of stories that I hear and believe that together, we can make their lives better.

CONCLUSION

The goal of therapy should be to provide culturally competent services to all clients (Comas-Díaz, 2013). I strive to do this whether I am working with individuals, couples, families, or groups. This chapter gave real-world therapeutic excerpts, with women working on individual, work problems, and interpersonal concerns with partners. All WOC who live and work in the United States have been exposed to some degree to various contemporary and historical traumas (Duran, 2006), and individual women arm themselves with diverse womanist coping strategies, outlined in Exhibit 3.3.

Womanist therapy offers a unique perspective to address the needs of WOC. It seeks to fully embrace the multiplicity of race, class, gender, sexual

EXHIBIT 3.3
Womanist Coping Strategies

1. Breaking down stoicism and silencing of feelings (Jack & Ali, 2010)
2. Discarding the Superwoman syndrome (Nabors & Pettee, 2003)
3. Exploring soul wounds from cultural trauma (Duran, 2006)
4. Acknowledging sexual, emotional and physical trauma (Bryant-Davis, 2005a, 2005b)
5. Practicing self-care (Evans, Kincade, Marbley, & Seem, 2005)
6. Actively using support systems, such as sisterhood, family, friends, spirituality/church, physicians, attorneys, and work and school personnel (Appleby, Colon, & Hamilton, 2001; Nabors & Pettee, 2003; Evans et al., 2005)
7. Shifting psychological responses depending on the situation (Nabors & Pettee, 2003; C. Jones & Shorter-Gooden, 2003)
8. Discussing financial and emotional security (Evans et al., 2005; Nabors & Pettee, 2003)
9. Empowering clients to help them see that the personal is political (Brown & May, 2009; Evans et al., 2005; Pinderhughes, 1995)
10. Doing *Conscientização* or Conscientization work to help clients gain self-insight through reflection and action (Comas-Díaz, 2013; Freire, 1970)
11. Reinforcing coping flexibility by allowing relevant responses to stressors (Lykes, 1983)
12. Pulling on the strength of ancestors by "standing on shoulders" (C. Jones & Shorter-Gooden, 2003)

orientation, spirituality, culture, ethnicity, physical disability, their intersection, and multiple identities and oppressions.

This therapy builds on the strengths that clients bring to therapy and works to change the person and her perceptions of the world that she lives in. Even as this approach seeks to be inclusive, the emphasis remains on viewing the individual with unique strengths and weaknesses. As the demographics of the United States continue to become more ethnically diverse, therapists must be culturally competent (Sue & Sue, 2008), and they must able to offer therapy that meets the needs of individual clients. More WOC are seeking therapy now than previously, as health insurance is more affordable and more believe that therapy can actually help them (Errickson et al., 2011).

Therapists must be prepared to provide the therapeutic assistance that these women need and facilitate positive changes in their lives. Therapists of any race or gender can practice successful womanist therapy if they are willing to take course work on Black women and have supervision that challenges their understanding of the worldviews, values, and oppressive forces that these women face.

I think often of Maya Angelou's quote "I've learned that people will forget about what you said, people will forget about what you did, but people will never forget how you made them feel" (as cited in Kelly, 2003, p. 263). The job we have as therapists is to help clients take steps toward empowerment and acquire more conscious control of their thoughts and actions so that they can feel empowered and live more fulfilling lives.

REFERENCES

Alcoff, L. (1988). Cultural feminism versus post-structuralism: The identity crisis in feminist theory. *Signs: Journal of Women in Culture and Society, 13*, 405–436. http://dx.doi.org/10.1086/494426

Al-Mateen, C. S., Christian, F. M., Mishra, A., Cofield, M., & Tildon, T. (2002). Women of color. In S. G. Kornstein & A. H. Clayton (Eds.), *Women's mental health* (pp. 568–583). New York, NY: Guilford Press.

Appleby, G. A., Colon, E., & Hamilton, J. (2001). Lesbian, gay, bisexual and transgender people confront heterocentrism, heterosexism, and homophobia. In G. A. Appleby, E. Colon, & J. Hamilton (Eds.), *Diversity, oppression and social functioning: Person in environment assessment and intervention* (pp. 145–178). Boston, MA: Allyn & Bacon.

Asante, M. K. (1987). *The Afrocentric ideal*. Philadelphia, PA: Temple University Press.

Asante, M. K. (1992). *Afrocentricity*. Trenton, NJ: Africa World Press.

Barnett, R. C., & Rivers, C. (2004). *Same difference: How gender myths are hurting our relationships, our children, and our jobs*. New York, NY: Basic Books.

Belenky, M. F., Clinchy, B. M., Goldberger, N. R., & Tarule, J. M. (1986). *Women's ways of knowing*. New York, NY: Basic Books.

Bohan, J. S. (1993). Regarding gender: Essentialism, constructionism, and feminist psychology. *Psychology of Women Quarterly, 17*, 5–21. http://dx.doi.org/10.1111/j.1471-6402.1993.tb00673.x

Boyd-Franklin, N. B. (1989). *Black families in therapy: A multisytems approach*. New York, NY: Guilford Press.

Boyd-Franklin, N. (2003). *Black families in therapy: Understanding the African American experience*. New York, NY: Guilford Press.

Brown, L. S. (1994). *Subversive dialogues: Theory in feminist therapy*. New York, NY: Basic Books.

Brown, S. L., & May, K. M. (2009). Counseling with women. In C. M. Ellis & J. Carlson (Eds.), *Cross-cultural awareness and social justice in counseling* (pp. 61–87). New York, NY: Routledge.

Bryant-Davis, T. (2005a). Coping strategies of African American adult survivors of childhood violence. *Professional Psychology: Research and Practice, 36*, 409–414. http://dx.doi.org/10.1037/0735-7028.36.4.409

Bryant-Davis, T. (2005b). *Thriving in the wake of trauma: A multicultural guide*. Westport, CT: Praeger/Greenwood.

Bryant-Davis, T. (2013). Sister friends: A reflection and analysis of the therapeutic role of sisterhood in African American women's lives. *Women & Therapy*, *36*, 110–120. http://dx.doi.org/10.1080/02703149.2012.720906

Bryant-Davis, T., Ellis, M. U., & Perez, P. (2013). Women of color and spirituality: Faith to move mountains. In L. Comas-Díaz & B. Greene (Eds.), *Psychological health of women of color: Intersections, challenges and opportunities* (pp. 303–315). Santa Barbara, CA: Praeger.

Cervantes, J. M. (2012). Brothers of color in couples therapy: Managing the rainfall and storms of discrimination and racism for Latino and African American men. In D. S. Shepard & M. Harway (Eds.), *Engaging men in couples therapy* (pp. 253–278). New York, NY: Routledge.

Chatters, L. M., Taylor, R. J., Jackson, J. S., & Lincoln, K. D. (2008). Religious coping among African Americans, Caribbean Blacks and non-Hispanic Whites. *Journal of Community Psychology*, *36*, 371–386.

Chodorow, N. (1978). *The reproduction of mothering*. Berkeley: University of California Press.

Collins, P. H. (1991). *Black feminist thought*. New York, NY: Routledge.

Comas-Díaz, L. (1991). Feminism and diversity in psychology: The case of women of color. *Psychology of Women Quarterly*, *15*, 597–609.

Comas-Díaz, L. (2008). 2007 Carolyn Sherif Award address: *Spirita*: Reclaiming womanist sacredness into feminism. *Psychology of Women Quarterly*, *32*, 13–21.

Comas-Díaz, L. (2013). Culturally competent psychological interventions with women of color. In L. Comas-Díaz & B. Greene (Eds.), *Psychological health of women of color: Intersections, challenges and opportunities* (pp. 373–408). Santa Barbara, CA: Praeger.

Comas-Díaz, L., & Greene, B. (Eds.). (1994). *Women of color: Integrating ethnic and gender identities in psychotherapy*. New York, NY: Guilford Press.

Constantine, M. G., Greer, T. M., & Kindaichi, M. M. (2003). Theoretical and cultural considerations in counseling women of color. In M. Kopala & M. A. Keitel (Eds.), *Handbook of counseling women* (pp. 40–52). Thousand Oaks, CA: Sage.

di Stefano, C. (1990). Dilemmas of difference. In L. J. Nicholson (Ed.), *Feminism/postmodernism* (pp. 63–82). New York, NY: Routledge.

Duckworth, K. (2009). *African American women and depression*. Arlington, VA: National Alliance on Mental Illness.

Duran, E. (2006). *Healing the soul wound: Counseling with American Indians and other native peoples*. New York, NY: Teachers College Press.

Enns, C. Z., & Byars-Winston, A. M. (2010). Multicultural feminist therapy. In H. Landrine & N. F. Russo (Eds.), *Handbook of diversity in feminist psychology* (pp. 367–388). New York, NY: Springer.

Errickson, S. P., Alvarez, M., Forquera, R., Whitehead, T. L., Fleg, A., Hawkins, T., . . . Schoenbach, V. J. C. (2011). What will health-care reform mean for minority health disparities? *Public Health Reports*, *126*, 170–175.

Espin, O. M., & Gawelek, M. A. (1992). Women's diversity: Ethnicity, race, class and gender in theories of feminist psychology. In L. S. Brown & M. Ballou (Eds.), *Personality and psychopathology: Feminist reappraisals* (pp. 88–107). New York, NY: Norton.

Evans, K. M., Kincade, E. A., Marbley, A. F., & Seem, S. R. (2005). Feminism and feminist therapy: Lessons from the past and hopes for the future. *Journal of Counseling and Development, 83,* 269–277.

Fine, M. (1985). Reflections on a feminist psychology of women: Paradoxes and prospects. *Psychology of Women Quarterly, 9,* 167–183.

Fine, M. (1997). Witnessing whiteness. In M. Fine, L. Weis, L. C. Powell, & L. M. Wong (Eds.), *Off white: Readings on race, power, and society* (pp. 57–65). New York, NY: Routledge.

Freire, P. (1970). *Pedagogy of the oppressed.* New York, NY: Seabury Press.

Gilligan, C. (1982). *In a different voice: Psychological theory and women's development.* Cambridge, MA: Harvard University Press.

Greene, B. (1994). African American women. In L. Comas-Díaz & B. Greene (Eds.), *Women of color: Ethnic and gender identities in psychotherapy* (pp. 10–29). New York, NY: Guilford Press.

Greene, B., & Sanchez-Hucles, J. (1998). Diversity: Advancing an inclusive feminist psychology. In J. Worrell & N. Johnson (Eds.), *The future of feminist psychology: Education, research and practice* (pp. 173–202). Washington, DC: American Psychological Association.

Golden, C. (1996). Relational theories of European American women's development. In J. C. Chrisler, C. Golden, & P. D. Rozee (Eds.), *Lectures on the psychology of women* (pp. 229–242). New York, NY: McGraw-Hill.

Henley, N. M., Meng, K., O'Brien, D., McCarthy, W. J., & Sockloskie, R. J. (1998). Developing a scale to measure the diversity of feminist attitudes. *Psychology of Women Quarterly, 22,* 317–348. http://dx.doi.org/10.1111/j.1471-6402.1998.tb00158.x

Jack, D. C., & Ali, A. (2010). Culture, self-silencing, and depression: A contextual–relational perspective. In D. C. Jack & A. Ali (Eds.), *Silencing the self across cultures: Depression and gender in the social world* (pp. 3–17). New York, NY: Oxford University Press.

Jones, A. C. (1993). *Wade in the water: The wisdom of the spirituals.* Maryknoll, NY: Orbis Books.

Jones, C., & Shorter-Gooden, K. (2003). *Shifting: The double lives of Black women in America.* New York, NY: HarperCollins.

Jordan, J. V., Kaplan, A., Miller, J. B., Stiver, I. P., & Surrey, J. L. (1991). *Women's growth in connection: Writings from the Stone Center.* New York, NY: Guilford Press.

Kelly, B. (2003). *Worth repeating: More than 5,000 classic and contemporary quotes.* Grand Rapids, MI: Kregel Academic and Professional.

Landrine, H. (Ed.). (1995). *Bringing cultural diversity to feminist psychology: Theory, research and practice*. Washington, DC: American Psychological Association.

Lykes, M. (1983). Discrimination and coping in the lives of Black women: Analyses of oral history data. *Journal of Social Issues, 39*, 79–100. http://dx.doi.org/10.1111/j.1540-4560.1983.tb00157.x

Matlin, M. (2000). *The psychology of women* (4th ed.). Fort Worth, TX: Harcourt Brace.

Mbiti, J. S. (1990). *African religions and philosophy* (2nd ed.). Portsmouth, NH: Heinemann.

McIntosh, P. (1992). White privilege and male privilege: A personal account of coming to see correspondences through work in women's studies. In M. L. Andersen & P. H. Collins (Eds.), *Race, class and gender: An anthology* (pp. 70–81). Belmont, CA: Wadsworth.

Miller, J. B. (1986). *Toward a new psychology of women*. Boston, MA: Beacon Press.

Miller, J. B. (1991). The development of women's sense of self. In J. V. Jordan, A. G. Kaplan, J. B. Miller, I. P. Stiver, & J. L. Surrey (Eds.), *Women's growth in connection: Writings from the Stone Center* (pp. 11–16). New York, NY: Guilford Press.

Moodley, R. (2005). Outside race, inside gender: A good enough "holding environment" in counseling and psychotherapy. *Counselling Psychology Quarterly, 18*, 319–328. http://dx.doi.org/10.1080/09515070500386356

Nabors, N. A., & Pettee, M. F. (2003). Womanist therapy with African American women with disabilities. *Women & Therapy, 26*, 331–341.

Nobles, W. W. (1991). African philosophy: Foundations for Black psychology. In R. L. Jones (Ed.), *Black psychology* (pp. 47–63). Berkeley, CA: Cobb & Henry.

Ogunyemi, C. O. (1985). Womanism: The dynamics of the contemporary Black Female novel in English. *Signs, 11*, 63–80.

Phillips, L. (2006). *The womanist reader*. New York, NY: Routledge.

Pinderhughes, E. (1995). Empowering diverse populations: Family practice in the 21st century. *Families in Society: The Journal of Contemporary Human Services, 76*, 131–140.

Pollitt, K. (1992, March 23). Are women morally superior to men? *The Nation, 28*, 799–807.

Reid, P. T. (1993). Poor women in psychological research: Shut up and shut out. *Psychology of Women Quarterly, 17*, 133–150.

Reid, P. T., & Kelly, E. (1994). Research on women of color: From ignorance to awareness. *Psychology of Women Quarterly, 18*, 477–486.

Sue, D. W., & Sue, D. (2008). *Counseling the culturally diverse: Theory and practice* (5th ed.). New York, NY: Wiley.

Tang, T. N., & Tang, C. S. (2001). Gender role internalization, multiple roles, and Chinese women's mental health. *Psychology of Women Quarterly, 25*, 181–186. http://dx.doi.org/10.1111/1471-6402.00020

U.S. Census Bureau. (2010). *Poverty main.* Retrieved from http://www.census.gov/hhes/www/poverty/

Walker, A. (1983). *In search of our mother's gardens.* New York, NY: Harcourt, Brace, Jovanovich.

Walker, A. (1995). Womanism. In A. Kesselman, L. D. McNair, & N. Schniedewind (Eds.), *Women images and realities: A multicultural anthology* (p. 18). Mountain View, CA: Mayfield.

West, C., & Zimmerman, D. H. (1991). Doing gender. In J. Lorber & S. A. Farrell (Eds.), *The social construction of gender* (pp. 13–37). Newbury Park, CA: Sage.

White, J. L. (1984). *The psychology of Blacks.* Englewood Cliffs, NJ: Prentice-Hall.

Williams, C. B. (2005). Counseling African American women: Multiple identities—Multiple constraints. *Journal of Counseling and Development, 83,* 278–283.

Williams, C. B. (2008). African American women, Afrocentrism, and feminism. *Women & Therapy, 22,* 37–41. http://dx.doi.org/10.1300/J015v22n04_01

Williams, C. B., & Wiggins, M. I. (2010). Womanist spirituality as a response to the racism-sexism double bind in African American women. *Counseling and Values, 54,* 175–186. http://dx.doi.org/10.1002/j.2161-007X.2010.tb00015.x

Williams, M. K., McCandies, T., & Dunlap, M. K. (2002). Women of color and feminist psychology: Moving from criticism and critique to integration and application. In L. H. Collins, M. R. Dunlap, & J. C. Chrisler (Eds.), *Charting a new course for feminist psychology* (pp. 65–90). Westport, CT: Praeger.

Williams, T. M. (2008). *Black pain: It just looks like we're not hurting.* New York, NY: Scribner.

4

LATINAS PODEROSAS: SHAPING MUJERISMO TO MANIFEST SACRED SPACES FOR HEALING AND TRANSFORMATION

ALBERTA M. GLORIA AND JEANETT CASTELLANOS

First and all alone—The first in her family to graduate from high school and attend college in the United States, Alma feels alone as a first-year college student on a predominantly White campus. She often feels uncertain, overwhelmed, panicky, and guilty for having left her mother and younger siblings at home to go to school. With her mother unemployed for the past year, Alma tries to send home money from her financial aid package, but her financial aid isn't much. Alma is unable to purchase books for class or buy a full-week meal plan, despite working a full 12 hours of work-study weekly, in additional to 15 hours as a cashier at the local grocery store. She is worried about keeping up academically, despite earning grades of B or better in her classes. She also worries about whether she should return home to help her mother by working a full-time job and taking care of her younger siblings. Torn about asking for advice from her mother, who is supportive of Alma's educational pursuits, Alma feels proud of how well her mother has supported the family, given her father's absence. More than two years ago,

http://dx.doi.org/10.1037/14937-005
Womanist and Mujerista Psychologies: Voices of Fire, Acts of Courage, T. Bryant-Davis and L. Comas-Díaz (Editors)

Alma's father was pulled over during a routine traffic stop for a broken car tail-light and was arrested and eventually deported. Alma's family started each day in prayer asking that they would all return home at the end of the day, and she was constantly afraid that her mother or father might not return home someday, because of their status in the United States. Alma's parents left their home country of El Salvador with the desire for increased opportunities for their family. Her mother's stories of sacrifice and going without motivate Alma to attend college and eventually help take care of her family. Feeling scared and uncertain has become an all-too-common experience for Alma at both home and school. As such, Alma sought assistance at a Latina/o community mental health clinic that offered sliding-scale services and had a good reputation for working with university students. Alma is assigned to a Latina therapist of Mexican descent who has practiced at the clinic for the last 10 years.

A frequent starting point for and about Latinas/os generally and to many Latinas specifically is the question *¿Quien somos?* (Who are we)? Yet, all too frequently the questions of who Latinas are or what cultural roles are available to them become the central focus subjugating self-discovery and self-affirmation (Miguela, 2001). The restrictive identities of sinner, saint, whore, mother, wife, and caretaker become the measure against which Latinas are dichotomously judged and admired (Arrizón, 2009; Gloria & Castellanos, 2013; Miguela, 2001).

Given the heterogeneity of experiences based on age, ethnicity, sexual orientation, generational level, acculturation, language ability, education, socioeconomic status, and a multitude of other identities, there is no "typical" Latina (Gloria, 2001). Although descriptive data may seemingly provide a typical narrative of many Latinas in the United States, it only assists in creating a context—the information does not offer cultural meaning or deep-structure value of Latinas and their realities. Instead, literature fully examining Latinas' processes is of greatest benefit. Further, it is incumbent upon each Latina to engage in self-exploration to find her voice and define her realities in the process of answering the questions of who, what, and how she is (Anzaldúa, 1987; Castellanos & Gloria, 2016; Comas-Díaz, 2013; Miguela, 2001).

Throughout this chapter, we share information and perspectives to address the questions of who, what, and how for Latinas. The chapter is not formulaic or prescriptive in addressing the process of healing or transformation but rather serves as a starting point for knowledge and self-awareness. To do so, we begin with a brief overview of salient informants of Latina identities and realities. Next, we address the challenges and processes of reclaiming *patrones culturales* and *espiritualidades* (cultural and spiritual blueprints; Gloria & Castellanos, 2013) and models by which Latinas can work toward transformation and self-awareness as they interweave their multiple realities and identities. We conclude the chapter with a discussion of ancestral wisdoms to bridge Latinas' realities of *una Latina poderosa* (a powerful Latina).

Latinas face multiple risk factors for health and wellness, including immigration status, adjustment and acculturative stress, discrimination, underemployment and low-paying positions, single parenthood, familial separation and change of familial roles, interpersonal loss, or caring for aged parents (National Alliance on Mental Illness, 2006, 2008). Understanding the values and beliefs that inform Latinas' realities and meanings is imperative in finding healing, transformation, and well-being for themselves, their families, and communities.

INFORMANTS OF LATINA REALITIES AND IDENTITIES: *VALORES CULTURALES* (LATINA/O CULTURAL VALUES)

Although Latinas uniquely navigate dynamically diverse communities and experiences (Aguirre & Turner, 2011), they are unified by cultural practices and beliefs (Santiago-Rivera, Arredondo, & Gallardo-Cooper, 2002). Latinas share a collective identity (Alexander, Eyerman, Giesen, & Smelser, 2004) and dimensions of common realities. Specifically, many Latinas hold the belief that individuals are interconnected more broadly to the environment and to others physically, mentally, and energetically or spiritually (Ramírez, 1991). Grounded in community, Latinas come from a culture that emphasizes interconnection, loyalty to others (Castellanos & Gloria, 2016), and collective responsibility to the group and family (Ramírez, 1991). These beliefs and traditional practices stem from a diverse set of ethnocultural and indigenous Latina/o communities (McNeill & Cervantes, 2008) and varying emic psychologies (Ramírez, 1991, 1998). Moreover, these culturally shared ethnic-specific beliefs, practices and values offer Latinas a common ground for their experiences, interpretations of life, and responses to their everyday challenges. As *familismo, comunidad,* extended family, *personalismo, confianza,* and *epiritualidad* are core values within the culture, these beliefs and practices are highlighted.

The values of familismo (familism) and comunidad (community) are arguably the most salient for Latinas/os (Gloria & Castellanos, 2009; Santiago-Rivera et al., 2002). *Familia* (family) is "the primary natural support system that provides physical, emotional, and social support for many Latinas/os" (Gloria & Castellanos, 2009, p. 14). The literature describes familismo as that of solidarity, loyalty, reciprocity, and interdependence (Falicov, 2013), which is identified as the chief cultural structure, mutual support system, and source of resource for Latinas (Lopez, 2010). Although the degree to which familismo is adhered to or manifested differs among Latinas, the value of *todo para la familia* (everything for family), holds a poignant cultural power.

Latinas are often socialized to place family first and take responsibility for others within the family (Santiago-Rivera et al., 2002).

Having care and obligation for family ultimately creates and expands the responsibility of interconnection to comunidad (community; Castellanos & Gloria, 2016). In that family includes extended kinship systems that reflect fictive and nonfictive family members, Latinas often hold a collective family identity that is broad and serves to integrate and connect (Lopez, 2010). In particular, the process of *compadrazgo* (coparentage) occurs by tasking *padrinos* (godfathers) or *madrinas* (godmothers) to care for the financial, spiritual, or well-being of others' children (Gill-Hopple & Brage-Hudson, 2012; Gloria & Castellanos, 2009). Compadrazgo links individuals and families in life-long relationships (Mintz & Wolf, 1950) whereby families hold a collective responsibility for the group's welfare (Gloria & Castellanos, 2013).

Directly connected to the processes and values manifesting family are the elements of connection and modes of interaction. Personalismo is a distinct interpersonal style that emphasizes the importance of personal connections (Ortiz, 2009). Commonly referred within the literature as a "cultural script," personalismo is an orientation in which personal exchanges are centralized and embodied by respect and dignity regardless of personal or social statuses (Gloria & Castellanos, 2009). Similarly, *simpatía* is the process of maintaining cordial and positive relationships (Arbona, 2006). By doing so, a sense of trust, intimacy, and familiarity within relationships engenders confianza (Gloria & Castellanos, 2009). As relationships *son de confianza* (can be trusted), engaging with *cariño* (affection and care) via verbal and nonverbal endearments (e.g., hug or kiss when greeted) is common.

Inherent to Latinas' cultural and collective values and identity is the role of espiritualidad and the creation of energies that directly emanate from the group (family, community) and culture. Cervantes and Ramírez (1992) described *Mestizo spirituality* as a life philosophy of Latinas/os that engages, protects, and connects for which a protective divine has influence and affirmation over all. In particular, the life approach emphasizes a relational orientation and stresses balance of connections among self, family, and community; engagement of subsequent responsibilities of the relationships; and insight and clarity of meaning that is avowed by a higher creative force or spirit (Cervantes, 2010).

Indeed, for many Latinas, espiritualidad is an approach to life that is innately intertwined with the person and culture (Nicolas, Gonzalez-Eastep, & DeSilva, 2010) and rooted within interpersonal interactions (Gloria & Castellanos, 2013). Permeating all elements of life (Comas-Díaz, 2006), Latinas are often socialized within a belief system rooted in religiosity (e.g., *si Dios quiere*/if God wills it) and spirituality (*Estoy conectada con el universo*/ I am interconnected with universe) and educated to attend *el espíritu* (the spirit or energy) through the practice of rituals, cultural osmosis, and language

(Comas-Díaz, 2006). In doing so, Latinas are drawn to their mothers' and grandmothers' generational wisdoms, life lessons, and perspectives on relational and communal interactions and mind–body interconnections (Arredondo, 2002; Cervantes, 2010; Comas-Díaz, 2013; Gloria & Castellanos, 2013).

MISLABELED AND MISUNDERSTOOD: UNDERSTANDING *LA MUJER'S* CULTURAL AND GENDER SCRIPTS

The cultural scripts ascribed to many Latinas span from self-deprecated and deficient-oriented to culture power-filled and strengths based (e.g., *chingonas/* badass warrioresses; Gloria & Castellanos, 2013). With a history of oppression, marginalization, and misrepresentation of processes (Anzaldúa, 1987; Isasi-Díaz, 2004, 2008) and subsequent disempowerment (Arrizón, 2009), Latinas are challenged to sift through social, cultural, and religious messages about themselves. One script (originally described as religious) Latinas encounter is the *marianista* perspective (Stevens, 1973). This perspective relegates Latinas as passive, in need of protection, divinelike, selfless, submissive, compliant, and with an asexual purpose of procreation. In contrast, Latinas were viewed preferentially upon motherhood as their value was linked to reproduction (Vasquez, 1994). In this way, Latinas have been metaphorically decapitated or silenced to follow patriarchal orders (Arrizón, 2009). The systemic silencing, along with the misunderstanding and misnaming of Latina processes (Anzaldúa, 1987; Arrizón, 2009; Isasi-Díaz, 1996, 2004) disengages and distances Latinas from personal power while reinforcing a false and limited sense of self-worth and enabling a fragmented process of existence.

Sensuality and sexuality is one dimension of Latinas about which perceptions, directives, and oppressions are salient (Lara, 2008). Latinas' sexuality is often dichotomized into a whore–virgin binary (Arrizón, 2009; Gaspar de Alba, 2005), while sexual exchanges are relegated to physical necessities and cultural scripts (Lara, 2008). The divine energetic exchange and transformed consciousness of reclaiming a Latina's emotional and physical self is dismissed (Gloria & Castellanos, 2013; Lara, 2008) and split from the physical and spiritual (Arrizón, 2009). In particular, the spiritual exchanges of sensuality or the "flexible structures of feelings" are overlooked, unaware, unarticulated, and not lived out (Arrizón, 2009, p. 192).

With modern times and the liberation of women through education and work representation (Nielsen Project, 2013), women are reclaiming their dimensionality, the complexity of their identities, and the strength and value within their practices (Comas-Díaz, 2008; Gloria & Castellanos, 2012). Close to two decades ago, Comas-Díaz, Lykes, and Alarcón (1998) addressed the need for Latina women's psychological liberation that affirms their *mujerista* identities through the blending of culture, values, and spirituality. Specifically, Comas-Díaz (2008) described the concept of *spirita* or "spirit of liberation among women of color" that "mobilizes women to take control of their lives, overcome their oppressed mentality, and achieve a critical knowledge of themselves" (p. 13). Arredondo (2002) also proposed the *santas y marquesas* (saints and royalty) thesis—an analysis centered in the understanding that Latinas must navigate cultural scripts and balance gender expectations. Specifically, to manage the complexity of identities, Latinas first need to (re) establish their cultural roots as a means to create new knowledge and identities (Arredondo, 2002). Inevitably, the process of identifying, reclaiming, defining, and making meaning of these identifies requires Latinas live *entre fronteras* (between borders) or *nepantla*, a *Nahuatl* (an indigenous language to Mexico) word meaning *tierra entre medio* (land or space in the middle; Anzaldúa, 1987).

In bridging and balancing Latinas' opposing worlds that are often unpredictable and ever-changing, Rodriguez (2004) presented the concept of Latina consciousness, identified as Mestiza espiritualidad, in which women experience "oppositional consciousness" as they are consistently in a transformative stage of becoming. Similarly, the notion of *mujerismo* (Comas-Díaz, 2008; 2012) underscores Latinas' resilience in navigating oppression, the role of culture and gender, and the value of liberation approaches. The resilience and power movement to correct cognitive distortions and recognize the role of colonization and oppression is proposed by the spirita consciousness (Comas-Díaz, 2008), which calls for a collective identity, liberation, and emancipation of oppression. A value on the past and present, inner strength and resilience, and a repositioning of la mujer has manifested a soul retrieval in women that reclaims and captures their full essence, and shapes a collective identity consisting of multidimensionality and embedded in personal empowerment—consistently reinforcing the role of strength and power (*poder*) through *la poderosa* paradigm (Gloria & Castellanos, 2012).

In a society in which women are identified as *libertisadas*/libretrarians or *feministas*/feminists (and sometimes even *traumadas*/traumatized, *amargadas*/embittered, *fieras*/fierce, *mujeres sin razon*/women without reason) when expressing their full identities, embracing their power, and asserting their position (as *brujas*/witches when tapping into their subconscious and creating divine spaces for vision and insight), a different platform of interpretation for these practices and processes must exist (Comas-Díaz, 2013; Espín, 1997; Gloria & Castellanos, 2012). More and specific work addressing Latinas' identities is needed, as interpretations of their identities have shifted to empowerment, inner strength, and healing (Arredondo, 2002; Comas-Díaz, 2006, 2008; Falicov, 2013). Moreover, the call is warranted to understand Latinas and their processes as healers and visionaries who are valued for insight, intuition, energetic connections, and spiritual interplay rather than as brujas or cultural and spiritual libertines. It is this call for a mind shift to interpret properly and understand their processes, practices, beliefs, powers, and identities that the following conceptualizations and models of being poderosa are offered.

LATINAS' REALIDADES: PATRONES CULTURALES Y ESPIRTUALIDADES (LATINAS' REALITIES: CULTURAL AND SPIRITUAL BLUEPRINTS)

Although Latinas may share some elements of their patrones, each has a unique patrón cultural y espiritual or blueprint seeded in her ancestral contributions and experiences formed through historical, spiritual, religious, moral, cultural, and sociopolitical outlook. It is through self-reflection and clarity of their blueprint that Latinas become aware and conscious of their identities as poderosas (Gloria & Castellanos, 2013).

Gloria and Castellanos (2013) described patrones as blueprints of the spiritual makeup that have been consciously and unconsciously transmitted across generations. From cultural learnings gained through direct daily encounters to basic tasks of sharing time (e.g., eating a meal, sitting and sharing space), it is the transmissions of ancestral *costumbres*, valores, and *practicas culturales* (customs, values, and cultural practices) that form a Latina's patrón. Consistent with Comas-Díaz's (2013) discussion of the healing process of *comadres*, it is often Latinas' *madres y abuelas* (mothers and grandmothers) who impart the wisdoms of *supervivencia* (survival) and *prosperidad* (prosperity).

Comas-Díaz (2006) described the process of "calling back the spirit" to reformulate Latina identity. It is the process of engaging one's strength and resilience to reconnect spiritually to one's native roots and practices. It is the process of achieving *sabiduría*, a spiritual and existential type of wisdom or collective consciousness that interconnect Latinas to themselves and their identities (and others) for integration and self-improvement (Comas-Díaz, 2006). When Latinas doubt themselves, the process leads to them to borrow from "external, oppressive, and nonnative systems" (Comas-Díaz, 2006, p. 176) and engage with patrones/blueprints that are extraneous to their true selves (Gloria & Castellanos, 2013).

SACRED SPACES AND HEALING: RECLAIMING PATRONES/BLUEPRINTS

Whether using the approach of spirita, sabiduría, mestizo espiritualidad, *conocimiento* (knowing), or collective consciousness for empowerment, a common element to transformation is that of reclaiming self. In doing so, sacred spaces are fundamental as they are spaces where energies are shared to support envisioned transformations and reclaim empowering scripts. Sacred spaces introduce divine breaks through to the mortal world (Ivakhiv, 2003). Spaces can be physical, metaphysical, conscious, or unconscious (Soto, Cervantes-Soon, Villarreal, & Campos, 2009). It is a place where Latinas engage their inner consciousness and connect to the collective consciousness. Latinas engage in self-discovery, rediscovery, and conocimiento (Facio & Lara, 2014; Soto et al., 2009). Specifically, Latinas create sacred spaces on a daily basis through personal reflections, intimate conversations, positive exchanges, shared intentions, prayer, connecting, and bonding with others via conversations, positive exchanges, shared intentions, and collective efforts.

Ultimately, it is from and through scared spaces that healing occurs. The process of healing is that of restoration and renewal—a process that Latinas must engage to create transformations that are rooted within their indigenous patrones. A multidimensional process, healing occurs consciously and unconsciously at the physical, metaphysical, emotional, and spiritual levels. For example, Nuñez (2008) described the process of spiritual healing as the liberation of one's soul from barriers and obstructions that could lead to physical or emotional suffering. Comas-Díaz (2006) held that espiritualidad is foundational to healing in which the mind, body, and spirit of the collective must be balanced to promote transcendence, change, and wellness. By engaging sacred spaces for healing, Latinas can tap into their patrones/blueprints with clarity and intent, pushing past the societal oppressions and scripts that disempower.

MODELS OF UNA LATINA PODEROSA

As Latinas find themselves in different situations and contexts that may be incongruent to their core cultural values, worldview, attitudes, and beliefs, they must find creative and sacred ways of owning and navigating power and success. Ultimately, each Latina owns and holds the power for healing, despite seeking assistance from helpers or therapists. As noted, numerous approaches and models (e.g., Acosta, 2008; Arredondo, 2002; Cervantes, 2010; Comas-Díaz, 2006, 2008, 2012; Rodriguez, 2004; Soto et al., 2009; Vasquez, 1994) lend insight and understanding of mujerismo or *marianismo*. One noteworthy model draws on the interpersonal bonds of women who create sacred and healing spaces of transformation as comadres (comothers; Comas-Díaz, 2013). In particular, Comas-Díaz (2013) shared the scared teachings conveyed through her grandmother's *cuentos* (stories), which focused on self-awareness; consciousness; and broader spiritual and cultural connection to past, present, and future, all the while bolstering resilience and wellness as a means for mujerismo. In particular, the 10 commandments of being mujerismo included poignant *consejos* (advice) of honoring inner divinity, asking for help, being aware of who one is yet being open to change, recalling that identity transcends oneself, transforming low self-esteem into self-love, empowering others, encouraging connectedness and solidarity, fighting oppression, becoming resilient and learning to overcome adversity, and dancing with life (Comas-Díaz, 2013).

Drawing from the collective work of other models, helping approaches, and writings about the realities and processes of Latinas, the following models set a working framework for helpers or clinicians to help Latinas develop strength and meaning through self-awareness and transformation toward mujerismo and being a Latina poderosa. In particular, the development of recommendations stemming from the ELLA and SOMOS models (described below) are situated within and emanate from the notions of mujerismo (Comas-Díaz, 2008, 2012, 2013). It is from the inextricably intertwined processes of *cultura,* valores culturales, espiritualidad (culture, values, and spirituality), and Latinas' inner processes and powers that these mujerista models of ELLA and SOMOS emphasize the meaning and application processes that Latinas can adopt and/or be applied within the therapeutic setting to assist them in finding empowerment and wellness via transformational healing, inner knowing, and conocimiento/knowledge.

ELLA

The ELLA model of engaging healing and wellness through the self, family, and community is a broad-based approach to assist Latinas seeking to reclaim their power and processes (see Figure 4.1). The four tenets are

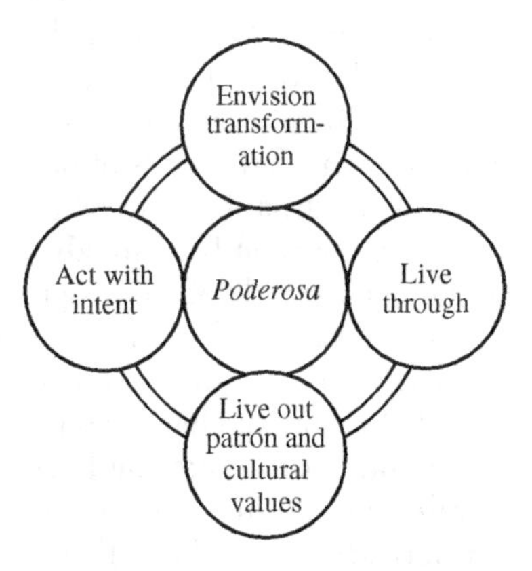

Figure 4.1. ELLA model (Envision transformation, Live through, Live out patrón/blueprint and cultural values, and Act with intent).

dynamic and flow in an unending circular process, and the acronym ELLA is taken from the first letter of each tenet:

- Envision transformation,
- Live through,
- Live out patrón/blueprint and cultural values, and
- Act with intent.

Next, each tenet is briefly described and applied to Alma, the Latina introduced at the chapter's start.

Envision Transformation

One of the first processes of transformation is to envision it. Believing transformation is possible and that one has the right to take on a different role or manifest change is central to the vision. Envisioning transformation is not about "wishing away" challenges or situations of one's life, family, or community. Instead, it is the recognition that change is needed and/or wanted for advancement while engaging the process of identifying how change can be achieved. More than insight is needed; transformational change also entails the belief that energies, past wisdoms, and strengths and a patrón are integral to the process.

> To begin the relationship, Alma's therapist described herself as working from an integrative approach, drawing from person-centered, cognitive behavior, and interpersonal processes theories. More specifically, she considers the interplay of culture, context, power, and oppression as it influences the client's identities, interconnections, mood, and behaviors. Early in her relationship with her therapist, Alma disclosed that her parents struggled to overcome great obstacles and sacrificed to create a better future for their family. Focused on immediate family concerns, Alma's therapist helped her understand how by earning a college education that she could assist her family with greater impact over the long term than by not earning a degree. Although she was pulled by the daily needs of her family (e.g., child care and supplemental income from her jobs while at home), Alma's therapist challenged her to envision how an advanced degree could allow her a greater earning potential and more options and choice for her family, model for her younger siblings the importance of education, and allow her to serve as a leader within her community. By accessing the same familial vision for change and focused strengths of her parents and grandparents to centralize family, Alma found that she could draw on her familial and cultural patrón of strength to envision and manifest her transformation. As Alma's therapist challenged her to connect more fully with her family and her patrón in a way that was strengths based, rather than to separate and choose change for herself

away from family, Alma felt closer and more comfortable in sharing her narrative. As Alma increasingly trusted that her therapist did not blame or pathologize her or her family, she was increasingly open to exploring what and how her transformation would unfold.

Live Through

Perhaps one of the most challenging negotiations of transformation and manifesting visions is living through subsequent responses, reactions, and interpersonal engagements as Latinas. As cultural expectations change and proscribed roles for Latinas are challenged, (re)storied, and (re)claimed to hold positive and strengths-based narratives, Latinas will frequently find themselves living through pushback and questioning from their families and communities. Familial loyalty may be questioned or positioned as defiance and cultural treason and betrayal (Acosta, 2008) as Latinas create their own scripts and processes for engagement. By living through the shifts and changes, they are able to remain consistent to envision and emulate transformations for empowerment and success.

As Alma became increasingly more aware that she wanted to persist in higher education, her dissonance and uncertainty increased about how her family would respond to her decision. To assist in living through the challenges that come with envisioned transformation, Alma and her therapist discussed her plan to return home for a few days to assist her mother with child care and as a reprieve from being on her own. Alma's therapist helped her to identify what feelings emerged as she was increasingly faced with family members, in particular her madrina, telling her that she needed to come home—that a good daughter would return home, assist her mother, and forgo her selfish educational endeavor that was directly adding to the family's demise. As Alma and her therapist sorted through the messages and resulting feelings, she gained the clarity and knowledge that the messages she was receiving were that of survival and strength of family. By making this connection, Alma knew that she would have to live through the challenge and draw on these same strengths to persist in higher education. As Alma doubted herself and struggled against owning a perception of herself that was culturally scripted and distanced her from her patrón and true sense of self, her therapist owned her biases and assumptions about Alma's inability to stand firm through her challenges. To remain empathetic to Alma's process, the therapist returned to her own struggles to maintain processes that were core to herself and her patrón. With a carefully timed self-disclosure, Alma's therapist shared with her that it was difficult for her to see Alma doubt and question herself and that she was committed to helping her find her power and identity as a poderosa in a way that was most helpful and healing for Alma.

Live Out Patrón/Blueprint and Cultural Values

As Latinas experience challenges or support for their transformations, they may have a tendency to move away from one's patrón or even return to the other-ascribed notion of who she is to be. Throughout the process of transforming roles and expectations, returning to one's *raices* (roots) is fundamental to maintain and engage in a different script (Arredondo, 2002), particularly as raices determine whether contexts are safe to her notion of self. It is important to note that not all contexts or spaces allow Latinas to live out their cultural values in ways that are accepted or valued (Delgado-Guerrero & Gloria, 2013), and thus they must gauge how safely and strategically they can live out particular values. Ultimately, Latinas can benefit from staying close to their core selves and can do so by finding their power or spaces that support and validate transformation and healing.

> As Alma lived out her cultural values, her therapist reviewed the different contexts in which she had the most frequent challenges. In discussion with her therapist, Alma described how she frequently found that her values about family were challenged and subtly dismissed in her educational climate. Alma was tearful and shared that several of her new peers questioned whether she was "college material" as she put her family first when making decisions about how to spend free time on weekends. Surrounded by relationships that were not collective oriented, Alma often felt disconnected. As Alma discussed her feelings with her therapist, she recognized that she was moving away from her patrón and that her power of collective identity and consciousness would be compromised. To stay close to her values, her therapist recommended that she seek out a Latina culture-based group while at school that would allow her *hermandad Latina* (Latina sisterhood). By finding others who shared similar struggles of being first (to attend college, to navigate the system, to balance home and school) and who also kept family centralized enabled Alma to engage and stay rooted to her cultural values and live through the challenges of engaging core values. In addition to seeking out the Latina student sorority, Alma's therapist encouraged her to consider other spaces and places where she could feel congruent with her values. Alma identified church as a possible space; however, she indicated that prayer, meditation, and seeking out the calming energies of genuine connections enabled her to feel the most congruent. She also noted that talking in Spanish with her grandmother when they cooked were times and spaces when she felt comfortable living out her values. Alma's therapist suggested that she consider how cooking a Sunday dinner with her "sisters" from her sorority could assist in creating such a space to live out her patrón.

Act With Intent

Acting with intent is steeped within the strength of conscious resolve and will to manifest or engage change (Nelson, 2003). The action of intent returns Latinas to the consistent process of envisioning transformation as intent steers the energies toward a belief that no other process or reality can exist (Castellanos & Gloria, 2016). Specifically, it is by aligning one's intent with other Latinas (Comas-Díaz, 2006), families, communities, and the divine or creative universal energies that power is envisioned and manifested (Gloria & Castellanos, 2013).

> With the support of her educational comadres from her Latina student sorority, coupled with her therapist's encouragement to maintain focus on her intent, Alma stayed persistent to her belief that her most valuable contribution to la familia was a college education. Alma and her therapist cocreated a behavioral plan by which she could act with intent and focus to be successful with school. They addressed her schedule for academics and time for her student group, while focusing on her major and longer term goals after graduation. The plan also involved time that Alma would take to reflect and create spaces of transformation. Alma suggested that she could burn sage and light *una veladora* (a prayer candle) as she engaged in reflection, much like her grandmother and mother do during times of personal challenge and familial struggle. As part of this process, her therapist also shared her own challenges and struggles in higher education, which validated and normalized Alma's experiences. By establishing a greater sense of clarity regarding her focus and plan, Alma envisioned how she would engage her day-to-day transformation of college with intent. Ultimately, her intentions manifested as her decision to return for a second year, as well as setting in motion dreams of college for her younger siblings. Alma identified that a college degree would allow her economic and social capital to assist her family more fully than if she had not persisted. Moreover, as Alma's therapist questioned her intention with supportive challenge and encouragement, Alma's resolve increased as she navigated college, and her resolve subsequently became the working platform from which her evolution as una mujer poderosa would occur.

SOMOS (We Are)

The SOMOS model of transformation and collective consciousness (see Figure 4.2) provides specific directives for Latinas; however, the model is not purposed as an imperative but rather as a way to make meaning. The SOMOS model draws from different indigenous and shamanic practices and systems that serve as points of reference within the model. The processes build on each other and are thus presented as steps yet are not intended to be sequential but cumulative, "building" toward being a Latina poderosa. As natural healers and helpers, Latinas should be encouraged to own their power within the steps of transformation and collective consciousness. Similarly, helpers (e.g., clinicians, therapists, psychologists) can assist as cohelpers to Latinas' transformations and self-owing processes.

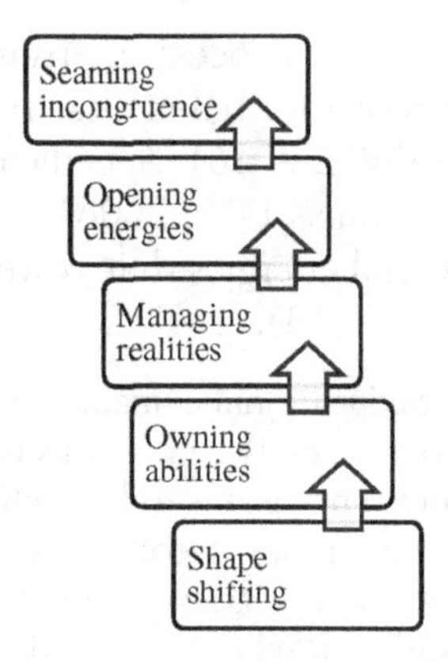

Figure 4.2. SOMOS model (Shape shifting, Owning abilities, Managing realities, Opening energies, and Seaming incongruence).

Latina poderosas are tool seekers for personal transformation transcending to higher processes in their quest to sustain their power, expand their personal strength, and create more pathways to transmit and attain cultural, spiritual, and ancestral wisdom. They engage in rituals and spiritual ceremonies to communicate and gain awareness. They explore the dimensionality of sacredness and sit in stillness for insight and centeredness. Una Latina poderosa creates through messages, dreams, and self-awakening. It is through creating unbeaten paths, pathways, and portals procreating spiritual forts hosting past memories, acceptance, reclaiming of the self, and self-love that she reaches transformation, sacredness, divinity, and awakening. It is these processes that can assist Latinas in traversing the road to power and healing. The processes build upon each other and are thus presented as steps, where one process is foundational for the next, yet they are not intended to be sequential, but cumulative: "building" upward, toward being a Latina poderosa. The first letter of each tenet forms the acronym SOMOS, to read:

- Shape shifting,
- Owning abilities,
- Managing realities,
- Opening energies, and
- Seaming incongruence.

Below, each tenet is briefly described and applied to Alma, the Latina introduced in the chapter's start.

Shape Shifting

Seeded in indigenous practices and shamanistic beliefs, shape shifting is the process of moving or shifting energy as well the way that we view it

(Perkins, 1997). Occurring at multiple levels, shape shifting can manifest physically (e.g., taking on a new physical form) or personally, such that one's beliefs or attitudes are shifted to be more congruent with one's true self. A key process of shape shifting is accepting the role of dreams (Perkins, 1997) and the connection between real time and dream time, the role of manifesting vision through intent, and merging of goals to reality.

> To engage the process of shape shifting, Alma's therapist asked her to identify the different identities and contexts in which they are held. By doing so, Alma was also asked to tune into her intuition and inner knowing as she sought to move, morph, and transcend within and between her multiple intersecting identities. In their discussion of identities, Alma expressed the most difficulty in holding those identities of being a student and a daughter simultaneously. By gaining clarity of the differing expectations and assumptions about who she is within the contexts and environments, she tapped into her ancestral conocimiento and noticed the commonalities, differences, and common spaces. For example, she recognized her different strengths and core values across contexts that lead to an unfolding of her unconsciousness, an increased connection to a greater presence, and a sense of healing. To assist in the process of shape shifting, Alma first had to identify and name her different identities that she held as most salient. As she listed these identities Alma's therapist assisted in helping her to delineate which of the identities were externally imposed by larger society, imposed by family, and internally assumed, as well as those that were transmitted to her via her patrón. By connecting her identities and having greater knowledge from where they came, and the resulting feelings and energies that came from each, Alma was able see what and how she needed to move between identities in connecting to her core self.

Owning Abilities

Poderosas engage life from the level of the soul, a sense of feeling and experiential exchanges that provides access to ancestral imprints and lending to spiritual gifts. Latinas' ability to be courageous and own their abilities facilitates their mastering of skills, engagement in creation, and creativity in curious states. Engaging similar energies to achieve and own one's abilities, such as the hummingbird who is noted for not being able to fly given its shape (Villoldo, 2008), Latinas nonetheless rise to challenging occasions, reclaim their power, and track past steps, ancestral wisdom, and intuition guidance to enter a new space.

> Alma's therapist helped her find the value and strengths in her collective and individual identities as a means to feel pride and own her abilities that are part of her patrón. By owning her abilities and finding power in her experiences, Alma began to generalize how her she could bring

this sense of ability to her experiences on campus. For example, she connected her parents and grandparents *ganas* (motivation and desire) to make a better life through sacrifice and hard work while maintaining a strong devotion to family as informing her own ganas to graduate from high school and go on to a four-year university. Further, she connected her prayer and espiritualidad as a means to calm her when she found herself in anxious situations on campus (e.g., in classes) that was directly tied to her history with *la Virgen* to feel protected and empowered. Specifically, by clarifying Alma's evolving relationship with power and ability to see herself as having abilities was seeded in understanding her role in everyday processes. Her therapist assisted her to make the connection between past and the present as she bridged past teachings with present learning. By embracing her practices of *eharle las ganas* (draw on one's motivation to succeed) prayer, gratitude, celebration, and praise, Alma sought to sustain sacredness and spiritual connection to recognize and own her abilities.

Managing Realities

The process of managing realities stems from understanding the courageous choice to create relationships with realities that are strength-oriented or filled with disempowered suffering (Villoldo, 2008). It is through the crafting of new stories and morphing through everyday processes with intent that Latinas function as transformers, connectors, and key or wisdom keepers to different realities. Poderosas work to restory or recreate their realities through vigilant focused to their new goal. Well-versed in feeling external energies, Latinas often know the future/what is coming and have a skill to track current vibrations in day-to-day experiences (Comas-Díaz, 2008).

To address how Alma was managing her different realities that were associated with her different yet intersecting identities and contexts, her therapist focused on relationships and collective processes that were important to her. With a deep value for personal her relationships, Alma and her therapist focused on how she could draw knowledge and strength from her interpersonal connections as she sought to navigate her environments as a comadre, *hija, y estudiante* (comother, daughter, and student). As Alma's therapist questioned her about how and when she created sacred spaces for herself, Alma clarified that she was building common spaces through family and community in her everyday exchanges. She also saw how she was a knowledge keeper as she constructed different possibilities through and within her multiple realities. Through this process, Alma tapped into her feelings of being angry and rejected as a student on campus and of being hurt and confused that her family perceived her as acting against them. By accessing and exploring her emergent feelings from her different contexts, Alma recognized how she could foreshadow and have insight into what might unfold within her relationships during her visit home. As part of her plan, Alma's therapist suggested that when she felt discouraged or overwhelmed, she could identify a family *dicho* (saying) that could assist her to restory her narrative and to find strength in her family wisdom and patrón.

Opening Energies

Latinas know how to move and transfer within the changing tapestry of their daily realities. In a quest to maintain wellness, they learn to be open and fluid to change and transformation. In their survival processes, poderosas are available in the present, have a deep understanding of feeling and love, show compassion, and seek understanding (e.g., demonstrating cariño/affection, expressing *amor*/love, emphasizing conocimiento).

As Alma returned to therapy after her trip home, she discussed the many emotion-filled conversations that she engaged with her mother and madrina about staying in school for the semester and for the longer term. Although she has cariño y amor for her family, she nonetheless revealed being particularly hurt, as they were critical of her having joined a sorority and calling her peers "sisters," as she has two biological sisters who they reminded her she was not taking care of with the same consideration and attention. Alma's familial loyalty and respect was questioned, and she felt ashamed, misunderstood, and secretly angry. In exploring the shame and critical response of Alma's madrina and mother, it came to light that Alma's grandmother had been particularly disapproving of Alma's mother in her decision to marry and come to the United States with her husband, as she was perceived as breaking up the family. It was not long after Alma's mother had left her home country that her father (Alma's grandfather) became gravely ill and she was no longer available to help care for him. After further discussion with her therapist, Alma disclosed that she had always felt that her mother had made a courageous and strong choice for her family, as her parents had always sent money and supplies to her grandparents every chance they could. As her therapist challenged Alma to make a similarly courageous and strong choice for family, Alma was able to view the exchanges with compassion, forgiveness, and self-acceptance. By slowing down, finding quiet, and looking inward (Stewart, 2009) to find her strengths, compassion, and love about and for her family, she began to access wisdoms, and connections with her patrón.

Seaming Incongruence

In managing multiple realities and identities, it is at the borders that Latinas seam and seek to draw connections (Anzaldúa, 1987). Latinas' internal ability to navigate incongruence and live within and between borders of identities, context, or realities is directly connected to her ability to anchor herself in the process and learn from the experiences.

> As Alma and her therapist neared the end of their sessions together, her skill of journeying through the differences (home and school, social expectations, personal processes) and creating personal nourishment from exchanges (sorority, time with family) served as a healing process as well as an assessment for her therapist that Alma was making the needed connections for herself. Although Alma and her therapist identified incongruences by which she felt most deeply hurt, Alma began making her own connections and seeing how she had to seam together opposing perspectives and approaches that, ultimately, emanated from the same space of care and concern. Alma's therapist suggested she keep a journal where she could write down and keep track of how such incongruences evolved and changed over time. As Alma committed her differences to paper, she found continued strength in naming them and knowing that she was part of weaving the tapestry of her family wisdom as that she could find common ground through shared values, emotion, and conocimiento. By connecting differences, she created a passage to her cultural and spiritual patrón, ancestors' wisdom, and lessons of past lives. Moreover, as she wove together incongruities (*soy mujer liberada y buena hija*/I am a mujerista and I am a good daughter) while staying connected to her feelings (e.g., worry, fear, confusion, elation, relief), she sought a strong position (I am worthy, I am healthy) to gain power while obtaining higher consciousness.

In essence, Latinas' internal blueprints stem from the ability to connect to the cultural consciousness through intuition, reflection, and mindfulness (Gloria & Castellanos, 2013). Latinas transmit information that is available in the larger cloak of knowledge that often goes unnoticed and untapped. Gifted with identities comprising multidimensionality and richness, Latinas have learned to be open to taking different forms, blending with the environment, and creating new and different realities. Within the patrón, Latinas access the fluidity of existence such that intentions can shift relationships and energies.

Living Through Dichos: Bridging Ancestral Teachings and Family Knowledge

As indicated throughout this chapter and specific to the above-presented models of transformation and healing, tapping into one's patrón cultural y espiritual facilitates for Latinas to gain self-awareness, healing, and transformation. Dichos are tangible and easily accessible way for Latinas, as well as the helpers and clinicians who are assisting them, to bridge the past and present and serve as an active means of reflection and self-transformation (Castellanos & Gloria, 2016). Dichos are cultural wisdoms and lessons frequently tied to early formative familial teachings (Zuniga, 1991) and core cultural beliefs within a culture (Flores-Torres & Ramirez, 2006). Dichos transmit Latina/o life lessons through short narratives, ideas, and reflections on daily activities (Aviera, 1996; Flores-Torres & Ramirez, 2006; Zuniga, 1991). The perspectives and wisdoms of dichos emanate from patrones, which have been passed across generations and a means of conocimiento translated into life lessons and serving as concrete directives to move through difficult experiences, as they accentuate ability, resilience, and endurance (Gloria & Castellanos, 2013; Zuniga, 1991). Comas-Díaz (2006) aptly argued that dichos can "offer subversive strategies as they express adaptive responses to oppression, colonization, and internalized oppression" (p. 444). By reframing and/or gaining new perspective, Latinas can tap into long-standing wisdom and familial energies to promote cultural resilience and situation management (Castellanos & Gloria, 2016; Comas-Díaz, 2006).

For poderosas, dichos "can be used as mechanisms of healing to show what is possible and to reveal truth and learn from the collective unconsciousness" (Castellanos & Gloria, 2016, p. 74). Used to address a range of daily issues (Flores-Torres & Ramirez, 2006), dichos can be readily implemented in the therapeutic setting by asking Latinas which dichos have the most meaning or relevance to them as they find their sources of strength and connection to their patrones. Central to the use of dichos is the ability of the therapist or helper to traverse roles and contexts (i.e., shape shift) and seam incongruities, such that the poderosa/client can inform and teach the lessons of her patrón to her therapist. In that dichos can be used within each of the models, they are explicitly and more fully addressed below relative to clinical intervention with Latinas to draw power and strength in being una ponderosa, as well as applied to Alma.

Lo Que Bien se Aprende, Nunca se Pierde *(What One Learns Well Will Never Be Lost)*

In a process filled with contact to the spirit and connection to ancestral knowledge and inner knowing, one has a deep acceptance that knowledge is gained through experience and time but wisdom comes from cyclical energy that is a representation of past ancestors, past life lessons, lineage, and connection to the tribe. Poderosas work from a power that enables them to travel through dreams and communication through the calling of their ancestors, abuelas (grandmothers) who have crossed over, and deceased family members (spirits) who continue to visit to assist in the creation of the communal purpose and family mission. The knowledge base is complemented with spiritual knowledge, intuitive messages, and spiritual direction. These lessons are imprinted in their blueprints, unforgettable to their experiences, and accessible in their subconscious and unconscious. The vision, foresight, and clarity poderosas possess is a collective knowledge and knowing that transcend time and space. It is a guiding force that is sought from within and found through the immersion of power and spirit.

> As a way to enact and maintain continued connection to her ancestral knowledge and inner knowing, Alma was encouraged to engage in rituals in the therapy session as well as in her daily life activities that reflected the essence of inner knowledge never being lost. In particular, she reframed mundane practices that she had learned from her mother, madrina, and grandmother into power practices as she connected to her core values. Alma's therapist questioned and challenged her to see beyond the mundane activity but rather to see how the practice of her daily prayers, lighting a candle, or even sharing a meal with familia physically and spiritually fed her sense of cultural power. Increasingly, it became apparent to Alma and her therapist and the therapeutic relationship that her sense of confianza was a critical element to her disclosure of such intensely personal engagements, despite initially being considered mundane.

El Que la Sigue la Consigue *(The Person Who Persists Is the Person Who Will Achieve It)*

The premise of persistence is steeped in *esperanza* (hope) and fortitude that if one stays the course toward an outcome or through a situation, one will achieve or succeed. It is the passion of commitment, belief, thought, and action that allows Latinas to draw on their inner strengths as poderosas to persist. Reflecting on familial hardships, the sacrifices of Latinas who engage their individual strengths and divinities can draw strength to persist during times of uncertainty and question. Although life's hardships may create stress, it is these processes that inherently engender the motivation and persistence to keep going to move through.

> When Alma's therapist asked what it was that she wanted to achieve, she quickly expressed the desire to make her family proud by being the first in her family to go to college. As a first-generation college student, Alma identified the different reference points of her family's hardships endured as the motivation to finish school. By honoring how her parents worked tirelessly in underpaid and difficult positions and lost cultural and family connection to secure a better life for their families and children, she found strength to persist through challenges when she questioned or doubted her educational abilities. To assist in circumventing Alma doubts, Alma's therapist questioned and reminded her about those places that she found inner strength. It is important to note that they also developed a working plan for her college persistence as Alma was able to identify those internal (prayer, naming her strengths) and external (family relationships, sorority sisters) sources of strength that could buffer against on-going and unexpected challenges.

Querer es Poder *(Where There Is a Will, There Is a Way)*

The notion of one's want being equated to having is built upon an individual's desire, drive, or *ganas* (motivation) to achieve the desired goal or outcome. The desire to explore and imagine possibilities of something different is a powerful process in and of itself. As envisioning transformation is often challenging and may move against or beyond the cultural assumptions, it requires Latinas to stay steadfast in transforming culturally restrictive assumptions and traditions and creating new fluid and flexible notions of self (Gloria & Castellanos, 2013). For example, Lara (2008) described the story of *la malinche* (the traitor), the ultimate Latina traitor, who provided interpretation in the conquest of Mexico for Hernán Cortés (Gaspar de Alba, 2005). *Malinztin* is re-claimed as *la mujer radicada* (a radical woman). A women who is a survivor, has inner strength and fortitude (Lara, 2008), and is a self-sufficient as she finds power rather than treason within her words (Miguela, 2001).

> As Alma's therapist asked her to envision and name aloud her desired transformation, she engaged in a process that enabled her a shedding of external notions of self to occur. Releasing the beliefs that she is a "bad" daughter, a traitor to her family, or that her family's demise rests on her shoulders was an important starting point and critical breakthrough. As a result, Alma released the notion that by going to school she is giving up her culture, which in turn enabled her to find her strength and vision for herself. Alma's therapist named the change occurring as Alma began reclaiming the power and desire within her vision and, in turn, allowed Alma a renewed and power-based notion of herself. Alma's ability to reference her family's strength, resilience and strength became the needed point of (re)connection to her espiritualidad, as well as to begin repositioning herself as a poderosa. In particular, it was Alma's ability to reference her mother's actions and reactions to her decision to go to school away from her family as a source of strength that enabled her to live out her culture and seam incongruence as she found and owned her connection to a familial history of strength and power.

Se Hace Camino al Andar *(The Path Is Made by Walking)*

In a collective web of existence, Latina poderosas are not walking alone but must walk with others (familia, community, ancestors) to make progress and create a path. Although Latinas work from a wholistic framework connecting with the upper or mortal world, they create pathways to navigate current realities and dream time (the passage to manifest change and envision a different reality). Latinas poderosas must have the courage to transcend gender scripts, gender roles, and gender expectations to maximize their power and evolve personally and spiritually. To be Latina poderosas sustaining their power, they must be willing to walk unchartered waters, be willing to engage the unknown, become fearless of unexpected outcomes, be creative problem solvers in their quest to survive, and be able to calm their spirit while feeding their soul.

> For Alma, envisioning and giving breath to her dream facilitated a process of transformation and healing. Within the therapeutic relationship, she had an initial space to sit with her fears and feel the discomfort of forging a new path as a means of finding strength and meaning within herself. Similarly, being challenged to seek out others who are walking similar uncharted and unscripted paths (student group "sisters") enabled her to access power beyond herself as part of her interconnectedness to and with others. In essence, as her therapist assisted Alma to recognize and own her inner power, a buffering and repositioning of the interpretation of her challenges while tapping into her collective consciousness emerged. At the time of termination, Alma felt grounded and centered within herself as she recognized that her choice for school was a new path that she was forging with and for her family. Alma relayed how she felt empowered as she committed to her choice and began planning and preparing for graduate studies as yet another way to assist her family. She identified how graduate studies was a means for her to continue her journey of strength as she expressed a desire and determination to serve as a community leader and educational *prometora* and poderosa. Alma made her own connection of how she wanted to forge a new path for her family, much in the same way that her mother and grandmother had by making challenging choices for and because of the family. Alma began exploring different career paths in which she could empower others to go to school. Although not certain of her plans, she spoke of wanting to merge areas of school counseling and advising, women's studies, nursing, and women's sexual health and/or public health. Alma was also interested in knowing more about the mind–body connection and began keeping a diary of her familial oral history with specific interest in identifying more of the familial dichos and related immigration stories. As she gained increased comfort and intention about her purpose, she began writing an e-journal blog for her social media outlet about her familial history and began making her family narratives the focus of her writing assignments in her college classes.

TRANSFORMATIONAL HEALING: PRACTICE IMPLICATIONS FOR THERAPISTS WORKING WITH PODEROSAS

Being una poderosa is a continuous process rather than a static outcome. Being powerful is a dynamic ever-changing process steeped in one's belief system that requires energy, knowing, increasing consciousness, and physical and meta-physical connections. It also requires sacred spaces in which to heal and engage self-awareness for transformation. As such, exploring how

Latinas can engage in ongoing self-reflections to allow for conocimiento and healing to emerge is needed. Next, as the transformation process unfolds, it is important to underscore that poderosas are their own healers. That is, therapists would do well to remind and work toward poderosas recognizing that they have within themselves the ability and power to engage their own healing processes. Therapists and clinicians must strive to implement culturally relevant and emic-centered services in provision of poderosa-based services. To assist in the self-reflection and transformation process both within the counseling setting and for individual self-reflection, Exhibit 4.1 provides questions that can assist with the goal of working toward clarity and insight about one's patrón. These questions are not intended as an exhaustive list but rather as a starting point from which Latinas and their therapists can build upon and deepen the needed reflections as they make meaning and find insight into their processes.

> As Alma and her therapist reflected on the therapeutic relationship and issues addressed over the course of their time, it was clear that Alma had gained insights about her strength and newfound identity as a Latina poderosa. Alma felt ready to end their therapy relationship but was worried that without the biweekly support, she would have difficulty implementing her hard-earned insights. To assist, Alma and her therapist developed

EXHIBIT 4.1
Questions for Clarity and Insight about One's *Patrón*

Spaces of healing and transformation	Inner strengths	Processes toward *Conocimiento*
• Where do you feel most validated to envision transformation? • How do you create sacred space for *conocimiento?* • What connections and exchanges validate your transformation and healing? • How do you engage your divergent and convergent realities and identities for transformation?	• What practices do you engage to access your inner strengths? • What connections assist your inner strength and healing? • How do you draw your personal strength and power? • What practices do you engage to access your power? • What are some of your power bases?	• When do you access collective consciousness, your ancestral wisdom, and your *patrón*? • What beliefs and practices do you engage to stay connected to ancestral wisdom and their teachings? • What beliefs and practices do you engage to attain *conocimiento*? • What are your *patrón's* ancient teachings of healing?

a plan in which she would return to her patrón as a first step, as well as to create a sacred space for herself in which she could have clarity of reflection. Alma was reminded that she could pose questions for herself and with her "sisters"/comadres such that they could create healing spaces while sharing support for each other's transformation. Although returning for additional counseling sessions was not financially realistic for Alma, her therapist reminded her of her inner power to heal and transform as a central element of being poderosa. She also reminded Alma of how through her relationships with others and in particular, to herself and her familial teachings/history, that she was una poderosa.

REFERENCES

Acosta, K. L. (2008). Lesbianas in the borderlands: Shifting identities and imagined communities. *Gender & Society*, *22*, 639–659. http://dx.doi.org/10.1177/0891243208321169

Aguirre, A., Jr., & Turner, J. H. (2011). *American ethnicity: The dynamics and consequences of discrimination* (7th ed.). New York, NY: McGraw Hill.

Alexander, J. C., Eyerman, R., Giesen, B., & Smelser, N. J. (2004). *Cultural trauma and collective identity*. Berkeley: University of California, Press. http://dx.doi.org/10.1525/california/9780520235946.001.0001

Anzaldúa, G. (1987). *Borderlands/La frontera: The new mestiza*. San Francisco, CA: Aunt Lute.

Arbona, C. (2006). Puerto Ricans. In Y. Jackson (Ed.), *Encyclopedia of multicultural psychology* (pp. 373–379). Thousand Oaks, CA: Sage. http://dx.doi.org/10.4135/9781412952668.n170

Arredondo, P. (2002). Mujeres Latinas: *Santas y marquesas*. *Cultural Diversity and Ethnic Minority Psychology*, *8*, 308–319. http://dx.doi.org/10.1037/1099-9809.8.4.308

Arrizón, A. (2009). Latina subjectivity, sexuality and sensuality. *Women & Performance: A Journal of Feminist Theory*, *18*, 189–198. http://dx.doi.org/10.1080/07407700802495928

Aviera, A. (1996). "Dichos" therapy group: A therapeutic use of Spanish language proverbs with hospitalized Spanish-speaking psychiatric patients. *Cultural Diversity and Mental Health*, *2*, 73–87. http://dx.doi.org/10.1037/1099-9809.2.2.73

Castellanos, J., & Gloria, A. M. (2016). Latina/os—Drive, community, and spirituality: The strength within (*SOMOS Latina/os—Ganas, comunidad, y el espiritu: La fuerza que llevamos por dentro*). In E. C. Chang, C. A. Downey, J. K. Hirsch, & N. J. Lin (Eds.), *Positive psychology in racial and ethnic groups: Theory, research, and practice* (pp. 61–82). Washington, DC: American Psychological Association.

Cervantes, J. M. (2010). Mestizo spirituality: Toward an integrated approach to psychotherapy for Latina/os. *Psychotherapy: Theory, Research, Practice, Training, 47*, 527–539. http://dx.doi.org/10.1037/a0022078

Cervantes, J. M., & Ramírez, O. (1992). Spirituality and family dynamics in psychotherapy with Latino children. In L. Vargas & J. Koss-Chioino (Eds.), *Working with culture: Psychotherapeutic interventions with ethnic minority children and adolescents* (pp. 103–128). San Francisco, CA: Jossey-Bass.

Comas-Díaz, L. (2006). Latino healing: The integration of ethnic psychology into psychotherapy. *Psychotherapy: Theory, Research, Practice, Training, 43*, 436–453. http://dx.doi.org/10.1037/0033-3204.43.4.436

Comas-Díaz, L. (2008). 2007 Carolyn Sherif Award address: *Spirita*: Reclaiming womanist sacredness in feminism. *Psychology of Women Quarterly, 32*, 13–21. http://dx.doi.org/10.1111/j.1471-6402.2007.00403.x

Comas-Díaz, L. (2012). Colored spirituality: The centrality of spirituality of spirit among ethnic minorities. In L. J. Miller (Ed.), *The Oxford book of psychology and spirituality* (pp. 197–206). New York, NY: Oxford.

Comas-Díaz, L. (2013). *Comadres*: The healing power of a female bond. *Women & Therapy, 36*, 62–75. http://dx.doi.org/10.1080/02703149.2012.720213

Comas-Díaz, L., Lykes, M. B., & Alarcón, R. D. (1998). Ethnic conflict and the psychology of liberation in Guatemala, Peru, and Puerto Rico. *American Psychologist, 53*, 778–792. http://dx.doi.org/10.1037/0003-066X.53.7.778

Delgado-Guerrero, M., & Gloria, A. M. (2013). *La importancia de la hermandad Latina*: Examining the psychosociocultural influences of Latina-based sororities on academic persistence decisions. *Journal of College Student Development, 54*, 361–378. http://dx.doi.org/10.1353/csd.2013.0067

Espín, O. M. (1997). *Latina realities: Essays on healing, migration, and sexuality*. Boulder, CO: Westview Press.

Facio, E., & Lara, I. (2014). *Fleshing the spirit: Spiritualty and activism in Chicana, Latina, and indigenous women's lives*. Tucson: University of Arizona Press.

Falicov, C. J. (2013). *Latino families in therapy: A guide to multicultural practice* (2nd ed.). New York, NY: Guilford Press.

Flores-Torres, L. L., & Ramirez, S. Z. (2006). Indigenous treatments: Dichos. In Y. Jackson (Ed.), *Encyclopedia of multicultural psychology* (pp. 250–251). Thousand Oaks, CA: Sage. http://dx.doi.org/10.4135/9781412952668.n126

Gaspar de Alba, A. (2005). Malinche's revenge. In R. Romero & A. N. Harris (Eds.), *Feminism, nation and myth: La malinche* (pp. 44–57). Houston, TX: Arte Público Press.

Gill-Hopple, K., & Brage-Hudson, D. (2012). *Compadrazgo*: A literature review. *Journal of Transcultural Nursing, 23*, 117–123. http://dx.doi.org/10.1177/1043659611433870

Gloria, A. M. (2001). The cultural construction of Latinas: Practice implications of multiple realities and identities. In D. B. Pope-Davis & H. L. K. Coleman

(Eds.), *The intersection between race, gender, and class: Implications for multicultural counseling* (pp. 3–24). Thousand Oaks, CA: Sage. http://dx.doi.org/10.4135/9781452231846.n1

Gloria, A. M., & Castellanos, J. (2009). Latinas/os and their communities. In Council of National Psychological Associations for the Advancement of Ethnic Minority Interests (Ed.), *Psychology education and training from culture-specific and multiracial perspectives: Clinical issues and recommendations* (pp. 12–18). Washington, DC: American Psychological Association.

Gloria, A. M., & Castellanos, J. (2012). *Desafíos y bendiciones*: A multi-perspective examination of the educational experiences and coping responses of first-generation college Latina students. *Journal of Hispanic Higher Education, 11*, 82–98. http://dx.doi.org/10.1177/1538192711430382

Gloria, A. M., & Castellanos, J. (2013). *Realidades culturales y identidades dimensionadas*: The complexities of Latina diversities. In C. Enns & E. Williams (Eds.), *Handbook of feminist multicultural counseling psychology* (pp. 169–182). New York, NY: Oxford University Press.

Isasi-Díaz, A. (1996). *Mujerista theology: A theology for the twenty-first century*. Maryknoll, NY: Orvis Books.

Isasi-Díaz, A. (2004). *Burlando al opresor*: Mocking/tricking the oppressor: Dreams and hope of Hispanas/Latinas and mujeristas. *Theological Studies, 65*, 340–363. http://dx.doi.org/10.1177/004056390406500205

Isasi-Díaz, A. (2008). *Se hace camino al andar*—The road is made by walking: What the future demands of women-centered theologies. *Feminist Theology: The Journal of the Britain & Ireland School of Feminist Theology, 16*, 379–382. http://dx.doi.org/10.1177/0966735008091404

Ivakhiv, A. (2003). Nature and self in new age pilgrimage. *Culture and Religion, 4*, 93–118. http://dx.doi.org/10.1080/01438300302812

Lara, I. (2008). Latina health activists-healers bridging body and spirit. *Women & Therapy, 31*, 21–40. http://dx.doi.org/10.1300/02703140802145169

Lopez, T. (2010). Familismo. In Y. Jackson (Ed.), *Encyclopedia of multicultural psychology* (p. 211). Thousand Oaks, CA: Sage.

Miguela, A. D. (2001, May 5). Re-inventing themselves: Forging a Latina identity in contemporary Latina narrative. *US Latino/a Literature*. Retrieved from http://www.uhu.es/antonia.dominguez/latinas/latina.pdf

Mintz, S. W., & Wolf, E. R. (1950). An analysis of ritual co-parenthood (*Compadrazgo*). *Southwestern Journal of Anthropology, 6*, 341–368.

National Alliance on Mental Illness. (2006). *Latino community mental health fact sheet*. Arlington, VA: Author.

National Alliance on Mental Illness. (2008). *Latina women and depression: Fact sheet*. Arlington, VA: Author.

Nelson, M. C. (2003). *Toltec prophecies of Don Miguel Ruiz*. Tulsa, OK: Council Oak Books.

Nicolas, G., Gonzalez-Eastep, D., & DeSilva, A. (2010). Spirituality. In Y. Jackson (Ed.), *Encyclopedia of multicultural psychology* (pp. 443–445). Thousand Oaks, CA: Sage.

Nielsen Project. (2013). *Latina power shift*. Retrieved from http://www.nielsen.com/us/en/insights/reports/2013/latina-power-shift.html

Nuñez, S. (2008). Brazil's ultimate healing resource: The power of spirit. In B. W. McNeill & J. M. Cervantes (Eds.), *Latina/o healing practices: Mestizo and indigenous perspectives* (pp. 139–174). New York, NY: Routledge.

Ortiz, F. A. (2009). Personalismo. In M. A. De la Torre (Ed.), *Hispanic American Religious Cultures* (p. 177). Santa Barbara, CA: ABC-CLIO.

McNeill, B. W., & Cervantes, J. M. (Eds.). (2008). *Latina/o healing practices: Mestizo and indigenous perspectives*. New York, NY: Routledge.

Perkins, J. (1997). *Shapeshifting: Shamanic techniques for global and personal transformation*. Rochester, VT: Destiny Books.

Ramírez, M. (1991). *Psychotherapy and counseling with minorities: A cognitive approach to individual and cultural differences*. New York, NY: Pergamon Press.

Ramírez, M. (1998). *Multicultural/multiracial psychology: Mestizo perspectives in personality and mental health*. Lanham, MD: Rowman & Littlefield.

Rodriguez, J. (2004). *Mestiza* spirituality: Community, ritual and justice. *Theological Studies, 65*, 317–339. http://dx.doi.org/10.1177/004056390406500204

Santiago-Rivera, A. L., Arredondo, P., & Gallardo-Cooper, M. (Eds.). (2002). *Counseling Latinos and la familia: A practical guide*. Thousand Oaks, CA: Sage.

Soto, L. D., Cervantes-Soon, C. G., Villarreal, E., & Campos, E. E. (2009). The Xicana sacred space: A communal circle of *compromiso* for educational researchers. *Harvard Educational Review, 79*, 755–776. http://dx.doi.org/10.17763/haer.79.4.4k3x387k74754q18

Stevens, E. P. (1973). *Marianismo*: The other face of machismo in Latin America. In A. Pescatello (Ed.), *Female and male in Latin American essays* (pp. 90–101). Pittsburgh, PA: University of Pittsburgh Press.

Stewart, W. B. (2009). *Deep medicine: Harnessing the source of your healing power*. Oakland, CA: New Harbinger.

Vasquez, M. J. T. (1994). Latinas. In L. Comas-Díaz & B. Greene (Eds.), *Women of color: Integrating ethnic and gender identities in psychotherapy* (pp. 114–138). New York, NY: Guilford Press.

Villoldo, A. (2008). *Courageous dreaming: How shamans dream the world into being*. Carlsbad, CA: Hay House.

Zuniga, M. E. (1991). "Dichos" as metaphorical tools for resistant Latino clients. *Psychotherapy: Theory, Research, Practice, Training, 28*, 480–483. http://dx.doi.org/10.1037/0033-3204.28.3.480

III

SPIRITUALITY

5

WOMANISM AND SPIRITUALITY/THEOLOGY

MARTHA E. BANKS AND STEPHANIE LEE

> In a stunning reversal of American societal order, it is an enslaved girl who is called to publicly proclaim the Gospel—her gender, race, and age all stand in contrast to the powers and structures that would otherwise render her silent. (Pierce, 2013, p. 47)

> *Even Me*
> Lord, I hear of show'rs of blessing, Thou art scatt'ring full and free;
> Show'rs the thirsty souls refreshing, Let some drops now fall on me!
> Even me, yes! Even me! Even me, Lord! Even me!
> Let some drops now fall on me.
>
> —Elizabeth Codner (1824–1919)

Considerable literature is available on the role of spirituality in the lives of African American women. Womanist psychologists and theologians have long recognized that spirituality and religion are critical to the well-being of African American women (Bryant-Davis, Ellis, & Perez, 2013). In this chapter, we encourage mental health practitioners and researchers to consider multiple perspectives on the impact of colonization and enslavement on the receipt and expression of African American women's spirituality and religion. Using a womanist theological perspective, we examine ways in which spirituality and religion can be used to attain psychological wellness for African American women. We also provide an overview of theological distortions inimical to women's well-being (Greene, 2008), as a caution against misuse of religion as a form of oppression. The predominant material used to support

http://dx.doi.org/10.1037/14937-006
Womanist and Mujerista Psychologies: Voices of Fire, Acts of Courage, T. Bryant-Davis and L. Comas-Díaz (Editors)

this chapter is based on literature arising from Christianity, with an emphasis on religious practices in the United States. We appreciate that womanism is reflected in other major religions, both within the United States and around the world.

UNDERSTANDING SPIRITUALITY AND WOMANIST THEOLOGY

Womanism

Based on Alice Walker's (1983) definition of a *womanist* as "a Black feminist or feminist of color" who is "committed to survival and wholeness of entire people, male and female" (p. xi), *womanism* is a school of philosophy designed "to dismantle systemic oppression in the face of ongoing assaults" and "to sustain themselves, womanists honor the spirit" (Comas-Díaz, 2008, p. 14). Womanism encompasses the spiritual, communal, and psychological aspects of a woman (Abernethy, Houston, Mimms, & Boyd-Franklin, 2006).

Spirituality, Religiosity, and Religion

It is important to understand what is meant by *spirituality*, *religiosity*, and *religion*. Much of the literature available is written by people with a heritage of colonizing and enslaving other people, attempting to reduce the humanity of those people (Robinson, 2012). This has been countered by Black liberation theologians (e.g., James H. Cone, Howard Thurman, Martin Luther King, Jr.) who confronted racism embedded in European-informed religion and by feminist theologians (including Rosemary Radford Ruether, Phyllis Trible, Elisabeth Schussler Fiorenza) who confronted sexism that is supported by religion in male-dominated societies. Womanist theologians (e.g., Delores S. Williams, Renita Weems, Cheryl Townsend Gilkes) have been more inclusive, recognizing the interrelatedness of multiple oppressions and working toward theology, scriptural interpretation, and application that leads to improved health and status of individuals and communities. Whereas Black, feminist, and womanist theologians have focused on relationships among people and cultures, Victorin-Vangerud (2003) challenged people to consider all of creation in the connectedness of people to each other and the earth, including the islands, continents (i.e., large islands), and the role and depth of the ocean in connecting, dividing, and constantly reshaping all of existence—deep examination increases understanding of the fluidity of boundaries among life, spirit, and creation observed and yet to be known.

For this chapter, we take definitions of *spirituality*, *religiosity*, and *religion* from a womanist perspective. It should be noted that few agree on what these terms mean, even among people sharing similar demographics. Mattis (2002) provided the following definitions in her work with African American women:

> *Religiosity* is defined as the degree to which individuals adhere to the prescribed beliefs and practices of an organized religion.
>
> *Spirituality* refers to an individual's belief in the sacred and transcendent nature of life, and the manifestation of these beliefs in a sense of connectedness with others (e.g., humans, spirits, and God), and in a quest for goodness. (p. 310)

Spirituality also involves reverence, awe, inspiration, and answers about the infinite (Richards & Bergin, 2005). Stek (1997) defined *religion* as

> ways in which humans relate to the divine. . . . All such "ways" include a system of beliefs about the divine and how it is related to the world. Most also involve an attitude of awe toward the divine, and a pattern of actions (rituals and an ethical code). By extension, *religion* is often used to refer to systems of belief and related practices that play an analogous role in people's lives (e.g., Buddhism, Confucianism, and even humanism).

Spirituality is often defined as an individual experience, with religion reflecting an organized, shared institution (Abernethy et al., 2006). Comas-Díaz (2008) defined *spirita* as women of color's spirituality that "mobilizes women to take control of their lives, overcome their oppressed mentality, and achieve a critical knowledge of themselves" (p. 13).

Religion and spirituality occur in relationship and interaction. Women do not passively receive religious teaching or spiritual events; they enter into searches for meaning and relationship using lenses reflecting their cultures and experiences. For African women, especially those in currently or historically colonized societies, the struggle between traditional African and European-influenced religion is overt, albeit seldom discussed (Kanyoro, 2001); a similar struggle is observed among Black people in the Caribbean Islands (Taylor, Chatters, & Jackson, 2009). Enslaved women of African descent, cut off from their families and culture, but exposed to European-influenced religion, experienced a different conflict. Today, the issues of multiple oppression (Banks, 2012) continue to create difficulties, as African American women seek spirituality in religions shaped largely by people who continue to benefit from the institutional oppression, the ongoing legacy of slavery, created by their ancestors (Frederick-McGlathery, 2006).

Womanist Theology

Theology, or the study of God, involves interpretation and application of religious scripture. It is faith-seeking understanding: "Womanist theology attempts to help Black women see, affirm, and have confidence in the importance of their experience and faith for determining the character of the Christian religion in the African American community" (D. S. Williams, 2013, Kindle locations 233–235). Womanist theology is closely connected with other theologies, and includes all humanity, while addressing the interaction of oppressions experienced by African American women, focusing on "the faith, survival and freedom-struggle of African American women. Thus womanist theology identifies and critiques Black male oppression of Black females while it also critiques White racism that oppresses all African Americans, female and male" (D. S. Williams, 2013, Kindle locations 239–249).

Although womanist theology is considered by some to be a combination of feminist theology and Black liberation theology, it is actually greater than the sum of those two contributing theologies:

> Womanist theology arose out of the need for a theology that would take seriously the perspectival lens African American women's experience brings to the theological enterprise. Womanist theology critiques the multidimensional oppression of African American women's lives, at a minimum, sexism, racism, classism, and heterosexism. It challenges structures, symbols, and sociopolitical realities that foster oppression/domination of Black women in particular, as well as Black men, humanity in general, and nature. (Crawford, 1998, p. 367)

Womanist theology has long roots, extending back to the time of slavery when Old Elizabeth, a freed slave without resources beyond limited literacy and ongoing divine direction, preached for 60 years in the late 18th and early 19th centuries in states along the mid-Atlantic coast (Pierce, 2013). Despite the role models of Old Elizabeth and many others, as well as scriptural support for preaching by women, Black churches have been slow to accord women access to the pulpit (Cary, 2008; Cooper, 2011) or invite/welcome/allow womanist theology in the church (Warnock, 2014). West (2006) observed that the restriction of Black women from the pulpit occurs in service of maintaining the illusion that church leadership is the province of Black men who face racism outside of the church but can serve as "patriarchal figures of authority" (p. 132) as pastors and preachers, whereas women are relegated to supportive roles (Griffin-Fennell & Williams, 2006) or leadership in service outside of the pulpit (Butler, 2006). African American clergywomen face challenges to their leadership, whether they use an independent or a competitive style admired in clergymen, or a collaborative or empowering style that matches the nurturing stereotype of women (Cary, 2008). This racialized sexism occurs across religions. In the United Methodist denomination, for example, Black clergywomen compose only 2.3% of the clergy and 1.8% of full-time local pastors (Kane, 2014). Visibility of African American women in the pulpit, especially in proportion with representation in the religious population, provides a powerful message of the inclusion of women as favored people, counteracts oppressive images of women as second-class, and increases the chance of womanist messages reaching congregants and members of the community (L. Lee, 2012).

Women of color experience spirituality as important in their lives and pursue religion in a variety of ways (Frederick-McGlathery, 2006). King (2009) found that, despite negative media portrayals of Islam as a terrorist and misogynist religion, British and American feminist women are reverting or converting to Islam "because it gives women rights and has less tolerance of the commercialization of sex and the sexual objectification of women" (p. 298). They differentiate between the religion itself and the cultural practices of some adherents.

SPIRITUALITY: A FOUNDATION OF HEALTH

Spirituality has been identified as a critical, integral part of physical and mental wellness (Holt, Schulz, Williams, Clark, & Wang, 2012), actually functioning as a buffer for African Americans exposed to individual and/or institutional racism (Bowen-Reid & Harrell, 2002; C. B. Williams & Wiggins, 2010). Research has been conducted on spirituality as a critical factor in the health of African American women, especially in coping with illness. That research includes coping upon diagnosis, treatment, and recovery from breast cancer (Tate, 2011); renal disease and dialysis (Tanyi & Werner, 2008); cardiovascular disease (Masters & Hooker, 2013); and diabetes (Polzer & Miles, 2007). These are all areas in which African American women's health is significantly worse than that of European Americans (Leigh & Li, 2014).

Suicide, the result of unrelenting and increasing depression, is seldom observed in African American women as compared with African American men and with women who are members of other ethnic groups. Griffin-Fennell and Williams (2006), however, showed that African American women "may complete suicide less frequently than men, but African American women do attempt suicide at a higher rate" (p. 312). Risk factors for suicide include chronic illness, violence and other trauma (Arnette, Mascaro, Santana, Davis, & Kaslow, 2007; Kaslow et al., 2010), and homelessness. For adolescent African American women, collaborative religious coping appears to provide reasons for living, minimizing suicidal ideation (Molock, Puri, Matlin, & Barksdale, 2006). Early research examined the role of religion as a buffer that minimized suicidal attempts, but inconsistent results led to exploration of the role of spirituality in the lives of African Americans experiencing severe depression (Griffin-Fennell & Williams, 2006). One issue raised by Goldston et al. (2008) is the barrier to clergy prevention of suicide in Black churches; clergy seldom recognize suicide lethality or refer people to mental health professionals, due in part to the belief that African Americans do not commit suicide and negative perspectives about mental health treatment.

As a result, it is important to assess levels of spirituality to develop culturally relevant treatments (Ambrose, 2006). Holt, Lukwago, and Kreuter (2003) found that a belief dimension of spirituality was more critical than a behavioral dimension in determining the best way to communicate with African American women about breast cancer and the use of mammography, so that "spiritual health communication should only be used if an individual self-identifies as a spiritual person" (p. 394) and that other approaches be developed for women with low spiritual belief. Holt et al. (2009) considered two other dimensions of spirituality, perceived religious influence on health behaviors and illness as punishment from a higher power, as important in increasing understanding of health disparities between African Americans and other ethnic groups. In similar research, Franklin, Schlundt, and Wallston (2008) examined three constructs of African American health fatalism: divine provision ("belief that God will provide good health"; e.g., answer to prayer), destined plan ("an individual's health status is part of a plan that God has determined"; e.g., purpose in one's life), and helpless inevitability ("belief that a person has little or no control over their health"; e.g., personal action is not important), as explanations for self-care and compliance with health treatment (p. 332).

Harvey and Cook (2010) found that spirituality provided a way for older women to deal with chronic illness by combining their emotional and cognitive processing about their circumstances. The participants in their research felt that spirituality gave them perspective that increased faith and strengthened their ability to take responsibility for and collaborate in their health and health care, rather than giving full control of their lives to God or health care professionals. Such collaboration is consistent with an African worldview and supports resilience observed in African American women despite lifelong oppression (Trotman & Tirrell, 2013).

African American women experience HIV/AIDS at disproportionately high rates. Dalmida, Holstad, DiIorio, and Laderman (2012) explored the detailed roles of spirituality and religiosity in the lives of African American women living with HIV/AIDS, who were more apt to endorse being spiritual than being religious, because of barriers created by many religious institutions. Their spirituality involved a journey that took them closer to God. The women used their spirituality by attending church (in person or by watching television), praying, helping other people, witnessing, and having faith in God. The power of telling their stories was liberating. As a result, they felt healthier, found inner peace, had the strength to keep going, experienced spiritual support, and discovered meaning for their lives (Dalmida et al., 2012). The importance of spirituality has been demonstrated to influence compliance with medical treatment. With the ability to control HIV and prevent full-blown AIDS through medical treatment, it is critical that infected people comply with prescribed medical regimens. Simoni, Frick, and Huang (2006) determined that spirituality in combination with low levels of negative affect significantly enhanced adherence to antiretroviral therapy.

A major health challenge for African American women is violence (Stockman, Hayashi, & Campbell, 2015). Spirituality has been critical in addressing the repeatedly traumatizing and intergenerational violence that dates back to the kidnapping of Black women from Africa, through centuries of enslavement, up to the domestic violence and human trafficking that characterize modern-day slavery (Gillum, 2009). Bryant-Davis (2005) found that spirituality was the most often acknowledged coping strategy used by African American adults who had survived violence during their childhoods. Throughout life, high levels of spirituality are correlated with good health (Paranjape & Kaslow, 2010).

Homelessness is a problem disproportionately experienced by African American women (Douglas, Jimenez, Lin, & Frisman, 2008), especially as they age. They pursue assistance from clergy and churches because the religious institutions and people are reputed to be compassionate. Homeless women are at very high risk for rape and other assault, with ensuing "depression, post-traumatic stress syndrome, alcoholism, and substance use. Sustained exposure to the threat of assault, as well as long term exposure to the elements, and poor nutrition can compromise dramatically the health of homeless women" (Washington & Moxley, 2008, p. 157). Given the limited information and invisibility of homelessness in many parts of the United States, it is important to learn about the experiences of homeless women in their own voices and understand that spirituality is a critical factor for these women as they seek to overcome homelessness. Incorporating that understanding into psychotherapy and social services is an important part of the ministry of religious organizations as they provide services for homeless African American women (Moxley, Washington, & McElhaney, 2012).

RELIGION: ADDRESSING SPIRITUAL HEALTH NEEDS

S. Lee (1999) identified six specific pastoral care needs experienced by African American congregations: free expression, family/community support, care in the face of extreme loss and separation, identity, self-esteem and self-determination, and identification with biblical images and biblical history that affirm and liberate.

Free Expression

When Europeans kidnapped Africans and brought them to North America, they deprived them of their languages and cultures, including religion and spiritual expression:

> As a spiritual people with a different world view, the Africans (and later the African Americans combating racism and oppression) needed a place—a free space—a place of refuge where they could embrace their African spiritual root—where they could pray and worship in their own way, where the community could experience freedom. (S. Lee, 1999, p. 4)

Weems (1988) opened the door for full expression for, by, and about African American women who had previously been denied significance and voice in the Black church. Womanist theologians gave women expression by reinterpreting scripture through African American women's experiences which had previously been silenced.

Testimony is the sharing and telling of lived experiences (Washington & Moxley, 2008). In church, this sharing is healing for the speaker and the listeners. Wimberly (1997) recognized the power of testimony as healing for clergy, as well as laypeople, and recommended internal review and reinterpretation of their own personal and professional testimonies. As African American women listen to testimony, they hear their own stories, learn of the survival and victories of others, and are empowered by messages of hope that they can incorporate into their own lives and situations. Testimony was contextualized in biblical terms by womanist theologians, increasing what could be shared by African American women in church.

Family/Community Support

African Americans give a high priority to belonging, so that an individual exists in relation to others and not separately. Relationships are all perceived as kinships. It is often stated, "To be healthy is to be connected."

Womanist theologians provide biblical examples of the importance of relationships. The story of Mary, the mother of Jesus, and her cousin, Elizabeth, involves Mary's helping Elizabeth with her late life pregnancy and Elizabeth's affirmation of Mary's role in God's Divine Plan (Luke 1:39–56; The Infancy Gospel of James 12:1–7; Davies, 2009). This is an example of friendship and kinship that was healthy for both women. Another example of healthy friendship and kinship is the sacrifice by Ruth of her citizenship in order to support her widowed and childless mother-in-law, Naomi (Ruth 1:16–19). Naomi, in turn, provided guidance and arranged for Ruth's security as an immigrant woman (Ruth 3:1–18).

Similar to Mary, Elizabeth, Naomi, and Ruth, African American women often find themselves on the margins of society. The womanist focus on the healthy relationships among women empowers African American women to support each other in a society that undervalues and stereotypes them through sexualized racism and racialized sexism (Speight, Isom, & Thomas, 2013; Townes, 2010; West, 2006).

Care in the Face of Extreme Loss and Separation

The loss and separation experienced by kidnapped Africans and African American slaves is paralleled today in the high rates of violence and incarceration in African American communities, as well as the targeted violence against African Americans crossing societal barriers. Biblical stories of women provide images of movement from the margins of society to reunification with community. These are Good News to African American women who have faced barriers to full participation in U.S. society.

Hagar, an African slave in Israel, was separated from everything and everybody when she was thrown out of her mistress's home; she was hated, but she received care directly from God (Genesis 21:9–19). From a womanist perspective, Hagar's situation is similar to that of trafficked/enslaved women who have no rights as slaves and, upon release from slavery, are at risk for arrest, deportation, and/or life-threatening violence (Murphy, 2014). Just as Hagar was thrown out of her home, so African American women experience being thrown out of their homes for being pregnant, being infected with HIV/AIDS, returning from incarceration, or being members of sexual minorities. Like Hagar, they receive no community support, but look to God for care. In Matthew 9:20–22, Mark 5:27–34, and Luke 8:42b–48, a woman who was hemorrhaging had been shunned by society because she had been bleeding for 12 years. Following her faith, she received care directly from Jesus; her healing restored her to the community. Jesus spoke with a shunned Samaritan woman who was marginalized for living with a man to whom she was not married (John 5:6–30). After her conversation with Jesus, she was restored to the community as she gave her testimony of receiving grace. These three women in the Bible were shunned: Hagar for being a slave perceived as aspiring to change her social status, the woman with hemorrhage for having a socially denounced disability, and the woman at the well for her lifestyle. Their marginalization is paralleled by African American women who are accused of being "uppity" (aspiring to change social status), experience disability (likely to have considerable worse health than European American women), and are less likely to marry than European American women (a combination of the impact of stereotypes and laws that limit resources for impoverished married women; West, 2006).

Identity

Using hegemony, European Americans have established a national culture that gives added value to European-informed culture and demeans other cultures. S. Lee (1999) noted, "Added to physical domination was the mental enslavement of Black people—the internalization of the values of slavemasters" (p. 7). African Americans were required to deny the African past and affirm European values, such as belief that God ordained slavery, and that drumming and dancing were not legitimate forms of worship. Hairstyles, skin color, chosen names, learning styles, and tattooing are perceived and evaluated using European American standards, impacting educational opportunities, employment, and other societal involvement.

These issues influence women more than men because women of all ethnicities in U.S. society are evaluated on their appearance for femininity, attractiveness, and social class (Banks, 2015). In the Black church, African American women are able to put on the trappings of prestige through dressing up, a major boost to self-esteem for women whose poverty is reflected in their dress and whose employment often limits them to dehumanizing uniforms. Those uniforms are a holdover from slave days when special cloth was woven so that slaves could be easily identified by the clothing they wore (Brown University Steering Committee on Slavery and Justice, 2006). Some Black churchwomen participate in promenades, with tailored outfits, including hats and gloves. Separate wardrobes are exclusively reserved for church. In addition to the use of clothing for image, African American women participate in church in ways that they cannot in other areas of society. Presence and membership in church serve as markers of respectability, indicators of having identity of being "somebody," as women serve as the backbone of the church and hold a variety of roles, albeit in the background relative to men (Gilkes, 2000, 2006). The respectable identity of the Black church was used in film to attract Black people to serve in the military during World War II; images included well-dressed people, educated preachers, and false images of an integrated military (Cripps & Culbert, 1979).

Despite the more than 200 years that have passed since 1810 when Sarah Baartman was kidnapped and put on display in London like an animal because her physique differed from that of stereotypical European women, African American women are still compared and contrasted, as she was (Roberts, 2010; Speight et al., 2013). Assembly at woman-affirming churches provides African American women the opportunity to affirm their body shapes as similar to those of other congregants; woman-affirmation is a critical component of womanist theology (Angelou, 1978).

Self-Esteem and Self-Determination

The Black church decided to

> distance itself from "Black worship" and anything that demonstrated traces of Africanisms, but becoming so adjusted to the White theology of Black oppression that when Dr. Martin Luther King, Jr. finally called for Blacks to stand up and stand against injustice and oppression, many refused fearing they would lose their "standing" in the White community. The reality was that most Black pastors that considered themselves respectable stood in accord with the dominant (i.e., White) American attitudes toward revolution. (S. Lee, 1999, pp. 9–10)

In so doing, such churches maintained an uncritical alignment with the European-influenced versions of Christianity that supported oppression (Phelps, 2000).

During the civil rights movement, employed Black women were teachers and day workers/maids who were at high risk of losing their jobs if they participated in social justice activities. Those women were members of the churches that were silenced during that period. Many churches that did not participate in social action five decades ago still do not in the 21st century. Some churches, however, were at the center of social action using a balance of protest and praise (McMickle, 2014); women were a significant part, albeit behind the scenes, of those protests (Barnes, 2006; Gilkes, 2000, 2006; Keller, 1993). Women, especially womanist theologians, are still not welcome in the pulpits of many Black churches; they are prevented from leading social action by organizing churches to employ bible-based justification to address social problems. Without the womanists in the pulpit, the needs of African American women are not being met in many churches.

Identification With Biblical Images and Biblical History That Affirm and Liberate

Since the Age of Enlightenment, many of the images and understandings of biblical figures are portrayed by, or presented as, European-descended people, despite the origin of Judaism and Christianity among people of Western Asian/North African descent. As S. Lee (1999) noted,

> Enslaved Blacks (and modern Blacks too) needed to find images of God and God's people that were empowering and not part of the system of oppression. This, the slave religion accomplished by identifying with God's chosen—the people of Israel and their story of liberation through God's mighty intervention, which they fully expected for themselves as well. (p. 11)

Many biblical stories are about women in abusive situations who are liberated by God. They are portrayed in the Bible as fallen women who generally would not be considered worthwhile. Hagar was a slave who had, at the bidding of her mistress, borne her master a child (Genesis 16:1–3); Tamar pretended to be a prostitute to become pregnant by her father-in-law, who did not want her to marry his last surviving son (Genesis 38:6–26); and Rahab, characterized in many translations as a prostitute but possibly an innkeeper at a time when women would not generally be allowed that role, provided protection for Israeli spies (Joshua 2:1–22; 6:21–25). These women serve as role models for girls coming of age, as each found ways to protect herself and her family. They were able, through faith, to take charge of their own bodies and their futures, despite the abusive situations they were in. In the biblical times, women's fates were primarily in the hands of men, yet, with the help of God, they were able to work around the men who would oppress them.

SPIRITUAL DAMAGE: RELIGION IN THE WRONG HANDS

One concern for mental health practitioners is the need for attention to the nature of the religion to which their clients might be exposed (Greene, 2008). For example, Potter (2007) reviewed extensive research revealing misinterpretation of the Torah, Talmud, Qur'an, and Bible to support abuse of women, including bullying within the context of the religious institution. This is particularly problematic in Black churches, where women's roles are often so proscribed that unhealthy competition has replaced spiritual nurturing and positive relationships, denying African American women's humanity, femininity, and self-worth (Cary, 2008). Plante (2011) identified multiple ways in which some approaches to religion can be harmful:

- Tragically, particular religious beliefs and practices have been used as ideological bases for war, to oppress women, to torture and murder people who do not share the same religious tradition and perspectives, and to instill guilt, depression, and anxiety among many.
- Religious leaders can also use their power, influence, and control over their congregations for abusive purposes.
- Religiousness is sometimes associated with harmful health behaviors, such as the rejection of medical and psychiatric care, that can have devastating and even fatal consequences. (p. 84)

Tragedies and serious illness, such as cancer and HIV/AIDS, are sometimes mischaracterized as punishment for sins (Salley, 2009). Taking medication and other pursuit of health care is portrayed as a lack of faith. Such religious practices can lead to depression, anxiety, and desire to hurt self or others.

Another concern is individualistic prosperity theology, "a Christian theology whose signature teaching is that God wants believers to be rich and enjoy good physical health" (Mumford, 2012, p. 371). It has become popular since the late 1970s, and predominates in popular Word (of Faith) churches. Tillotson (2010) described materialistic Christianity as psychologically toxic to African Americans, as such religion seeks to divide rather than strengthen relationships and a collective sense of belonging.

Allen (2012) cautioned against the sexist rhetoric that can characterize Black sermons and the need to attend to the negative impact of such preaching on African American women's spiritual and mental health. Singh, Garnett, and Williams (2013) provided an example of a woman whose perspective about the Black church included "they continually told me at church, 'How dare you question. . . .' I think my strongest problem was the vulnerability of Black women in the churches" (p. 1109). Such a sense of vulnerability under the aegis of religion is clearly antithetical to healthy spirituality; it also interferes with childhood and adult revealing of abuse. McMickle (2014) observed,

> When a passionate time of praise and worship is disconnected from a disciplined and determined time of service and even sacrifice in the name of God, the worship itself becomes invalid and inauthentic. . . . At no point do people feel the need to speak up about war and peace, bias and discrimination, the increase in such pain indices as poverty, incarceration, teen and out-of-wedlock birth, HIV/AIDS infection rates, drug and alcohol abuse, failing public schools in inner cities, unemployment and the outsourcing of jobs, and/or domestic violence and divorce. (p. 338)

Contrary to the benefits of spirituality, religion has been problematic with respect to violence experienced by African American women. Crawford (1998) observed that "the church's silence suggest [sic] that talking about abuse and violence are greater offenses than the acts themselves!" (p. 380). Potter (2007) found that women seeking support of clergy were advised to remain in abusive relationships and believed they would be rejected if they shared experiences of being trafficked. Further, "the existence of sexism and promotion of patriarchy and traditional marital roles within some Black churches may inadvertently serve to facilitate perpetration of IPV [intimate partner violence] and survivors' suffering" (Gillum, 2009, p. 5). Bent-Goodley (2011) explored the concept of spiritual abuse, which involves a level of abuse that is different from physical and psychological abuse examined in most research. Spiritual abuse includes misinterpretation of scripture by both perpetrators and religious people, including clergy, to force victims to stay in abusive relationships.

In addition to the concern about messages in religious institutions, attention must be paid to potential harm by family members and health professionals who inappropriately use their own religion, spirituality, or theology that differs significantly from those of a person whom they are trying to support (Simon, Crowther, & Higgerson, 2007). The harm can take the form of self-hatred or lead to hopeless confusion, anxiety, and depression. When individuals and groups are not allowed access to full spirita, hurt people hurt people.

FOLLOWING GOD'S PATH TO HEALTH: PROPHETIC PREACHING FOR SOCIAL JUSTICE

A collective approach of religious institutions is important for supporting African-descended Americans in jointly pursuing social justice (Tillotson, 2010). In particular, as Mumford (2012) put it: "Of African Americans are to meet the challenges of the twenty-first century, we must adopt preaching that incorporates the best of both the prophetic and prosperity preaching traditions" (p. 381). Contrary to individualistic prosperity theology, prophetic preaching is based on justice and calls for collaboration and collective action: "Prophetic preaching speaks up for God's justice in a way that is different and relevant to the needs or plight of hearers. Prophetic preaching critically challenges the status quo. Prophetic preachers are not preoccupied with being politically correct" (Morris, 2011, p. 6). Gilbert (2014) referred to prophetic preaching as involving *conscientization* (naming reality) and aesthetic poetry, addressing both the horrors of the world and the promise of God's grace. Whereas prosperity theology encourages adherents to adjust their lives to fit extant cultural hierarchies, prophetic preaching raises awareness of injustice:

> Prophetic preaching not only challenges the status quo but offers theological and biblical insights into the current human situation from an individual's enslavement to sin to current cries for freedom echoed around the world in massive protests. It provides divinely orchestrated strategies on how to move out of despair with determination and hope. (Morris, 2011, pp. 6–7)

Prophetic preaching includes critiques of the un-Godly world and describes the promise of God's new reality (Powery, 2014), as described earlier by Morris (2011): "Prophetic preaching requires the preacher to name both what is not of God in the world (criticizing) and the new reality God will bring to pass in the future (energizing)" (p. 8). Allen (2012) encouraged a "womanist orientation in prophetic preaching" (p. 394), consistent with spirita (Comas-Díaz, 2008):

> In terms of content, *womanist prophetic preaching* refers to sermons that address social justice issues in the larger society, critique the ethical practices of the tradition in which the preaching is performed, and include a paradigm for listeners to critique sermon content and discourse about emancipatory praxis. (Allen, 2012, pp. 387–388)

Such a social justice approach allows religious institutions to become places of safety.

In the Black church, prophetic preaching takes place not only in the sermons but also in the music (Fox, 2014). Kirk-Duggan (2014) described several womanist themes in spirituals and hymns, including divine (agape) love ("He's Got the Whole World in His Hands"), search for empowerment ("We Shall Not Be Moved"), community building ("Didn't My Lord Deliver Daniel?"), and champions of women's rights ("Give Me Yo' Hand"). Abbington (2014) explored congregational hymn singing of such freedom songs as "I Want Jesus to Walk with Me," "Woke Up This Mornin' With My Mind Stayed on Jesus," and "Oh, Freedom!" He described the importance of this communal act:

> Most importantly, each member should depart the sanctuary worship vowed to say and mean, in the words of Thomas A. Dorsey, "I'm Going to Live the Life I Sing about in My Song," as the African American church continues to "Lift Every Voice and Sing!" remembering and affirming that "If It Had Not Been for the Lord on My Side, Where Would I Be?" (Abbington, 2014, p. 149)

Black prophetic preaching has been important in collective movement toward social justice: "The communal nature of Black prophetic preaching enabled Blacks in the United States to maintain their humanity when the dominant culture sought to deny it" (Mumford, 2012, p. 368) and led to equal rights laws and antidiscrimination decisions by the U.S. Supreme Court. Ideal prophetic preaching acknowledges systemic oppression, while encouraging and supporting individual responsibility (Mumford, 2012); this is similar to the empowerment characteristic of womanist psychological practice.

RENEWAL: SPIRITA, PSYCHOTHERAPY, AND THE BLACK CHURCH

We've Come This Far By Faith

> We've come this far by faith, Leaning on the Lord;
> Trusting in His Holy Word, He's never failed me yet.
> Oh, can't turn around, We've come this far by faith.
>
> —Albert A. Goodson

Despite the flaws in religion, African American women continue to join, attend, and compose the majority membership of Black churches. Black women empathize with the triple bondage of Jesus Christ, whose image was distorted through the oppressors' sins of patriarchy (sexism), White supremacy (racism), and privilege (classism). They do not experience a dispassionate third person appraisal:

> Jesus has been used to keep women in their proper place; Blacks meek, mild and docile in the face of brutal forms of dehumanization; and he has also been used to insure the servility of servants. African American women heard twice (and sometimes three times) the mandate "Be subject. . . ." for it is sanctioned by Jesus and ordained by God. . . . Consequently, they (African American Women and Jesus) have suffered from the sins of racism, sexism and classism.
>
> However, in spite of this oppressive indoctrination, Jesus Christ has been a central figure in the lives of African American Women. They obviously experienced Jesus in ways different from what was intended by the teaching and preaching by White oppressors [and other oppressors]. (Grant, 1994, pp. 30–31)

Womanist psychology and liberation theology have been combined to support the spirituality that has helped African American women escape from sexism, racism, and other oppressions (Pinn, 2012; Potter, 2007; Valandra, 2007; C. B. Williams & Wiggins, 2010). Wiggins (2011), for example, provided guidelines for using spiritual journaling to help clients deal with their beliefs, reflect on meditation, examine transcendent experiences, communicate with God (sometimes conceived as a higher power), reflect on scriptures and other sacred writing, and deal with emotional reactions to life experiences, ultimately creating a paper trail of personal growth. Plante (2011) addressed the need to assist clients in focusing on the positive, healthful aspects of their religions and suggests that this be done in consultation with the clients' spiritual leaders. Religious and spiritual cultural competence is key to effective psychotherapy, especially when working with clients whose beliefs differ from those of the therapists. Psychologists endorse being religious at significantly lower rates than the U.S. population, so development of religious and spiritual cultural competence is a challenge that, if unmet, can result in misdiagnosis of clients as "repressed, defended, insecure, or deluded" (Plante, 2011, p. 96). Such competence is seldom attained through graduate training in psychology but must be sought separately during or after traditional psychological training (McMinn et al., 2014; Vogel, McMinn, Peterson, & Gathercoal, 2013). However, psychological competencies and ethics specific to clients' spiritual or religious beliefs and practices are being developed (Hathaway, 2011; Vieten et al., 2013).

It is critical to avoid painting the Black church with a broad brush. Churches tend to vary according to inclusion and worship style. Social class plays an important role in the Black church, as reflected in such matters as education (LaRue, 2000) and skin color (Norwood, 2014). Therapists must be careful not to assume that womanist and other liberation theologies have been incorporated into all local religious institutions. In attempting to refer women of color to religious institutions, practitioners should be aware of the nature of the specific institutions to determine whether they provide womanist support for attendees, both visitors and parishioners, or whether their practices are oppressive, classist, misogynist, racist, or a combination thereof (West, 2006). Plante (2011) explicitly described the challenge of being respectful of religious diversity while maintaining a posture of doing no harm and not allowing a client to do harm.

Black churches must address the problem of domestic violence from a womanist perspective to avoid revictimizing abused women (Bent-Goodley, 2011). Gillum (2009) explained that messages from the pulpit provide education, open discussion, contextualize abuse as un-Godly and intolerable, increase congregational support for victims, and confront misinterpretation of scripture. Messages from the pulpit can be augmented through extant gendered ministries. Age-appropriate materials should be provided to children and youth to prevent abuse and support those who have already been victims and/or witnesses.

Pastoral care integrates a combination of spirita and psychotherapy for healing. This involves a conversion process from a worldly or material focus to organization around a spiritual center. In the process, people moved from being self-serving to serving others, following God's will

> The impact of the conversion experience and the new understanding it brought was the reason Blacks could not comprehend how White slave masters could claim salvation and yet continue the practice of slavery and their brutal, inhuman treatment of other humans. No wonder they concluded that there was something wrong with the White man's religion! (S. Lee, 1999, p. 17)

APPLYING WHAT WE HAVE LEARNED: A PROGRAM OF SPIRITUAL NURTURING FOR HOMELESS WOMEN

Drawing on the six needs experienced by African American congregations (S. Lee, 1999, as outlined previously) and incorporating a spiritual application of the arts (Abbington, 2014; Shapiro & Modestin, 2013), Reverend Stephanie Lee created "Inspirational Singing," a nurturing, spiritual healing program for homeless women, manifesting God's love by letting them know that they mattered. The women served by the program were, in most cases, reduced to the worst conditions they had ever experienced. Many of them had mental illness, some were wrestling with different addictions, and some had had their children removed from their custody because of their circumstances. All had experienced the frustration of a social service system that, at best, was impersonal and insufficient for the dire needs they were experiencing; at worst, it was abusive. The Inspirational Singing program provided them a place where they could finally be heard! Their story and their feelings mattered. Rather than hearing how they had failed, which was often the message they confronted daily, they were affirmed, loved, and valued by those who came faithfully to minister to them—and be ministered to by them. The program provided those participating a place of community, connection, and comfort—and self-esteem. Some who had been separated from their children expressed finding a source of comfort in the ministry of Reverend Lee, who often ministered together with her college-aged daughter. Most also found comfort and validation knowing that the prayer requests, which they wrote out, would be faithfully and fervently prayed for during the upcoming weeks. They steadfastly believed, as the Apostle James, the brother of Jesus wrote, "The prayer of the righteous is powerful and effective" (James 5:16).

The program consisted of traditional gospel hymns of faith, sharing of stories—their testimonies and individual-specific intercessory prayer, augmented by healing touch, building of relationships, and the freedom to worship with full expression of spirituality. Giving these silenced women a voice, a sense of connection, and hope were the most important aspects of the program. Hope was gained by listening to other women's testimonies and knowing that they had survived adversities that some of the women were still experiencing. That sense of hope is captured by one of the favorite hymns used in the program:

The Lord Will Make a Way Somehow

> The Lord will make a way somehow when beneath the cross I bow.
> He will take away each sorrow; let Him have your burdens now.
> When the load bears down so heavy the weight is shown upon my brow,
> There's a sweet relief in knowing the Lord will make a way somehow.
>
> —Thomas A. Dorsey (1899–1993)

We close with an anonymous testimony that illustrates the benefits of experiencing practical womanist theology, with access to the healing spirita in religious settings:

> Worship in the Pentecostal tradition was in many ways very freeing and healing for me. It was there that I, a shy introverted wounded person who had until recently communicated only through my musical instrument, began to realize that I could "belong" and could outwardly express what was deep within—not in my words necessarily but through the psalmody of gospel music, which by its very nature allows the singer to put everything held within into the hands of a powerful God who is willing and able to help. Here I was encountering a loving, approachable God rather than the remote, judgmental deity of my childhood. (It would be quite a long time, however, before I would be able to inter-

nalize that love. That did not happen for me within the fundamentalist Pentecostal perspective.) It was also there that I began to hear the testimonies of others who had achieved victory in their lives—usually spiritual victories but sometimes physical and material ones as well. Those testimonies helped me to realize that many others had had similar experiences and that, with God, there could and would be victory after all—even for someone like me, who felt my life had hit bottom. In fact, it was at this bottom that God worked best! This was a wonderful dawning of hope!

—Anonymous

Higher Ground

I'm pressing on the upward way,
New heights I'm gaining every day
Still praying as I onward bound,
"Lord, plant my feet on higher ground."
Lord, lift me up and let me stand,
By faith on heaven's table land
A higher plane than I have found
Lord, plant my feet on higher ground.

—Johnson Oatman, Jr. (1856–1922)

REFERENCES

Abbington, J. (2014). If it had not been for the Lord on my side: Hymnody in African American churches. In J. Abbington (Ed.), *Readings in African American church music and worship* (Vol. 2, pp. 129–150). Chicago, IL: GIA.

Abernethy, A. D., Houston, T. R., Mimms, T., & Boyd-Franklin, N. (2006). Using prayer in psychotherapy: Applying Sue's differential to enhance culturally competent care. *Cultural Diversity & Ethnic Minority Psychology, 12*, 101–114. http://dx.doi.org/10.1037/1099-9809.12.1.101

Allen, D. E. (2012). Womanists as prophetic preachers. *Review & Expositor, 109*, 387–396. http://dx.doi.org/10.1177/003463731210900306

Ambrose, S. D. (2006). *Religion and psychology: New research*. Hauppauge, NY: Nova Science.

Angelou, M. (1978). Phenomenal woman. In *And still I rise* (pp. 8–10). New York, NY: Random House.

Arnette, N. C., Mascaro, N., Santana, M. C., Davis, S., & Kaslow, N. J. (2007). Enhancing spiritual well-being among suicidal African American female survivors of intimate partner violence. *Journal of Clinical Psychology, 63*, 909–924. http://dx.doi.org/10.1002/jclp.20403

Banks, M. E. (2012). Multiple minority identities and mental health: Social and research implications of diversity within and between groups. In R. Nettles & R. Balter (Eds.), *Multiple minority identities: applications for practice, research, and training* (pp. 35–58). New York, NY: Springer.

Banks, M. E. (2015). Whiteness and disability: Double marginalization. *Women & Therapy, 38*, 220–231. http://dx.doi.org/10.1080/02703149.2015.1059191

Barnes, S. L. (2006). Whosoever will let her come: Social activism and gender inclusivity in the Black church. *Journal for the Scientific Study of Religion, 45*, 371–387. http://dx.doi.org/10.1111/j.1468-5906.2006.00312.x

Bent-Goodley, T. B. (2011). *The ultimate betrayal: A renewed look at intimate partner violence*. Washington, DC: National Association of Social Workers Press.

Bowen-Reid, T. L., & Harrell, J. P. (2002). Racist experiences and health outcome: An examination of spirituality as a buffer. *Journal of Black Psychology, 28*, 18–36. http://dx.doi.org/10.1177/0095798402028001002

Brown University Steering Committee on Slavery and Justice. (2006). *Slavery and justice*. Providence, RI: Brown University.

Bryant-Davis, T. (2005). Coping strategies of African American adult survivors of childhood violence. *Professional Psychology: Research and Practice, 36*, 409–414. http://dx.doi.org/10.1037/0735-7028.36.4.409

Bryant-Davis, T., Ellis, M. U., & Perez, B. (2013). Women of Color and spirituality: Faith to move mountains. In L. Comas-Díaz & B. Greene (Eds.), *Psychological health of Women of Color: Intersections, challenges, and opportunities* (pp. 303–315). Santa Barbara, CA: Praeger.

Butler, A. D. (2006). "Only a woman would do": Bible reading and African American women's organizing work. In R. M. Griffith & B. D. Savage (Eds.), *Women and religion in the African diaspora: Knowledge, power, and performance* (pp. 155–178). Baltimore, MD: Johns Hopkins University Press.

Cary, F. T. (2008). Why women treat female clergy differently than their male counterparts. *American Baptist Quarterly, 27*, 271–287.

Comas-Díaz, L. (2008). 2007 Carolyn Sherif Award address: *Spirita*: Reclaiming womanist sacredness into feminism. *Psychology of Women Quarterly, 32*, 13–21. http://dx.doi.org/10.1111/j.1471-6402.2007.00403.x

Cooper, B. A. (2011). *Under the stained glass ceiling: Sexual harassment of United Methodist clergywomen by laity*. San Diego, CA: Frontrowliving Press.

Crawford, A. E. (1998). Womanist Christology: Where have we come from and where are we going? *Review & Expositor, 95*, 367–382. http://dx.doi.org/10.1177/003463739809500305

Cripps, T., & Culbert, D. (1979). The Negro soldier (1944): Film propaganda in black and white. *American Quarterly, 31*, 616–640. http://dx.doi.org/10.2307/2712429

Dalmida, S. G., Holstad, M. M., DiIorio, C., & Laderman, G. (2012). The meaning and use of spirituality among African American women living with HIV/AIDS. *Western Journal of Nursing Research, 34*, 736–765. http://dx.doi.org/10.1177/0193945912443740

Davies, S. (2009). *The infancy gospels of Jesus: Apocryphal tales from the childhoods of Mary and Jesus—Annotated & explained*. Woodstock, VT: SkyLight Paths.

Douglas, A. N., Jimenez, S., Lin, H.-J., & Frisman, L. K. (2008). Ethnic differences in the effects of spiritual well-being on long-term psychological and behavioral outcomes within a sample of homeless women. *Cultural Diversity & Ethnic Minority Psychology*, *14*, 344–352. http://dx.doi.org/10.1037/1099-9809.14.4.344

Fox, M. (2014). Don't nobody know my troubles but God: Discursive, social, and aesthetic connections and distinctives in "sacred" and "secular" Black music. In J. Abbington (Ed.), *Readings in African American church music and worship* (Vol. 2, pp. 377–398). Chicago, IL: GIA.

Franklin, M. D., Schlundt, D. G., & Wallston, K. A. (2008). Development and validation of a religious health fatalism measure for the African-American faith community. *Journal of Health Psychology*, *13*, 323–335. http://dx.doi.org/10.1177/1359105307088137

Frederick-McGlathery, M. (2006). "But, it's Bible": African American women and television preachers. In R. M. Griffith & B. D. Savage (Eds.), *Women and religion in the African diaspora: Knowledge, power, and performance* (pp. 266–292). Baltimore, MD: Johns Hopkins University Press.

Gilbert, K. R. (2014). Making the unseen seen: Pedagogy and aesthetics in African American prophetic preaching. In J. Abbington (Ed.), *Readings in African American church music and worship* (Vol. 2, pp. 291–305). Chicago, IL: GIA.

Gilkes, C. T. (2000). *If it wasn't for the women . . .: Black women's experience and womanist culture in church and community*. Maryknoll, NY: Orbis Books.

Gilkes, C. T. (2006). Exploring the religious connection: Black women community workers, religious agency, and the force of faith. In R. M. Griffith & B. D. Savage (Eds.), *Women and religion in the African diaspora: Knowledge, power, and performance* (pp. 179–196). Baltimore, MD: Johns Hopkins University Press.

Gillum, T. L. (2009). *The intersection of spirituality, religion, and intimate partner violence in the African American community*. St. Paul, MN: Institute on Domestic Violence in the African American Community.

Goldston, D. B., Molock, S. D., Whitbeck, L. B., Murakami, J. L., Zayas, L. H., & Hall, G. C. N. (2008). Cultural considerations in adolescent suicide prevention and psychosocial treatment. *American Psychologist*, 63, 14–31. http://dx.doi.org/10.1037/0003-066X.63.1.14

Grant, J. (1994). "Come to my help Lord for I'm in trouble": Womanist Jesus and the mutual struggle for liberation. *Journal of Black Theology in South Africa*, 8, 21–34.

Greene, B. (2008). African American women, religion, and oppression: The use and abuse of spiritual beliefs. In C. A. Rayburn & L. Comas-Díaz (Eds.), *Women's psychology. Woman soul: The inner life of women's spirituality* (pp. 153–166). Westport, CT: Praeger/Greenwood.

Griffin-Fennell, F., & Williams, M. (2006). Examining the complexities of suicidal behavior in the African American community. *Journal of Black Psychology*, 32, 3–319. http://dx.doi.org/10.1177/0095798406290469

Harvey, I. S., & Cook, L. (2010). Exploring the role of spirituality in self-management practices among older African-American and non-Hispanic White women with chronic conditions. *Chronic Illness*, 6, 111–124. http://dx.doi.org/10.1177/1742395309350228

Hathaway, W. L. (2011). Ethical guidelines for using spiritually oriented interventions. In J. D. Aten, M. R. McMinn, & E. L. Worthington, Jr. (Eds.), *Spiritually oriented interventions for counseling and psychotherapy* (pp. 65–81). Washington, DC: American Psychological Association. http://dx.doi.org/10.1037/12313-003

Holt, C. L., Clark, E. M., Roth, D., Crowther, M., Kohler, C., Fouad, M., . . . Southward, P. L. (2009). Development and validation of instruments to assess potential religion-health mechanisms in an African American population. *Journal of Black Psychology*, 35, 271–288. http://dx.doi.org/10.1177/0095798409333593

Holt, C. L., Lukwago, S. N., & Kreuter, M. W. (2003). Spirituality, breast cancer beliefs and mammography utilization among urban African American women. *Journal of Health Psychology*, 8, 383–396. http://dx.doi.org/10.1177/13591053030083008

Holt, C. L., Schulz, E., Williams, B. R., Clark, E. M., & Wang, M. Q. (2012). Social, religious and spiritual capital and physical/emotional functioning in a national sample of African Americans. *Journal of Community & Applied Social Psychology*, *22*, 346–362. http://dx.doi.org/10.1002/casp.1116

Kane, E. (2014, April). Women of color less than 4% of UMC clergy. *Women by the numbers*. Retrieved from http://www.gcsrw.org/Portals/4/WBN%20April%202014.pdf

Kanyoro, M. (2001). Engendered communal theology: African women's contribution to theology in the twenty-first century. *Feminist Theology*, 9, 36–56. http://dx.doi.org/10.1177/096673500100002704

Kaslow, N. J., Leiner, A. S., Reviere, S., Jackson, E., Bethea, K., Bhaju, J., . . . Thompson, M. P. (2010). Suicidal, abused African American women's response to a culturally informed intervention. *Journal of Consulting and Clinical Psychology*, *78*, 449–458. http://dx.doi.org/10.1037/a0019692

Keller, R. S. (1993). *Spirituality and social responsibility: Vocational vision of women in the United Methodist tradition*. Nashville, TN: Abingdon Press.

King, A. (2009). Islam, women, and violence. *Feminist Theology*, *17*, 292–328. http://dx.doi.org/10.1177/0966735009102361

Kirk-Duggan, C. A. (2014). Womanist musings. In J. Abbington (Ed.), *Readings in African American church music and worship* (Vol. 2, pp. 747–794). Chicago, IL: GIA.

LaRue, C. J. (2000). *The heart of Black preaching*. Louisville, KY: Westminster John Knox Press.

Lee, L. (2012). An encounter with God. In G. B. Brooks (Ed.), *Black United Methodists preach!* (pp. 1–10). Nashville, TN: Abingdon Press.

Lee, S. (1999). *Investigation into the history & practice of African American pastoral care*. Unpublished manuscript, Methodist School of Theology in Ohio.

Leigh, W. A., & Li, Y. (2014). *Women of color health data book* (4th ed.). Bethesda, MD: National Institutes of Health Office of Research on Women's Health.

Masters, K. S., & Hooker, S. A. (2013). Religiousness/spirituality, cardiovascular disease, and cancer: Cultural integration for health research and intervention. *Journal of Consulting and Clinical Psychology*, *81*, 206–216. http://dx.doi.org/10.1037/a0030813

Mattis, J. S. (2002). Religion and spirituality in the meaning-making and coping experiences of African American women: A qualitative analysis. *Psychology of Women Quarterly*, *26*, 309–321. http://dx.doi.org/10.1111/1471-6402.t01-2-00070

McMickle, M. A. (2014). When prophetic preaching gives way to praise. In J. Abbington (Ed.), *Readings in African American church music and worship* (Vol. 2, pp. 327–340). Chicago, IL: GIA.

McMinn, M. R., Bufford, R. K., Vogel, M. J., Gerdin, T., Goetsch, B., Block, M. M., . . . Wiarda, N. R. (2014). Religious and spiritual diversity training in professional psychology: A case study. *Training and Education in Professional Psychology*, *8*, 51–57. http://dx.doi.org/10.1037/tep0000012

Molock, S. D., Puri, R., Matlin, S., & Barksdale, C. (2006). Relationship between religious coping and suicidal behaviors among African American Adolescents. *Journal of Black Psychology*, *32*, 366–389. http://dx.doi.org/10.1177/0095798406290466

Morris, D. (2011, July). Prophetic preaching: An interview with Hyveth Williams. *Ministry: International Journal for Pastors*, *83*, 6–9.

Moxley, D. P., Washington, O. G. M., & McElhaney, J. (2012). "I don't have a home:" Helping homeless people through faith, spirituality, and compassionate service. *Journal of Religion and Health*, *51*, 431–449. http://dx.doi.org/10.1007/s10943-010-9363-6

Mumford, D. J. (2012). Prosperity gospel and African American prophetic preaching. *Review & Expositor*, *109*, 365–385. http://dx.doi.org/10.1177/003463731210900305

Murphy, L. T. (2014). *Survivors of slavery: Modern-day slave narratives*. New York, NY: Columbia University Press.

Norwood, K. J. (2014). Colorism and Blackthink: A modern augmentation of double consciousness. In K. J. Norwood (Ed.), *Color matters: Skin tone bias and the myth of a post-racial America* (pp. 158–181). New York, NY: Routledge.

Paranjape, A., & Kaslow, N. (2010). Family violence exposure and health outcomes among older African American women: Do spirituality and social support play protective roles? *Journal of Women's Health*, *19*, 1899–1904. http://dx.doi.org/10.1089/jwh.2009.1845

Phelps, J. T. (2000). Communion ecclesiology and Black liberation theology. *Theological Studies*, *61*, 672–699. http://dx.doi.org/10.1177/004056390006100404

Pierce, Y. (2013). A public praise with neither purse nor scrip: Old Elizabeth and womanist theological ways. *Theology Today*, *70*, 46–53. http://dx.doi.org/10.1177/0040573612473631

Pinn, A. B. (2012). Looking like me? Jesus images, Christology, and the limitations of theological blackness. In G. Yancy (Ed.), *Christology and Whiteness: What would Jesus do?* (pp. 169–179). New York, NY: Routledge.

Plante, T. G. (2011). Addressing problematic spirituality in therapy. In J. D. Aten, M. R. McMinn, & E. L. Worthington, Jr. (Eds.), *Spiritually oriented interventions for counseling and psychotherapy* (pp. 83–106). Washington, DC: American Psychological Association. http://dx.doi.org/10.1037/12313-004

Polzer, R. L., & Miles, M. S. (2007). Spirituality in African Americans with diabetes: Self-management through a relationship with God. *Qualitative Health Research, 17,* 176–188. http://dx.doi.org/10.1177/1049732306297750

Potter, H. (2007). Battered Black women's use of religious services and spirituality for assistance in leaving abusive relationships. *Violence Against Women, 13,* 262–284. http://dx.doi.org/10.1177/1077801206297438

Powery, L. A. (2014). Walkin' the talk: The Spirit and the lived sermon. In J. Abbington (Ed.), *Readings in African American church music and worship* (Vol. 2, pp. 323–326). Chicago, IL: GIA.

Richards, P. S., & Bergin, A. E. (2005). *A spiritual strategy for counseling and psychotherapy* (2nd ed.). Washington, DC: American Psychological Association. http://dx.doi.org/10.1037/11214-000

Roberts, D. (2010). The paradox of silence and display: Sexual violation of enslaved women and contemporary contradictions in Black female sexuality. In B. J. Brooten (Ed.), *Beyond slavery: Overcoming its religious and sexual legacies* (pp. 41–60). New York, NY: Palgrave Macmillan.

Robinson, E. A. (2012). *Race and theology*. Nashville, TN: Abingdon Press.

Salley, B. B. (2009). Excerpts from *Meditations of the heart on the workings (or not) of the hand*. In C. A. Marshall, E. Kendall, M. E. Banks, & R. M. S. Gover (Eds.), *Disabilities: Insights from across fields and around the world: Vol. 1. The experience: Definitions, causes, and consequences* (pp. 243–248). Westport, CT: Praeger.

Shapiro, E. R., & Modestin, Y. (2013). Women of color and the arts: Creativities in everyday life as wellsprings of resistance and resilience. In L. Comas-Díaz & B. Greene (Eds.), *Psychological health of women of color: Intersections, challenges, and opportunities* (pp. 317–336). Santa Barbara, CA: Praeger.

Simon, C. E., Crowther, M., & Higgerson, H.-K. (2007). The stage-specific role of spirituality among African American Christian women throughout the breast cancer experience. *Cultural Diversity & Ethnic Minority Psychology, 13,* 26–34. http://dx.doi.org/10.1037/1099-9809.13.1.26

Simoni, J. M., Frick, P. A., & Huang, B. (2006). A longitudinal evaluation of a social support model of medication adherence among HIV-positive men and women on antiretroviral therapy. *Health Psychology, 25,* 74–81. http://dx.doi.org/10.1037/0278-6133.25.1.74

Singh, A. A., Garnett, A., & Williams, D. (2013). Resilience strategies of African American women survivors of child sexual abuse: A qualitative inquiry. *The Counseling Psychologist, 41,* 1093–1124. http://dx.doi.org/10.1177/0011000012469413

Speight, S. L., Isom, D. A., & Thomas, A. J. (2013). From Hottentot to Superwoman: Issues of identity and mental health for African American women. In C. Z. Enns & E. N. Williams (Eds.), *Oxford library of psychology. The Oxford handbook of feminist multicultural counseling psychology* (pp. 115–130). New York, NY: Oxford University Press.

Stek, J. H. (1997). Religion. In W. A. Elwell (Ed.), *Baker's evangelical dictionary of Biblical theology online*. Grand Rapids, MI: Baker Books. Retrieved from http://www.biblestudytools.com/dictionaries/bakers-evangelical-dictionary/religion.html

Stockman, J. K., Hayashi, H., & Campbell, J. C. (2015). Intimate partner violence and its health impact on ethnic minority women. *Journal of Women's Health, 24*, 62–79. http://dx.doi.org/10.1089/jwh.2014.4879

Tanyi, R. A., & Werner, J. S. (2008). Women's experience of spirituality within end-stage renal disease and hemodialysis. *Clinical Nursing Research, 17*, 32–49. http://dx.doi.org/10.1177/1054773807311691

Tate, J. D. (2011). The role of spirituality in the breast cancer experiences of African American women. *Journal of Holistic Nursing, 29*, 249–255. http://dx.doi.org/10.1177/0898010111398655

Taylor, R. J., Chatters, L. M., & Jackson, J. S. (2009). Correlates of spirituality among African Americans and Caribbean Blacks in the United States: Findings from the National Survey of American Life. *Journal of Black Psychology, 35*, 317–342. http://dx.doi.org/10.1177/0095798408329947

Tillotson, M. (2010). A critical location of the contemporary Black church: Finding a place for the Word Church formation. *Journal of Black Studies, 40*, 1016–1030. http://dx.doi.org/10.1177/0021934709349212

Townes, E. T. (2010). From mammy to welfare queen: Images of Black women in public-policy formation. In B. J. Brooten (Ed.), *Beyond slavery: Overcoming its religious and sexual legacies* (pp. 61–74). New York, NY: Palgrave Macmillan.

Trotman, F., & Tirrell, M. (2013). Elder women of color: Considerations for mental health professionals. In L. Comas-Díaz & B. Greene (Eds.), *Psychological health of women of color: Intersections, challenges, and opportunities* (pp. 81–100). Santa Barbara, CA: Praeger.

Valandra. (2007). Reclaiming their lives and breaking free: An Afrocentric approach to recovery from prostitution. *Affilia: Journal of Women & Social Work, 22*, 195–208. http://dx.doi.org/10.1177/0886109907299052

Victorin-Vangerud, N. M. (2003). Thinking like an archipelago: Beyond tehomophobic theology. *Pacifica, 16*, 153–172.

Vieten, C., Scammell, S., Pilato, R., Ammondson, I., Pargament, K. I., & Lukoff, D. (2013). Spiritual and religious competencies for psychologists. *Psychology of Religion and Spirituality, 5*, 129–144. http://dx.doi.org/10.1037/a0032699

Vogel, M. J., McMinn, M. R., Peterson, M. A., & Gathercoal, K. A. (2013). Examining religion and spirituality as diversity training: A multidimensional look at training in the American Psychological Association. *Professional Psychology: Research and Practice, 44*, 158–167. http://dx.doi.org/10.1037/a0032472

Walker, A. (1983). *In search of our mothers' garden: Womanist prose*. New York, NY: Harcourt Brace Jovanovich.

Warnock, R. G. (2014). *The divided mind of the Black church: Theology, piety, and public witness*. New York, NY: NYU Press.

Washington, O. G. M., & Moxley, D. P. (2008). Telling my story: From narrative to exhibit in illuminating the lived experience of homelessness among older African American women. *Journal of Health Psychology, 13*, 154–165. http://dx.doi.org/10.1177/1359105307086702

Weems, R. (1988). *Just a Sister Away: A womanist vision of women's relationships in the Bible*. Philadelphia, PA: Innisfree Press.

West, T. C. (2006). *Disruptive Christian ethics: When racism and women's lives matter*. Louisville, KY: Westminster John Knox Press.

Wiggins, M. I. (2011). Spiritual journaling. In J. D. Aten, M. R. McMinn, & E. L. Worthington, Jr., (Eds.), *Spiritually oriented interventions for counseling and psychotherapy* (pp. 303–321). Washington, DC: American Psychological Association. http://dx.doi.org/10.1037/12313-012

Williams, C. B., & Wiggins, M. I. (2010). Womanist spirituality as a response to the racism-sexism double bind in African American women. *Counseling and Values, 54*, 175–186. http://dx.doi.org/10.1002/j.2161-007X.2010.tb00015.x

Williams, D. S. (2013). *Sisters in the wilderness: The challenge of womanist God-talk* (Kindle ed.). Maryknoll, NY: Orbis Books.

Wimberly, E. P. (1997). *Recalling our own stories: Spiritual renewal for religious caregivers*. Hoboken, NJ: Jossey-Bass.

6

MUJERISTA PSYCHOSPIRITUALITY

LILLIAN COMAS-DÍAZ

We are the feminists among the people of our culture.
—Cherrie Moraga

Mujerismo is a Latina feminism infused with a strong spiritual base. The conceptual and psychopolitical translation of mujerismo is Latina womanism (see Introduction, this volume). An emergent *mujerista* psychology is based on a liberation approach, critical cultural/feminist analysis, and a secular syncretistic spirituality. When mujeristas examine the intersectionality of Latinas' oppressions, they create a feminist perspective nurtured by their realities as ethnic minority women, ancestral wisdom, decolonization, and liberation. Consequently, mujerista psychologists oppose (neo)colonizing theories, methods, practices, and aesthetics. They appropriate cultural and spiritual/religious symbols to construct new ones for empowerment, emancipation, and transformation.

I advance a mujerista psychospirituality as a foundation for a mujerista psychology. Within this conceptualization, I define *mujerista psychology* as a Latina feminism infused with a spiritual-feminist liberation approach and a

http://dx.doi.org/10.1037/14937-007
Womanist and Mujerista Psychologies: Voices of Fire, Acts of Courage, T. Bryant-Davis and L. Comas-Díaz (Editors)

commitment to social justice for all oppressed people. In this context, psychospirituality entails the belief in interconnectedness, holism, communality, solidarity, global liberation, and transformation. The mujerista psychospiritual approach combines mainstream psychology with spiritual tools to foster healing, liberation, spiritual development, and spiritual activism. I begin this chapter with a discussion of the emergence of a mujerista psychospirituality. Then, I introduce a mujerista psychospiritual theory and practice. Subsequently, I present a mujerista identity development. Afterward, I discuss the mujerista psychospiritual healing, followed by a case illustration. I end the chapter with a discussion of the mujerista spiritual activism.

NAMING THEMSELVES: MUJERISTAS' PSYCHOSPIRITUAL BAPTISM

> The first act of liberation is to name ourselves.
>
> —Ana Castillo

The mujerista theology emerged out of the intersection of cultural theology, feminist theology, and liberation theology. Mujeristas owe a conceptual debt to theology of liberation because this orientation considers justice, social action, and love as inseparable. However, mujeristas joined other Latina feminist theologians in criticizing liberation theology for its absence of gender equality (Díaz-Stevens, 1994). In this vein, the mujerista approach fosters Latinas' resistance, subversion, reconstruction, activism, and liberation (Isasi-Díaz, 1996). Inspired by womanist theologians, Isasi-Díaz (1994) exhorted Latina feminist theologians to name themselves mujeristas to develop a new consciousness. Through this process, mujeristas resist oppression, recover their voice, reauthor their life story, chart their own journey, and engage in social justice action. In particular, mujeristas fight structures of domination that relate to the intersection of race, ethnicity, culture, class, sexual orientation, language, nativity, cultural trauma, and location in the construction of a racialized gender identity. Moreover, mujeristas' psychospiritual baptism strengthens their resilience, agency, and self-determination. Even more important, mujeristas give birth to themselves. Through this process, they acknowledge their ancestral legacy; recover their cultural memory; affirm their collective unconsciousness; change negative cognitions, emotions, and behaviors; and deepen their gendered spiritual gifts. In sum, mujeristas embark on a psychospiritual journey toward personal and collective transformation.

A central mujerista value is the representation of the everyday Latina. Based on women's lived experience, mujeristas create a Latina feminist worldview grounded in their condition as women of color, ancestral wisdom, spiritual traditions, and cultural beliefs. In this way, mujeristas focus on alternative forms of knowledge and engage in oppositional strategies to survive, resist, decolonize, and optimize their personal and collective development. Within this framework, Isasi-Díaz (2004) interpreted Latina survivalist resilience as "*la lucha* continues"—the daily self-actualizing struggle.

Spirituality permeates mujeristas' lives. Greetings, farewells, prayers, stories, teachings, sayings, proverbs, songs, and *testimonios* echo psychospirituality on a daily basis. Mujeristas interact with the invisible realm through contact with deities, saints, ancestors, spirits, and energy. They engage in spiritual practices, such as praying, altar making, and lighting candles as coping mechanisms (Castellanos & Gloria, 2008). Indeed, most Latinas/os have reported experiencing supernatural and metaphysical events, including visions, intuitions, and prophetic dreams (Pew Hispanic Center and Pew Forum on Religion & Public Life, 2007; Pew Research Hispanic Trends Project, 2012). In this way, mujeristas honor myth, ritual, tradition, ceremony, service to humanity, and creativity. Within this psychocultural context, mujerista psychologists developed theory and practice based on Latinas' worldviews, herstory, struggles, spirituality, voice, life circumstances, place, and lived experience.

MUJERISTA PSYCHOSPIRITUALITY: THEORY AND PRAXIS

> The act of writing is the act of making soul, alchemy.
>
> —Gloria Anzaldúa

Mujerista psychospirituality is an interdisciplinary system that fosters cultural resistance, reconstruction, and transmutation. As such, it is a vehicle for spiritual regeneration, transformation, liberation, and decolonization. A psychospiritual decolonization recognizes the contexts of (neo)colonization, and coloniality of power, as well as coloniality of gender. The construct *coloniality of power* refers to how the structures of power, control, dominance, and privilege that emerged during the European colonization continue to affect Latin Americans (Quijano, 2000). As a result, coloniality of power functions as a control that imposes Eurocentric ideals over individuals with a legacy of colonization and exposure to neocolonization (Comas-Díaz, 2016). Within this framework, the living legacy of colonialism supports a social discrimination system based on the intersection of race, politics, and class; one that assigns privilege to groups of people while disenfranchising racialized groups. Following this analysis, Lugones (2008) advanced the concept of *coloniality of gender* to explain how the coloniality of power ranks women as inferior to men. Moreover, she asserted that the coloniality of gender designates how the colonial/modern system oppresses both women and men of color, leading to the disruption of solidarity. Using a therapeutic decolonization, mujerista psychologists help individuals to reformulate personal and collective identities and to foster self- and social mastery (Comas-Díaz, 2000). Within this framework, they help Latinas to deconstruct colonizing stories, work toward racial equality, and promote sociopolitical change (Comas-Díaz, 2007). Indeed, therapeutic decolonization promotes the recovery of Latinas' ancestral wisdom, including the use of ethnic and gender specific beliefs in self-healing. Moreover, mujerista practitioners advocate for holistic healing through the integration of indigenous and spiritual perspectives into mainstream treatment. Indeed, Latinas/os recognize the sacredness in daily existence (Koerner, Shirai, & Pedroza, 2013). Isasi-Díaz (1994) called this phenomenon *lo cotidiano*.

The infusion of sacredness in lo cotidiano is congruent with a personal and intimate relationship with the divinity on a regular basis, as opposed to a vassal–serf or lord–subject connection (Estés, 2011). Mujeristas integrate the sacred with the secular. In fact, many, Latinas/os endorse a horizontal religiosity/spirituality, an orientation where individuals believe that the divine acts through them leading to social liberation (Baró, as cited in Aron & Corne, 1994). Along these lines, mujeristas endorse a contextual locus of control, one that enables them to choose a locus of control (internal or internal) depending on what is required in a particular situation (Comas-Díaz, 2006). To illustrate, researchers found that Latinas reported both an internal and an external locus of control in their relationship between spirituality and health depending of what was needed (Jurkowski, Kurlanska, & Ramos, 2010). Indeed, a contextual locus of control enables Latinas to interact with spiritual forces in the cocreation of reality, fostering a sense of self-determination (Comas-Díaz, 2006).

Mujeristas frequently express their psychospirituality in a Christian style because Christianity was the colonizing religion imposed on Latinas' ancestors. Notwithstanding this legacy, Latinas' spirituality functions independently of the church (Campesino & Schwartz, 2006). Regardless of religious affiliation, many Latinas endorse a syncretistic spirituality anchored in their legacy of colonization and oppression (Comas-Díaz, 2008). Certainly, a Latina syncretistic spirituality is rooted in the pre-Conquest spiritual traditions that preceded Christianity (Anzaldúa, 1987; Castillo, 1995), European Christianity, African traditions (Isasi-Díaz & Tarango, 1988), and Eastern approaches (Comas-Díaz, 2014). The Latina syncretistic spirituality foments a collective responsibility for the interconnected well-being of self, community, and nature. Such a spiritual amalgamation fosters mujeristas' recovery of their discounted wisdom (Holiday, 2010) and empowers them to become wise Latinas. Furthermore, a syncretistic spirituality promotes mujeristas' connection to their divine feminine within. For instance, mujeristas identify with the Virgin Mary's subversive and liberating aspects, as opposed to the patriarchal clergy's view of a virtuous Virgin Mary. An example, *las Guadalupanas*, a Latina organization devoted to the Virgin of Guadalupe, find empowerment, develop leadership, and commit to social activism (Torres, 2013). Notably, Estés (1996), a self-identified Guadalupana, described the Virgin of Guadalupe as a "girl gang leader in heaven," highlighting her feminist divine power. Consistent with this notion, mujeristas identify with a divinity that physically looks like them. To illustrate, many Latina feminists syncretize Tonantzin (Aztec goddess, Our Mother) into the Virgin of Guadalupe (a Black Madonna), transforming her into a feminist icon of indomitable strength and power (Estés, 2011), a protector of the oppressed, and a sacred freedom fighter (Castillo, 1996). What's more, a syncretistic Tonantzin/Guadalupe is the subject of many Latina feminist artistic expressions (Román-Odio, 2013).

A syncretistic spirituality fosters retraditionalism among mujeristas. *Retraditionalism* refers to the archeological unearthing of cultural ancestry, knowledge, and wisdom. As Lugones (2015) asserted, oppressed individuals have *conocimiento* (knowledge). In other words, a syncretistic psychospirituality grounds mujeristas to their ancestral roots to foster conocimiento—a holistic understanding nurtured by self-reflection, imagination, senses, rational thoughts, and social justice action (Keating, 2006). Accordingly, mujeristas exercise generativity when they share their conocimiento with other women, children, and men. Conocimiento and *sabiduría* (wisdom) impart alternative forms of knowledge to mujeristas, helping them to enact oppositional subversive strategies (Sandoval, 2000). In this fashion, mujerista psychologists construct theory and practice from a "knower and being" perspective (Collins, 1998) to develop a coalitional consciousness.

Following this analysis, mujerista psychologists subscribe to liberation psychology, an approach developed by Martín-Baró (as cited in Aron & Corne, 1994), a Jesuit priest who was also a psychologist. Liberation psychologists recognize the centrality of Spirit among communities of color (Comas-Díaz, Lykes, & Alarcon, 1998). Although mujerista psychologists engage in critical feminist analyses of liberation psychology (Moane, 2011), they favor liberation approaches because justice, equality, and love are considered indivisible within this orientation. Therefore, mujerista psychologists side with the oppressed to foster liberation. Moreover, they encourage *conscientización*, a process that helps oppressed individuals to raise their sociopolitical consciousness, practice self-reflection, think critically, and work toward social change (Freire, 1970).

Of particular importance, Moraga (1981) advanced a theory in the flesh within a liberation framework. She proposed a nonessentialist feminist Latina theory to addresses the sociopolitical and psychological implications of oppression. Within this conceptualization, *flesh* refers to Latinas' status of marginalized women of color in a specific sociopolitical situation. In particular, a theory in the flesh signifies the intersectional effects of Latinas' physical realities, such as skin color, phenotype, place (including where they grow up as well as where they live), and sexuality, on their conscientización and, thus, resulting in the development of a psychopolitical consciousness (Moraga, 1981). Moraga (1981) added that these perspectives allow Latinas to "actively deconstruct by constructing." Hurtado (2003) asserted that the theory in the flesh uncovers and legitimizes alternative forms of feminist cultural analyses. One of these alternative forms, Hurtado declared, is spirituality. Indeed, mujerista psychologists use the theory in the flesh as a psychospiritual approach to infuse faith, hope, and a moral foresight into their psychological practice.

Another Latina feminist theory integral to a mujerista psychospirituality is Anzaldúa's (1987) concept of *nepantla*—a *Nahuatl* word meaning "in between." Nepantla is a construct that represents how marginalized and colonized people engage in culturally resilient strategies to survive and subvert domination (Comas-Díaz, 2008). According to this theory, when the new *mestiza/mulata* inhabits a nepantla, she initiates healing from oppression, colonization, and soul wounds (Hernández-Wolfe, 2011). Specifically, new mestiza/mulatas (a) are inner exiles, because American-born Latinas are assigned an alien status; (b) examine their psychological shadow though their hybrid identity lens; (c) develop an alternative vision of the world; (d) nurture *la facultad*, an intuition that moves ordinary functioning to a deeper and unconscious state; and (e) engage in *autohistoria* (assemblages), as a process to integrate the fragmented self (Anzaldúa, 2002, as cited in Román-Odio, 2013). Anzaldúa (2002) called this process *nepantlismo*, a development that imparts a dialogical dimension into Latina feminist theory. Therefore, when mujeristas engage in nepantlismo, they cross in-between spaces and travel from one identity to a new one. Simply put, Latinas engaged in nepantlismo develop a dialectical identity through a psychospiritual development.

MUJERISTA PSYCHOSPIRITUAL DEVELOPMENT

I change myself, I change the world.

—Gloria Anzaldúa

Mujeristas embark in a psychospiritual journey throughout their life. Many cross borders and acquire a *transfronteriza*/borderland identity—a dynamic and evolving status (Anzaldúa, 1987). Following a similar line of reasoning, Cisneros (1991) asserted that transfronterizas challenge the White mainstream feminism's "geopolitical and elitist mappings" (p. 448). Transfronterizas become inherent cultural travelers when they inhabit a nepantla. As such, they develop a mobile consciousness, one that instead of being nomadic, is kaleidoscopic and cinematographic in nature (Sandoval, 1998). Similarly, Lugones (1992, 2003) observed that because women's identity is frequently built on maps of the world that are oppressive to women, identity becomes compartmentalized. However, as women travel geographically, culturally, and spiritually, they are able to negotiate multiple maps of the world and, as a result, become empowered. Moreover, Lugones stated that a world traveler identity helps women to develop a compassionate and transformative perspective, helping Latinas to integrate sociopolitical, ethical, and spiritual dimensions into their identity development.

In a similar fashion, Comas-Díaz (2008) proposed a womanist/mujerista model of psychospiritual development. In this model, a womanist path values moral agency as an important gendered racial developmental component of Latinas spiritual development. The womanist/mujerista path involves five spiral phases: (a) rejection of oppression, (b) reclaiming sacredness, (c), endorsement of universal healing, (d) international solidarity, and (e) reevolution. Research seemed to provide evidence for the womanist/mujerista path development of social justice action after remembering their cultural and spiritual traditions (Tisdell, 2002). To this end, a mujerista psychospirituality provides a vehicle for healing the self, healing others, and healing the world. In the next section, I discuss mujerista psychospiritual healing. I follow the discussion with a case illustration.

MUJERISTA PSYCHOSPIRITUAL HEALING

> If you wish to heal your sadness or anger, seek to heal the sadness or anger of others.
>
> —Ana Castillo

Spirituality is a fountain of healing and wellness. Various research findings have acknowledged the positive influence of spirituality on mental health (Johnstone et al., 2012). For instance, Miller et al. (2014) studied individuals at high risk for familiar depression, and found that participants' spirituality, as opposed to their religiosity, was associated with a thicker cerebral cortex. Based on these findings, the researchers suggested that spirituality confers protection against depressive illness in individuals with a high risk for major depression. Additionally, Cordero (2011) found that spirituality promoted the development of posttraumatic growth among Latinas/os. Moreover, Jurkowski, Kurlanska, and Ramos (2010) found that Latinas envision and use spirituality as a vital component of their health. Even more, other research has revealed that many Latinas/os use spirituality as an alternative healing approach combined with mainstream therapies (Ortiz, Shields, Clauson, & Clay, 2007; Reyes-Ortiz, Rodriguez, & Markides, 2009).

Fortunately, the Latino culture is rich in holistic folk healing. These healing approaches emerged out of psychosocial and political oppression to empower Latinas/os through the reconnection to their ancestry and history. Indeed, many Latinas/os reclaim their indigenous spiritual beliefs when they cope with adversity, oppression, immigration, and dislocation. Some of Latino healing practices include *curanderismo*, *espiritismo*, and *Santería*, among others (Comas-Díaz, 2012). Curanderismo is an indigenous based folk healing, medicine, and psychotherapy. *Curanderas* (female practitioners) are shamanic healers who function as medical intuitive and use a diversity of healing techniques (Avila & Parker, 1999). Espiritismo (Latino folk spiritualism) is a religion, philosophy, and folk psychotherapy. Therefore, *espiritistas* (mediums) heal through spirit communication, counseling, and psychospiritual approaches (Comas-Díaz, 2012). Another folk healing, Santería, is a Yoruba- (African-) based religion transplanted to the Americas. When African slaves were prohibited from practicing their original religion, they syncretized Yoruba deities into Catholic saints, or *santos*, hence the name Santería (Zea, Mason, & Murguia, 2000).

The above-mentioned Latino healing traditions share several commonalities, such as a shamanistic cosmology, holism, contact with spirits, magical realism (the infusion of the supernatural into the natural), metaphysics, the channeling of universal energy into the healing process, commitment to spiritual development, and service to humanity (Comas-Díaz, 2012). The promotion of the spiritual development of the sufferer, healer, and spirits provides a basis for a Latino folk healing. In addition to affirming cultural continuity, Latino healing develops through syncretism. For example, *santerismo* is an integration of Santería and espiritismo (Baez & Hernandez, 2001).

Mujeristas anchor their spirituality in a gendered cultural context. It is instructive to note that three out of four Latina/o healers are women (Koss-Chioino, 2013). Indeed, women are also the majority of the complementary and alternative medicine users in Latino communities (Mikhail, Walli, & Ziment, 2004). This gendered phenomenon is not surprising, because Latinas' well-being is often compromised when they are exposed to intersecting oppressions. For instance, historical trauma, in the form of soul wounds, compounded with contemporary oppression (e.g., microaggressions) leave indelible marks among many Latinas. As a result, these emotional footprints create a psychological cartography in Latinas' flesh, mind, and soul—one that is in need of healing.

Certainly, many Latina healers heal their sadness and anger by healing the sadness and anger of others. They learn healing from older women, usually grandmothers, and other female ancestors (Comas-Díaz, 2013). Indeed, female healers are highly respected and considered powerful and effective in many Latina/o communities (Zapata & Shippee-Rice, 1999). Surely, most of the desired qualities in healers are consistent with Latinas' socialization. For instance, Latina gender norms dictate that females take care of others, and consequently, are in charge of the family health and well-being. Moreover, women are expected to nurture the family members' spirituality. In this way, Latinas healers are required to be compassionate, humble, and to engage in service to humanity. Moreover, the Latino culture acknowledges that feminine qualities such as love, compassion, *misericordia* (mercy) tending, and nurturing are crucial to spiritual development (Comas-Díaz, 2006).

Anzaldúa (2002) recognized the pivotal role of spirituality among Latina feminists. She envisioned nepantla as both a cultural–spiritual space and a process of transformation. Anazaldúa observed that inhabiting a nepantla opens up a shamanistic force for healing and transformation. Moreover, she identified *nepantleras* (women in a nepantla) as contemporary shamans who use visioning and imagination to heal and liberate the self and community. For Anazaldua, nepantleras are unique visionary cultural workers who as liminal (threshold) individuals, move within and among multiple and conflicting worlds, without aligning themselves with a single group or ideology. In Anazaldua's words, nepantleras

> act as intermediaries between cultures and their various versions of reality. . . . They try to overturn the destructive perceptions of the world that we've been taught by our various cultures. . . . Nepantleras think in terms of the planet, not just their own racial group, the U.S. or Norte America. (Keating, 2009, p. 293)

A nepantla spirituality is a liminal space where Latinas identify their source of healing as their connection with their inner feminine divine (Medina, 2014). Consequently, most Latina healers infuse a nepantla spirituality into their practice. In this fashion, Latina healers use ritual, herbal remedies, visualization, prayer, meditation, intuition, divination, possession, and consultation with spirits, and cultivate a positive energy, among other spiritual approaches. Similar to psychologists, Latina healers use *plática* (conversation), a *corazón to corazón* (heart to heart) counseling grounded in a sacred environment of trust, safety, and compassion. In essence, pláticas help the sufferer to think with her heart. In a heart-to-heart manner, Latina healers establish a strong bond with the sufferer. In other words, Latina healers exhibit radical empathy, a capacity to heal through the embodiment of the sufferer's pain and distress (Koss-Chioino, 2013). Latinas believe that their healing ability is a *don*—a gift that requires spiritual cultivation to develop. Throughout their spiritual development, most Latina healers experience (a) a spiritual transformation in their worldview, attitudes, and behavior; (b) the wounded healer syndrome—a shamanist concept in which the individual emerged out of a near-death experience or life-threatening experience with a healing capacity; and (c) communion with the sacred (Koss-Chioino, 2013).

Mujerista psychologists learn from Latina healers. They become familiar with folk healing and, thus, incorporate psychospiritual elements into their psychological practice. In this manner, mujerista psychologists use psychospirituality as a holistic cultural- and gender-relevant approach to heal and transform the lives of their clients and loved ones. Accordingly, they engage in nonverbal, verbal, symbolic interactions, and in mind–body–soul healing. Moreover, Latina healers commit to their own spiritual development as they honor visions, prophetic dreams, sensorial modes of connection, emphatic identification, and many other nonrational forms of knowledge. For example, mujerista psychologists use la facultad in combination with psychological knowledge in their work. La facultad nurtures therapists' radical empathy and enhances their attunement with their clients. Furthermore, mujerista psychologists engage in intuitive inquiry in their healing practice. *Intuitive inquiry* refers to the analysis of objective and subjective data though successive hermeneutic cycles of data collection and reflection (Anderson, 2004).

The following case vignette illustrates how the author, a mujerista psychologist, used psychospirituality in her psychotherapy with a Latina client.

CASE ILLUSTRATION: LUZ RETRIEVES HER SOUL

> With intuition we see like a starry night, we gaze at the world through a thousand eyes.
>
> —Clarissa Pinkola Estés

Luz, a 40-year-old Mexican American divorced heterosexual woman, came to see me after experiencing her first panic attack. She was diagnosed after going to the emergency room because of experiencing chest pains. Dr. Guerrero, Luz's internist, referred her to me because "Luz wanted to see a Latina psychologist who could understand her culture."

Dressed in professional clothes, Luz was tall, with brown hair, and was well oriented to place, time, and person. A financial advisor, she greeted me, saying, "I checked you out in the Internet." She smiled and said, "You seemed OK." Luz's positive review notwithstanding, my first therapeutic task was to provide a safe and trusting environment to facilitate the emergence of a positive alliance. I allowed intuition and Latino culture (many Latinas use their middle name as first name) guide me: "Do you have a middle name?"

"Estela," Luz replied, and started to cry.

After a while I asked, "What happened to you?"

"I lost my only child, Estela, in a car accident," Luz said. "She was coming home from a party with friends. The accident occurred 6 months after her *quinceañera* [sweet 15] party."

We worked on Luz's complicated bereavement during the first stage of therapy. Raised Catholic, Luz disclosed that she did grief work with a nun immediately after Estela's death. "You never get over the death of your only child," Luz explained,

> I divorced John, my German American husband. We had many cultural conflicts, but I tried to make the marriage work. However, we ended our marriage after we began to blame each other for Estela's death. Fortunately, my mother Consuelo moved in with me after John left.

Luz continued her story in a testimonio:

> Life has been challenging since Estela's death 5 years ago. I don't go out with friends anymore. I don't see my extended family. I'm not interested in dating. I get up in the morning only for two reasons: my mother and my clients. Even though I don't enjoy work anymore, my clients tell me that I am helpful to them. I have a hard time believing them. Recently, I had a small car accident. That's what sent me here. Sometimes I want to leave it all and be with Estela.

Luz stopped for a moment and stared at me: "Don't worry. I'm not suicidal. My soul left my body when Estela died. My mother said I suffer from *susto*."

Prevalent in Latin America and among U.S. Latinas/os, susto (fright) is a culture-bound syndrome characterized by anxiety, depression, and somatic complaints. Consistent with this perspective, susto is caused by early abandonment, rape, loss of loved ones through death, divorce, or immigration, as well as unresolved grief, and trauma (Weller, Baer, Garcia de Alba Garcia, & Salcedo Rocha, 2008). Treatment of susto aims to retrieve the lost parts of the self, separated by trauma, to integrate the sufferer's disconnected aspects.

During the initial stage of therapy, Luz asked me, "Are you a *bruja* [witch]?"

"What do you mean?" I asked.

"Brujas are psychics," Luz answered. "Like a bruja, you seem to read my mind."

"I'm not a mind reader. Rather, I try to use intuition to connect with you," I replied.

"That makes sense," Luz said. "I believe in la facultad."

It is interesting that Latina feminists have reinterpreted the meaning of bruja to designate a woman who uses her intuitive gifts for healing (Castillo, 1995). Luz's comment allowed me to further explore her spiritual and religious background. In addition to a spiritual/religious assessment (Comas-Díaz, 2012), I used the *Ayleli* approach. A psychospiritual assessment technique, Ayleli is a Cherokee practice based on the belief in the Native Circle, a figure that represents balance between mind, body, spirit, and environment (Garrett & Garrett, 1994). Ayleli practitioners ask sufferers to look into the four winds to become aware of their healing needs, life lessons, and spiritual gifts (Garrett & Garrett, 1994). In this fashion, I asked Luz questions related to the East (ancestry, roots, belonging), South (agency, mastery, self-determination), West (decolonization, autonomy, independence), and North (wisdom, compassion, generosity). Luz's responses were consistent with an endorsement of holism, a contextual locus of control, and a belief in animism. A lapsed Catholic, Luz reported that she became interested in Mexican indigenous spirituality while attending college: "I visited Mexico many times and consulted curanderas and brujas," she added.

With this information in mind, I suggested a psychospiritual approach to treat Luz's susto. Because Luz's testimonio reenacted her traumatic loss, I used desensitization to help her self-modulate. After our therapeutic alliance was cemented, I invited Luz to consider guided imagery. Familiar with this technique, Luz accepted. During the visualization exercise, she saw herself pregnant. Luz became anxious. "What's happening?" I asked.

Luz responded,

> I see myself as two women sitting next to each other. One, dressed in black, is crying, and the other, dressed in white, is praying. This is like the Frida Kahlo painting *The Two Fridas*. Therefore, *Las dos Luces* [plural of *Luz*] are holding hands with each other. We are connected by blood through our exposed hearts.

Luz became so disturbed by the las dos Luces image that she started to hyperventilate. I asked her to imagine an ally who could offer succor. After a while, Luz's breathing calmed down. I slowly brought her back from the exercise. "What happened?" I asked.

"La Guadalupe came to my rescue," Luz replied.

I asked Luz to do the eye movement desensitization and reprocessing (EMDR) butterfly hug (Shapiro, 1995) to help her ground herself. She reacted well to this technique and calmed down.

"I still I get upset when I think of las dos Luces," Luz said.

"Contact your inner wisdom," I suggested. "Bring Guadalupe into your heart. Use your breath to calm yourself and ask what your visualization means. You may not receive an answer immediately. Pay attention to your dreams, hunches, and other nonrational messages."

During our next session, Luz reported that she visited Socorro, a Latina Tarot card reader. "I wanted to explore the meaning of las dos Luces," Luz said. "Socorro used the *Santísimo Corazón* [most Holy Heart], a Guadalupaana Tarot card reading pattern. *La Virgin de Guadalupe lo puede todo* [Our Lady of Guadalupe can do everything], Socorro told me."

According to Devine (2000), the Santísimo Corazón Tarot reading pattern is an invocation to Our Lady of Guadalupe for help. On the basis of Socorro's reading, Luz learned that she had buried a painful secret in the past, one that Estela's death uncovered. As a result, Luz's soul left her body.

"You need to retrieve your soul," Socorro advised Luz. "Do a *novena* and wear a Guadalupe *milagro*."

A novena is a type of Catholic praying ritual lasting nine successive days. A milagro is a symbol of hope in the shape of a pendant made of metal, wood, or cloth. Luz wore a cloth milagro with a Guadalupe image during the novena days. Consuelo accompanied Luz in the ritual: "Faith nurtures strength, courage, and hope," Consuelo told her daughter.

Luz had a dream after she completed the novena. She described this dream during a talk therapy session: "I saw myself pregnant, but not with Estela. I remembered my first pregnancy. I was young, single, and afraid. John, my boyfriend, pressured me to have an abortion. I was so ashamed after I did the abortion that I forgot it." Luz began to cry. "When Estela died, my anguish returned. I cannot bear my guilt. Now I know that this is the meaning of las dos Luces."

"Did you name your first child?" I asked intuitively.

"You are reading my mind again. Yes, I named her Lucero."

We processed Luz's traumatic memory during talk therapy. Luz offered an interpretation: "I love starry nights. Who knows, maybe it is because of my name." Luz continued: "I chose Lucero as the name for my first baby. A *lucero* is a bright star that always gives *luz* (light)."

After retrieving her repressed memory, Luz began to experience terrifying nightmares. She saw herself being punished for her abortion. Luz asked Consuelo to move into her bedroom. Although this arrangement reduced Luz's nightmares, it did not completely eliminate them. I suggested a mind–body approach to address Luz's guilt. *Feeding your demons* (Allione, 2008) is a Tibetan Buddhist shamanistic healing. Within this psychospiritual perspective, the client reinterprets her Shadow (problem or distress) as a demon (ignorance in Buddhist terms). In brief, Luz entered into a meditative stage, visualized the demon (guilt), personified it, and looked into its eyes. Afterward, she engaged in conversation with the demon. Luz found out what her guilt (demon) needed from her. She fed the demon what it needed (compassion), and transformed the demon into an ally. In other words, by feeding her demon, Luz began to transform her guilt into self-compassion.

We spent several sessions processing Luz's feeding your demons experience. In addition, I used a cognitive behavioral trauma therapy to address her guilt. Luz's mood began to improve. She socialized, started a yoga practice, and meditated on a regular basis. "I am beginning to feel alive again, but my soul has not returned to me yet," Luz informed me.

After the feeding your demons exercise, Luz visited Milagros, a curandera. Luz reported that Milagros did several *limpias* (spiritual cleansings), prescribed *baños* (herbal baths), and helped Luz to increase her positive energy. Luz began to feel better. She visited her relatives and socialized with friends. As a result, Consuelo returned to her own bedroom. Notwithstanding Luz's progress, guilt continued to visit her, particularly, at night. "It's like the Goya painting *Caprichos: The Sleep of Reason Produces Monsters*," Luz said.

I suggested *brainspotting* to address Luz' traumatic symptoms. Based on a profound therapist–client attunement, brainspotting helps clients to locate, process, and release neurobiological sources of emotional pain and trauma (Grand, 2013). In my clinical experience, this trauma therapy is similar to EMDR but requires the therapist's radical empathy. Luz agreed to try brainspotting. During these sessions, Luz saw a series of images related to defining moments in her development. "It's like a Mexican mural showing my life story," she said.

We alternated brainspotting sessions with talk therapy, to further process her experience. Even though Luz improved her mood, she did not feel that her soul had returned. Upon Luz's request, I guided her in a creative visualization. She identified her intention as calling her soul back. Luz described the first image: "Estela is smiling at me. She looks happy." Luz remained silent for several minutes. She smiled throughout the whole visualization. Toward the end of the session Luz said, "I'm seeing las dos Luces. They are changing now. Las dos Luces became Lucero and Estela." Luz placed her right arm on her heart: "They are holding hands and are connected at the heart."

To cement Luz's therapeutic integration, I invited her to try another psychospiritual approach—mandala drawing. A mandala is an archetype of wholeness within the Eastern and Native American traditions. Indeed, research showed that drawing the circular shape of a mandala encourages integration and is an active ingredient in enhancing individual's mood (Babouchkina & Robbins, 2015). Luz enthusiastically agreed with my suggestion: "I will draw a Huichol mandala. My mother is a Huichol (Wixéritani) Indian and in this way I connect with my maternal ancestry."

Luz brought a beautiful mandala to our next session. "You know, I always wanted to be a painter," she said. "I don't have susto anymore," Luz declared, "I retrieved my soul."

I believe that the therapeutic alliance was crucial in Luz's treatment. Certainly, the therapeutic relationship in the mujerista psychology is like any other multicultural therapeutic relationship. For example, mujerista therapists follow West's (2005) advice and cross the line between talking therapies and spiritual healing. Similar to the healer–sufferer bond, a mujerista therapeutic relationship focuses on cultural, gender, and psychospiritual attunement. Likewise, Comas-Díaz (2012) described the concept of cultural resonance as the therapist's ability to obtain client information beyond verbal means. This process entails a combination of intuition, clinical acumen, and cultural competence. Indeed, mujerista psychologists commit to develop cultural competence throughout their life. In this regard, they learn from folk healing and integrate this conocimiento into their psychological practice. When appropriate, mujerista psychologists collaborate with the folk healers who work with her client. Even more, they nurture la facultad and, thus, aim to develop radical empathy. Moreover, mujerista psychologists embrace a plurality of roles, including therapist, healer, mentor, guide, teacher, fellow spiritual seeker, among others. Likewise, mujerista psychologists commit to their own spiritual development. In this process, they invoke a nepantla spirituality to help their clients to heal and liberate their soul (Nunez, 2008).

Luz remained in treatment with me for 2½ years. Six months after she completed therapy, I received a small package in the mail. When I opened it, I found a Guadalupe milagro with a note: "I just learned about post traumatic growth. After the trauma of losing my two daughters, and nearly losing myself, I discovered my creative gift. Now my days are bright and my nights are full of stars. I'm sending you *luz*."

MUJERISTA SPIRITUAL ACTIVISM

> Spiritual activism begins with the personal yet moves outward, acknowledging our radical interconnectedness. This is spirituality for social change, spirituality that recognizes the many differences among us yet insists on our commonalities, and uses these commonalities as catalysts for transformation.
>
> —AnaLouise Keating

Gloria Anzaldúa defined *spiritual activism* as a combination of a social activism with a spiritual vision (Keating, 2006). A spiritual activism requires self-reflection, development, and engagement in compassionate acts designed to achieve social change (Anzaldúa, 2002; Keating, 2006). Following this reasoning, mujerista psychologists engage in spiritual activism. They commit to being of service to their communities because as Ramsey (2012) noted, service to others is a form of activism rooted in compassion and love.

Similar to sacred activists (Harvey, 2009), mujerista psychologists embrace their own specific forms of service and develop "networks of grace" composed of like-minded women who behave with passion, heart, and love. In this capacity, mujerista psychologists act with dignity and compassion as means of coping with oppression. They examine the nefarious effects of oppression and assist women in developing a coalitional consciousness and a "collective state of being" (Castillo, 1995) to endorse a global solidarity with all oppressed people. Moreover, mujeristas immerse themselves in hope. According to

Anzaldúa (2002), spiritual activists' immersion or *empapamiento* refers to the use of hope to uncover possibilities to engage in transformation. Furthermore, mujerista psychologists pledge to not participate in and to not benefit from oppressive structures.

Mujerista psychologists seek to honor and develop their spiritual vision. A *spiritual vision* refers to an inner knowledge of one's purpose in the universe. Consistent with these notions, a spiritual vision is a type of intuition, or in Anzaldúa's (1987) terms, *la facultad*. Within this context, la facultad is a survivalist mechanism involving an innate "seeing" and understanding of power dynamics, allowing mujeristas to engage in a positive and functional coping. This intuitive process helps mujeristas to nurture their psychic abilities. In doing so, they are transformed into visionaries, seers, and prophets (i.e., tellers of truth). In short, when mujerista psychologists become nepantleras, they engage a unique type of visionary cultural work (Anzaldúa, 2002). Indeed, mujerista psychologists use their spiritual gifts to engage in a sacred service toward their communities and to work toward leaving a legacy of peace and equality for future generations.

CONCLUSION

> The wild woman is fluent in the language of dreams, images, passion, and poetry.
>
> —Clarissa Pinkola Estés

A mujerista psychospirituality is emotionally tattooed into Latinas' flesh and soul. The mujerista psychospiritual tools are vehicles for survival, subversion, optimal development, solidarity, and liberation. Mujerista psychologists help Latinas to reclaim their ancestral self, recover their voice, and empower themselves. Moreover, mujerista psychologists promote decolonization and the development of a new consciousness. In other words, they help Latinas to become fluent in the language of dreams, images, passion, and creativity (Estés, 1996). To achieve these goals, mujerista psychologists endorse a liberation approach, engage in cultural/feminist analyses, and subscribe to a secular syncretistic spirituality.

Mujerista psychologists seek shelter for themselves and others under a psychospiritual *rebozo* (shawl). They nurture their clients' spiritual development to become spiritual visionaries who engage in social justice activism. In this way, mujerista psychologists endorse a coalitional, transnational, and international solidarity. Ultimately, when mujerista psychologists assist women in giving birth to themselves, they engage in generativity toward others, their communities, and the world.

REFERENCES

Allione, T. (2008). *Feeding your demons: Ancient wisdom for resolving inner conflict*. New York, NY: Little, Brown and Company.

Anderson, R. (2004). Intuitive inquiry: An epistemology of the heart for scientific inquiry. *The Humanistic Psychologist, 32*, 307–334.

Anzaldúa, G. (1987). *Borderlands/la frontera: The new mestiza*. San Francisco, CA: Spinster/Aunt Lute.

Anzaldúa, G. (2002). Now let us shift . . . the path of conocimiento . . . inner work, public acts. In G. E. Anzaldúa & A. L. Keating (Eds.), *This bridge we call home: Radical visions for transformation* (pp. 540–570). New York, NY: Routledge.

Aron, A., & Corne, S. (Eds.). (1994). *Writings for a liberation psychology: Ignacio Martín-Baro*. Boston, MA: Harvard University Press.

Avila, E., & Parker, J. (1999). *Woman who glows in the dark: A curandera reveals traditional Aztec secrets of physical and spiritual health*. New York, NY: Jeremy P. Tarcher/Putnam.

Babouchkina, A., & Robbins, S. J. (2015). Reducing negative mood through Mandala creation: A randomized controlled study. *Art Therapy: Journal of the American Art Therapy Association, 32*, 34–39. http://dx.doi.org/10.1080/07421656.2015.994428

Baez, A., & Hernandez, D. (2001). Complementary spiritual beliefs in the Latino community: The interface with psychotherapy. *American Journal of Orthopsychiatry, 71*, 408–415. http://dx.doi.org/10.1037/0002-9432.71.4.408

Campesino, M., & Schwartz, G. E. (2006). Spirituality among Latinas/os: Implications of culture in conceptualization and measurement. *Advances in Nursing Science, 29*, 69–81. http://dx.doi.org/10.1097/00012272-200601000-00007

Castellanos, J., & Gloria, A. M. (2008). *Rese un Ave Maria y encendí una velita*: The use of spirituality and religion as a means of coping with educational experiences for Latina/o college students. In B. W. McNeill & J. M. Cervantes (Eds.), *Latina/o healing practices: Mestizo and indigenous perspectives* (pp. 195–222). New York, NY: Routledge.

Castillo, A. (1995). *Massacre of the dreamers: Essays on Xicanisma*. New York, NY: Penguin.

Castillo, A. (Ed.). (1996). *Goddess of the Americas/La Diosa de las Américas: Writings on the Virgin of Guadalupe*. New York, NY: Riverhead Books.

Cisneros, S. (1991). *Woman hollowing creek and other stories*. New York, NY: Random House.

Collins, P. (1998). *Fighting words: Black women and the search for justice*. Minneapolis, MN: University of Minnesota Press.

Comas-Díaz, L. (2000). An ethnopolitical approach to working with people of color. *American Psychologist, 55*, 1319–1325. http://dx.doi.org/10.1037/0003-066X.55.11.1319

Comas-Díaz, L. (2006). Latino healing: The integration of ethnic psychology into psychotherapy. *Psychotherapy: Theory, Research, Practice, Training, 43*, 436–453. http://dx.doi.org/10.1037/0033-3204.43.4.436

Comas-Díaz, L. (2007). Ethnopolitical psychology: Healing and transformation. In E. Aldarondo (Ed.), *Promoting social justice in mental health practice* (pp. 91–118). Hillsdale, NJ: Erlbaum.

Comas-Díaz, L. (2008). Spirita: Reclaiming womanist sacredness in feminism. *Psychology of Women Quarterly, 32*, 13–21. http://dx.doi.org/10.1111/j.1471-6402.2007.00403.x

Comas-Díaz, L. (2012). *Multicultural care: A clinician's guide to cultural competence*. Washington, DC: American Psychological Association. http://dx.doi.org/10.1037/13491-000

Comas-Díaz, L. (2013). *Comadres*: The healing power of a female bond. *Women & Therapy, 36*, 62–75. http://dx.doi.org/10.1080/02703149.2012.720213

Comas-Díaz, L. (2014). *La Diosa*: Syncretistic folk spirituality among Latinas. In T. Bryant-Davis, A. Austria, D. Kawahara, & D. Willis (Eds.), *Religion and spirituality for diverse women: Foundations of strength and resilience* (pp. 215–231). Santa Barbara, CA: Praeger/Greenwood.

Comas-Díaz, L. (2016). Racial trauma recovery: A race-informed therapeutic approach to racial wounds. In A. N. Alvarez, C. T. H. Liang, & H. A. Neville (Eds.), *The cost of racism for people of color: Contextualizing experiences of discrimination* (pp. 249–272). Washington, DC: American Psychological Association.

Comas-Díaz, L., Lykes, M. B., & Alarcon, R. D. (1998). Ethnic conflict and the psychology of liberation in Guatemala, Peru, and Puerto Rico. *American Psychologist, 53*, 778–792. http://dx.doi.org/10.1037/0003-066X.53.7.778

Cordero, D. (2011). Spirituality has been positively associated with post-traumatic growth among Latinos' posttraumatic growth in Latino men: The influence of familismo, personalismo, and spirituality. *Dissertation Abstracts International: The Sciences and Engineering, 72B*, 526.

Devine, M. V. (2000). *Magic from Mexico*. St. Paul, MN: Llewellyn.

Díaz-Stevens, A. M. (1994). Latinas and the Church. In J. P. Dolan & A. F. Deck (Eds.), *Hispanic Catholic culture in the U.S.: Issues and concerns* (pp. 240–277). Notre Dame, IN: University of Notre Dame Press.

Estés, C. P. (1996). *Women who run with the wolves*. New York, NY: Ballantine Books.

Estés, C. P. (2011). *Untie the strong woman: Blessed mother's immaculate love for the wild soul*. Boulder, CO: Sounds True.

Freire, P. (1970). *Pedagogy of the oppressed*. New York, NY: Seabury Press.

Garrett, J. T., & Garrett, M. W. (1994). The path of good medicine: Understanding and counseling Native American Indians. *Journal of Multicultural Counseling and Development, 22*, 139–144. http://dx.doi.org/10.1002/j.2161-1912.1994.tb00459.x

Grand, D. (2013). *Brainspotting: The revolutionary new therapy for rapid and effective change*. Boulder, CO: Sounds True.

Harvey, A. (2009). *The hope: A guide to sacred activism*. Calsbad, CA: Hay House.

Hernández-Wolfe, P. (2011). Decolonization and mental health: A mestiza journey in the borderlands. *Women & Therapy*, *34*, 293–306. http://dx.doi.org/10.1080/02703149.2011.580687

Holiday, J. M. (2010). The word, the body, and the kinfolk: The intersection of transpersonal thought with womanist approaches to psychology. *International Journal of Transpersonal Studies*, *29*, 103–120.

Hurtado, A. (2003). Theory in the flesh: Towards an endarkened epistemology. *Qualitative Studies in Education*, *16*, 215–225.

Isasi-Díaz, A. M. (1994). *Mujeristas*: A name of our own. Sisters struggling in the spirit. In N. B. Lewis (Ed.), *A women of color theological anthology* (pp. 126–138). Louisville, KY: Women's Ministries Program, Presbyterian Church.

Isasi-Díaz, A. M. (1996). *Mujerista theology: A theology for the twenty-first century*. Maryknoll, NY: Orbis Books.

Isasi-Díaz, A. M. (2004). *La lucha continues: Mujerista theology*. Maryknoll, NY: Orbis Books.

Isasi-Díaz, A. M., & Tarango, Y. (1988). *Hispanic women: Prophetic voice in the church*. New York, NY: Harper & Row.

Johnstone, B., Yoon, D. P., Cohen, D., Schopp, L. H., McCormack, G., Campbell, J., & Smith, M. (2012). Relationships among spirituality, religious practices, personality factors, and health for five different faith traditions. *Journal of Religion and Health*, *51*, 1017–1041. http://dx.doi.org/10.1007/s10943-012-9615-8

Jurkowski, J. M., Kurlanska, C., & Ramos, B. M. (2010, September–October). Latino women's spiritual beliefs related to health. *American Journal of Health Promotion*, *25*, 19–25. http://dx.doi.org/10.4278/ajhp.080923-QUAL-211

Keating, A. L. (2006). From borderlands and new mestizas to *nepantlas* and *nepantleras*: Anzaldúan theories for social change. *Human Architecture: Journal of the Sociology of Self-Knowledge*, 5–16.

Keating, A. L. (2009). *The Gloria Anzaldúa reader*. Durham, NC: Duke University Press.

Koerner, S., Shirai, Y., & Pedroza, R. (2013). Role of religious/spiritual beliefs and practices among Latina family caregivers of Mexican descent. *Journal of Latina/o Psychology*, *1*, 95–111.

Koss-Chioino, J. (2013). Religion and spirituality in Latino life in the United States. In K. I. Pargament (Ed.), *APA handbook of psychology, religion, and spirituality: Vol. 1. Context, theory, and research* (pp. 599–615). Washington, DC: American Psychological Association.

Lugones, M. (1992). On borderlands/la frontera: An interpretive essay. *Hypatia*, *7*, 31–37. http://dx.doi.org/10.1111/j.1527-2001.1992.tb00715.x

Lugones, M. (2003). *Pilgrimages/peregrinajes: Theorizing coalition against multiple oppressions*. New York, NY: Rowan & Littlefield.

Lugones, M. (2008). The coloniality of gender. *Worlds & Knowledge Otherwise*, 1–17. Retrieved from https://globalstudies.trinity.duke.edu/wp-content/themes/cgsh/materials/WKO/v2d2_Lugones.pdf

Lugones, M. (2015, April 11). *Mestizaje and communality*. Keynote address at The Feminist Architecture of Gloria Anzaldúa: New Translation, Crossings, and Pedagogies in Anzaldúan Thought. Institute for Humanities Research, University of California, Santa Cruz.

Medina, L. (2014). Nepantla spirituality: My path to the source(s) of healing. In E. Facio & I. Lara (Eds.), *Fleshing the spirit: Spirituality and activism in Chicana, Latina, and indigenous women's lives* (pp. 167–186). Tucson: University of Arizona Press.

Mikhail, N., Walli, S., & Ziment, I. (2004). Use of alternate medicine among Hispanics. *Journal of Alternative and Complementary Medicine, 10*, 851–859. http://dx.doi.org/10.1089/acm.2004.10.851

Miller, L., Bansal, R., Wickramaratne, P., Hao, X., Tenke, C. E., Weissman, M. M., & Peterson, B. S. (2014). Neuroanatomical correlates of religiosity and spirituality: A study in adults at high and low familial risk for depression. *JAMA Psychiatry, 71*, 128–135. http://dx.doi.org/10.1001/jamapsychiatry.2013.3067

Moane, G. (2011). *Gender and colonialism: A psychological analysis of oppression and liberation* (2nd ed.). New York, NY: Palgrave/MacMillan.

Moraga, C. (1981). Entering the lives of others: Theory in the flesh. In G. A. Anzaldúa & C. Moraga (Eds.), *This bridge called my back: Writings by radical women of color* (pp. 85–90). Watertown, MA: Persephone Press.

Nuñez, S. (2008). Brazil's ultimate healing resource: The power of spirit. In B. W. McNeill & J. M. Cervantes (Eds.), *Latina/o healing practices: Mestizo and indigenous perspectives* (pp. 139–174). New York, NY: Routledge.

Ortiz, B. I., Shields, K. M., Clauson, K. A., & Clay, P. G. (2007). Complementary and alternative medicine use among Hispanics in the United States. *The Annals of Pharmacotherapy, 41*, 994–1004. http://dx.doi.org/10.1345/aph.1H600

Pew Hispanic Center and Pew Forum on Religion & Public Life. (2007, April 27). *Latinos and the transformation of American religion*. Retrieved from http://www.pewhispanic.org/2007/04/25/changing-faiths-latinos-and-the-transformation-of-american-religion/

Pew Research Hispanic Trends Project. (2012, April 4). Politics, values and religion. In *When labels don't fit: Hispanics and their views of identity*. Retrieved from http://www.pewhispanic.org/2012/04/04/v-politics-values-and-religion/

Quijano, A. (2000). Coloniality of power, Eurocentrism and Latin America. *Nepantla: Views from South, 1.3*, 533–580. Retrieved from www.unc.edu/~aescobar/wan/wanquijano

Ramsey, S. (2012). Caring is activism: Black southern womanist teachers theorizing and the careers of Kathleen Crosby and Bertha Maxwell-Roddey, 1946–1986. *Educational Studies: Journal of the American Educational Studies Association, 48*, 244–265. http://dx.doi.org/10.1080/00131946.2012.660667

Reyes-Ortiz, C. A., Rodriguez, M., & Markides, K. S. (2009). The role of spirituality healing with perceptions of the medical encounter among Latinos. *Journal of General Internal Medicine, 24*(Suppl. 3), 542–547. http://dx.doi.org/10.1007/s11606-009-1067-9

Román-Odio, C. (2013). *Sacred iconographies in Chicana cultural productions*. New York, NY: Palgrave/Macmillan. http://dx.doi.org/10.1057/9781137077714

Sandoval, C. (1998). *Mestizaje* as method: Feminists-of-color challenge the canon. In C. Trujillo (Ed.), *Living Chicana theory* (pp. 352–370). Berkeley, CA: Third Woman Press.

Sandoval, C. (2000). *Methodology of the oppressed*. Minneapolis: University of Minnesota Press.

Shapiro, F. (1995). *Eye movement desensitization and reprocessing: Basic principles, protocols, and procedures*. New York, NY: Guilford.

Tisdell, E. J. (2002). Spiritual development and cultural context in the lives of women adult educators for social change. *Journal of Adult Development, 9*, 127–140. http://dx.doi.org/10.1023/A:1015737429914

Torres, T. L. (2013). *The paradox of Latina religious in the Catholic Church: Las Guadalupanas of Kansas City*. New York, NY: Palgrave. http://dx.doi.org/10.1057/9781137370327

Weller, S. C., Baer, R. D., Garcia de Alba Garcia, J., & Salcedo Rocha, A. L. (2008). *Susto* and *nervios*: Expressions for stress and depression. *Culture, Medicine and Psychiatry, 32*, 406–420. http://dx.doi.org/10.1007/s11013-008-9101-7

West, W. (2005). Crossing the line between talking therapies and spiritual healing. In R. Moodley & W. West (Eds.), *Integrating traditional healing practices into counseling and psychotherapy* (pp. 38–50). Thousand Oaks, CA: Sage. http://dx.doi.org/10.4135/9781452231648.n4

Zapata, J., & Shippee-Rice, R. (1999, April). The use of folk healing and healers by six Latinos living in New England: A preliminary study. *Journal of Transcultural Nursing, 10*, 136–142. http://dx.doi.org/10.1177/104365969901000207

Zea, M. C., Mason, M., & Murguia, A. (2000). Psychotherapy with members of Latino/Latina religions and spiritual traditions. In P. S. Richards & A. E. Bergin (Eds.), *Handbook of psychotherapy and religious diversity* (pp. 397–419). Washington, DC: American Psychological Association. http://dx.doi.org/10.1037/10347-016

IV
CREATIVITY

7

WOMANISM, CREATIVITY, AND RESISTANCE: MAKING A WAY OUT OF "NO WAY"

DANIELLE DRAKE-BURNETTE, BRAVADA GARRETT-AKINSANYA, AND THEMA BRYANT-DAVIS

The *womanist* perspective has been the catalyst for social change in and beyond the African American community across generations. From the times of enslavement, through the powerful struggles of the civil rights movement, to modern day advances, the narratives of Black women have described creative resistance strategies that have moved them from places of pain to places of power. Despite systemic attempts to marginalize, devalue, and erase their existence, the socially constructed realities and lived experiences of Black women under oppressive conditions of exploitation and violence have yielded coping strategies that contribute to their resilience in the fight for social justice.

In this chapter, we first explore the role of creative resistance in womanism as redress of sociocultural abuse. We then explore creative artistic expression as a key component of African American culture, with particular emphasis on its connections for womanists. Next, we examine creative

http://dx.doi.org/10.1037/14937-008
Womanist and Mujerista Psychologies: Voices of Fire, Acts of Courage, T. Bryant-Davis and L. Comas-Díaz (Editors)

expression from the perspective of its current use for psychological coping and healing in recent empirical studies. Finally, we offer a case example to highlight the efficacy of expressive art therapy with an African American adolescent in foster care with a history of trauma and abuse. We identify how the womanist creative resistance strategies developed by various Black women have enabled them to "make a way out of no way" for them to continue to love, grow, and thrive.

WOMANISM WITHIN THE CONTEXT OF A SOCIOCULTURAL MODEL OF ABUSE OF POWER

Hill Collins (1990) stated that "Black feminism [is] a process of self-conscious struggle that empowers women and men to actualize a humanist vision of community" (p. 39), and Guy-Sheftall (1986) asserted that the dual experiences of Black women with sexism and racism distinguishes them from other types of feminists. In her book, hooks (1984) contended that

> feminist theory lacks wholeness, lacks the broad analysis that could encompass a variety of human experiences. . . . At its most visionary, it will emerge from individuals who have knowledge of both margin and center. (p. xviii)

Consequently, Black feminism is inclusive in nature, recognizing no hierarchy of oppressions (Lorde, 1983) and advocates that all oppressions must be eliminated: "It is the space where race, gender, class, and activism converge and emerge creating a positive and powerful multidimensional vision of how to implement strategies and opportunities for Black women" (Hall, Garrett-Akinsanya, & Hucles, 2007, p. 37).

Womanism is a term coined by Alice Walker, and it describes the essence and expansive nature of Black feminism. A. Walker's (1983) concept of womanism (vs. feminism) conveys the full-bodied expression of feminism, enhancing its substance and conceptually merging race and gender. Her description of womanism demonstrated the commitment of Black women to eradicate the socioculturally abusive and oppressive experiences that they and other disempowered groups have endured.

Womanism is deeply steeped in the generative nature of Black women to creatively undo systemic inequalities in multiple life areas—especially in conditions in which access to racial and gender equity are challenged. More important, at its root, the term is the embodiment of activism, spirituality, and relational empowerment of a woman's commitment to herself, other women and her community. Alice Walker is credited for the original voice of womanism, and other scholars, such as Clenora Hudson-Weems and

Chikwenye Okonjo Ogunyemi, have contributed resounding voices to the resistance struggles of Black women in the diaspora. It is within this womanist framework that Black women through the ages have defied boundaries to overcome systemic abuses of power.

THE SOCIOCULTURAL MODEL OF ABUSE OF POWER AND WOMANIST CREATIVE RESPONSE

The context of resistance encountered by womanist activism involves an ability to create a counternarrative that combats the negative environment that relegates Black women and others to the margins. Garrett-Akinsanya (2000) introduced a model of the sociocultural abuse of power and control that describes the process of marginalization within multiple areas of these sociocultural abuses. The model was originated during the course of therapy with an African American female client who described problems at her work site, including experiences of isolation, sexual harassment, and lack of economic opportunities. During a previous course of therapy, the client had been introduced to the Power and Control Wheel created through the Domestic Containment Program in Duluth, Minnesota (Pense & Paymar, 1993). In essence, this wheel describes eight forms of psychological abuse, consisting of specific behaviors associated with intimate partner domestic violence. It then occurred to Garrett-Akinsanya that as a Black woman living in America, her client had experienced a form of sociocultural violence that presents itself as inequities and disparities in multiple life areas.

L. E. A. Walker (1994) highlighted the similarities that exist between sociocultural abuse and domestic violence. She suggested that domestic violence researchers and practitioners incorporate the definitions of psychological violence or terrorism endorsed by Amnesty International, as they closely resemble the ways that male batterers control and intimidate their female partners. Thus, to capture the constructs of psychological violence, the current sociocultural model of abuse of power and control (see Figure 7.1) is characterized by eight oppressive elements that contribute to the development and maintenance of discrimination and prejudice: (a) isolation; (b) emotional abuse; (c) economic abuse; (d) sexual abuse; (e) use of their children; (f) threats; (g) intimidation; and (h) using White, male, and American privilege. Because oppression is institutionalized in society, women and other members of marginalized groups often believe and internalize the oppressive messages created about them. Thus, oppression incorporates the development of multiple "-isms," including externalized and internalized biases, such as heterosexism, ableism, classism, sexism, racism, sizeism, ageism, and religious oppression (Public Agenda, 2004).

Figure 7.1. Sociocultural model of abuse of power and control.

Some authors, such as Kammer (2002), have contended that the major source of oppression and sickness in society is unresolved, unhealed personal trauma that becomes institutionalized as oppressive forces that propagate more personal trauma. Van der Kolk (1987) also described the deleterious social impact of personal trauma, and the recent American Psychological Association report *Dual Pathways to a Better America* (APA Presidential Task Force on Preventing Discrimination and Promoting Diversity, 2012) showed that the brain activity patterns associated with physical pain are similar to those associated with social exclusion (Eisenberger, Lieberman, & Williams, 2003). This report contended that the "psychological consequences of physical assault can be similar to those of social rejection, exclusion, and discrimination based on marginalized group status" (p. 2).

Finally, Miller and Stiver (1995) attempted to address the formation of oppressive reactive syndromes by referring to the cultural relational paradox, applied to marginalized groups within the dominant culture. Specifically, in this model, people from nondominant groups long to be connected but they experience repeated violations and disconnections within the dominant culture. In response, members of the nondominant group consciously keep parts of their experience away from their interactions with the dominant group, or unconsciously distance from their own cultural and ethnic experiences. Thus, Black women have historically been challenged to engage in womanist activism to address elements (a) through (h) listed above.

Womanists have demonstrated creativity as a form of healing, resistance, and problem solving throughout the history of Africans in America. They have used creativity in protests and rebellion, political mobilization, business, industry, and artistic expression. Black feminist and womanist writers have emerged to document successes and include Angela Davis, Patricia Hill Collins, Beverly Guy-Sheftall, and Paula Giddings. One prevalent group of activist feminists is the Combahee River Collective in Boston, founded in 1974. The book *All the Women Are White and All the Blacks Are Men, but Some of Us Are Brave* (Hull, Scott, & Smith, 1982) suggested that the battles fought by womanist leaders for race and gender equality and for social justice, although changed, continue to be a priority as the need to have the collective voices of Black women heard continues.

HISTORICAL AND CURRENT CENTRALITY OF THE ARTS IN BLACK CULTURE

Womanists define and speak for themselves with boldness and courage. Women of African descent have found voice through multiple vehicles, with artistic expression being one of the most pervasive and profound. Womanist expressive arts can take multiple forms to achieve a range of goals related to awareness, communication, healing, and resistance. Given womanists love for their culture and for the arts, particularly given the silencing and isolation resulting from systemic abuses of power, it is fitting that artistic expression has been central to the lives of African American women. The following section describes the historical and contemporary presence and role of the arts in African American culture.

Historical Centrality of the Arts in Black Culture

Creativity has always existed in African American communities, often in the midst of severe hardship, and is widely accepted as an act that is inseparable not only from spirituality but also from all other forms of creative expression (A. C. Jones, 2001; F. Jones, 2001). This creativity has historically been manifest in African indigenous healing practices that both incorporate multiple uses of the arts in healing and have a foundation in the historical and current arts by the African American community. Indigenous healing encompasses the cultural, traditional knowledge used to promote health and well-being before the introduction of modern medicine (Edwards, 2011; Harley, 2006). Indigenous healing practices acknowledge the interrelatedness of all life and typically combine spiritual, physical, and mental health to affect the individual and the community in relation to the environment and the universe (Edwards, 2011). In mediating the various levels of community and environment, creativity and arts-based practices (e.g., ritual, drum rhythms, oral tradition, storytelling, singing and chanting, breath, dance and movement, circle-based communion) were woven together with herbal medicine (known also as *root working*) and meditative/contemplative practice to secure the health and well-being of the community (Edwards, 2011; Harley, 2006).

Slave traders inadvertently brought together disparate healing traditions from a variety of African communities, which communities of enslaved African then used to counter the oppressive conditions under which they survived (Harley, 2006). Emerging from these various arts-based healing traditions came African American art forms, including field songs, spirituals, dance and movement practices, and storytelling, which eventually led to the creation of the gospel, blues and jazz music, dance traditions of the Harlem Renaissance, and a rich oral and written literature tradition. The historical centrality of music, dance, and literature/poetry for the African American community is further explored in this section.

Music

Rhythmic music facilitates connection and healing through a vibrational quality to health and wellbeing in the community. As illustrated by Edwards (2011),

> African healing typically includes a focusing of energy through movement as in rhythmic, musical, hand clapping, singing, and dancing in some form of ceremonial spiritual-communal context. . . . [It] is not an event in itself, but a connectedness with others and the external world. People dance in groups, singing, clapping and whistling. (p. 340)

Singing in the African American tradition has long been considered to be an inherent form of resilience because of the emotional and physiological changes that go together with the production of sound in the body (A. C. Jones, 2001). For example, the communal healing process enacted by blues artists begins with the performer singing his or her pain and using the vibrational quality of singing and musical instruments, with storytelling within the words of the song adding an additional healing element; the entire process being witnessed and understood by an empathetic audience provides a cathartic mirroring for both performer and audience (Aschoff, 2001). Hill Collins (1986) further elucidated the centrality of singing from the perspective of gospel singer Willie Mae Ford Smith, who noted,

> "It's just a feeling within. You can't help yourself. . . . I feel like I can fly away. I forget I'm in the world sometimes. I want to take off." For Mother Smith, her creativity is a sphere of freedom, one that helps her cope with and transcend daily life. (p. 23)

The vibration and tone involved in humming and moaning that comes from the field songs, spirituals, and gospel music both descends from African singing and chanting practices and was enacted as a way to cope with the oppressive effects of slavery and racism.

The Harlem Renaissance, the bosom of Black life and culture, was a magnet for Black professionals and hopeful artists of all genres. According to Davis (1998), Minnie Smith, a Black songstress, was the first to record a blues song in 1920. However, the success of Black female blues singers was eclipsed by Black men in the 1930s. Nonetheless, the entertainment industry was fueled by the feminist leadership of Black women, including Ma Rainey, Bessie Smith, and Billie Holiday. These women emerged from a Black-male-dominated musical tradition—the blues and jazz—and carved out their own careers in a time when men reigned supreme. Submerged in their music were the life stories and struggles of poor and working-class women, a group of invisible women from whom they themselves emerged.

Within the jazz tradition is what F. Jones (2001) termed the *challenge attitude*. Jazz as a music form is punctuated by the improvisational stance it takes to the standard piece of music. He suggested that for the given piece of music, similar to the positioning of the African individual in America, the reality is not static but is rather dynamic and available for personal interpretation. F. Jones posited,

> The challenge attitude in African American culture is expecting that there is another, perhaps opposite, meaning to what White authority presents as truth, especially as it pertains to the challenger's self-identity. It prepares Black Americans to screen stimuli for their potential threat. The individual interprets others' words, norms, and givens from a skeptical position. The others' "truth" can therefore be either redefined or accepted unaltered. The action of interpretation is the key element in the interchange. It affirms the interpreter's subjective autonomy and therefore spares the individual from psychological dominance even when he or she cannot control the physical circumstance. (p. 133)

This ability to challenge the dominant standard, to subjectively interpret a seemingly objective reality, is the freedom that African Americans imbued into the jazz form as an inherent offshoot of the attitude carried by the people to maintain a positive sense of self-esteem in the face of racism and oppression. This improvisational attitude is taught formally and informally in the African American community, and it contributes to the ability to successfully code switch to navigate the often ambiguous milieu of the dominant culture (F. Jones, 2001). The womanist perspective goes a step further by empowering Black women to screen for systemic abuses from the dual perspective of gender and race, providing a culturally based platform to speak out against purported societal truths and create very specific contextualized meanings of any given situation.

Dance

Dance and movement are central to the African cultural aesthetic and are inextricably linked to the rhythmic music tradition. In West African dance, the movement is a direct result of the rhythm played by the drum. In this way, the dancer cannot express without the drum as the initiator.

Further, engagement with both sound and movement helps to acculturate the individual to their environment. As explained by dancer, anthropologist, and activist Katherine Dunham about her work with the underserved communities in East St. Louis, "It is our aim here to socialize the young and old through 'culturization,' to make the individual aware of himself and his environment, to create a desire to be alive" (Anderson, 2006, p. 2). The culturization process occurring within the movement associated with cultural dance forms, as in the challenge attitude in jazz previously described, imbues a cultural self-awareness that contributes to an increased self-esteem in the individual.

Dance, from a womanist perspective, additionally supports the reclamation of the Black female body from the clutches of racist and patriarchal ideals by reconnecting to African-centered aesthetics that celebrate the specific movement and rhythmic qualities often deemed salacious and/or inappropriate from White male, White female, and Black male perspectives. It is a "physical medium that allow[s] the body to express what oppressed voices [cannot]" (Gittens, 2012, p. 51).

Literature/Poetry

Literature in the African American community stems from the oral history traditions of the griots in West Africa. As the history keepers of the community, griots held the stories of each family and presented their histories through stories, song, and dance. Africans continued the tradition of storytelling for many years after arrival in America, in large part because of the formalized censure and lethal consequences of learning to read and write during slavery. As such, a tenuous relationship existed with African Americans and standard writing practices. As elucidated by author and anthropologist Zora Neale Hurston (2000),

> His very words are action words. His interpretation of the English language is in terms of pictures. One act described in terms of another. Hence the rich metaphor and simile. . . . No little moment passes unadorned. . . . So we can say the White man thinks in a written language and the Negro thinks in hieroglyphics. . . . The will to adorn is the second most notable characteristic in Negro expression. Perhaps his idea of adornment does not attempt to meet conventional standards, but it satisfies the soul of its creator. (pp. 31–32)

It is both the act of creative adornment and resistance that imbue the African American literary tradition with its unique identity. This aspect of resistance in creative writing was further explicated by A. Walker (2014, as cited in Parmar, 2014):

> Creation is really a sustained period of bliss—even though the subject can still be very sad. Because there's the triumph of coming through and

understanding that you have, and that you did it the way only you could do it—you didn't do it the way somebody told you to do it, you did it just the way you had to do it. And that is what makes us, us.

It is important to note, given the griot tradition of storytelling through song, the womanist literary tradition has been propagated not only through poetry and literature but also through song lyrics. From these varied artistic explorations, one begins to understand the African American artistic aesthetic tradition, and more specifically, a womanist perspective, as centered on a desire for self-identity, resistance, and creative flourish and adornment.

Current Centrality of the Arts in Black Culture

The centrality of the African American creative tradition pervades contemporary art forms and continues to be prominent in hip-hop culture, spoken word, and personal style—particularly the natural hair movement for women in the community. These contemporary African-American-derived artistic aesthetics continue to embrace the challenge attitude and link with womanist values by defying dominant discourses, resisting invisibility through flourish and adornment, and celebrating self-identification by setting its own standards of definition.

Hip-Hop Culture

Hip-hop grew out of 1970s New York street culture as a music form that simultaneously cultivated its own speech, dance, fashion, and visual art culture (Fernando, 1994; Keyes, 2001). At the core of its beginnings was a discourse led by urban youth that addressed the prevailing social issues, including high levels of unemployment, poor housing quality, and inadequate education (Keyes, 2001; Fernando, 1994). Hip-hop's artistic aesthetic lies on the continuum of African American expressive culture and through the "hip-hop attitude," a direct descendent of the challenge attitude in jazz, brazenly critiqued the social conditions that many youth in urban communities across the United States were facing. As such, this art form became a voice for the voiceless.

Ironically, while hip-hop has come under fire for its often misogynistic content, African American women, who are often located on the margins of the genre, have engaged in some of the most challenging discussions. As Fernando (1994) emphasized,

> Women have a right to be rabid. They also have the right to pick up the mike and set the record straight, which is exactly what they have done. Rap after all is a form of verbal combat and from the beginning female rappers have added their voices to the battle of the sexes. They defined themselves as strong and able women who appeal to the strictly street

> audience as much as any of their male counterparts they also add an important perspective in a male dominated world. (p. 271)

Because of their marginalized position in hip-hop, women recognized and accepted their position as role models and set out to defy many of the misogynistic themes within the art form (Fernando, 1994). The lyrical content of Black female rappers, such as MC Lyte, Queen Latifah, and Lauryn Hill, have consistently set out to challenge both American dominant culture and patriarchal perspectives, offering instead the unique perspectives of the challenges faced by Black women.

Spoken Word

Spoken word emerged as a political offshoot of hip-hop that was fueled and supported by many of the social justice activities of the 1960s and 1970s. Rooted in arts activism, spoken word and poetry slam gained prominence in the late 1990s and early 2000s, and continued the political statements that mainstream hip-hop had moved away from making. Poets, defining themselves separately from dominant stereotypes of the day, wanted to be seen as both individual and part of a community, to be independent and interdependent. As spoken word poet, psychotherapist, and educator Danielle Drake-Burnette (2009) wrote,

> I found it . . . / in hard conversations with ethereal home / & sonic vibrations of lonely moans found / first in fragmented pieces of peace . . . / then stretched long and wide like impatient spaces / Then by changing the lonely time / to spending time, I made friends / . . . with myself / And y'all, I found out that if you can't spend time / by yourself, you probably don't like yourself / And I know some of you may not understand this / but I do not miss the crowds and parties / relishing instead my peace time / I found it . . . (p. 101)

Drake-Burnette is creating a definition that lies outside of her social groupings yet simultaneously recognizes womanist values of interdependence through her connection to a higher power.

Hair Styling

Of burgeoning contemporary significance in the African American cultural and artistic aesthetic is the reclamation of the natural coil in Black hair from Eurocentric beauty standards. In an effort to both celebrate and redefine an identity solely from an African aesthetic, African American women are foregoing relaxers and "going natural" or "doing the big chop" (cutting off one's relaxed or processed hair). As a result, Internet blog sites have been inundated with "naturals" (women who wear their hair naturally) who share inventive and creative hair styles that both revel in the natural coil patterns in African hair, and showcase the flourish and adornment that bespeaks the African American artistic aesthetic. Nikki Walton (2010), a psychotherapist and founder of the popular natural hair site Curly Nikki, stated

> It's not just about the styling and the aesthetic, it's also about the psychology because it's very much wrapped up in body image and self-esteem. Our hair is everything. . . . So allowing people to vent and talk about their family's response, their friends' response, to them Big Chopping or going natural, it's very cathartic to be able to do that in a safe place.

Beyond the expressive creative aesthetic of natural hair and styling, naturals often support womanist perspectives of resisting dominant cultural messages about the nature of beauty, resulting in a greater focus on the self-esteem of Black women, men and children. It is evident that the centrality of the arts appears in nearly every aspect of life for African Americans. Given the almost inseparable link between creativity and healing, it becomes clear that working with the African American community, using strengths already demonstrated through community artistic expression, is a culturally competent method of working.

MENTAL HEALTH BENEFITS OF THE ARTS FOR AFRICAN AMERICAN WOMEN

As demonstrated in the previous sections, the mental health benefits of the arts have been implicit in the ways in which African Americans, particularly African American women, have navigated issues of identity, methods of communication, and resistance, and have responded to trauma and oppression. However, contemporary psychological theory and research now explicitly demonstrate the efficacy of using expressive arts in therapy, particularly for trauma responses. Expressive arts are efficacious in their ability to symbolize an experience, emotion, or idea that had been previously unformed or ineffable (Stepakoff, 2007). This ability to verbalize emotion holds several areas of importance for African American women.

First, it addresses a deep-seated issue within the history of oppression among African American women: invisibility and silencing, which comes with the simultaneity of race-based and gender-based oppression (Hill Collins, 1986). Second, it addresses one of the dissociative effects of trauma, alexithymia, which impedes the identification and ability to name affective states (Gantt & Tinnin, 2009; Perry, 2006). According to Levine (2005), *trauma* is an external act invading the psyche, which happens to the individual and for which that individual carries no responsibility. Using this definition, the trauma response is frequently experienced by African American women because of their subjugated position from a racial and gendered perspective, which increases their exposure to experiences of oppression.

Third, the arts provide a unique platform for African American women to engage in arts-based social justice action using methods that prioritize their own values and voices (Hill Collins, 1986; Smith, 2000). From this standpoint, the mental health benefits of the arts facilitate and align with key themes in womanist theory and practice by (a) providing opportunities to explore identity, (b) creating healthy and effective responses to trauma and oppression, (c) accessing multiple methods of communicating, and (d) providing alternative platforms for resistance and social action (Hill Collins, 1986; Smith, 2000).

MULTIMODAL USE OF THE ARTS

Much of the field of expressive arts therapy is based on intermodal expressive arts therapy theories. Expressive arts therapy theory focuses on the commonality of all arts, and as such forgoes specialization to draw on the combined benefit of the interrelatedness among the arts (Knill, Barba, & Fuchs, 2004). Expressive art therapy theory further uses Roscher's (1976, as cited in Knill et al., 2004) theory of polyaesthetics, which emphasizes the arts as engaged in all sensory and communicative modalities, and incorporates crystallization theory, which highlights the basic human need to crystallize, or precisely clarify, the individual's thoughts and feelings (Knill et al., 2004). From this theoretical perspective, expressive arts have the ability to engage all the senses, toward precisely clarifying an experience, which can be communicated through one or multiple creative modalities. The nuanced expression of experience available through multimodal expressive arts aligns seamlessly with the goals of womanist theory in its ability to assist in exploring, responding to, and communicating the specific experiences of Black women to a larger audience.

THERAPEUTIC USE OF THE ARTS FOR TRAUMA RECOVERY AND RESISTANCE

Although empirical research studies specifically focusing on expressive arts, either through individual or multimodal arts processes, with all populations, and particularly with African American women, are undoubtedly lacking, a few studies using both groups and individual case studies have begun to elucidate the efficacy of using the arts. In this section, we discuss the few studies that use expressive arts specifically with African American women.

Therapeutic Use of Music

A qualitative ethnographic analysis of Nina Simone's womanist song lyrics demonstrates using music to raise racial and gender consciousness; to prepare for activism; to empower; and to address psychological issues, such as love, stress, and the destigmatization of emotional pain (Mena & Saucier, 2014). In an essay highlighting hip-hop soul as a contemporary form of urban feminism, Lindsey (2013) examined the lyrics and performance of Mary J. Blige as representative of the "embodied performance of African American women's sociopolitical and interior lives" (p. 87). Her exploration suggests that the uniquely African American female perspective of the hip-hop soul genre speaks directly to the dissonance and dissent of contemporary Black womanhood (Lindsey, 2013).

Therapeutic Use of Dance/Movement

Murrock and Gary (2008) conducted a physical-health-related study that supported using a culturally specific dance intervention to increase the functional capacity (distance walking abilities) of African American women. They conducted another study that demonstrated the efficacy of the culturally specific dance intervention to decrease obesity among their African American women participants (Murrock & Gary, 2010). The success of their interventions lie in using gospel music selected by the study participants, having an African American choreographer and dance instructor, and integrally partnering with African American churches in the design and administration of the study. It is important to note the multimodal nature of these studies, as music plays an essential role in movement-based interventions in this population.

Therapeutic Use of Visual Art

Mindfulness-based art therapy has been found effective with Black female cancer survivors in reducing stress and improving quality of life after the intervention and at a 6-month follow-up (Monti et al., 2013). Black feminist or womanist visual art has also been used as a form of self-reflection for Black women and to stimulate self-reflection on issues of race and gender in the viewer (Bowles, 2007). Riley (1997) presented a visual-arts-based case study of an African American family of women (a grandmother, mother, aunt, and four children) that demonstrated the equalizing effects of art therapy when communicating across a wide range of developmental abilities. The researcher in this study, a Caucasian clinician, used an art-therapy-based mapping intervention to communicate across culture to more fully understand the adaptive nature of the family's coping mechanisms, so that she could more effectively advocate for the family to the Department of Child Services.

Therapeutic Use of Expressive Writing

African and African American womanist novelists have used their literary craft as a vehicle to address sexuality, cultural, religious, and racial issues (Ogunyemi, 1985). Creative writing, including poetry, letter writing, and journaling, has also been used in therapy to help Black women heal and cope in the aftermath of abusive relationships (Few, 2002).

Therapeutic Use of Multimodal Expressive Arts

A mixed-method, longitudinal participatory action research study explored African American women's experiences of coming out of homelessness in the Detroit, Michigan, area using a variety of arts interventions, including quilting, narrative, poetry, expressive writing, photography, performance, and arts exhibit (Moxley, Feen-Calligan, Washington, & Garriott, 2011; Washington & Moxley, 2008). Through the variety of arts methods, the researchers uniquely captured the experiences of trauma, resistance, and resilience experienced by their coresearcher/research participants through richly textured first-person accounts. Bryant-Davis (2011), a womanist psychologist, discussed her use of the expressive arts in trauma-focused psychotherapy as a tool of empowerment, survival, thriving, coping, and resistance. Holiday (2014) used womanist research models to integrate the arts, specifically storytelling, digital collage, and short filmmaking to study women who are depressed and to create opportunities for transformation.

CASE STUDY: A HEART LOST AT SEA

One of the authors of this chapter, Danielle Drake-Burnette, is an African American womanist expressive arts therapist who worked with an African American female adolescent client experiencing trauma in a school-based setting in the San Francisco Bay Area, California. This case describes the trajectory of clinical work using expressive arts, including visual art, expressive writing, and music, with the client over a 9-month period.

The client was a 16-year-old African American adolescent girl who self-identified as bisexual. Although she had a history of trauma and multiple foster care placements beginning in early childhood, she exuded a resilient confidence and walked with what she called "swag" (a swagger). The period in which the therapeutic work took place was in her longest foster care placement to that point, approximately 11 months in a group home setting.

At school she exhibited multiple anger and behavioral issues involving classmates and teachers, including being involved in multiple verbal and physical confrontations, multiple absences, and considerable academic concerns. Additionally, early in our work she revealed she had been sexually abused at the age of 10, when her mother, in a drug-induced state, sold her to two men. She did not tell anyone about her sexual abuse experience for 6 years in an attempt to protect her mother. One of the first tasks required was submitting a Child Protective Services report to ensure the client's safety. This action also immediately disrupted the burgeoning trust and confidentiality that client and therapist were beginning to build. In the long run, however, filing the report may have demonstrated that she was in the care of a responsible, trusting adult. Even after the report was filed, her main concern was ensuring that her relationship with her mother would not be affected.

Upon commencing treatment, the client was beginning to develop a close, trusting relationship with her foster mom. Another highly significant relationship for the client was her ex-girlfriend, another 16-year-old bisexual African American girl. This intimate partner relationship was the subject of most of the therapeutic work.

Although she struggled academically, the client was very intelligent, emotionally perceptive, and extremely hypervigilant—a resilient protective strategy often keenly developed in people experiencing complex trauma. Her mood frequently fluctuated between intense anger and/or sadness or very lighthearted and upbeat. Her upbeat moods usually happened on days when her relationship with her ex-girlfriend was working well for her. Building trust was a major theme of the work, and because she experienced betrayal and abuse from her mother, her trauma was developmental and pervasive. Therefore, the primary therapeutic goal was to increase her feelings of safety with trustworthy adults.

The client's mood was often dysregulated when attending therapy sessions, often due to discord in her relationships with her ex-girlfriend or other peers at school. To work with the fluctuations in her mood, a process was developed in which the therapist led the client through mindful breathing or progressive relaxation activities. Once the client was more regulated, she could displace her feelings into an artistic expression by engaging in a 3- to 5-minute free write. The client would then review her writing, find words and phrases that she liked or found interesting, and create visual images of the themes that surfaced. Finally, she would create a poem or some other piece of writing that captured the essence of her affective states during the session. In our second session, she created vivid imagery that emerged from her writing with a phrase "paddle lost at sea." She then created an image of a heart and a boat on the sea with rain clouds in the corners and in the center. The client titled this drawing "Heart Lost at Sea," stating that the heart in the drawing represented her love and the boat represented her mother. This visual image depicted her relationship with her mother, illustrating that although the client experienced closeness with her mother, they were also separated by an ocean. In the subsequent weeks and months, the poignancy of the longing in that image began to become clearer. The client desired a warm, secure relationship with her mother; however, because of the divide of the unspoken, unacknowledged betrayal between the client and her mother, a painful rift existed in their relationship.

In what was thought to be the final therapy session, music was used as the primary method of communication. The client entered the session unwilling to verbally discuss any material from her life in the previous week because all of it would make her think of what she did not want to think about. Noticing that the client had been listening to music on her phone when she came into the session, the therapist asked her if she wanted to her music into the portable speaker in the room and be the deejay for the session. She brightened at the idea and created a nine-song playlist in the session.

Although the session was primarily nonverbal, through listening to the lyrics of the songs the client played, the therapist was able to understand her affective state in the session. The session did not require words from the client but instead a willingness to follow her lead as she explored and defined her experience, with the therapist present as witness to the process. Through the arts processing over the 9 months in which client and therapist worked, the client was able to reveal parts of herself that she had never shown anyone and to have her experiences of betrayal, anger, and sadness witnessed and acknowledged. The ability of the therapist to hold the client's experience and assist in naming and mirroring back her emotional states helped to develop a trusting therapeutic relationship.

Throughout the course of the therapeutic relationship, the client made references to the relief she felt at the similarity of our cultural backgrounds. This was especially evident in the sessions where music references came up. That the therapist knew many of the songs played in the music session was important to the client, demonstrated by the way her face would light up when the therapist recognized a song.

The insightful nature of the transformational power of the arts demonstrated the way engaging in a multimodal expressive arts process enabled the client to deeply access her emotions and be witnessed in them. This work fits within a womanist framework in its focus on the empowerment that comes from self-definition and its use of creative expression to explore and voice ideas of the self.

IMPLICATIONS OF THE USES OF CREATIVITY FOR WOMANISTS

African American women have historically suffered from simultaneous gender- and race-based oppression, which often silenced their voices and rendered their experiences invisible. Resisting these threats of silence and invisibility have been hallmarks of the African American creative tradition. By providing enhanced avenues for expression, the symbolization available in creativity and expressive arts expands the possibility for both enhanced self-understanding and being understood by another (Stepakoff, 2007). Poet Audre Lorde (1984) urged,

> As they become known to and accepted by us, our feelings and the honest exploration of them become sanctuaries and spawning grounds for the most radical and daring of ideas. They become a safe-house for that difference so necessary to change and the conceptualization of any meaningful action. (p. 37)

Further, as demonstrated in the research studies in the previous section, the benefits of engaging in art and creativity can reduce anxiety; increase feelings of unity, openness, and sharing; improve sleep quality; promote resilience; increase appreciation of the body; increase positive feelings; and improve overall quality of life. These qualities connect directly to the goals of the indigenous healing practices previously outlined and speak to a return to well-being. Certainly, more expressive arts-based research in general, and with African American women in particular, is required to provide enhanced empirical support; however, it is evident that creative arts expression provides a much needed alternative that can continue to light a path for women whose experiences have been pushed to the margins.

REFERENCES

American Psychological Association Presidential Task Force on Preventing Discrimination and Promoting Diversity. (2012). *Dual pathways to a better America: Preventing discrimination and promoting diversity*. Washington, DC: American Psychological Association. Retrieved from http://www.nytimes.com/2006/05/22/arts/dance/22cnd-dunham.html

Anderson, J. (2006, May 22). Katherine Dunham, dance pioneer, dies at 96. *The New York Times*. Retrieved from http://www.nytimes.com/2006/05/22/arts/dance/22cnd-dunham.html?pagewanted=all

Aschoff, P. R. (2001). The poetry of the blues: Understanding the blues in its cultural context. In F. Jones & A. C. Jones (Eds.), *Triumph of the soul: Cultural and psychological aspects of African American music* (pp. 35–67). Westport, CT: Praeger.

Bowles, J. (2007). "Acting like a man": Adrian Piper's mythic being and Black feminism in the 1970s. *Signs, 2*, 621–647.

Bryant-Davis, T. (2011). The birthing of a womanist psychologist: On becoming a guide to healing and empowerment. In L. Comas-Díaz & M. B. Weiner (Eds.), *Women psychotherapists: Journeys in healing* (pp. 1–13). Lanham, MD: Rowman & Littlefield.

Davis, A. Y. (1998). *Blues legacies and Black feminism: Gertrude "Ma" Rainey, Bessie Smith, and Billie Holiday*. New York, NY: Pantheon.

Drake-Burnette, D. (2009). *Cast iron life: A collection of poems and recipes*. Mill Valley, CA: Planetize the Movement.

Edwards, S. D. (2011). A psychology of indigenous healing in Southern Africa. *Journal of Psychology in Africa, 21*, 335–347. http://dx.doi.org/10.1080/14330237.2011.10820466

Eisenberger, N. I., Lieberman, M. D., & Williams, K. D. (2003, October 10). Does rejection hurt? An fMRI study of social exclusion. *Science, 302*, 290–292. http://dx.doi.org/10.1126/science.1089134

Fernando, S. H. (1994). *The new beats: Exploring the music, culture, and attitudes of hip-hop*. New York, NY: Doubleday.

Few, A. (2002). Grounding our feet and hearts: Black women's coping strategies in psychologically abusive dating relationships. *Women & Therapy, 25*, 59–77. http://dx.doi.org/10.1300/J015v25n03_05

Gantt, L., & Tinnin, L. W. (2009). Support for a neurobiological view of trauma with implications for art therapy. *The Arts in Psychotherapy, 36*, 148–153. http://dx.doi.org/10.1016/j.aip.2008.12.005

Garrett-Akinsanya, B. (2000, August). *Too legit to quit: A look at African American female leaders African-centered wellness: Self-care as a success strategy for African American women*. Paper presented at the American Psychological Association 108th Annual Convention, Washington, DC.

Gittens, A. F. (2012). Black dance and the fight for flight: Sabar and the transformation and cultural significance of dance from West Africa to Black America (1960–2010). *Journal of Black Studies, 43*, 49–71. http://dx.doi.org/10.1177/0021934711423262

Guy-Sheftall, B. (1986, Fall). Remembering Sojourner Truth: On Black feminism. *Catalyst*, 54–57.

Hall, R. L., Garrett-Akinsanya, B., & Hucles, M. (2007). Voices of Black feminist leaders: Making spaces for ourselves. In J. L. Chin, B. Lott, J. K. Rice, & J. Sanchez-Hucles (Eds.), *Women and leadership: Transforming visions and diverse voices* (pp. 281–296). Oxford, England: Blackwell. http://dx.doi.org/10.1002/9780470692332.ch13

Harley, D. A. (2006). Indigenous healing practices among rural elderly African Americans. *International Journal of Disability, Development and Education, 53*, 433–452. http://dx.doi.org/10.1080/10349120601008605

Hill Collins, P. (1986). Learning from the outsider within: The sociological significance of Black feminist thought. *Social Problems, 33*, 14–32. http://dx.doi.org/10.2307/800672

Hill Collins, P. (1990). *Black feminist thought: Knowledge, consciousness and the politics of empowerment*. New York, NY: Routledge.

Holiday, J. (2014). Stories are medicine: Responding to deep sadness with spirit. *Dissertation Abstracts International: The Sciences and Engineering, 75B*, 2014.

hooks, b. (1984). *Feminist theory: From margin to center*. Boston, MA: South End.

Hull, G. T., Scott, P. B., & Smith, B. (Eds.). (1982). *All the women are White, all the Blacks are men, but some of us are brave: Black women's studies*. New York, NY: Feminist Press.

Hurston, Z. N. (2000). Characteristics of Negro expression. In W. Napier (Ed.), *African American literary theory: A reader* (pp. 31–44). New York, NY: New York University Press.

Jones, A. C. (2001). Upon this rock: The foundational influence of the spirituals. In F. Jones & A. C. Jones (Eds.), *Triumph of the soul: Cultural and psychological aspects of African American music* (pp. 3–34). Westport, CT: Praeger.

Jones, F. (2001). Jazz and the resilience of African Americans. In F. Jones & A. C. Jones (Eds.), *Triumph of the soul: Cultural and psychological aspects of African American music* (pp. 127–151). Westport, CT: Praeger.

Kammer, B. J. (2002). *The cycle of devolution: A psychological inquiry into the relationship between personal trauma & social oppression*. Montpelier, VT: The Union Institute and University.

Keyes, C. L. (2001). The meaning of rap music in contemporary Black culture. In F. Jones & A. C. Jones (Eds.), *Triumph of the soul: Cultural and psychological aspects of African American music* (pp. 153–179). Westport, CT: Praeger.

Knill, P. J., Barba, H. N., & Fuchs, M. N. (2004). *Minstrels of soul: Intermodal expressive therapy*. Toronto, Ontario, Canada: EGS Press.

Levine, S. K. (2005). The philosophy of expressive arts therapy: Poesis as a response to the world. In P. J. Knill, E. G. Levine, & S. K. Levine (Eds.), *Principles and practice of expressive arts therapy: Toward a therapeutic aesthetics* (pp. 15–74). London, England: Jessica Kingsley.

Lindsey, T. B. (2013). If you look in my life: Love, hip-hop soul, and contemporary African American womanhood. *African American Review, 46*, 87–99, 200. http://dx.doi.org/10.1353/afa.2013.0004

Lorde, A. (1983). There is no hierarchy of oppressions. *Interracial Books for Children Bulletin, 14*, 9.

Lorde, A. (1984). *Sister outsider: Essays and speeches*. Trumansburg, NY: The Crossing Press.

Mena, J., & Saucier, P. (2014). "Don't let me be misunderstood": Nina Simone's Africana womanism. *Journal of Black Studies, 45,* 247–265. http://dx.doi.org/10.1177/0021934714528512

Miller, J. B., & Stiver, I. P. (1995). *Relational images and their meanings in psychotherapy* (Work in Progress No. 74). Wellesley, MA: Stone Center Working Paper Series.

Monti, D. A., Kash, K. M., Kunkel, E. J., Moss, A., Mathews, M., Brainard, G., . . . Newberg, A. B. (2013). Psychosocial benefits of a novel mindfulness intervention versus standard support in distressed women with breast cancer. *Psycho-Oncology, 22,* 2565–2575. http://dx.doi.org/10.1002/pon.3320

Moxley, D. P., Feen-Calligan, H. R., Washington, O. G. M., & Garriott, L. (2011). Quilting in self-efficacy group work with older African American women leaving homelessness. *Art Therapy: Journal of the American Art Therapy Association, 28,* 11–122.

Murrock, C. J., & Gary, F. A. (2008). A culturally-specific dance intervention to increase functional capacity in African American women. *Journal of Cultural Diversity, 15,* 168–173.

Murrock, C. J., & Gary, F. A. (2010). Culturally specific dance to reduce obesity in African American women. *Health Promotion Practice, 11,* 465–473. http://dx.doi.org/10.1177/1524839908323520

Ogunyemi, C. (1985). Womanism: The dynamics of the contemporary Black female novel in English. *Signs: Journal of Women in Culture and Society, 11,* 63–80. http://dx.doi.org/10.1086/494200

Parmar, P. (Writer & Director). (2014, February 7). Alice Walker: Beauty in truth [Television series episode]. In P. Parmar & S. Haq (Producer), *American masters.* Los Angeles, CA: Public Broadcasting System.

Pense, E., & Paymar, M. (1993). *Education groups for men who batter: The Duluth model.* New York, NY: Springer.

Perry, B. (2006). Applying principles of neurodevelopment to clinical work with maltreated and traumatized children: The neurosequential model of therapeutics. In N. Boyd-Webb (Ed.), *Working with traumatized youth in child welfare* (pp. 27–52). New York, NY: Guilford Press.

Public Agenda. (2004). *Issues guide.* Retrieved from http://www.publicagenda.org/pages/issue-guides

Riley, S. (1997). Conflicts in treatment, issues of liberation, connection, and culture: Art therapy for women and their families. *Art Therapy: Journal of the American Art Therapy Association, 14,* 102–108. http://dx.doi.org/10.1080/07421656.1987.10759264

Smith, B. (2000). Toward a Black feminist criticism. In W. Napier (Ed.), *African American literary theory: A reader* (pp. 132–146). New York, NY: New York University Press.

Stepakoff, S. (2007). The healing power of symbolization in the aftermath of massive war atrocities: Examples from Liberian and Sierra Leonean survivors.

Journal of Humanistic Psychology, 47, 400–412. http://dx.doi.org/10.1177/0022167807301787

Van der Kolk, B. (1987). *Psychological trauma*. Washington, DC: American Psychiatric Press.

Walker, A. (1983). *In search of our mothers' gardens: Womanist prose*. New York, NY: Harcourt Brace.

Walker, L. E. A. (1994). *Abused women and survivor therapy: A practical guide for the psychotherapist*. Washington, DC: APA Press. http://dx.doi.org/10.1037/10153-000

Walton, N. (2010, August 17). *Biography*. Retrieved from http://www.curlynikki.com/2010/08/biography.html

Washington, O. G. M., & Moxley, D. P. (2008). Telling my story: From narrative to exhibit in illuminating the lived experience of homelessness among older African American women. *Journal of Health Psychology, 13*, 154–165. http://dx.doi.org/10.1177/1359105307086702

8

MUJERISTA CREATIVITY: LATIN@ SACRED ARTS AS LIFE-COURSE DEVELOPMENTAL RESOURCES

ESTER SHAPIRO AND DARCY ALCÁNTARA

> The snow-covered windshield of my car became like a movie screen where I could see my next-door neighbor in Lima, a woman who lived in extreme poverty yet never lost her sense of dignity and purpose of life. I remember the steadiness of her struggle: day after day she dealt with the reality of the present and survived that day in order to be able to face the next. That reflection has led me to develop the category of *lo cotidiano* as the main site for struggle, as the site that reveals oppression at the same time it illumines the preferred future. (Isasi-Díaz, 2004, p. 17)

> In the ethnopoetics and performance of the shaman, my people, the Indians, did not Split the artistic from the functional, the sacred from the secular, art from everyday life. The religious, social and aesthetic purposes of art were all intertwined. Before the Conquest, poets gathered to play music, dance, sing and read poetry in open-air places around the *Xochicuahuitl, el Arbol Florido, Tree-in-Flower*. . . . The ability of story (prose and poetry) to transform the storyteller and the listener into something or someone else is shamanistic. The writer, as shape-changer, is a *nahual*, a shaman. (Anzaldúa, 1987, p. 66)

Creativity and the arts support Latin@s[1] and other women of color in transforming human hardships and resourcefully creating spaces of refuge, resistance, and resilience. Through creative expression, these women challenge

[1]We use the term *Latin@* throughout the chapter, following U.S. transnational and gender-neutral/gender-queer writings, except when using preferred naming and spelling by cited authors, recognizing that terms used for *Hispanic, Chicano/a,* or *Latina/o* groups imply uniformity or cohesion with racialized political histories.

http://dx.doi.org/10.1037/14937-009
Womanist and Mujerista Psychologies: Voices of Fire, Acts of Courage, T. Bryant-Davis and L. Comas-Díaz (Editors)

patriarchy, racism, colonialism, and other oppressions and promote liberation and positive shared life-course development. These healing artistic traditions have a long history of intertwining with sacred traditions for Latin@s and other women of color. In particular, Latin@ creativity is often grounded in spiritual worldviews that link everyday life to social justice.

In this chapter, we explore the central cultural/developmental role of creativity and the arts for Latin@s, focusing on how creativity expresses and reflects a spirituality that challenges oppression and promotes liberation. The chapter is grounded in *mujerista* theology, which is a feminist liberation theology that opposes colonialism. In particular, we draw from Isasi-Díaz's (2004) decolonizing theories and qualitative research methods and from Anzaldúa's theory of *la frontera* (borderlands), which explores the role of guiding cultural myths and spiritual activism (Anzaldúa, 1987, 1990; Anzaldúa & Keating, 2002; Anzaldúa & Moraga, 1981). Isasi-Díaz and Anzaldúa developed their perspectives in the 1980s, at a time when activist Chicana and Latina writers challenged patriarchal, racist, and colonial orthodoxies that impose definitions of self and spirit designed for domination. Their highly influential work provides a meaningful lens for examining Latin@ creativity.

In the sections that follow, we first introduce mujerista theology and la frontera/borderlands theory. These critical, culturally informed perspectives show how everyday spirituality is central in understanding Latinas' creative resources for responding to life challenges. Then, using this theoretical lens, we examine examples of Latin@ creativity. We review how Latin@s draw from ancestral spirits and culturally meaningful divinities through storytelling, testimonies, household altars, nourishing recipes, and celebrations, as well as drawing from and creating folk or popular media arts in their home and community. We suggest that Latin@ spiritualities in contexts of inequality support improvisation and personally meaningful interpretation within collective cultural traditions, or folk religion.

MUJERISTA AND BORDERLANDS METHODS FOR COCREATING TRANSFORMATIVE KNOWLEDGE

Mujerista theology is grounded in *la lucha*—the struggle—to recognize and resist multiple forms of oppression in ordinary women's lives while illuminating pathways and actions toward a more just society. In describing how she developed mujerista theology, Isasi-Díaz (1993) reflected on her own journey as a Cuban American departing from traditional, patriarchal Catholicism toward radical revisionings synthesizing feminism, women of color perspectives, and social justice theologies. With these reflections, she used the metaphor of film and critical moments/catalyzing images on the road to *conocimiento y conciencia*, visionary and transformative knowledge animated by a deep sense of ethics. One critical moment and catalyzing image for Isasi-Díaz occurred when she was driving in blinding snow through Rochester, New York, far from the Havana of her childhood. Suddenly, Isasi-Díaz visualized her neighbor in Peru and this neighbor's strategies for preserving dignity in facing the harsh demands of lo cotidiano (everyday life), sustaining family life in contexts of overwhelming poverty. Isasi-Díaz used this vision as a catalyst to bridge divisions created by gender, economic, and societal equity. For Isasi-Díaz, lo cotidiano—as an embodied crossroads of personal, cultural and historical time and life settings grounding Latin@ lived experiences of la lucha—offers a generative space for confronting and transcending life challenges. Regardless of individuals' histories or current contexts of privilege or oppression, everyone can choose to define and transform these life challenges in a way that advances solidarity and equity. Isasi-Díaz particularly focused on *popular religion*, a term used for beliefs and practices incorporating the sacred outside religious institutions, often synthesizing practices when diverse communities come together in challenging contexts (Isasi-Díaz, 1993; Isasi-Díaz & Mendieta, 2012). Until her death from cancer in 2012, Isasi-Díaz worked in communities devoted to creating new forms of decolonizing feminist knowledge(s) and accountability for social justice.

Anzaldúa's (1987) *Borderlands/La Frontera: The New Mestiza* also draws on film as metaphor for *la facultad*, a spiritual awareness violently severed and marginalized by an unjust society, which can be made whole again through arduous, deeply creative processes of critical confrontation, recognition, and synthesis (Anzaldúa, 2002). She described visionary, transformative trancelike states opening up channels of experience suppressed by domination, reclaiming them toward new storying, enabling more complex, critical border-crossing consciousness and capacity for ethical action. Shamanistic receptivity brings great pain but also rich rewards, revealing new ways of healing from oppression's violent sunderings: worlds of light and dark; human experience and nature; the living and the dead; and imposed knowledge(s) designed for domination and transformative knowledge(s) reweaving connections between self, community, spirit, and cosmos. Anzaldúa's cross-genre work of scholarship, politics, and poetics supported the groundbreaking collective projects *This Bridge Called My Back* (Anzaldúa & Moraga, 1981) and *This Bridge We Call Home* (Anzaldúa & Keating, 2002). Although Eurocentric feminist scholarship has overlooked spiritual dimensions in work by Anzaldúa and others, Latin@ scholar Pérez (2007, 2014) suggested that *Making Face, Making Soul*, Anzaldúa's (1990) edited collection of narratives and poetry by women of color, reclaims the deeply social Nahua concept of personhood and integrity (*in ixtli in yollotl*; face, heart = person), aligning spirit-directed heart with social face or public presence.

Both Isasi-Díaz and Anzaldúa, drawing from unique life experiences, worked from different institutional locations toward distinctive goals.

Isasi-Díaz traveled outward, toward empathic understanding of poor Latina lives, and Anzaldúa traveled inward, reclaiming societally devalued aspects of self. Each used singular tools for theorizing, asking new questions about aspects of self/soul in relation to culture/spirituality made invisible by rules of gender-centered social oppression, colonization, racial and economic privilege in specific Latin American, Caribbean, and U.S. colonial contexts. Both explored multifaceted complexities and contradictions of their own and others' lived experiences under conditions of social injustice. Both emerged with common themes and transdisciplinary methods of inquiry centered on gender equity as requisite for undivided social justice, with culturally informed spirituality as central to their social justice activism.

Below, we draw from Isasi-Díaz's (2004) feminist liberation theology, decolonizing theories, and qualitative research methods of ethnomethodology and meta-ethnography. We also draw from Anzaldúa's borderlands explorations of guiding cultural myths and spiritual activism (Anzaldúa, 1987, 1990; Anzaldúa & Keating, 2002; Anzaldúa & Moraga, 1981). Mujerista/borderlands perspectives on spirituality, creativity, and social justice are expanded through dialogue with Latin@-centric cultural/developmental perspectives on shared growth in the intergenerational life course (Falicov, 2014; García Coll & Marks, 2012; Shapiro, 1994, 2007, 2013a, 2013b) and Latin@ psychologies of wholeness/wellness linked to spiritualities (Comas-Díaz, 2008b; Hernández-Wolfe, 2013; Koss-Chioino, 2013). Using examples, we illustrate how Latin@s draw from culturally meaningful divinities to improvise household *altares*, tell ancestral stories, invoke intimate relationships with saints, embellish household arts, and bring creativity to shared cultural and community traditions supporting wellness and resilience. Spiritual resources provide strength during times of hardship while helping comfort others, affirm a sense of purpose and hope through ethical *compromiso*/commitments to the enduring beauty of social justice. Understanding sacred arts in everyday life as wellsprings for resistance and resilience linked to social justice is not for Latin@s only or for women of color only. Rather, this perspective offers a generative space for sharing transformative conocimientos, recovered/discovered sacred healing arts emerging from Latin@-centric approaches to creative spirituality.

TRANSDISCIPLINARY CULTURAL/DEVELOPMENTAL PERSPECTIVES: PERSONAL AND PROFESSIONAL SOURCES OF TRANSFORMATIVE KNOWLEDGE

Both authors of this chapter are Latin@ clinical psychologists and represent different generations, professional experiences, and immigrant family life-course journeys. We are now forever connected through mentorship and collegiality, and we came together through our focus on Latin@s and resources for wellness within the intergenerational life course. Consistent with social-justice-informed perspectives in clinical, cultural, and developmental psychology, we draw on our own life experiences, on critical theories and transdisciplinary methods, and on our dialogues with each other and across multiple communities of knowledge to inform our work. As a Cuban Eastern European Jewish American clinical psychologist, Ester Shapiro has studied how societal ideologies and inequalities impact family life-course transitions, including birth, death, and adolescence/early adulthood, and how cultural resources promote positive shared development. As a child- and family-centered clinical psychologist, Darcy Alcántara specializes in multisystemic, culturally informed child assessment and in research on how Mexican American and Latin@ youth and families respond to anti-immigrant contexts with culturally meaningful resources for resilience (Alcántara, 2013).

Both of us have learned a great deal from the "world traveling" (Lugones, 2004) that comes from encounters with the complexity of cross-cultural conversations, including the diversity of Latin@ experiences, supporting transformative listening as foundational to personal and collective change. Although we come from very different backgrounds that capture the complexity of Latin@ lives, we share a sense of spirituality best captured by Medina's (2014) words:

> My definition of spirituality at this time is one's relationship with self, with others, with nature, with the universe, with the ancestors, and with the sacred source and great mystery of life and death. Spirituality is fundamentally about being in relationship; being aware of one's interdependence or connectedness to all that can be seen and all that is unseen. (p. 167)

Where mainstream understandings of selfhood impose borders around dimensions of oneself, indigenous spirituality teaches that one exists as a whole. Connectedness with oneself and internal experience reveals connectedness with others.

Our personal stories are one source of transformative knowledge. Another source is the stories gleaned from our professional, transdisciplinary research. The synthesizing theory and methods of transdisciplinary research (Leavy, 2011) offer psychologists an approach focused on methods for generating conocimiento, or knowledge, consistent with mujerista/borderlands methods and ethics. Transdisciplinary inquiry begins with the topic needing to be better understood, rather than a single discipline/subdiscipline and its particular theories or methods for reducing complexity of phenomena. This approach recognizes that disciplinary tools carry legacies of collusion with domination and that academics and professionals are not the sole experts offering relevant knowledge. Transdisciplinary inquiry includes participatory methods, ensuring those impacted by the problem or question are involved as empowered equals at every phase of inquiry and fully benefit from the acquired knowledge. This approach rigorously incorporates critical theories and investigator reflexivity, identifying knowledge gained through social position, creating dialogues across disciplines and communities promoting shared learning. The knowledge gained highlights accountability to impacted communities and commitment to social change. Transdisciplinary or border-crossing methods highlight how contexts cocreate possibilities within evolving interdependent lives as personal and collective histories, material and social realities, and creative individual interpretations come together in alchemical and unpredictable ways throughout the life course.

Working with diverse graduate and undergraduate students on the Health Promotion Research Team in Psychology at the University of Massachusetts, our team's research explores how diverse families and communities draw on collective cultural traditions to support creativity and innovation in response to challenging contexts of change, mobilizing culturally meaningful resources for resilience, including self-definitions, relationships and actions transforming arduous, unjust life circumstances. Rather than focus on diagnosis and psychopathology, we explore definitions of personal and collective wellness consistent with indigenous philosophies of *el buen vivir* (the good life; Leon, 2012). Creativity within cultural traditions supports both their preservation and reinvention, expanding ways of being within culture while transforming relationships and settings toward greater equity. Our inquiries take place in classroom, clinical, and community settings, highlighting critical theories; holistic, intersectional approaches; and participatory methods of inquiry focused on lo cotidiano and knowledge gained as oppressed groups strive to solve problems of everyday survival, achieving personal and collective goals while transforming contexts toward greater equality.

In our research, we consider the spiritual basis of transformative knowledge. For example, indigenous cosmologies of Latin America share an image of the sacred tree of life as *axis mundi*, the stable center or navel of the world, its trunk connected to earth and sky, linking the four orienting directions in the sun's rising and setting, the cycle of seasons, and the cycles of birth, growth, death, and rebirth. Most cultures view the passage of intergenerational time, how the present connects to an ancestral past and a future we protect today for generations to come, as a sacred trust. We attend to the spiritual and ethical leadership offered by border-crossing knowledge, building bridges to psychology.

PSYCHOLOGY, SPIRITUALITY, AND CREATIVITY: FINDING CULTURAL/DEVELOPMENTAL CONNECTIONS

Scientific psychology has historically stood apart from religious and spiritual beliefs, seeing religion and faith as objects of study but considering these as worldviews contradicting the critical perspectives required to test scientific hypotheses. However, the field has increasingly embraced studies of religion and spirituality as multidimensional, incorporating public/institutional and private/personal practices with both beneficial and potentially destructive beliefs and practices impacting well-being and health (Pargament, 2013). For example, psychology of life-course rituals has taken two major directions, one studying benefits of rituals and routines of everyday family life (Fiese et al., 2002) and another studying religious ritual as organizing different phases of life-course development (Idler, 2013), supporting transformation of self within cultural expectations.

In clinical and health psychology, interventions using Buddhist meditation practices to reduce stress, as well as to target specific symptoms of anxiety or posttraumatic stress, have been tested in randomized controlled trials and found to be highly effective. However, most of this work teaches meditation as a practice uprooted/removed from its holistic religious traditions. Multicultural psychology has more systematically recognized religious differences associated with cultural diversity, expanding the ways to think about culturally adapting psychotherapies so they are more consistent with culturally based religious beliefs and practices (Bernal & Domenech-Rodriguez, 2012; Comas-Díaz, 2012).

Psychology increasingly recognizes the value of culturally grounded spiritual traditions as resources for socially oppressed groups seeking the comfort, connection, and courage nourishing resistance and resilience (Comas-Díaz, 2008b; Falicov, 2014). However, many religions have supported patriarchal social institutions, including strict enforcement of highly unequal gender roles and of prohibitions against queer sexualities. Psychologists supporting equity within cultural traditions have become interested in better understanding the transformation of religious and spiritual institutions, beliefs, and practices, as well as alternative communities created by feminists, communities of color, and lesbian, gay, bisexual, transgender, and queer individuals as believers, scholars, and activists.

Working at the crossroads of clinical and multicultural psychology, Comas-Díaz (2008b) offered the concept of *Spirita* as a synthesizing, women of color spirituality challenging Eurocentric feminist spirituality in critical domains. This concept is especially meaningful in understanding creativity in lo cotidiano. Comas-Díaz (2008b) argued that in contrast to the eclecticism and cultural borrowing of feminist spirituality, Spirita emphasizes integrative, cultural/transcultural analysis and cultural acknowledgment leading to inclusion. Although feminist spirituality focuses on the self in historical contexts and a heroine's journey of personal development and liberation, the Spirita journey emphasizes service, collective liberation, and a shared path toward social justice. Finally, particularly meaningful in understanding spirituality and creativity, whereas feminist spirituality highlights opportunities for personal healing and empathic joy, Spirita recognizes shared traumatic experiences and draws joy from empathic connections and commitment to creating communities for universal healing through increased social justice.

In a previous work, Shapiro and Modestin (2013) explored the sacred as a foundational component of the culturally grounded, collective emancipatory work of women of color artists. Women of color feminisms in psychology have used intersectionality to address effects of gender, race, ethnicity, social class, sexualities, and educational oppression and privilege as dynamic dimensions of social contexts that are simultaneously shared and uniquely interpreted lived experiences (Comas-Díaz, 2012; Hurtado, 2007). Interdisciplinary works exploring connections between U.S. multicultural feminist studies and third-world women of color feminisms emphasize complexities and challenges of displacements and diasporas in diverse women's lives. Reaching across borders, and involving artists in their explorations of women creating culture, these writers use transnational perspectives and innovative, genre-crossing methods integrating scholarly, testimonial/autoethnographic, creative and activist writing to generate and celebrate *fronteriza*/border-crossing conocimientos/ understandings.

If psychology research is approached with an open mind to seeing bridges between psychology, spirituality, justice, and creativity, one finds many connections, some of which are surprising. Recent influential work in positive psychology identified spirituality and creativity as practices enriching everyday life (Pedrotti & Edwards, 2014). Fredrickson, whose research explores the ways positive experiences "broaden and build" positive emotions, suggested that everyday spirituality, by creating spaces of peace, appreciation, and joy, helps cultivate the positive emotions associated with physical and mental well-being (Catalino & Fredrickson, 2011). Developmental and positive psychologists, among others, have begun to focus on processes associated with resilience in response to challenges, including stress-related growth and posttraumatic growth. However, bridging theoretical perspectives toward useful synthesis requires critical theory sensitive to the ways power dynamics, particularly biomedical models of psychopathology individualizing and decontextualizing symptoms of distress, have become incorporated into disciplinary theories, research methods, and practice assumptions (Hernández-Wolfe, 2013). For example, posttraumatic growth theories often assume that clinical levels of distress are required to stimulate growth. In contrast, prospective developmental perspectives on impacts of potentially traumatic events suggest that symptoms of distress and processes associated with positive coping immediately co-occur. Further, the societal and clinical frameworks used to tell others the story of challenging experiences themselves significantly contribute to journeys of resistance, recovery, and resilience (Hernández-Wolfe, 2013; Shapiro, 2007). Culturally meaningful spiritual solutions to challenges of living cannot be imposed by others, however well-intentioned, but must be discovered through sociopolitically critical, emotionally meaningful processes of respectful inquiry into life circumstances, purpose, and meaning.

Mujerista and borderlands spiritual beliefs/practices and methods of inquiry and discovery are deeply rooted in women's own creative expressions of spirituality, as connected to powerful, embodied life forces and *conciencia* in its multiple meanings: knowledge or awareness of the world, with consequences for moral agency. These perspectives on the life course link the flow of time in the rise and setting of the sun, birth, growth, death and regeneration, the cycles of seasons and of generations, and love in its many dimensions as a life force nurturing self and others. Often working with modest materials, women bring their heart/soul to household and table, gathering in daily communion. Creative acts nourish the courage and strength for la lucha/the struggle for social justice in confronting intersecting social oppressions of sexism, racism, and poverty, through both psychospiritual journeys and social justice actions. Ethical revisionings of gender, culture, sexualities and spiritualities by Latin@/Chicana feminists creatively communicated hard-won knowledge gained at intersections/borderlands of women's lived experiences, viewing spirituality and representations of the sacred, grounded in lo cotidiano as central in caring for self and others while enriching and transforming arduous circumstances (Facio & Lara, 2014).

ANZALDÚA'S BORDERLANDS AS CULTURAL, SPIRITUAL AND ETHICAL DEVELOPMENT

In *Borderlands/La Frontera*, Anzaldúa (1987) explored her own deeply mystical experience of personal development within nature and culture. She discussed the sometimes violent process of rebirth required to shed the images and terms of domination—sometimes violently imposed, sometimes willingly embraced—designed to control unruly women of color, queer men, and all the poor mestizos and *mojados*/"wetbacks"—defining relations of gender, race, sexuality, and social class both within and outside the family. She described seven unfolding steps in reclaiming disavowed knowledge:

1. *El arrebato*: an angry, passionate often traumatic experience rupturing the familiar;
2. *nepantla*, the space between inner and outer worlds and zone of possibilities;
3. the *Coatlicue* depths, accompanied by the terrifying presence of the goddess of life and death, despair, and distress dominating with the familiar world confronted and dismantled;

4. call to action through compromise/commitment and spiritual conversion;
5. *Coyolxauhqui*, a daughter of *Coatlicue* who represents reflection, resistance and transformation;
6. the blow-up or clash of realities as new conocimientos/knowledge are explored often in spaces of domination; and
7. an achievement of transformation and wholeness through shifting realities (Anzaldúa, 2002; Bobel, Sieber, Suyemoto, Tang, & Tork, 2006).

Anzaldúa's chapter on the Coatlicue state of confronting contradictions in *Borderlands/La Frontera* credited Jung's work on archetypes, and Jungian analyst Hillman's work, as instrumental in the development of her thought, particularly regarding archetypes as representing the presence of the divine in the psyche (Anzaldúa, 1987, p. 95). Indeed, Anzaldúa's transformative work reached for mythic images, necessary yet forbidden, supporting her unique critical vision and journey to a more multifaceted wholeness capturing her experience as a queer Mestiza. In his influential essay "The Stages of Life," Jung (1914–1930/2011) argued that in adolescence, individuals discover a complex self in which tensions between valued aspects of self, such as gender complexity or nontraditional spirituality, may create inner conflict, especially because society prescribes normative rather than creative solutions to these "problems." Jung suggested that at midlife, both men and women achieve the maturity to explore alternative aspects of self, an insight confirmed in life-course development research. Jung (1914–1930/2011) himself explored aspects of gendered self and spirituality forbidden by his historical times and societal position. Hernández-Wolfe (2013) used Anzaldúa's *Borderlands* and the Nepantla state of liminality to explore a decolonizing mental health emphasizing cultural resources for resilience.

Although Anzaldúa (1987) made only brief mention of what she termed *spiritual mestizaje*, focusing more on spiritual activism (Keating, 2008), her exploration of border-crossing consciousness used cultural archetypes to connect personal with collective journeys toward wholeness. She described undertaking personal journeys of development linked to ancestral beliefs, yet simultaneously being free to create new forms of conciencia/ethical knowledge. Combining these cultural explorations with a critical perspective on multiple forms of oppression, Anzaldúa (1987) recovered childhood mystical experiences embedded in indigenous cultural/spiritual beliefs and created her own lineage within these traditions, making space for embodied connection to matriarchal myths supporting gender complexity and queer sexuality.

Delgadillo (2011) explored and expanded on Anzaldúa's vision of spiritual transformation resulting in new mestiza consciousness, applying the concept of "spiritual mestizaje" to the work of Chicana writers: "*Nuestra alma el trabajo* [our soul the work], the great alchemical work; spiritual mestizaje, a 'morphogenesis', an inevitable unfolding" (Anzaldúa, 1987, as cited in Delgadillo, 2011, p. 81). She suggested that Anzaldúa (1987) incorporated indigenous cosmologies/worldviews and rituals of transformation to create an innovative text and narrative methodology, termed *autohistoria*, or theorizing through self-study in historical context. Her innovative method yielded new ways of theorizing the interface of sociopolitical contexts and self, transforming contexts for self-definition. Delgadillo went on to explore journeys of spiritual mestizaje in the creative writing of contemporary Chicanas, and the ways their work incorporates innovative inquiries using mixed-method narratives incorporating historical analysis, autobiographical *testimonio*, poetry, and fiction to create a Borderland ethos or sensibility.

Delgadillo (2011) used the term *spirituality* to capture full indigenous religious/spiritual worldviews, in contrast to the term *religion*, which she and other scholars outside of Christian Western traditions associate not only with institutional practices but also with a totalizing, Eurocentric understanding of the place of the sacred in society that does not correspond to the role of the sacred in other cultures and eras. This Eurocentric practice of elevating Western, monotheistic traditions can be problematic, as many of the world's popular and syncretic spiritual/religious traditions are poorly understood and unappreciated as "primitive" or animistic forms, as, for example, the Afro Yoruba traditions brought to Cuba, Haiti, and Brazil by African slaves (Santeria, Vudu, and Candomble, respectively). In *Decolonizing Epistemologies*, Isasi-Díaz and Mendieta (2012) presented a much more complex picture of Amerindian, African, and other immigrant diaspora contributions to Latina/o theology and underlying philosophies by using principles of decolonization to address the Catholic, Christian, and Eurocentric bias and its incorporation of multiple forms of intersecting social class, racial, ethnic, and gender oppressions. Isasi-Díaz and Mendieta argued that confronting regional legacies of colonization by directly engaging indigenous, Afro, and other diasporic communities enables one to locate his or her understanding of spirituality in the deeply ethical cosmologies of belief supporting *el buen vivir*, the conditions that permit the flourishing of all life in its full interdependence and wholeness fundamental to the sacred in these and the world's communities. Delgadillo suggested Anzaldúa's "queering" of spirituality to transcend binaries of gender, sexuality, and power in religious traditions regards multiple ways of knowing the sacred in the world as an ethical responsibility.

MARTÍNEZ: LITERARY LIBERATION THEOLOGY AS MENTAL HEALTH PRACTICE

One illustration of creative, mixed-method writing connected to spiritual activism is offered by the life and work of journalist, poet, novelist, and activist Demetria Martínez, whose novel *Mother Tongue* (1997) Delgadillo (2011) explored for historical/cultural spiritual themes. Martínez's multifaceted creative works are especially valuable in reconceptualizing Latin@ spirituality within psychology, as she has written and spoken publicly about her mental health. Particularly relevant is what she termed *literary liberation theology*, a resource for personal wellness and societal change. Martínez regularly visits the University of Massachusetts (UMass) Boston Joiner Center for the Study of War and Its Consequences, teaching creative nonfiction and poetry writing workshops. Ester Shapiro joined her writing workshops and participated in discussions of writing, activism and healing. The following discussion of the activist psychospiritual foundations of Martínez's creative work draws from her published writing and public interviews, including a presentation at UMass Boston about her struggles with bipolar disorder and using cultural, political, and spiritual resources, as well as holistic health care, in her journey toward wholeness (Martínez, 2014).

In her book of personal essays, *Confessions of a Berlitz-Tape Chicana*, Martínez (2005) described the fateful histories in the U.S. Southwest that led to her loss of Spanish-language and indigenous cultures as "mother tongues." The novel *Mother Tongue* (Martínez, 1997) is based on her experiences in 1986–1988 when she was writing for the *National Catholic Reporter* about Central American refugees and the Sanctuary movement. Through this work, she accompanied a Lutheran minister and two pregnant Salvadoran women on their journey to Albuquerque, where the governor had declared New Mexico a Sanctuary State. She was arrested and brought to trial by the U.S. government for conspiracy in connection with alleged smuggling of Salvadoran refugees into the United States and was threatened with a 25-year prison sentence. The government presented her poem "Nativity for Two Salvadoran Women" (Gaspar de Alba, Herrera-Sobek, & Martínez, 1989) as evidence of the conspiracy. This poem, which speaks to the tragedy of U.S.-supported civil war in the region, draws parallels between the religious imagery of Jesus' birth and the courage with which these Salvadoran mothers-to-be undertook an arduous journey to offer their children a better life. Both she and the minister she accompanied were acquitted, but the experience was personally terrorizing. She felt that the silence imposed by the government's persecution (she was warned that her phones were tapped), the need to protect the Sanctuary movement, and the legal requirements of her defence made her feel deeply silenced, as for years afterwards she struggled with the criminalization of her journalism, poetry and politics, yet she emerged with an eloquent voice and distinctive style (Lomas, 2006). Martínez's (1997) novel *Mother Tongue* is based on the experience of the trial, telling Maria's story as one that connected her flight from El Salvador to indigenous women and communities in their struggle for the conditions of wholeness in supporting and sustaining life. For Martínez, as for many women, the mythic image of Mary as mother of Jesus represents the creation of life through the spark of divinity that must be nurtured, too often in harsh conditions. Her image helps many endure the suffering due to poverty and violence, while incorporating possibilities of transcendence and transformation.

In her essay "Birth Day," Martínez (2005) described her experiences with extreme psychological states from childhood and her use of literary, psychological, cultural, and spiritual traditions to understand and transform them. She recalled, "Any sense of a center, or a stable identity, has long eluded me. Routines—the loom upon which one weaves a life—fell apart whenever I did" (Martínez, 2005, p. 27). After the trial, she became convinced her testimony had exposed a Sanctuary activist who was subsequently killed by U.S.-trained Salvadoran death squads, precipitating a crisis. She found relief and a path toward healing when a friend suggested she might be experiencing bipolar disorder and referred her to a trusted physician, who helped her find the right medication and supports enabling her to stabilize. She found it useful to distinguish her creative and activist work (i.e., constructive attempts to draw on intense emotionality and culturally meaningful visions act on, and heal, a fractured world) from her bipolar illness, which intensified her emotional responses, particularly depression and self-blame, beyond what she could bear. She contrasted her bipolar states of mind, especially the darkness, exhaustion, and self-blame of her debilitating depression, and "the observer in me—that is to say, my spirit—broke off from my manic-depressive mind, and it is to that observer that I owe my life" (Martínez, 2005, p. 30). She felt grateful that timely diagnosis and responsive treatment during her crisis enabled her to moderate her emotional intensity while channeling her spirituality and activism through her writing. Her use of cultural/spiritual healing practices combined with medication and culturally grounded healing within extended family, creative, and activist communities, helping stabilize her emotional states while preserving her creativity. Healing into wholeness enduringly requires continuing, close attention to her wellness as a holistic mind/body/spiritual/cultural process. When asked about her treatment, she said she never sought psychiatric care, as she did not find that that framework spoke to her personal journey toward wellness (Martínez, personal communication, April 25, 2006). Working from a culturally grounded, holistic mind/body/spirit perspective permitted her to heal and continue her work of the spirit, which is psychological, narrative, spiritual, and activist work. Martínez

(2005) viewed healing from her bipolar illness as requiring commitment to the work of the spirit: "We are the ones whose spirits dribble out of us like blood . . . we are the artists of spirit retrieval" (p. 32). Throughout her creative work, Martínez has explored healing through self-expression within supportive communities that share common cultural, spiritual, and activist values and work toward wholeness with justice.

HEALING, CULTURE, AND THE SACRED: LATIN@ ARTISTS BRIDGING FOLK AND FORMAL ARTS

Artistic, sacred, and healing traditions have a long history of intertwining for Latin@s and other women of color (Shapiro & Modestin, 2013). Women of color artists have historically contributed to new spaces within which other women can see themselves reflected in new, more emancipatory ways. Two major themes in these artistic community works are (a) a focus on multiple media representations of lived experiences of sexism and racism that offer alternative visions and (b) a refusal of traditional boundaries of artistic expression and deliberate use of hybrid forms drawing from sources in everyday life, as well as those recognized in formal art criticism. Patriarchal and colonizing theologies emphasize sumptuous spaces and formal, hierarchical structures, reinforcing a social order protecting privilege. The spiritual practices of women's everyday lives incorporate aesthetics designed to both reflect and enrich arduous life journeys through images, icons, and rituals connecting ancestral time and the sacred to daily life and life-course transitions.

Introducing Facio and Lara's (2014) collection of essays, *Fleshing the Spirit*, Hernandez-Avila (2014) invoked the ancient Mesoamerican image from Teotihuacan of the Great Mother, the female principle of the universe, present in all of life, birthing Coyote, representing the trickster whose role is creative disruption. She suggested that in Chicana/Latina/indigenous cosmologies, the act of birthing has to do not only with the physical act but also with personal creativity, as it connects to the creative spirit of the universe. She noted that the image also includes the divine hands of the female principle, representing the creativity and wholeness in everything women do with their hands and heart, the embodied wisdom required to do, write, live, love, and be in ways that challenge and radically transform our understandings of spirituality. Facio and Lara organized chapters using the guiding principles of the four directions and the centering practices of *testimonio* traditions, designed to use one's own life story and spiritual journey as a means of inspiring communities of connection, healing, and wholeness for others and/in the world. Consistent with principles of mujerista/borderlands spirituality, creative and healing arts offer practical resources for linking lo cotidiano to the sacred, illuminating pathways connecting personal, community, and societal change toward preferred futures committed to justice. These rhythms of daily life are organized in synchrony with intersections of time and space in both the ordinary life cycle and extraordinary, challenging events.

Pérez's (2007) exploration of Chicana arts through the lens of politically informed spirituality also organized her presentation of "aesthetic altarities" using the Nahual textual poetics, in which the juxtaposition of elements expands the metaphorical space for their reception and interpretation. Her wide-ranging review of Chicana artists, many of whom incorporate humble elements and private rituals into their public artistic work, mirrored and expanded on intergenerational practices they observed, preserved, and transformed in their own homes and communities. Pérez explored how Chicana artists use multimedia to represent the actual and imaginary places, lost to dispossession and diaspora, yet preserved through seemingly mundane cultural practices that capture the continuity of ancestral traditions rooted in the earth's cycles. One area of artistic work bridging formal arts and folk arts is the altar to the ancestors, gracing many homes and public places. Pérez suggested that the freedom to create hybrid spiritualities or otherness offered by domestic altars has inspired a widely varied Chicana artistic use of altars using installation, painting, photography, film, and mixed media. Others explore, and expand on, cultural traditions common in household and community arts. For example, artist and psychologist Amalia Mesa-Bains creates altar-based installations focused on dress and domestic arts as social and transgressive spaces of possibility. Through installations using dress, mirrors, furniture, and paintings, such as the *Black Madonna of Monserrat*, she exposes imposed images of patriarchy, uncovering images of women's gynocentric power hidden by projections of Eurocentric and male dominance.

Pérez (2007) also explored the large body of work by Chicana artists reinterpreting the Virgin of Guadalupe as a means of reclaiming multiple dimensions of the Virgin, whose power to accompany the poor and disenfranchised is expanded to include feminist empowerment, erotics, and queer sexualities. She included emotionally striking evocations of the Virgin by Yolanda Lopez, who depicts herself, in *Portrait of the Artist as the Virgin of Guadalupe*, as a vanquishing caped crusader and other archetypal heroines, including Margaret Stewart sewing the Virgin's cape and Botticelli's Venus as a love goddess. She also noted that a great deal of Chicana's sacred/bleeding heart imagery seemingly based primarily on Catholic sources is often hybridized with the alignment of the Face and Divinized Heart, or *yolteotl* in the Nahua concept. Maya Gonzalez's painting *The Love That Stains* invokes Frida

Kahlo's famous painting *The Two Fridas*, seated side by side: one Frida dressed in humble indigenous clothing connected to a second Frida, dressed in luxurious White European garments, her heart pumping and bleeding out as with scissors in hand she severs the chord connecting them. Yet in Gonzalez's painting, the cover art for the hardback edition of Martínez's (2014) memoir, the European self with the exposed bleeding heart sits in foreground, held and comforted by the translucent mirror/spiritual self behind her, both accompanied by the hummingbird as representing *yolteol*/spirit, the duality of the figures depicted as a source of inner/spiritual strength and peace rather than of suffering. As in Anzaldúa's (1987) concept of la facultad, these artists acknowledge the violence of transformation.

In exploring Latin@ creativity and spirituality as expressed through popular religion, sacred arts in home and community settings offer meaningful, accessible spaces for innovation, improvisation, and self-expression connected to cultural and ancestral traditions. These creations include use of household saints and ancestral altars in both indigenous and Afro-diaspora traditions, the updating of iconic spiritual images through an exploration of La Virgen de Guadalupe in the Mexican/Chicana traditions and of Yemayá or the syncretic images of the Black Madonna in the Afro-diaspora traditions, home altars, and public arts and murals. Household altars offer a great deal of space for creative improvisation. To an uneducated eye, an altar may have a sculpture or image representing the Virgin Mary, along with photographs of beloved family members, perhaps with a special place for the deceased and often including images of deceased loved ones with living family members during times of happiness and celebration. Altars and their configuration of *ofrendas* (offerings) look and feel very different depending on whether you find the Catholic images infused with Afro Latin@ deities, the Orishas Yemayá and Oshun, as you find in the Caribbean and Brazil; with the European spiritism found in Cuba and Puerto Rico; or with the indigenous traditions associated with Mexico and La Virgen de Guadalupe.

The Afro Cuban American artist Maria Magdalena Campos Pons offers an example of artistic creativity and transculturation rooted in the Afro Catholic syncretism of Santeria, which invests Catholic saints with the identities and powers of Orishas in the Yoruba traditions of Ifa. She draws on performative and aesthetic characteristics of both religions with her own creative reclaiming of devalued sacred and domestic arts in the hands and homes of Cuban women of African descent. Campos Pons uses evolving multimedia installations, as well as large-scale Polaroid photography, constantly learning new techniques to creatively convey her understanding of African diaspora legacies in women's domestic lives. For one of her early installations, building on the realization that her family home just outside of Matanzas, Cuba, was built on the ruins of a slave quarters/*barracon*, she learned how to make bricks to recreate the physical space as a deep well of history. Looking inside the well, viewers could see and hear video images and sounds of children playing a Cuban version of "Ring Around the Rosy." Another mixed-media installation using film and sculpture showed a larger-than-life video image of her mother sewing and ironing a white dress, the material now rich and sumptuous, her image surrounded by handmade objects, including intricate, lacelike blown glass versions of the iron and trivet. Recurring images in Campos Pons's work are the Orishas Yemayá and Ochún, both feminine representation of the waters: Yemayá, of sea and maternity; Ochún, of sweet river waters and marriage/partnerships. Campos Pons's installations and photographs directly incorporate ritual elements, blurring the boundary between quotidian, sacred, and profane spaces (West-Durán, 2013). Her installation *Las Siete Potencias/ The Seven Powers* invokes the Middle Passage using hand-decorated wooden planks depicting the slave ships and the many lives lost to the unspeakable cruelty of enslavement. Yemayá is depicted in a drawing invoking her oceanic and maternal roles, embracing the dead and caring for survivors in a spiritual unity of tragic past and enduring survival. Campos Pons uses sculpture and photographs as both aesthetic and ritual objects, transforming the room-sized exhibition into a sacred space resembling an altar, in which viewers can bear witness to the horror, honor lives lost to enslavement and the Middle Passage, yet feel comforted by life's continuity through the sacred. In this and other work, Campos Pons photographs and represents her own body and those of other women to articulate and redefine aesthetic spaces, mindful of performative and ritual dimensions of spirituality.

West-Durán (2013) suggested Campos Pons's work could be viewed within the Yoruba concept of *ori*, representing the head of the body, mindfulness, consciousness: the internal experience revealing (and questioning) the self and identity, relationships (family, community), examining the past (history, public and private), and envisioning the future (creation of art). West-Durán noted the significance of Campos Pons's use of ori as she draws on the association between memory and water, especially within the context of Yemayá and water spirits. The Orishas can be understood as archetypes with multifaceted manifestations, embodying energies, relationships, forces in nature, and principles interwoven in daily life. Adding to their magnificent complexity as resources for living, an individual orisha has different *avatares o caminos* (avatars or paths), offering a rich spiritual and aesthetic vocabulary Campos Pons uses in her work and millions of believers draw on, enriching and guiding their lives. Latina psychologists Comas-Díaz (2008a) and Espín (2008) have both explored how images of saints supported their psychological and spiritual development at critical moments.

MUJERISTA THEOLOGY, SPIRITUAL MESTIZAJE AND ACTIVISM: THIS BRIDGE WE CALL HOME

Mujerista theology and borderlands spirituality in the United States and Latin America have inspired social movements connecting religion and spirituality; creative arts; women's reproductive health and rights; respect for racial, cultural, and sexual diversities; elimination of discrimination, violence, and poverty; and environmental protection as sacred trusts. As Comas-Díaz (2008b) noted in *Spirita,* Latina feminisms are grounded in a vision of spirituality integral to their social justice activism. Shapiro (2005) first became aware of the very different way that Latin American feminist movements, particularly movements for women's health and reproductive rights, incorporated religion and the sacred into their work when working as coordinating editor on a Spanish-language transnational edition of the feminist text *Our Bodies, Ourselves* (Shapiro, 2000). She discovered that the book in English completely avoids religion and spirituality, out of fear that this would expose its editors, the Boston Women's Health Book Collective, to both religious and scientific critiques. In contrast, Latin American women's health movements were grounded in spirituality that viewed mind–body–spirit and environment holistically, so that the ethics of reproductive choice used the position of Catholics for Choice, recognizing women's responsibility for bearing and sustaining life and for making the needed ethical decisions on behalf of all their future children (Shapiro, 2005). One early example of this political/spiritual unity was the Chilean activist group Con-spirando, which did environmental justice work from a spiritual perspective starting in the 1990s shortly after the end of the dictatorship. Creating *Nuestros Cuerpos, Nuestras Vidas,* the editors infused the text with this spiritually based vision of Latin American/Latin@ social justice activism.

In the Chican@ activist circles in Los Angeles, California, spirituality and social justice are the foundation for community building and activism. The understanding is that one cannot divide one's spirituality from their activism because through this connection to others, one develops a sense of collective responsibility. A major focus of these spaces is artistic exploration of popular arts. Mujeres de Maiz, an all-women artist's collective in Los Angeles, created a space for women of color artists and activists to organize together around issues affecting communities of color. The mission of this collective is the healing of the artists, communities, and Mother Earth through arts as prayer conveyed through their zines, art, multimedia exhibits, and performances. Their creative and artistic calling addresses resistance, healing, and change to "make visible the invisible." The intertwining of art, spirituality, and activism can also manifest through more subtle acknowledgment of spiritual practices and rituals. The Ovarian Psycos Bicycle Brigade, a more recent Chicana/

Latina organization in the Los Angeles area, comes together to address issues of oppression and creation of sisterhood through the shared practice of cycling in the city, organizing highly visible critical mass rides to create space for women of color on bicycles. In addition to their activism centered on the politicization of space and creating an alternative narrative for cyclists in Los Angeles, they organize community events for women that often include introduction or re-education of indigenous spiritual practices through workshops on rituals and artistic expression of spirituality. These activist circles place the role of women at the forefront as agents of change and spiritual growth. Through these creative, activist spaces, mujerista/borderlands spiritual mestizaje and activist practice of spirituality continues, infusing women's participation in community social engagement through transformative activism with the intent of creating safety and visibility, practicing communally, and rebuilding severed connections with self, others, and one's place in the world.

CONCLUSION

Defining creativity from within the spiritual and ethical foundations of mujerista theology highlights the importance of spiritually meaningful "folk arts" and their uses in household and community to solve problems of la lucha en lo cotidiano through connections to the sacred. The folk arts of popular religion bring new forms and meanings to rituals and routines of everyday life and spaces offering aesthetically rich colors, aromas, and flavors, the miracle of abundance. These explorations support new discoveries of ways human development into wholeness. They are unique to our time, place, and experiences yet inextricably connected to the flow of ancestral time and rhythms of nature. Life-course challenges both anticipated and unexpected, sometimes random acts of fate too often intertwined with willful impositions of injustice require one to discover new ways of reconciling ancestral traditions, new environmental demands, and a personal, unique voice/vision and capacity for agency within relational and collective interdependence. Latin@ spiritual beliefs and practices creatively synthesize indigenous, Afro-diasporic, European Catholic, Christian, Spiritist, Jewish, and Muslim practices, as well as Buddhist, Confucian, and other Asian beliefs and practices, woven together with woman-centered curandera/healer traditions deeply rooted in concern for the earth and protection of its abundance. As Isasi-Díaz (2004) noted, rigorous methodological and ethical accountability to Latin@ lived experiences of lo cotidiano helps discover creative spiritual resources and moral agency emerging from, and responsive to, challenges of daily life. This approach to creativity illuminates new ways of understanding religion and spirituality as cultural/developmental resources transforming life challenges toward healing, growth, and justice.

REFERENCES

Alcántara, D. (2013). *Latino youth experiences of immigrant policy, enforcement, and exclusion: Exploring risk and resilience* (master's thesis). Available from http://scholarworks.umb.edu/masters_theses/180/

Anzaldúa, G. (1987). *Borderlands/la frontera: The new Mestiza*. San Francisco, CA: Aunt Lute Books.

Anzaldúa, G. (Ed.). (1990). *Making face, making soul/haciendo caras: Creative and critical perspectives by women of color*. San Francisco, CA: Aunt Lute Books.

Anzaldúa, G. (2002). Now let us shift . . . the path of conocimiento . . . inner works, public acts. In G. Anzaldúa & A. Keating (Eds.), *This bridge we call home: Radical visions for transformation* (pp. 549–572). New York, NY: Routledge.

Anzaldúa, G., & Keating, A. (2002). *This bridge we call home: Radical visions for transformation*. New York, NY: Routledge.

Anzaldúa, G., & Moraga, C. (Eds.). (1981). *This bridge called my back: Writings by radical women of color*. Watertown, MA: Persephone Press.

Bernal, G., & Domenech-Rodriguez, M. (2012). *Cultural adaptation of evidence-based treatments*. Washington, DC: American Psychological Association.

Bobel, C., Sieber, T., Suyemoto, K., Tang, S., & Tork, A. (2006). Introduction: This bridge we are building: "Inner work, public acts." *Human Architecture, 4*, 333–338. Retrieved from http://scholarworks.umb.edu/humanarchitecture/vol4/iss3/30

Catalino, L. I., & Fredrickson, B. L. (2011). A Tuesday in the life of a flourisher: The role of positive emotional reactivity in optimal mental health. *Emotion, 11*, 938–950. http://dx.doi.org/10.1037/a0024889

Comas-Díaz, L. (2008a). Illuminating the Black Madonna: A healing journey. In C. Rayburn & L. Comas-Díaz (Eds.), *WomanSoul: The inner life of women's spirituality* (pp. 85–95). New York, NY: Praeger.

Comas-Díaz, L. (2008b). Spirita: Reclaiming womanist sacredness into feminism. *Psychology of Women Quarterly, 32*, 13–21. http://dx.doi.org/10.1111/j.1471-6402.2007.00403.x

Comas-Díaz, L. (2012). *Multicultural care: A clinician's guide to cultural competence*. Washington, DC: American Psychological Association. http://dx.doi.org/10.1037/13491-000

Delgadillo, T. (2011). *Spiritual mestizaje*. Durham, NC: Duke University Press.

Espín, O. (2008). My "friendship" with women saints as a source of spirituality. In C. Rayburn & L. Comas-Díaz (Eds.), *WomanSoul: The inner life of women's spirituality* (pp. 71–84). New York, NY: Praeger.

Facio, E., & Lara, I. (2014). *Fleshing the spirit: Spirituality and activism in Chicana, Latina, and indigenous women's lives*. Tucson: University of Arizona Press.

Falicov, C. (2014). *Latino families in therapy* (2nd ed.). New York, NY: Guilford Press.

Fiese, B. H., Tomcho, T. J., Douglas, M., Josephs, K., Poltrock, S., & Baker, T. (2002). A review of 50 years of research on naturally occurring family routines and rituals: Cause for celebration? *Journal of Family Psychology, 16*, 381–390. http://dx.doi.org/10.1037/0893-3200.16.4.381

García Coll, C., & Marks, A. (2012). *The immigrant paradox in children and adolescents: Is becoming American a developmental risk?* Washington, DC: American Psychological Association.

Gaspar de Alba, A., Herrera-Sobek, M., & Martínez, D. (Eds.) (1989). Three times a woman: Chicana poetry. *Bilingual Review Press, 5*, 132–133.

Hernandez-Avila, I. (2014). Foreword: A meditation. In E. Facio & I. Lara (Eds.), *Fleshing the spirit: Spirituality and activism in Chicana, Latina, and indigenous women's lives* (pp. xii–xix). Tucson: University of Arizona Press.

Hernández-Wolfe, P. (2013). *A borderlands view on Latinos, Latin Americans, and decolonization: Rethinking mental health*. San Francisco, CA: Jason Aronson.

Hurtado, A. (2007). Multiple lenses: Multicultural feminist theory. In H. Landrine & N. Russo (Eds.), *Handbook of diversity in feminist psychology* (pp. 29–54). New York, NY: Springer.

Idler, E. (2013). Rituals and practices. In K. Pargament (Ed.), *Handbook of the psychology of religion and spirituality* (pp. 329–347). Washington, DC: American Psychological Association. http://dx.doi.org/10.1037/14045-018

Isasi-Díaz, A. (1993). *Elaborating a* mujerista *theology—En la lucha/in the struggle: A Hispanic women's liberation theology*. Minneapolis, MN: Fortress Press.

Isasi-Díaz, A. (2004). *La lucha* continues: *Mujerista theology*. Minneapolis, MN: Fortress Press.

Isasi-Díaz, A., & Mendieta, E. (2012). *Decolonizing epistemologies: Latina/o theology and philosophy*. New York, NY: Fordham University Press.

Jung, C. G. (2011). *The red book*. New York, NY: Norton. (Original work published 1914–1930)

Keating, A. (2008). I'm a citizen of the universe: Gloria Anzaldúa's spiritual activism as catalyst for social change. *Feminist Studies, 34*, 53–69.

Koss-Chioino, J. (2013). Religion and spirituality in Latino life in the United States. In K. Pargament (Ed.), *Handbook of the psychology of religion and spirituality* (pp. 599–615). Washington, DC: American Psychological Association. http://dx.doi.org/10.1037/14045-033

Leavy, P. (2011). *Essentials of Transdisciplinary Research: Using Problem-Centered Methodologies*. Walnut Creek, CA: Left Coast Press.

Leon, M. (2012). *Feminist perspectives towards transforming economic power: Economic redefinitions toward* buen vivir *in Ecuador: A feminist approach*. Toronto, Ontario, Canada: Association for Women's Rights in Development.

Lomas, L. (2006). "The war cut out my tongue": Domestic violence, foreign wars, and translation in Demetria Martínez. *American Literature, 78*, 357–388.

Lugones, M. (2004). *Pilgrimages/pregrinajes: Theorizing coalitions against multiple oppressions*. New York, NY: Rowman & Littlefield.

Martínez, D. (1997). *Mother tongue*. New York, NY: Ballantine.

Martínez, D. (2005). *Confessions of a Berlitz-tape Chicana*. Norman: University of Oklahoma Press.

Martínez, D. (2014). *Secrets of joy*. Retrieved from http://demetriaMartínez.wordpress.com/

Medina, L. (2014). Nepantla spirituality: My path to the sources of healing. In E. Facio & I. Lara (Eds.), *Fleshing the spirit: Spirituality and activism in Chicana, Latina, and indigenous women's lives* (pp. 167–185). Tucson: University of Arizona Press.

Pargament, K. (Ed.). (2013). *Handbook of the psychology of religion and spirituality*. Washington, DC: American Psychological Association.

Pedrotti, J., & Edwards, L. (Eds.). (2014). *Perspectives on the intersection of multicultural and positive psychology*. New York, NY: Springer. http://dx.doi.org/10.1007/978-94-017-8654-6

Pérez, L. (2007). *Chicana art: The politics of spiritual and aesthetic altarities*. Chapel Hill, NC: Duke University Press. http://dx.doi.org/10.1215/9780822389880

Pérez, L. (2014). Writing with crooked lines. In E. Facio & I. Lara (Eds.), *Fleshing the spirit: Spirituality and activism in Chicana, Latina, and indigenous women's lives* (pp. 23–33). Tucson: University of Arizona Press.

Shapiro, E. R. (1994). *Grief as a family process: A developmental approach to clinical practice*. New York, NY: Guilford Press.

Shapiro, E. R. (Ed.). (2000). *Nuestros cuerpos, nuestras vidas* [Our bodies, ourselves]. New York, NY: Seven Stories Press.

Shapiro, E. R. (2005). Because words are not enough: Transnational collaborations and Latina revisionings of health promotion for gender justice and social change. *NWSA Journal, 17*, 141–172.

Shapiro, E. R. (2007). Whose recovery, of what? Relationships and environments promoting grief and growth. *Death Studies, 32*, 40–58. http://dx.doi.org/10.1080/07481180701741277

Shapiro, E. R. (2013a). Culture and socialization in assessment and treatment in thanatology. In D. Balk (Ed.), *Handbook of thanatology* (2nd ed., pp. 193–208). Oak Brook, IL: Association of Death Education and Counseling.

Shapiro, E. R. (2013b). Family resilience and chronic illness. In D. Becvar (Ed.), *Handbook of family resilience* (pp. 385–408). New York, NY: Springer.

Shapiro, E., & Modestin, Y. (2013). Women of color and the arts: Creativities in everyday life as wellsprings for resistance and resilience. In L. Comas-Díaz & B. Greene (Eds.), *Psychological health of women of color* (pp. 317–336). New York, NY: Palgrave.

West-Durán, A. (2013). What the water brings and takes away: The work of Maria Magdalena Campos Pons. In S. Otero & Y. Falola (Eds.), *Yemoja: Gender, sexuality, and creativity in the Latina/o and Afro-Atlantic diasporas* (pp. 197–214). Albany, NY: SUNY Press.

V

SOCIAL JUSTICE ACTION

9

A PSYCHOCULTURAL EXPLORATION OF WOMANISM, ACTIVISM, AND SOCIAL JUSTICE

THEMA BRYANT-DAVIS AND TYONNA ADAMS

2013 to 2015 has seen a reemergence of mass protest, boycotts, marches, and strategic planning within the African American community and across cultural and national lines. African American women have been at the forefront of this movement, leading local, national, international, and social media action (Sakuma, 2014). This movement has focused on addressing police brutality, violence in all of its forms, and the dysfunction of the criminal justice system. This is not a new tradition for the African American community or for African American women in particular. The identity, presence, role, and agency of Black women in their historical and contemporary struggle for liberation are worthy of scholarly womanist investigation and application (Gaines, 2013). Black women have seen themselves as capable agents of change and have played central roles in slave rebellions; in the civil rights movement; in the Black Power movement; in their socialization of their children; in transforming systems of oppression from within; in the creation and

http://dx.doi.org/10.1037/14937-010
Womanist and Mujerista Psychologies: Voices of Fire, Acts of Courage, T. Bryant-Davis and L. Comas-Díaz (Editors)

maintenance of separatist communities outside of mainstream America; in religious, legal, and educational systems; and in organizing and implementing protests, revolts, and rebellions (Gaines, 2013).

In this chapter, we present an overview of womanism broadly and discuss ways that womanist identity serves a liberating functioning for women of African descent. We explore the diverse expressions of womanism, along with our reflections about our journeys toward embodying a womanist, activist spirit. Last, we discuss how African American women can become empowered and take action to fight aforementioned oppressive agents.

ACTIVISM AS INTEGRAL TO WOMANISM

Walker (2003), who coined the term *womanism*, noted that a *womanist* is a woman of color who loves the struggle and brings to it a feminism that is racialized, class contextualized, and historically rooted. Activism is an intentional act to bring about justice and transformation. Womanism is defined in part as being "outrageous, courageous, and willful" in one's behavior as a result of the socialization messages Black women receive to be competent, responsible, and self-reliant (Bell & Nkomo, 1998; Walker, 2003). Womanists affirm their Blackness and their feminism and both of these traditions are based in commitments to the promotion of social justice (Coleman, 2013). Womanism goes beyond the fight for the rights of Black people exclusively or the fight for women's rights exclusively to call for the wholeness of all people, male and female around the globe (Walker, 2003). This concern for all does not however erase or minimize the care for herself, for Black women, and for the Black community. Womanist activism is rooted in a womanist caring ethic which requires that one recognize good intentions are insufficient; we must actively resist systems of oppression to protect the rights of all (Cozart & Gordon, 2006). Womanist activism appreciates women's strengths and is committed to working for survival and wholeness; this wholeness is a holistic sense of well-being which includes the mind.

"A womanist loves the Spirit, loves the folk, and loves herself" (Walker, 2003, p. xii). A womanist does not fall into the trap of people who focus on spirituality to the exclusion of contemporary world issues. Instead, the spirituality of a womanist is one that motivates her to act for justice and to create sustainable peace. It is the kind of spirituality that nurtured slave rebellions and the civil rights movement. The spirituality of womanists is intertwined with their activism. Although womanist activism has multiple expressions, the one that is most unique is the spiritual expression of womanist activism (Taylor, 2004). Additionally it is her love for the folk that motivates a womanist to speak up against injustice, oppression, and violation in every form. Womanists are family oriented, community oriented, and communally minded; they resist feelings of powerlessness and apply themselves to the empowerment of self, family, and community (Boyd-Franklin, 2003). They see the individual but also honor and work for the benefit of the larger community. Additionally, in keeping with the feminist idea that the personal is political, womanists love themselves and this self-love is a revolutionary, radical act of resistance; self-love for Black women is activism.

Womanism is based in a call to love and care, with an understanding that these words mandate action. Acts of social justice and activism for womanists are born in a fundamental desire for the wholeness of people. Within this framework, it is important to note that all acts that are life affirming for the oppressed are acts of revolutionary activism. It is radical to love yourself in a culture that dismisses you. It is an act of resistance to love your community in the midst of a society that seeks to dehumanize and pathologize you daily. It is activism to stand up for the dignity and security of those who have been systematically discarded educationally, economically, legally, socially, physically, and psychologically.

Activism for womanists is rooted in a deep culturally contextualized caring for the self and for humanity. Womanism is a racialized view of caring as opposed to a colorblind view (Thompson, 2003). Race and racism, as well as gender and sexism, are centralized in opposition to the view that the experience of White Americans is the universal norm and standard. Acts of resistance and social justice need to promote culturally relevant policies and critique systems with an appreciation for the role of multiple forms of systemic oppression. Activism for womanists is race conscious and gender conscious, and it starts from the place of the activist herself being aware of the role of privilege, power, and oppression in her life. Womanist activists give voice to race, gender, culture, social class, and sexuality issues. Phillips (2006) outlined key components of womanism. The first relates directly to activism; it is an antioppression stance. The other components are grassroots oriented, spiritually based, inclusive, and community oriented. Much womanist activism has emerged from grassroots movements, been nurtured by faith communities, and aimed to include a broad range of activists.

THE DIVERSE EXPRESSIONS OF WOMANIST ACTIVISM

Women of African descent have engaged in a range of activist resistance strategies throughout history. Enslaved African women used such resistance strategies as destroying farm equipment, pretending to be ill, jumping off slave ships, killing their offspring, escaping, assisting in the escape of others, and participating in plantation rebellions (Davis, 1983). In the

19th century, examples of womanist spiritual activism include the mystics Jarena Lee, Sojourner Truth, and Rebecca Cox Jackson, who engaged spiritual power to influence sociopolitical power (Bostic, 2013). Also, in the 19th and 20th centuries, women of African descent engaged in activism through organizing women's clubs focused on community improvement and self-development, public speaking, fundraising, starting businesses for economic development, building educational institutions, building political organizations, and raising children who loved themselves despite the larger society that did not love them (Giddings, 2007). Key Black women activists before and during the civil rights movement included Ida B. Wells, Mary McLeod Bethune, Anna Julia Cooper, and Mary Church Terrell. They fought against racial, gender, and class oppression, addressing issues such as voting rights, lynching, rape, educational and employment disparities, and labor conditions (Giddings, 2007). African American women participated and played key roles in the civil rights movement, the suffragist movement, and the Black Power movement. Within these movements they held leadership positions, organized and participated in marches and boycotts, and created and maintained programs to nurture and develop leaders within the community (Stewart, Settles, & Winter, 1998). Key Black women in the Black Power movement included Fulani Sunni Ali, Gloria Richardson, Elaine Brown, and Kathleen Cleaver (Collier-Thomas & Franklin, 2001).

Some feminists, Black and White, have promoted a one-sided understanding about Black women's participation in the civil rights and Black Power movements, focusing on the problems of patriarchy they faced and not fully recognizing Black women's influence and agency overall. Sexism has been a reality in these organizations, as racism has been a reality in the women's movement. In the face of these real challenges, Black womanist activists have had a voice and presence that is undeniable.

In contemporary times, womanist activists continue to address a range of issues, from reproductive rights to human trafficking and modern day slavery, and from environmental racism to education reform. Womanism combats patriarchy with an awareness of the key role that racism plays in blocking the liberation of Black people and other racially marginalized peoples. Womanism advocates for liberation for all from every form of oppression and seeks to build communities and individuals who can thrive. Womanists engage in activism from a racialized, gendered perspective that acknowledges history, as well as current sexual and socioeconomic factors. Womanists engage in multiple forms of womanist activism, including kitchen discourse, testifying discourse, and liberatory emergence to empower people of diverse backgrounds to thrive (Bryant-Davis, 2011; Coleman, 2013; Gaines, 2013; Weems, 1991). This activism also includes resistance of oppression and social justice promotion through the arts, teaching, writing, mothering, preaching, advocacy, live and online protest, and political mobilization (Everett, 2004; Harris, 2010; Loder-Jackson, 2012). The use of new media forms, such as Internet sites, to promote and organize protests have demonstrated to Black women that they are not dependent on mainstream media sources to validate their events or themselves (Everett, 2004). These modalities have been used to protest a range of issues, including but not limited to police brutality, sexual and community violence, poverty, inadequate housing and employment, political disenfranchisement, racism, sexism, education reform, immigration reform, heterosexism, health, and corruption in the criminal justice system (Jenkins, 2002; Lau, 2011; West, 2011). Advocacy efforts benefit from social media platforms, such as twitter and Facebook, because they easily facilitate discussions among organizations, news media, and the public and help sustain movement mobilization already taking place (Brown, 2014). Activists working for social justice, including justice issues around race, gender, sexuality, and poverty, have successfully used twitter to disseminate information for awareness raising, education, fundraising, and mobilization purposes (Bonilla & Rosa, 2015; Harp, Bachmann, Rosas-Moreno, & Loke, 2010; Rapp, Button, Fleury-Steiner, & Fleury-Steiner, 2010). Activism serves not only to eradicate oppression but also to empower, mobilize, and raise the morale of the oppressed (Jenkins, 2002).

EXPLORING THE PSYCHOLOGY OF WOMANIST ACTIVISM

Along with political action, womanists recognize a range of place in which activism is necessary, including in the therapy office and the school system. Ramsey (2012) noted that womanist teachers are more than gatekeepers put in place to protect a broken education system but instead are critical decision makers. Teachers as womanist activists understand their role in promoting equity in schools and transformative emotional growth that is rooted in their ethic of care (Ramsey, 2012).

Womanist care stretches us to constructive activism. Three principles of womanist action that were proposed for womanist teaching apply to social justice work for more globally (Cozart & Gordon, 2006). The first principle is *embracing the maternal*—that is, seeing people as connected to us instead of through the lens of the "other" to work for transformation. The second principle is *political clarity*, which is based on not only being motivated to help people as individuals but also seeing the oppression that is systemically reducing their lives. Political clarity also means taking responsibility for the ways in which harm is done by being silent supporters of systems that do harm. As Herman (1997) noted, it is easy to side with perpetrators: All they require is silence, and with silence, people have each supported systems of oppression. Political clarity means seeing oppression on a systemic level and seeing the ways inactivity has done harm. The third principle is *adopting an ethic of risk*: engaging in activism even when one is not guaranteed support or even success. In other words, womanists engage in activism because it is the right thing to do, not because of the benefits it will bring them. They speak up and stand up despite the costs and penalties that can and do come their way. And tomorrow, they do it again. Womanist activism is not a one-time petition or a one-day march. It is a lifelong commitment to working for social justice, even when it is not popular. Womanist activism is not ahistorical; on the contrary, it is deeply rooted in the cultural and historical perspective and it recognizes the urgency of now (Cozart & Gordon, 2006). Contrary to the stereotype that Black women who are concerned with women's rights are less committed to racial justice, a quantitative study found that Black women activists endorsed high rates of feminist and racial identities (White, 2006).

Womanist activism thrives on the participation of everyday women, as opposed to activism of a few charismatic leaders. Based in part on the Black Power movement, it seeks to affirm the culture, heritage, and aesthetics of African Americans and to counter systems that promote inequity. One historical example of womanist activism is the work of womanist teachers during the time of desegregation. These teachers aimed to build and protect the self-esteem of African American children while also working to challenge and disrupt racist educational systems (Ramsey, 2012). From the analysis of this historical example, we argue that womanist activists advocate for gender equality and for positive racial identity, particularly among children. Qualitative womanist research on activism, such as the Ramsey (2012) study, has used oral history interviews, newspapers, government documents, and archival records to centralize the voices and experiences of these womanist teacher activists. The findings from this study uncover the engagement of womanist teachers in combating both racism and sexism, as African American women live at the intersection of multiple forms of oppression (Collins, 2000; Crenshaw, 1989).

Quantitative findings reveal that midlife activism of Black women is predicted by student activism and a high sense of social responsibility (Cole & Stewart, 1996). In an additional study with midlife African American women, those who engaged in collective action felt their work had more of an impact than those who engaged in individual efforts and overall the women thought the civil rights movement had made more of a social impact that the women's movement (Hodari, 1999). It is interesting to note that marital status did not predict level of participation. In a qualitative study that included African American female and male antirape activists, the activists were motivated to act on the basis of race and gender political consciousness, as well as a felt need to speak up and a need to support Black women (White, 2001). In our reading of the qualitative data of womanist activists in Ramsey (2012), we make note of 14 factors about the cognitions, identities, and experiences of womanist activists that provide a framework for understanding the psychology of womanist activists. All 14 factors, listed next, may not exist in the lives of every womanist activist but a number of them may be consistent across persons.

1. Womanist activists are aware of the realities of contemporary oppression as a result of individuals being both direct targets and bearing witness to the trauma of oppression within their communities.
2. Womanists see the reality of oppression but still believe excellence is possible.
3. Womanists activist often have had prior exposure to remarkable womanist leaders who inspired their path.
4. Womanist activists have personal experiences with oppression from which they have shown resistance.
5. Womanists show an early capacity to engage without intimidation across cultural lines, including acts of resistance in childhood or adolescence.
6. Womanist activists demonstrate courage and confidence in the face of discrimination.
7. Womanists activists seek out exposure to knowledge that will assist in the empowerment of their community.
8. Womanists activists have often been exposed to positive racial socialization from family and/or community members such as teachers.
9. Womanist activists embody struggle and success, similar to the conception of posttraumatic growth which highlights the coexistence of despair and thriving.
10. Womanists who engage in activism do so at a cost, emotionally, socially, and economically. They have been penalized through isolation, rejection, stigma, violence and threats of violence, as well as loss of employment.
11. Womanists activists recognize and build on the gains of the civil rights movement and the feminist movement.
12. Womanists activists possess an anticipatory lens. On the basis of prior experience with subjugation, they can and do foresee experiences of oppression and work to prevent them or lessen their impact. This can be demonstrated in the aftermath of legalization of integrated schools. Womanist teachers and parents knew that the African American children who were sent to White schools would face difficult racist environments and individuals that could damage them physically and psychologically. With this knowledge, they made attempts to build up the

psychological and spiritual resources of their youth to protect them and assist them with the adjustment to their new contexts while seeking to maintain their knowledge of their worth.

13. Womanist activists recognize the value of and work to develop skills for meditation and difficult dialogues by adopting leadership styles based on honesty, boldness, and fairness.
14. Womanist activists appreciate a holistic, interdisciplinary approach to transformation.

Research examining social activism, volunteerism and altruism remains in its infancy. The predominant literature that has examined these practices has not focused on the way in which sociocultural factors may influence the expression of activism, volunteerism, and altruism. Womanism, defined as a commitment to the fusion of multiple identities, is chiefly concerned with combating multiple oppressions (DeBlaere & Bertsch, 2013; Garth, 1994). When observed from a womanist framework, it is easier to anchor such abstract, multifaceted concepts of prosocial engagement. Engagement in social activism and helping behavior underscores the womanist's commitment to the survival and thriving of all people. Womanist theology as a liberation theology emphasizes strengths and connectedness, and calls for proactive participation in the dismantling of various forms of oppression, including but not limited to racism, sexism, and classism. In the following section, we use a womanist framework to provide an overview of prosocial activities, such as activism, volunteerism, and altruism, to highlight the way in which engagement affects well-being.

COMMUNITY ENGAGEMENT

Research related to which individuals are most likely to engage in activism, volunteerism, and altruistic endeavors has not always considered the importance of contextualized factors. As Williams (2004) asserted in social movement–based literature, culture was typically presented as a mediating variable between structural opportunity and action. Culture was assumed to have little or no direct influence on mobilization of social action. However, newer approaches to conceptualizing social engagement have considered the role of cultural values (Williams, 2004). When various cultural values, including gender, ethnicity, and socioeconomic status, are considered, notable demographic differences in community engagement are observed (Cruce & Moore, 2007; Lopez et al., 2006; Rosenthal, Feiring, & Lewis, 1998). Generally speaking, female, ethnic minorities, and other marginalized groups (e.g., lesbian, gay, bisexual, and transgendered; those with a disability) are more likely to participate in community engagement than males and Caucasians.

Civic engagement has been associated with purpose and meaning-making processes. Several scholars have observed the association between religiosity and social engagement, whereby belonging to religious groups increases adolescents' (McLellan & Youniss, 2003) as well as adults' (Garland, Myers, & Wolfer, 2008) likelihood of participating in community activities. Peer, as well as familial, contexts also influence civic engagement, with individuals whose parents engage in volunteerism and activism being more likely to do so themselves (McLellan & Youniss, 2003). Levels of religiosity, as well as familial influence, are associated with increasing volunteer-oriented individuals' sense of purpose such that they are able to make greater sense of the world around them and instigate changes.

One of the pillars of African identity is a commitment to communalism. The African-derived belief "I am because we are; and since we are therefore I am" underscores the notion of communalism, whereby one's community is also one's extended family (Asante, 1987; Hord & Lee, 1995; White, 2001). This saying serves as an anchor for understanding African Americans' participation in community engagement activities. As White (2001) suggested, this creed describes a political consciousness that has proven integral to African American survival and resistance to oppression. The desire for racial solidarity coupled with a yearning to combat oppression serves as a vehicle for community engagement within the African American community.

Below are our testimonies, in poetic and narrative form. The goal of sharing our stories is to provide context about the various experiences that shape, transform and ignite a womanist spirit.

TESTIMONY: THEMA BRYANT-DAVIS

As a womanist, I know it is important to acknowledge my identity and journey as it intersects with this chapter. The following is my (previously unpublished) poetic testimony and it reveals the spiritual roots that led to my evolution as a womanist, artist, scholar, and activist.

Train up a child in the way she should go and when she grows old she will not depart

It starts in the heart
In the seeds that are planted but unspoken
that spring forward into thoughts, words, and actions
Creating reactions for years to come
As I think back on what it took for me to become who I am today
I flip back through the pages and remember the early stages that made a difference
My mother brought me journals to pen my thoughts asked me from the age of 5 what I thought it would take to heal the world

I was only a girl but one who was trained to believe my life could and should make a difference
Decades later I write and think and work for solutions to address spiritual, political, and emotional pollution that tarnishes the air
I am the daughter of two ministers, and the word they planted in me came through
Years after running from the call, I took my soul off of hold and answered
Responding to the fire that was burning within making me speak out even when I tried to hide
The overflow that was dancing inside my throat
But years before that it was my mother, one of the first African American praise dancers, who put me in African and ballet classes before I could form complex sentences
It is no mystery dance became my first language
When life happened in ways for which I had no words I could contract and release
Plié and relevé, pirouette through the pain and jete over stumbling blocks
She gave me dance and it became my medicine and my weapon, my tool and my vocabulary
She did not give me lessons in home economics, never learned to sew or to make homemade pie crust
She gave me scriptures and verbs, synonyms and antonyms, geography and theology
I have no memories of sitting at sewing machine with my mother over my shoulder
Only memories of going with my mother to visit those bound in bed in nursing homes and hospitals
I would dance, my brother would pray, and my mother would serve communion
These are the days of my life
My mother never taught me to flirt
She taught me to think
Once when my mother was hospitalized for a surgery
My father picked out my hair in an Afro
He tied a big yellow ribbon on it and told me I was a queen
I felt like royalty until I got to school and everyone laughed at me
I cried
Confused, ashamed, angry that I been set up for this letdown
My parents didn't give into my pleadings for Revlon until high school
But 6 years later I returned to my roots
Celebrating my natural hair required supernatural courage for some
For me it was just a homecoming
A remembering of the woman I was divinely created to be

Free to be me
I grew up seeing my father sitting at the dining room table writing and then rewriting and then practicing his sermons
I would hear his faint, rhythmic voice going over each point
I saw the background work required for what others simply attributed to glossy shine
I saw integrity and care were needed for excellence
I remember one night in Baltimore hearing a woman crying outside for help
My mother was the only one on the block who called the police
Carving action into my cerebellum that manifests today in petals of domestic violence activism
Sitting on the sidelines was never an option
My father told us about his years in the Peace Corps and always had voter registration at our church sitting upon layers of Kwanzaa celebrations, job fair icing, and fired up protest marches with me on his shoulders
Service and pride in my people were served to me with the love that some parents serve apple pie
All of this
Their words and their songs
Their sermons, their standing up, and their speaking out
Have carved out the woman standing here today
We are echoes of yesterday manifesting in today's realities
We have choices yet our tools have been handed to us from those who came before us
We must be ever careful, ever mindful of the unspoken lessons we are downloading in the spirits of our seeds
For whatsoever you sow, that you shall also reap
and the good news is the harvest you pull up you can also keep

TESTIMONY: TYONNA ADAMS

The moment I began accepting my intersecting identities is the moment I began accepting and embracing an activist spirit. The role of spirituality as well as social interactions were paramount to the development of my own Black, female, womanist consciousness, profoundly impacting my worldview.

Growing up, I always felt stuck between two different worlds. Rich and poor. White and Black. So many labels were assigned to me upon my birth, and as a child and adolescent, it was extremely difficult, sometimes even painful, to make sense of my identity. The most painful experiences were assumptions made about me due to the color of my skin, the way I talked, and the clothes I wore. As a young Black girl, I did not, and still do not, fit into society's definition of how a Black woman is supposed to act, talk, or look.

For this reason, labels such as "White-washed" and "oreo," and sentiments of "not being Black enough" were frequently bestowed upon me growing up. I spent countless nights wrestling with what it meant to "be Black" and trying to fit into society's narrow definition of Blackness. Through this exploration, I developed an increased sense of self and discovered strength, hidden beneath years of feeling inadequate.

School provided me with my first experience of difference. This experience of difference in school had a profound influence on my decision to pursue psychology. I attended elementary school in an affluent community with a large Caucasian population, an area outside of my neighborhood. I remember looking around and only seeing one other student who looked like me. This feeling of difference remained with me for many years and was brought to the forefront (in a different way) when I moved to Southeast San Diego, an area primarily populated by African American and Mexican American families. The perceived notion of difference related to socioeconomic status tainted my interactions with several of my peers, who labeled me as "White washed" and assumed that I had money. This experience was particularly troubling for me, as it highlighted intraracial conflict. In high school, I was one of three African Americans who participated in honors and advanced placement classes, which posed a unique set of challenges. Whenever we discussed literature such as *Beloved* (Morrison, 1987) or *Native Son* (Wright, 1940), I felt pressure to describe the African American perspective to my Caucasian peers, which led to several microinvalidations.

College provided me with an opportunity to explore Afrocentricity, affiliate with Pan-African organizations, and learn about African American history. I was angered at not learning about the contributions of my people in America and across the world. During a multicultural counseling course, my peers maintained a strong reliance on a Eurocentric worldview and an unwillingness to consider unique experiences and perspectives. I was the most outspoken and perhaps the most different of the three people of color in the classroom, because of coming from socioeconomic life experiences that were the most divergent from those of the other class members. I remember getting into an argument with a fellow classmate who implied that I was colluding with the professor simply because we were both ethnic minorities. This experience marked another instance of tiredness as it relates to dealing with societal strife.

College afforded me the opportunity to explore a new aspect of my identity: my womanhood. Having been raised by several strong Black women, I knew what strength was; however, it was not until I was in college and encountered greater discrimination and struggles that I was challenged to find my own strength. I enrolled in numerous ethnic studies as well as women's studies courses, participated in the *Vagina Monologues* (Ensler, 1996), and joined a service organization with a strong feminist focus. This progression seemed natural in some ways, given the pervasiveness of violence experienced by women in my family. However, having been known as a shy, quiet, insecure girl, this signaled a progression into an activist world. As part of Marians Service Organization, I served on the executive board and helped stimulate conversations about gendered identity, sexual violence, culture, and women's health issues. We held demonstrations across campus centered on intimate partner violence, sexual violence, breast cancer, and a forums about feminism: Deconstructing the F Word.

Despite affiliating with like-minded people with similar views about gendered identity, voices of feminists of color were not as prominent. I remember attending a specific Deconstructing the F Word forum, which focused on feminists of color, their unique challenges, and the ways in which they overcome racial as well as gendered subjugation. This was a defining moment because it prompted deeper exploration of my identity as and ways of navigating my intersecting ethnic, gender, and social identities. Some of the questions that I found myself reflecting on following the discussion were, What am I passionate about? What is my identity? What centers and motivates me?

I found myself seeking out conversations with other feminists of color, as well as reflecting about my intersecting identities. I began engaging in conversations about the intersectionality of identity and exploring what it means to be a feminist as well as a Black woman, subject to racial and gendered discrimination. This exploration led me to discover inspirational works by Black, female authors, poets, spiritualists and activists. Ultimately, I found that the term that best fits me is *womanist*. Womanism seems more fitting because it most clearly encapsulates my experience as a woman of color experiencing a double-burdened existence. As I explored my identity as a womanist, I became interested in feminist psychology as a discipline. I became grossly aware of intergenerational racial norms and the privileges I hold as a light-skinned, heterosexual Black woman. I also began examining my own biases about gender norms and sexuality and working on challenging readily held and accepted schemas within the African American community.

CONCLUSION

Nurturance and empowerment of the African American community through caring activism, resistance training, positive gender and racial socialization, and community service are continually needed, as is combating forces and systems of oppression. Noting that a change of times can require a change of strategy, Crosby (1993, as cited in Ramsey, 2012) advised,

> I don't advise anybody to be quite as outspoken as I have been. It doesn't work now. . . . They need to be firm, but tread in a way that will not hurt

them. But, I would always tell them not to be afraid to tell the truth, even though it hurts. I don't have any regrets. (p. 263)

Throughout their history in the United States and the history of their foremothers in Africa, Black women have communally examined issues of race, class, and gender oppression and have organized political agendas, held press conferences, taught and learned paramilitary training, and worked in decision-making circles in their organizations (Gaines, 2013). Womanists have engaged in liberation work in informal kitchen settings and on the front lines of protest movements. The spirit and fire of womanist activism continues to burn and can be seen in the contemporary efforts of new millennium womanists who continue to rise and roar.

We end this chapter with a poem that I (Thema Bryant-Davis) wrote in response to an event in 2014. A 16-year-old African American girl named Jada was sexually assaulted, and images of her while she was undressed and unconscious were spread on social media. Instead of outrage and compassion, people made jokes about Jada. But instead of hiding, Jada came forward, did interviews, and led marches to address violence against women and girls. Her activism, at such a young age and in the aftermath of a vicious and public assault, inspired many to engage in social justice and to resist silence and shame.

I am Jada
I refuse to live in exile from myself
Will not hide my face
Will not run in disgrace
I am volcano
Angry at injustice
yet resisting the lava of self-destruction
My silence will not be an obstruction
To my resurrection
Phoenix rising from the ashes
They thought they ruined me
Assumed they could shame me into silence
But silence no more I was born to roar
Born to soar
My mind floats to places far beyond the prison of their assumptions
Their opinion of me is irrelevant
My voice is significant
Violated victim is not the sum total of my identity
Look a little deeper
Fist raised
Shoulders back
Head up

Voice steady
Eyes seeing beyond the mud they threw at my face
Exposed my vulnerability
Exposed their false masculinity
I counter their punch with a knock out
Because I refuse to go away
I will not be swayed by those who blame me for their desecration of my temple
I am sacred space
I am valuable
I woke up this morning still hungry for justice
I will sleep tonight dreaming of the me I was meeting the woman I shall be despite my current reality
I am storm survivor
I did not chase this storm but since they picked me
I will paint rainbows in the future and cast my gaze there
I see a place where my sisters and I can laugh loudly, dance freely, speak openly, live safely
Come on
I'll take you there

REFERENCES

Asante, M. (1987). *The Afrocentric idea*. Philadelphia, PA: Temple University Press.

Bell, E. L. J. E., & Nkomo, S. M. (1998). Armoring: Learning to withstand racial oppression. *Journal of Comparative Family Studies*, *29*(2), 285–295. Retrieved from http://www.jstor.org/stable/41603565

Bonilla, Y., & Rosa, J. (2015). #Ferguson: Digital protest, hashtag ethnography, and the racial politics of social media in the United States. *American Ethnologist*, *42*, 4–17. http://dx.doi.org/10.1111/amet.12112

Boyd-Franklin, N. (2003). *Black families in therapy: Understanding the African American Experience* (2nd ed.). New York, NY: Guilford Press.

Bostic, J. (2013). *African-American female mysticism: Nineteenth-century religious activism*. London, England: Palgrave. http://dx.doi.org/10.1057/9781137375056

Brown, R. R. (2014). *Trayvon Martin and election 2012 social media messaging: An analysis of framing, rhetoric, and media types in online messages by civil rights organizations*. Retrieved from http://aquila.usm.edu/dissertations/164/

Bryant-Davis, T. (2011). The birthing of a womanist psychologist: On becoming a guide to healing and empowerment. In L. Comas-Díaz & M. B. Weiner (Eds.), *Women psychotherapists: Journeys in healing* (pp. 1–13). Lanham, MD: Jason Aronson.

Cole, E. R., & Stewart, A. J. (1996). Meanings of political participation among Black and White women: Political identity and social responsibility. *Journal of Personality and Social Psychology, 71*, 130–140. http://dx.doi.org/10.1037/0022-3514.71.1.130

Coleman, M. (2013). *Ain't I a womanist too? Third wave womanist religious thought*. Minneapolis, MN: Fortress Press.

Collier-Thomas, B. & Franklin, V. P. (2001). *Sisters in the struggle: Black women in the Civil Rights-Black Power movement*. New York, NY: New York University Press.

Collins, P. H. (2000). *Black feminist thought: Knowledge, consciousness, and the politics of empowerment* (2nd ed.). New York, NY: Routledge.

Cozart, S., & Gordon, J. (2006). Using womanist caring as a framework to teach social foundations. *The High School Journal*, 90, 9–15. http://dx.doi.org/10.1353/hsj.2006.0010

Crenshaw, K. (1989). Demarginalizing the intersection of race and sex: A Black feminist critique of antidiscrimination doctrine, feminist theory, and antiracist politics. *University of Chicago Legal Forum, 149*, 139–167.

Crosby, K. (1993, June 9). *Interview by Sonya Ramsey* [Audiotape recording]. Durham, NC: Special Collections of the Duke University Library.

Cruce, T. M., & Moore, J. V. (2007). First-year students' plans to volunteer: An examination of the predictors of community service participation. *Journal of College Student Development*, 48, 655–673. http://dx.doi.org/10.1353/csd.2007.0063

Davis, A. Y. (1983). *Women, race, and class*. Visalia, CA: Vintage Press.

DeBlaere, C., & Bertsch, K. N. (2013). Perceived sexist events and psychological distress of sexual minority women of color: The moderating role of womanism. *Psychology of Women Quarterly*, 37, 167–178. http://dx.doi.org/10.1177/0361684312470436

Ensler, E. (1996). *Vagina monologues* [Episodic play]. New York, NY: HERE Arts Center.

Everett, A. (2004). On cyberfeminism and cyberwomanism: High-tech mediations of feminism's discontents. *Signs: Journal of Women in Culture and Society*, 30, 1278–1286. http://dx.doi.org/10.1086/422235

Gaines, R. (2013). *"I am a revolutionary Black female nationalist": A womanist analysis of Fulani Sunni Ali's role as a new African citizen and minister of information in the provisional government of the Republic of New Africa* (Doctoral dissertation). Georgia State University, Atlanta. Retrieved from http://scholarworks.gsu.edu/communication_diss/44

Garland, D. R., Myers, D. M., & Wolfer, T. A. (2008). Social work with religious volunteers: Activating and sustaining community involvement. *Social Work*, 53, 255–265. http://dx.doi.org/10.1093/sw/53.3.255

Garth, P. H. (1994). A new knowledge: Feminism from an Afrocentric perspective. *Thresholds in Education*, 20, 8–13.

Giddings, P. J. (2007). *When and where I enter: The impact of Black women on race and sex in America*. New York, NY: Williams & Morror.

Harp, D., Bachmann, I., Rosas-Moreno, T. C., & Loke, J. (2010). Wave of hope: African American youth use media and engage more civically, politically than Whites. *Howard Journal of Communications, 21*, 224–246. http://dx.doi.org/10.1080/10646175.2010.496662

Harris, M. (2010). *Gifts of virtue, Alice Walker, and womanist ethics*. London, England: Palgrave. http://dx.doi.org/10.1057/9780230113930

Herman, J. (1997). *Trauma and recovery: The aftermath of violence—from domestic abuse to political terror*. New York, NY: Basic Books.

Hodari, A. J. (1999, November). Social action and Black women of the protest generation at mid-life: Issues of participation, effect orientation, and impact (Civil Rights Movement, Women's Movement, social movements). *Dissertation Abstracts International: The Sciences and Engineering, 60B*, 2409.

Hord, F. L., & Lee, J. S. (Eds.). (1995). *I am because we are: Readings in Black philosophy*. Amherst: University of Massachusetts Press.

Jenkins, E. J. (2002). Black women and community violence: Trauma, grief, and coping. *Women & Therapy, 25*, 29–44. http://dx.doi.org/10.1300/J015v25n03_03

Lau, K. J. (2011). *Body language: Sisters in shape, black women's fitness, and feminist identity politics*. Philadelphia, PA: Temple University Press.

Loder-Jackson, T. L. (2012). Hope and despair: Southern Black women educators across pre- and post-Civil Rights cohorts theorize about their activism. *Educational Studies: Journal of the American Educational Studies Association, 48*, 266–295. http://dx.doi.org/10.1080/00131946.2012.660665

Lopez, M. H., Levine, P., Both, D., Kiesa, A., Kriby, E., & Marcelo, K. (2006). *The 2006 civic and political health of the nation: A detailed look at how youth participate in politics and communities*. College Park, MD: The Center for Information and Research on Civic Learning and Engagement.

McLellan, J. A., & Youniss, J. (2003). Two systems of youth service. Determinants of voluntary and required community service. *Journal of Youth and Adolescence, 32*, 47–58. http://dx.doi.org/10.1023/A:1021032407300

Morrison, T. (1987). *Beloved*. New York, NY: Knopf.

Phillips, L. (2006). Womanism: On its own. In L. Phillips (Ed.), *The womanist reader* (pp. 405–450). New York, NY: Routledge.

Ramsey, S. (2012). Caring is activism: Black Southern womanist teachers theorizing and the careers of Kathleen Crosby and Bertha Maxwell-Roddey, 1946–1986. *Educational Studies, 48*, 244–265.

Rapp, L., Button, D. M., Fleury-Steiner, B., & Fleury-Steiner, R. (2010). The Internet as a tool for Black feminist activism: Lessons from an online antirape protest. *Feminist Criminology, 5*, 244–262. http://dx.doi.org/10.1177/1557085110371634

Rosenthal, S., Feiring, C., & Lewis, M. (1998). Political volunteering from late adolescence to young adulthood: Patterns and predictors. *Journal of Social Issues, 54*, 477–493. http://dx.doi.org/10.1111/j.1540-4560.1998.tb01231.x

Sakuma, A. (2014, October 12). Women hold the front-lines in Ferguson. *MSNBC*. http://www.msnbc.com/msnbc/women-hold-the-front-lines-ferguson

Stewart, A. J., Settles, I. H., & Winter, N. G. (1998). Women and the social movements of the 1960s: Activists, engaged observers, and nonparticipants. *Political Psychology, 19*, 63–94. http://dx.doi.org/10.1111/0162-895X.00093

Taylor, J. Y. (2004). Moving from surviving to thriving: African American women recovering from intimate male partner abuse. *Research and Theory For Nursing Practice: An International Journal, 18*, 35–50. http://dx.doi.org/10.1891/rtnp.18.1.35.28056

Thompson, A. (2003). Caring in context: Four feminist theories on gender and education. *Curriculum Inquiry, 33*, 9–65. http://dx.doi.org/10.1111/1467-873X.t01-1-00249

Walker, A. (2003). *In search of our mothers' gardens: Womanist prose*. Orlando, FL: Harvest.

Weems, R. (1991). *Just a sister away: A womanist's vision of relationships in the bible.* Philadelphia, PA: Innisfree Press.

West, C. M. (2011). Black women and intimate partner violence: New directions for research. *Journal of Interpersonal Violence, 19*, 1487–1493. http://dx.doi.org/10.1177/0886260504269700

White, A. M. (2006). Racial and gender attitudes as predictors of feminist activism among self-identified African American feminists. *The Journal of Black Psychology, 32*, 455–478. http://dx.doi.org/10.1177/0095798406292469

White, A. M. (2001). I am because we are: Combined race and gender political consciousness among African American women and men anti-rape activists. *Women's Studies International Forum, 24*, 11–24. http://dx.doi.org/10.1016/S0277-5395(00)00167-9

Williams, J. E. (2004). Vanguards of hope: The role of culture in mobilizing African American women's social activism in Arkansas. *Sociological Spectrum, 24*, 129–156. http://dx.doi.org/10.1080/02732170490271753

Wright, R. (1940). *Native son*. New York, NY: Harper & Brothers.

10

MUJERISTAS AND SOCIAL JUSTICE: *LA LUCHA ES LA VIDA*

CARRIE L. CASTAÑEDA-SOUND, SUSANA MARTINEZ, AND JOSEFINA E. DURÁN

> Mujerista is one who knows how to be faithful to the task of making justice and peace flourish, who opt for God's cause and the law of love. (Isasi-Díaz, 1989, p. 560)

With scholarly origins in the field of feminist theology, Isasi-Díaz was the renowned theologian who gave voice to Latina spirituality and the lived experience of *mujerismo* for "grassroots Latinas." *Mujerista* theology (Isasi-Díaz, 1996) blends culture, gender, and spirituality with liberation and social consciousness. Although previous chapters in this volume presented her groundbreaking work and its relevance to Latina spirituality, this chapter shifts the lens from mujerista theology and proposes a mujerista psychology of social justice by drawing from scholarly literature about social justice in psychology (e.g., participatory action research [PAR]), Latina feminist psychology, and *testimonio* (testimony) as a form of resistance and as a tool for healing in therapeutic contexts. The lived experience of mujeristas in the community as *promotoras* or as participants in *Las Guadalupanas* is also be presented. We conclude the chapter with a testimonio by one of the coauthors of this chapter (Josefina E. Durán) and a subsequent discussion of the themes from her

http://dx.doi.org/10.1037/14937-011
Womanist and Mujerista Psychologies: Voices of Fire, Acts of Courage, T. Bryant-Davis and L. Comas-Díaz (Editors)

testimonio that illustrate mujerista psychology and social justice. Josefina's life is particularly relevant to this discussion because of her experiences of liberation theology in Latin America, the feminist movement in the United States, and a friendship and collaboration with Dr. Isasi-Díaz. Because there is no "typical" Latina, this discussion demonstrates that mujerista psychology deepens an understanding of the diverse lives of Latinas.

LATINAS IN THE UNITED STATES

Inherent in the process of contextualizing the experiences of Latinas residing in the United States is the challenge to accurately capture the complexity of their identities. In this chapter, *Latinas/os* refers to women and men in the United States with ancestry from a Latin American country. *Latina* refers to women, and *Latino* refers to men. Almost half of the nearly 53 million individuals of Hispanic origin residing in the United States are women (Brow & Patten, 2014), composing 15% of all women in the United States (U.S. Census Bureau, 2010). Although they are the largest female ethnic group of color, not all Latinas with ancestry descending from Spanish-speaking countries identify with the pan-ethnic terms *Hispanic* or *Latina/o*. Surveys of Latinas/os indicate a preference to identify with the country of origin of their family (e.g., Salvadoran, Puerto Rican; Pew Hispanic Center [PHC], 2012). In fact, 43% of second-generation Latinas/os living in the United States still prefer to identify with their family's country of origin. Furthermore, the racial identification of individuals of Hispanic origin is complex, with comparable differences between the PHC's (2012) survey and the U.S. Census survey (Humes, Jones, & Ramirez, 2011). In response to PHC's survey, 51% of Latinas/os reported they are "some other race"; 36% identified as White; 25% volunteered that their race was Hispanic or Latino; and 10% chose Black, Asian, or mixed race. This contrasts with the U.S. Census Bureau's (2010) results indicating that only 37% of Latinas/os chose "some other race" and 53% identified as White. These examples of the difficulty in presenting a "profile" of Latinas underscores the importance of examining intersecting identities in addition to race and ethnicity such as generational status within the United States, socioeconomic status (SES), and religion.

Although more Latinas/os (64.5%) are U.S. born than are foreign born (35.5%), experiences of xenophobia, the fear or hatred of foreigners, affects both native and foreign born, and is a serious social justice concern (Lopez, Morin, & Taylor, 2010). A Latina could be any race, but because of Eurocentric conceptualizations equating Whiteness with Americanness within the United States, Latinas/os often have been racialized and deemed un-American and foreign (Golash-Boza, 2006). Racialization, coupled with colorism, and privilege afforded a person solely based on the color of their skin (Hunter, 2005), between and within different ethnic groups, has implications for racial self-identification of Latinas and may help explain the variability in responses to questions about race. Essentially, the valuing of lighter skin and prejudice against those with darker skin is a phenomenon evidenced in many cultures, but it is particularly salient for Latinas/os who descend from Latin American countries where hierarchies based on skin color have a historical precedent and are salient for access to privilege and power (Chavez-Dueñas, Adames, & Organista, 2014).

Also salient to the lives of Latinas are socioeconomic factors, which have been linked to physical and mental health outcomes (Gallo et al., 2013; Xu, 2011). In particular, the relationship between low SES and stress has been identified as a component in physical health disparities such as cardiovascular disease and Type 2 diabetes (Thoits, 2010). Gallo et al. (2013) examined the relationship of Mexican American women's SES level on their self-reported stress levels. Although women with high SES reported less perceived stress and more control in their lives, they did have higher chronic stress associated with chronic work and caregiving stress. The researchers also found a negative association between income and chronic housing and financial stress. Furthermore, many of the relationships of SES and stress were stable across levels of acculturation. Thus, it is important to acknowledge that high levels of stress can affect Latinas of both high and low SES, and different generational statuses. These results have implications for both physical and mental well-being of Latinas.

Differentiating within-group differences of Latinas/os is also critical when considering the relationship between SES and mental health. For example, although Cubans tend to be higher educated and have higher income earnings than do other Latinas/os, they too have within-group differences based on the qualitatively different experiences in the United States due to the different waves of immigration, premigration economic status, colorism, and postmigration access to resources. Xu (2011) examined ethnic variations of Cubans, Puerto Ricans, and Mexicans in relation to SES and psychological distress by measuring income, education, and wealth as indicators of SES. *Wealth* refers to "accumulated assets that people can use in time of emergencies or economic shocks" (Xu, 2011, p. 213) and is distributed more unequally than income in the United States (Keister & Moller, 2000). Results indicated that for all three groups wealth was stronger than education and income in predicting psychological distress. As Xu explained, "Wealth captures the financial wellbeing and security of a family, which income is not capable of measuring" (p. 221). In fact, people can have the same income level, yet have divergent levels of wealth. A conceptualization of SES that includes income, educational level, and wealth provides a multidimensional understanding of the effects of SES on psychological functioning.

Clearly, the demographic portrait of Latinas is rich with diversity, and examining every area of diversity (e.g., sexual orientation, education, generational status) is beyond the scope of this chapter. Most important is an understanding of intersectionality of these identities and the resulting effects on the lives of Latinas as they grow in consciousness. Fortunately, mujerista psychology provides a rich framework for this area of research and theoretical conceptualization that is often overlooked by mainstream Eurocentric psychology. Informed by both Latina feminism and liberatory paradigms, mujerista psychology weaves the spiritual, relational, and historical with social justice and political action.

LATINA FEMINIST PSYCHOLOGY AND MUJERISMO

Just as Isasi-Díaz (1996) identified the exclusion of Latina experiences in feminist theology, women of color noticed the same gap within the feminist movement in psychology in the 1970s (Russo & Vaz, 2001). Womanism and Chicana/Latina feminism developed as a result of these gaps in the 1980s and inspired a new generation of feminist psychologists. Although Latina feminisms and mujerismo substantially overlap, the role of spirituality is much more prominent in mujerista perspectives, reflecting its origins in theology. Nevertheless, Isasi-Díaz (1996) characterized the shift of consciousness of mujeristas as a call for "mutuality" and shared power with White feminists. Russo and Vaz (2001) described the subsequent multicultural feminist theories as having "diverse definitions, ideologies, and analyses of the political, economic, and social inequalities experienced by women" (p. 281). This movement also (de)centered objective science as the only source of legitimate knowledge and focused on the complex, subjective experiences of oppression and consciousness.

Major influences on the psychological conceptualization of Latinas' experiences have originated from the literary world, such as the work of Gloria Anzaldúa (1987). Anzaldúa developed a theory of the borderland not only to refer to the shared border of the United States and Mexico but also to illustrate the borderlands of identity, language, and spirituality for Latinas. Although initially applied to the lives of Mexican American women, her theoretical work has been adopted to conceptualize the oppressive experiences (as well as resilience) of Afro-Peruvian women (Falcón, 2008), and the mental health of bisexual individuals (Brewster, Moradi, DeBlaere, & Velez, 2013). Anzaldúa coined the construct *mestiza consciousness*, which addresses the awareness of injustice, the flexibility to shift between identities and the demands of the environment, and a tolerance for ambiguity and contradictions that Latinas use to successfully navigate the shift from personal and professional contexts. That the theory originated out of the lived experience of a Chicana who embraced many identities (Tejana, lesbiana, mestiza, feminist, poet, scholar, etc.) underscores the applicability to a collective identity of individuals from all walks of life and a variety of scholarly disciplines.

TESTIMONIO

Another example of a literary tradition that has informed understandings of Latinas is testimonio. Testimonio involves firsthand accounts, or life stories, that are transcribed by another person and recount personal and collective experiences of oppression. Smith (2010) explained that the different genres of testimonies include nonfiction and historical fiction, and are "resistance text" (p. 26). For example, through testimonio literary works, Latin American women have taken on abusive governmental regimes in countries such as Argentina, Guatemala, and Chile by bringing to light stories of oppression, exile, and extreme violence. Unfortunately, within Eurocentric circles of the literary world, authors of testimonies have been met with critique bordering on disdain. In addition to challenges with categorizing testimonios in the preexisting categories of fiction, nonfiction, or history, issues of the legitimacy and ownership of voice (e.g., who tells and who retells the story) are central issues (Smith, 2010). Historically, the voice of the other and the self is a concern for both feminist researchers and psychologists, and Brabeck (2003) contended that disrupting otherness requires examination of "our own positions in addition to the positions of others, and to explore how these positions interact and intersect" (p. 253). By centering often-untold stories, testimonio facilitates engagement by giving voice to both the oppressive story and the resistance narrative (Brabeck, 2003).

Although a testimonio is one person's story, it often reflects a communal experience of systemic oppression that includes violence and terror. Cienfuegos and Monelli (1983) implemented testimonios in their treatment of survivors of systematic abuse and torture by the Chilean military. Using a psychodynamic framework, the psychologists applied testimonio to their clinical work by audio recording clients' stories. The method of recording the testimonio required three to six sessions and involved explaining to the patients that the process of telling the story helps clinicians understand the emotions associated with the trauma, while providing the space for patients to "denounce, through a written essay, the violence and injustice to which they have been subjected" (Cienfuegos & Monelli, 1983, p. 48). The testimonios were in the client's own words, and the clinician asked questions solely for clarity of important events. The clinicians then integrated the patient's pretrauma history to create a historical context for the testimonio, transcribed the testimonio to text, and reviewed and edited it with the patient. The authors reported that initially their goal was to record the stories of the instances of torture for purposes of cataloging the abuses, but they quickly learned that providing testimonio was therapeutic for their patents. Specifically, patients that had experienced extreme torture and imprisonment benefitted most from testimonio, whereas the least success was with relatives of victims who were missing. The authors note that an important differentiation of testimonio from other forms of life story is that the trauma story "helps patients to integrate the traumatic experience into their lives by identifying its significance in the context of political and social events as well as the context of their personal history" (Cienfuegos & Monelli, 1983, p. 50).

The clinical implications of testimonio for the field of psychology are tremendous but should be considered with care, so as not to favor a single-story explanation of trauma. Cienfuegos and Monelli (1983) captured this in their method of framing the testimonio as process for denouncing the oppression. White (2000), an innovator in narrative therapy, explained the importance of identifying the multiple stories of trauma, and examining positions of power and meaning,

> [It is] in single-storied conversations that are informed by modern notions of catharsis that there is always the risk of contributing to re-traumatization and to renewed distress, and to the reinforcement of those negative identity conclusions that are so often the outcome of being in a subject position in relation to experiences that are traumatic or disqualifying. I do not believe that it is acceptable for therapeutic conversations to contribute to re-traumatisation or renewed distress, or to the reinforcement of people's negative identity conclusions. (p. 41)

Delineating the theoretical foundations of narrative therapy is beyond the scope of this chapter, but it is important to note that movement toward emphasizing the interpersonal, historical, and sociocultural contributions is the heart of a mujerista psychology.

Comas-Díaz (2000, 2006), who has provided notable contributions to understanding the needs of Latinas/os in psychotherapy, noted the importance of spiritual, community, and cultural connection to healing. Of particular relevance to mujerista perspectives is her work about Latina/o healing (Comas-Díaz, 2006) and the importance of using an ethnopolitical approach with people of color (Comas-Díaz, 2000). These frameworks compel practitioners to be knowledgeable of and place culturally congruent healing at the center of psychological practice. Examples include (a) the use of language to create new meanings through *cuentos* (storytelling) and *dichos* (idioms and sayings), (b) an understanding of the implications for well-being and psychotherapy of cultural values such as *familismo* (familism), *respeto* (respect), *simpatía* (social harmony), and *sabiduría* (a spiritually informed wisdom), and (c) contextualizing clients' lives using a sociopolitical framework that addresses historical and interpersonal colonization. Comas-Díaz's scholarly work continues to empower psychologists, in particular, Latina feminist psychologists, to respond to the call of returning to our ethnic sabiduría as a form of social justice within the Latina/o community.

SOCIAL JUSTICE WORK IN PSYCHOLOGY

Social justice has been an area of much debate in the field of psychology, as researchers and practitioners balance psychology's scientific background with the field's responsibility to promote human welfare. Social justice perspectives also challenge the long-standing individualist models by focusing on the social realities of individuals and communities. In recent years the field has become increasingly committed to addressing social justice issues in psychological research and practice (Ali & Lees, 2013; Hook & Davis, 2012; Vasquez, 2012). Much of this commitment to social justice exists from the recognition of an unjust history in psychology of racist themes and theories that maintained oppressive discourses in society (Vasquez, 2012). The field has also been gaining a greater appreciation for the social realities of individuals and how these realities impact psychological well-being.

Although the efforts to integrate social justice and psychology have been greater in the past few decades, the history of advocacy and passion for social change in the field is extensive. Kurt Lewin is noted as one of the founders of social psychology and is influential in the discipline with his views against oppression and for egalitarianism (Jost & Kay, 2010). Inspiration for a socially just practice also dates back to the work and passion of psychologists confronting the experience and consequences of war. For example, World War II influenced the development of a social justice framework in social psychological theory and research to address issues, such as morality, prejudice, and social injustice (Jost & Kay, 2010).

Ignacio Martín-Baró was another social psychologist who was influenced by the atrocities of violence and oppression. He was a Jesuit priest in El Salvador and was the head of the psychology department of the University of Central America. In 1989, he and six other priests, a housekeeper, and young girl were assassinated by Salvadoran soldiers because of their views of critical consciousness, liberation, and empowerment of the oppressed. He developed the psychology of liberation and aimed to bring awareness to the contextual and historical realities of those being studied while moving away from the focus on individual factors (Vera & Speight, 2003). Martín-Baró

(1994) believed it was the field's responsibility to create a praxis of social change, advocacy for empowerment, and explained,

> What we need is the revision, from the bottom up, of our most basic assumptions in psychological thought. But this revision cannot be made from our offices; it has to come from a praxis that is committed to the people. Only through such a praxis of commitment will we be able to get a new perspective on the people of our communities, with a view not only of what they positively are but of the negativity as well—of all they could be, but have been kept by historical conditions from becoming. (p. 23)

Conversations about social injustice have led to concentrated research on social factors that significantly impact the lives of individuals. Research has shown that several psychosocial factors are directly linked to mental health outcomes and well-being (Goodman, Pugach, Skolnik, & Smith, 2013). Poverty is a social factor most often addressed, with a focus on the power imbalance experienced between those with limited resources and those who distribute resources (Goodman et al., 2013). This means that resources closely tied to wellness are not distributed fairly among groups of people; therefore, marginalized groups are often at the bottom in terms of well-being (Prilleltensky, 2012). In an attempt to pursue the topic of wellness as fairness and power, Prilleltensky (2008) introduced the concept of psychopolitical validity. Psychopolitical validity is used in community psychology to evaluate whether research and interventions focus on power; it suggests that power is both political and psychological.

Prilleltensky (2008) argued that a framework is needed that aids in integrating political and psychological power to create social change. An important aspect of such a framework includes the idea that one must be aware of one's own power and how it influences research and practice. Feminist research and practice places great focus on issues of power and addresses the power imbalance directly (Brady-Amoon, 2011). Feminist therapists and researchers have for many years advocated for including political goals in counseling and psychotherapy; these goals are said to empower the client to challenge and overcome oppressive forces. Feminist research has also been one of the first disciplines to embrace qualitative methods in research, which seems to mirror some of the aspirations of Martin-Baró for research that focuses on more than individual factors (Brady-Amoon, 2011).

PAR is another way that social justice translates to praxis within psychological research, and PAR continues to challenge the status quo and work toward a more just way of learning about people's realities (Ali & Lees, 2013). Inspired by the revolutionary work of Freire (1982), PAR is grounded in the ideals of mutuality, colearning and coaction, and a deep commitment to transforming colonizing notions of researching the other. Freire (1982) explained that this approach is not passive: "We have to be very clear about the objective of this work: it is the people themselves, not the advancement of science" (p. 34). Thus, research is coenvisioned as an empowering process for coresearchers in community, and dismantles top–down processes characteristic of oppressive research paradigms.

This transformation of oppressive and colonizing research methods also applies to counseling approaches. The antioppression advocacy model places the therapist as an advocate and integrates therapeutic change and social change in an attempt to address poverty and other social factors that compromise the mental health of clients (Ali & Lees, 2013). It focuses on social factors, such as poverty, at a systemic level rather than an individual level (Goodman et al., 2013). This means that therapists are called to collaboratively approach problems with clients, inviting them to participate in social advocacy.

The multicultural counseling movement has also played a major role in the integration of social justice and counseling. Multicultural competence was originally deemed as an awareness of cultural differences and diversity, but its continued evolution has placed social justice at the core of training and practice. The movement has addresses the need for advocacy for underprivileged groups (Hook & Davis, 2012). This advocacy should be based on the client's needs and should be explored collaboratively with the client, developing self-advocacy skills and increasing the client's sense of power (Kiselica & Robinson, 2001). According to Kiselica and Robinson (2001), this form of advocacy often requires counselors to have an appreciation for human suffering, as well as a commitment to end it. Multicultural competence is now evaluated in terms of a consciousness and commitment to advocacy (Vera & Speight, 2003), thus requiring trainees to engage in self-reflection and an examination of attitudes, beliefs, and values that encourage or impede awareness of oppression. Multicultural competence also requires counselors to engage in prevention and outreach as a way of approaching social issues systemically.

Some Latina psychologists integrate social justice into their work by taking a political stance and becoming involved through governance and organizational structures to create waves of change and give voice to oppressed and silenced voices. Guzman (2012) discussed her experience as a Latina feminist community psychologist who sees activism as a major part of her professional identity. She also spoke to her experience as an undocumented child in the United States and how this began to shape her passion for activism and disrupting a pattern of silence around issues of discrimination. Furthermore, Guzman used a community psychology approach to pay particular attention to broader contextual barriers for people of color.

Another way that Latinas engage in social justice work is through a systemic approach. Koskan, Hilfinger Messias, Friedman, Brandt, and Walsemann (2013) focused on increasing access to health care and social services to immigrant communities. They created community health worker positions for members of the communities that help bridge the gap between the community and healthcare. These workers, known as *promotoras de salud*, provide interventions that fit with the community culturally and linguistically (Koskan et al., 2013). Promotoras are said to have the ability, sensitivity, and knowledge to translate care from a medical model to one that is more empowering for communities. Often, promotoras share a strong passion for advocating for their own communities, as they too have experienced social and health inequities (Squires & O'Brien, 2012). This approach to social justice work also fits within a community-based approach but includes a participatory aspect that gives greater voice to the communities being served.

The work of Guadalupanas is yet another example of mujeristas in action. Guadalupanas are religious organizations of Mexican and Mexican American Catholic women devoted to La Virgin de Guadalupe (T. L. Torres, 2013). These women, for decades, have engaged in various works of charity as a way of honoring what La Virgin de Guadalupe represents to the Mexican community: abnegation, sacrifice, kindness, and hope (Spinola, 2013). Guadalupanas have a communitarian worldview working in solidarity to address the needs of those in the community who are in need (T. L. Torres, 2013). Those in need are often marginalized groups of women, children, older people, or people who are ill. The Guadalupanas have in some ways given a voice to women in the Catholic Church, encouraging leadership and engagement in social concerns (T. L. Torres, 2013). Communities of Mexican American women across the United States gather to form and maintain Guadalupana societies that continue to promote the Catholic Church's mission for social justice. Setting up health campaigns, volunteering at battered women's shelters, ministering to prisoners, and organizing social activities for church youth are examples of the work that Guadalupanas do.

When faced with tragedy and oppression, mujeristas have a long history of organizing grassroots human rights movements to counter oppression. Examples include Las Madres de la Plaza Mayo in Argentina, who organized in response to the military dictatorship's practice of abducting men and women who were a threat to the government. The mothers of these children organized and led demonstrations in the capitol city, increasingly gaining attention to the injustice both nationally and internationally (Bouvard, 1994).

Another grassroots movement is Chilean women's resistance to the Pinochet dictatorship through the *Arpillera* movement (Walker, 2008).

Arpilleras are beautiful tapestries made with bright colors and with a backing made of burlap. During these oppressive years under the dictatorship, these beautiful and colorful tapestries depicted the horrific experiences of abduction of family members as well as community violence and terror. Arpillera workshops originated as a form of income for many women who could not find work or who were the sole providers to their families, but these workshops also became the center for healing as community through resistance and protest. Walker (2008) identified these workshops as the precursors to "political protest activities beyond simply creating the arpilleras" (para. 14).

Although it is important to situate social justice within psychology and the researcher and therapist's role as social justice advocates, it is critical to understand how mujeristas live social justice daily. As a means of centralizing these experiences outside of academia, the following section is a testimonio written by Josefina, which illustrates Isasi-Díaz's (1996) conceptualization of how "Hispanic women are very conscious of how the world we live in is defined for us, without taking us into consideration" (p. 137). Although Josefina never set out to be a social justice worker, she has lived a life defined by this work in Latin America, the United States, and with First Nations people. A discussion connecting her story to mujerista meanings of identity, critical consciousness, social ministry, and social action follows her testimonio.

MI TESTIMONIO

> *Caminante no hay camino, se hace camino al andar.* (Traveler, there is no path, your footsteps make the path.)
>
> —Antonio Machado, Spanish Poet

"What are you?" My university professor asked as we chatted before class. I was in Mexico City in 1959 attending a college semester course. The question took me by surprise. "I'm Mexican," I replied. She laughed and said, "No, you're a *gringita*." I stared in surprise. True, I was born and raised in the United States, of immigrant Mexican parents, but in my Arizona environment gringitas were White and blond—I was neither. In Phoenix, I self-identified and was community identified as Mexican, with Spanish being my first language. My professor had a follow-up question: "If the U.S. and Mexico went to war, on whose side would you be?" I paused and replied, "Probably the U.S." "You see," she said, "but your parents would be on the other side."

My professor's comment reminded me of a conversation with my mother when I asked her why she and my dad did not become U.S. citizens. She stated that the United States was not their country. I then suggested that we go live in Mexico. She looked at me, smiled and said, "Mexico is not your country." My parents lived in Arizona as naturalized green-carders for the rest of their lives, more than half a century, but they never felt that the United States was their country.

My parents each came to the United States fleeing the effects of the Mexican Civil War of 1910 and the lawlessness across the country. Revolutionary troops would enter towns, pilfer, and rape and kidnap some of the young girls. When the *revolucionarios* entered the town, my grandmother and her employer hid their daughters in a large crate, where they remained for three days. These experiences prompted my grandmother (Petra), my mother (Elvira), and my great aunt (MiVita) to flee to the United States and continue their boarding house enterprise in the Arizona mining towns. My father, Jose Durán, was 19 years old and working on his father's cattle ranch in Chihuahua when he was caught by Pancho Villa's men. With the aid of a cousin who was part of Villa's men, he escaped. He had never gone to school or traveled beyond their ranch, but using his survival skills, he managed to get to the Texas border and enter the United States. He found work on the railroad and after some time wound up in Phoenix.

My parents met in Phoenix, and in 1922, married and raised seven children, of whom I am the youngest. They bought a large, two-story rooming house, established a restaurant on the bottom floor with family quarters in back, and with it became self-employed for the rest of their lives. The house was located in an African American and Mexican semi-industrial neighborhood. Most Southwestern towns have legal or understood racial boundaries in housing, education, and health institutions. Real estate redlining patterns generally defined groupings of people. "Negroes" were in segregated schools; Mexicans were grouped in minority schools; the first hospital in Phoenix's minority community was not built until 1944 through the efforts of a progressive priest. For years, the only African American doctor served minorities, and he home delivered all of us Duráns.

Our family's life was insulated and consisted of work, school, and church. Everyone in the family worked in our restaurant from 5:00 a.m. to 1:00 a.m. By the age of 12, I was rising before 5:00 a.m. to help my mother with the breakfast crowd, and my older siblings helped with the night crowd. Our restaurant also served other community needs. People would bring letters for us to translate or to write, or they would ask us to make a phone call for them, as my siblings and I spoke English. In our environment, people did not have phones, nor did they speak English. There was never a question of whether we would help; the task fell to whichever child was handy. I began to learn the concept of "the more you know, the more you owe."

My parents were always housing people in need. People knew they could get help at Los Duráns, including free room and board. My dad did church visitations to hospitals and homes and would bring needy persons to live with us. "Tía" Juana was wheelchair-bound and her family couldn't care for her. She came to stay a few days, but stayed 4 years. Two blind men lived with us for 5 years. A young man from Nicaragua, whom my dad met at the Tuberculosis Sanitarium, lived with us for 2 years. I don't think my parents evaluated what they were doing; they just did it. I would later recognize this as my early introduction to social ministry.

After sowing wild oats in his youth, my father became a religious conservative and served as an elder in the Mexican Baptist Church in Phoenix. Our family's entire social interaction was woven into that church, and culture and religion defined our family life. Both were restrictive; nevertheless, my father ruled the family, particularly his daughters, with stoic discipline. Since early childhood, I saw things through a different prism from the acceptable cultural norm. Our home was a typical Mexican home, with defined gender roles. Cleaning, washing, and so on, were girl chores, which allowed the boys more freedom. My mother worked tirelessly as the cook in the restaurant and with the help of Petra and MiVita, who always lived with us, managed to raise a family. My father handled the money and the purchase of restaurant supplies. I grumbled and saw these same gender roles extended in the wider community. In church, men were officers and set church policy; women prepared communion, but only men could serve it. Religion was something accepted, not challenged; yet, I found myself questioning. As an intrepid teen, I posed the following questions to one of our pastors: "What if God was 'Negro' or a woman?" "Why did each faith group think that only they had the right answers?"

Education and school attendance were clear priorities in my family. Our parents did not understand or question what we were being taught, but they understood the numbers on a report card. In the 1950s, there were questionable school policies. In grammar and high school, speaking Spanish on the school grounds was prohibited. Yet, in high school, learning a foreign language was a requirement, so then, speaking Spanish in the classroom was allowed. As high school graduation neared, I met with my high school advisor. College was never suggested. The role for young Mexican women, even in the early 1960s, was that they remain living at home until they marry. College or joining the workforce were not common options. Following high school and while still living at home, I worked for 4 years, got an older brother to teach me how to drive, started college, and borrowed another brother's car. According to my father, women should not drive. He was furious when he found out, yet one day he came home with an old Studebaker he had purchased for $200 and handed me the keys—no words, just keys.

How do we know when it is time to move on? During college I began to question my path. I knew I did not want the typical path of getting married, having children, and raising a family. I wanted to travel and expand my horizons. I decided to go to Mexico for a semester of study. My father forbade it. He stated that if I left home, he would disown me. In his eyes, the only reason a Mexican woman would leave home was because she wanted to "run around." My mother hoped that I would be reasonable. I worked, saved money, and left for Mexico.

I loved Mexico. I felt a freedom there that I did not feel in my home or in my country. I embraced history, language, and the arts with a different fervor. I delved into Mexico's history, its geography, and its historical sites. I learned about U.S.-Mexico history that had not been in my U.S. history books at home. I became aware of my political naiveté and the need to be open to different political perspectives. During my stay in Mexico, my father again surprised me by sending me $20—no words, just $20. This was his unspoken support, if not acceptance.

I was beginning to spread my wings. I returned to the United States to continue my education. In the interim, my closest and next-older brother was also spreading his wings. After college, he had gotten a job in Colombia, South America, and kept urging me to come visit. In 1962, at age 26, and in the middle of my senior year of college, I decided I could not pass up this opportunity and left for Colombia. My friend, and future sister-in-law, joined me.

My father was furious about any trip I took. Each time I left, he told me that I could not return to his home. And each time my mother was caught in between. She could not understand or relate to my strange goals. She referred to me as *la rara* (the strange one) and kept hoping I would change my mind and follow more closely our family's cultural and religious norms. She was emotionally conflicted but supportive, and amidst her tears was buying and stashing away clothes for my trip.

In 1962, the U.S. Peace Corps programs had just begun. My brother's employer, CARE (an international humanitarian organization), was selected to oversee the placement and work of volunteers after establishing a new agency named CARE-Peace Corps. It was dealing in uncharted territory and scrambling. The director, upon learning that my friend and I had just arrived, immediately asked whether we would be willing to volunteer our services for a few days. He never asked about our skills, he simply saw two bilingual women. We agreed, and I began a new path in my life.

Those few days of volunteerism extended into 3 years in Colombia and subsequently into 2 more years in Chile as the Peace Corps' Administrative Officer. The Peace Corps' pace was feverish, with extremely long workdays involving idealistic people committed to President John F. Kennedy's vision of international community service. Through a political lens, I was experiencing yet another side of U.S. foreign policy. Through my religious/faith lens, the Peace Corps was somewhat akin to the social gospel—doing good works.

Liberation theology was surfacing at this time in Latin America. Its focus was addressing issues of social and economic justice for the poor. This movement, led by progressive Catholic priests and nuns, sought to change the Catholic Church's social hierarchy and its close alignment with repressive governments. One of our CARE-Peace Corps colleagues was a Colombian University sociology professor and a priest, Father Camilo Torres. Father Torres was an academician but became a people's priest who fought the government's repressive oligarchy and the church's lack of community involvement. He did student and community organizing work in poor communities and was a precursor to the social activism of later priests, such as Archbishop Romero of El Salvador. Eventually he was excommunicated and joined the rebel guerillas in the mountains, where he was subsequently killed (C. Torres & Gerassi, 1971). Faith-based social activism was very far removed from my own religious upbringing, yet these beliefs and approaches gave life to the biblical calls for justice I had learned in Sunday school.

While I was in Latin America, important historical and social justice events were also happening in the United States. President Kennedy was assassinated in 1963, the Revered Martin Luther King Jr. was addressing civil rights issues, and the feminist movement had begun. After 5 years overseas, I returned to the United States for a more personal reason—my father was dying. The strong disciplinarian was now weakened by advanced lung cancer. It was our family's first experience with this dreaded disease, but it would not be the last. Cancer would eventually take the lives of both my parents and four of my siblings.

Soon after my father's death, my mother was diagnosed with intestinal cancer. Reluctantly I returned to live in my home state of Arizona to care for her. This was what was expected in a Mexican family, and I realized that I also expected it of myself. But I also felt that my wings had been clipped. After an 11-year absence, I returned to the university and changed my business major to Spanish. The need for Spanish in the U.S. marketplace was beginning to surface. The U.S. federal court system also recognized a need to set standard criteria for Spanish–English interpreters throughout its court system. I was invited to join the U.S. government's first team of certified court interpreters and then to conduct certification testing throughout the United States and Puerto Rico.

I subsequently found employment as a translator with the Arizona state government, which needed to address a growing clientele of monolingual Spanish speakers. Although federal programs required that clients be served in a language they understood, Arizona had passed an English-only law, reflecting the state's historical political anti-immigrant climate. Federal requirements were more prescient, yet battling local institutionalized racism was a challenge. After establishing a translation unit with additional translators, I moved on to become a trainer of Native American staff working on the Navajo and Hopi Nations. Working with Native Americans and traveling on the reservations felt akin to traveling in Latin America while continuing to expand my awareness of the richness of other cultures. I also found it interesting that Native Americans detected some of my Indian ancestry and would ask for my tribal affiliation.

I returned to my home church, but with vastly different perspectives. Over time, I assumed a leadership role. In my years away, I had become ecumenical and open to other faith walks. I now found a rich connection with women's groups and recognized a religious sisterhood, particularly with nuns and ex-nuns involved in social action. I also was appointed to the national board of my denomination, American Baptist Churches, and found that I could give voice to national policy that affected minority and social issues. One of the issues was immigration. Having a voice on the board enabled me to advocate for, including the support of, undocumented persons, not just legal refugees. Undocumented persons were considered "illegals," outside U.S. laws, so a policy including them was risky, but I had a vested interest as my local church was now serving them.

In the early 1980s, in El Salvador, political unrest erupted and a 10-year civil war began. People fled El Salvador, making their way to the United States. A group of 13 young Salvadoran men fleeing the civil war tried to cross the Arizona desert in the middle of summer; all but one perished from heat and dehydration. Three protestant pastors and a nun, never having met each other, came together to wrestle with the question, What is the church's responsibility? My pastor and mentor was one of the three and as his assistant, I joined the group.

We faced difficult issues. It was against the law to harbor persons who were here illegally. Historically, Mexican Protestant churches and Roman Catholic churches did not trust each other. However, welcoming the stranger and feeding the hungry was no longer scripture to be read on Sundays but had become a reality in our lives. Without resources but with determination, we learned how to help people apply for political asylum and began leading clinics for applicants. This was at the forefront of what later would be known as the Sanctuary Movement—church groups assisting immigrants who were in the United States without legal documents, a nonstandard role for churches. The immigrant policy I had helped craft for my denomination gave national support to our efforts.

I was invited to join the board of a progressive national ecumenical organization of women, Church Women United, where I met an ex-nun, Ada María Isasi-Díaz. She was a very progressive theologian and an ethicist who worked tirelessly on issues, particularly as they affected Latinas within and outside the Church. She and I not only worked together but also became *hermanas*. It was Ada María who birthed the term *mujerista*, not to be confused with *feminista*. Although the feminist movement had gained momentum, its appeal and its leadership was of Anglo middle- to upper-class women. I was fortunate to work with Ada María on several of her research projects. She became a professor of ethics at Drake University until her sudden death in May 2012. Cancer had found another victim, and mujeristas lost their hermana.

A dozen years ago, I became a licensed pastor. I have a house church where family and friends gather in my living room most Sundays and I reach out to others via Skype and e-mail. I share with them religious, social justice, and spiritual issues as I see them and continue to wrestle with as I walk my walk. I have watched the generations after me struggle with some of the same identity issues that I struggled with. They, like me, are trying to answer my Mexican professor's query. Although their use of the Spanish language has diminished, their value system remains strong. I cherish their love and their trust. As I reflect on my life, I am thankful for great experiences. I am thankful for my parents' model of always being there for others. I am thankful for my strict upbringing, as it gave me discipline and grit. I am most thankful for that spirit that lives within us that enables us to claim our voice. That spirit, once freed, created my pathway and allowed me to make choices of what to discard and what to retain, when to flee and when to return. The *jornada* (journey) to discover the answer to "Who are you?" is a lifelong search for everyone. The answers may be elusive, but I find strength in the questions.

FROM A MUJERISTA THEOLOGY TO MUJERISTA PSYCHOLOGY

Josefina's narrative, and the very act of including this testimonio to illustrate theoretical concepts, embodies a mujerista psychology by weaving principles from Latina feminism, liberation psychology, and PAR. She discusses explorations of identity of self and community, the development of consciousness and questioning the status quo, and action through social ministry. This testimonio is both historical and personal, and it reflects the embedded nature of the self in relation to family history and culture, as well as the ethnopolitical influences on her life.

Exploration of Identity

Josefina's journey illustrates the exploration and development of her gender and ethnic identity. She discusses challenges to her ethnic identity when she studied in Mexico, and although not the first time she considered how her U.S. citizenship made her different from her parents, she realized it was a phenomenologically different experience growing up in the United States. Moreover, even though she experienced sexism and racism, and lived a childhood before the civil rights movement, she still was afforded privileges that she could not deny. Her parents reinforced this belief in giving to those less fortunate not only with words ("the more you know, the more you owe") but also through their actions serving the community. Thus, from a young age, Josefina internalized as an identity her duty to family and community. She also had an awareness of the social fabric and social dynamics of her environment. She knew that she lived in a mixed-race neighborhood where serving the community was the norm. Being available to assist with any need, such as reading and writing, was expected. This is very similar to the experiences of children of recent immigrants to the United States who serve as language and cultural brokers. Through exposure to the English language in school, they are able to assist their parents, extended family members, and neighbors with translation and interpretation (Morales & Hanson, 2005).

Thus, Josefina's dynamic social identity shifted based on context, (co)responding to the demands of her environment. Isasi-Díaz's (2008) conceptualization of a "praxis of care and tenderness for all" characterizes Josefina's upbringing and the driving force for her social justice work the rest of her life: "Community calls for a politics of identity within which we refuse to benefit at the expense of others, convinced that no one can be free until we all are free" (p. 380).

Mujerista Consciousness

Consciousness is an important construct in the work of most social justice and liberatory approaches. For Josefina, her consciousness began with questions. She questioned the status quo of gender within her home and church, and was often met with admonishment for being, as her mother put it, la rara. Gender and cultural expectations intertwined to create a context where she was expected to be obedient, virtuous, and self-sacrificing. The construct of *marianismo* has been used by researchers in Latina feminism and Latina/o psychology to describe this phenomenon, but it cannot be understood without also considering the values of *familismo* (familism), *respeto* (respect), and *simpatía* (promoting smooth interactions; Castillo, Perez, Castillo, & Ghosheh, 2010). A mujerista perspective challenges the value placed on "suffering and self-effacement" as a virtue and encourages Latinas to not internalize oppression by systems of power (Isasi-Díaz, 1996, p. 65). Thus, Josefina's struggle and shift to liberation were to balance the respect and duty to her family with her *sabiduría* to expand beyond the boundaries of her life in Phoenix.

Her travels with the Peace Corps took her to South America, where she expanded her global consciousness. Not only did she have a deeper understanding of Latin American history but she also gained a deeper understanding of U.S. history in relation to these countries. It was in Chile, Columbia,

El Salvador, and Guatemala that she truly understood poverty, violence, oppression, and resistance and was exposed to liberation theology. Josefina admits that much of her social justice work at this time was separate from her faith development but that these experiences planted the seeds for future integration of faith and social justice.

Social Ministry and Social Action

Upon returning to the United States, Josefina realized that the global experience of oppression existed in her backyard. When learning that Salvadoran immigrants fleeing the civil war in their country died in the desert, her faith community could no longer be silent. They were proactive and demonstrated their value of human life by placing water at critical points in the desert and initiated the Sanctuary Movement. Josefina never plans her next life project but instead responds to the call from the oppressed. Isasi-Díaz explains, "*La lucha*—the struggle—is never ending. That is why we have to see it as a way of life and not something that we do: It is part of who we are" (Isherwood, 2011, p. 12).

Josefina's friendship and subsequent collaboration with Isasi-Díaz had a profound impact on her life, and although she never identified with the label mujerista, or any labels for that matter, she certainly felt connection with the construct of *hermanista*, similar to the notion of "sisterhood" for womanists. This is a sisterhood imbued with solidarity to seek liberation from oppressive practices, and when "the fullness of God becomes a reality, we will all be sisters and brothers—kin to each other" (Isasi-Díaz, 1996, p. 163).

CONCLUSION

Latinas in the United States are rich in their diversity, and creating a profile of a typical Latina experience would essentialize their various identities and life journeys. This chapter demonstrates how mujerista perspectives of gender, consciousness, and liberation overlap and intertwine with Latina feminist and social justice theories in psychology. This provides a framework for conceptualizing how *mujeristas* live social justice, and live within (and between) the labels applied based on their ethnicity, race, political ideology, and religious belief system.

Josefina mentioned the Holy Spirit once in her narrative, and she never makes sense of her experience using religious terminology. This is consistent with Isasi-Díaz's (1996) assertion in conceptualizing a mujerista theology that is less about holiness, ritual, and prayer, but more about the experiences of Latinas as they "reflect on their everyday life and the struggle to survive against very difficult obstacles" (p. 69). Thus, understanding how spirituality can inform and drive the lives of Latinas who work toward social justice increases clinicians' and researchers' capacity for competent practice.

Finally, resilience was a common thread in Josefina's life story, and clinicians should recognize the value in exploring clients' understanding of ancestral stories of resilience and perseverance. Descending from families who sacrificed for the better lives of their offspring can create a sense of pride, duty, and inspiration in future generations. In addition, these ancestors model reframing struggle and sacrifice as tests of inner strength. In Josefina's experience, surpassing internalized and external limitations helped form the building blocks of her social justice work.

As clinicians and researchers travel their own journeys of social justice and liberation from oppressive practices, they should be mindful that their clients might be on similar journeys. Embodying a mujerista perspective of seeking parallels or a convergence of stories is not only a point where cultural humility is practiced but also a place where connectedness and solidarity are shared. In the words of Isasi-Díaz (2008),

> Without justice, without a praxis of care and tenderness toward all persons and the biosphere in which we "live and move and have our being," we have nothing to live for, we have nothing to die for. This points to the very heart of justice—solidarity—a deep sense of community that does not do away with diversity but, on the contrary, affirms and is enriched by it. (p. 380)

REFERENCES

Ali, A., & Lees, K. E. (2013). The therapist as advocate: Anti-oppression advocacy in psychological practice. *Journal of Clinical Psychology*, 69, 162–171. http://dx.doi.org/10.1002/jclp.21955

Anzaldúa, G. (1987). *Borderlands-la frontera: The new mestiza*. San Francisco, CA: Spinsters/Aunt Lute.

Bouvard, M. G. (1994). *Revolutionizing motherhood: The mothers of the plaza de mayo*. Lanham, MD: Rowman & Littlefield.

Brabeck, K. (2003). *Testimonio*: A strategy for collective resistance, cultural survival and building solidarity. *Feminism & Psychology*, 13, 252–258. http://dx.doi.org/10.1177/0959353503013002009

Brady-Amoon, P. (2011). Humanism, feminism, and multiculturalism: Essential elements of social justice in counseling, education, and advocacy. *Journal of Humanistic Counseling*, 50, 135–148. http://dx.doi.org/10.1002/j.2161-1939.2011.tb00113.x

Brewster, M. E., Moradi, B., DeBlaere, C., & Velez, B. L. (2013). Navigating the borderlands: The roles of minority stressors, bicultural self-efficacy, and cognitive flexibility in the mental health of bisexual individuals. *Journal of Counseling Psychology*, 60, 543–556. http://dx.doi.org/10.1037/a0033224

Brow, A., & Patten, E. (April, 2014). Statistical portrait of Hispanics in the United States, 2012. *Pew Research Hispanic Trends Project, Hispanic Research Center*. Washington, DC: Pew Hispanic Center. Retrieved from http://www.pewhispanic.org/2014/04/29/statistical-portrait-of-hispanics-in-the-united-states-2012/

Castillo, L. G., Perez, F. V., Castillo, R., & Ghosheh, M. R. (2010). Construction and initial validation of the Marianismo beliefs scale. *Counselling Psychology Quarterly*, 23, 163–175. http://dx.doi.org/10.1080/09515071003776036

Chavez-Dueñas, N. Y., Adames, H. Y., & Organista, K. C. (2014). Skin color prejudice and within-group racial discrimination: Historical and current impact on Latino/a populations. *Hispanic Journal of Behavioral Sciences*, 36, 3–26. http://dx.doi.org/10.1177/0739986313511306

Cienfuegos, A. J., & Monelli, C. (1983). The testimony of political repression as a therapeutic instrument. *American Journal of Orthopsychiatry*, 53, 43–51. http://dx.doi.org/10.1111/j.1939-0025.1983.tb03348.x

Comas-Díaz, L. (2000). An ethnopolitical approach to working with people of color. *American Psychologist*, 55, 1319–1325. http://dx.doi.org/10.1037/0003-066X.55.11.1319

Comas-Díaz, L. (2006). Latino healing: The integration of ethnic psychology into psychotherapy. *Psychotherapy: Theory, Research, Practice, Training*, 43, 436–453. http://dx.doi.org/10.1037/0033-3204.43.4.436

Falcón, S. M. (2008). Mestiza double consciousness: The voices of Afro-Peruvian women on gendered racism. *Gender & Society*, 22, 660–680. http://dx.doi.org/10.1177/0891243208321274

Freire, P. (1982). Creating alternative research methods: Learning to do it by doing it. In B. Hall, A. Gillette, & R. Tandon (Eds.), *Creating knowledge: A monopoly* (pp. 29–37). New Delhi, India: Society for Participatory Research in Asia, New Delhi.

Gallo, L. C., Shivpuri, S., Gonzalez, P., Fortmann, A. L., de los Monteros, K. E., Roesch, S. C., . . . Matthews, K. A. (2013). Socioeconomic status and stress in Mexican-American women: A multi-method perspective. *Journal of Behavioral Medicine*, 36, 379–388. http://dx.doi.org/10.1007/s10865-012-9432-2

Golash-Boza, T. (2006). Dropping the hyphen? Becoming Latino(a)-American through racialized assimilation. *Social Forces*, 85, 27–60. http://dx.doi.org/10.1353/sof.2006.0124

Goodman, L. A., Pugach, M., Skolnik, A., & Smith, L. (2013). Poverty and mental health practice: Within and beyond the 50-minute hour. *Journal of Clinical Psychology*, 69, 182–190. http://dx.doi.org/10.1002/jclp.21957

Guzman, B. (2012). The educational journey of a Latina feminist community psychologist. *Journal of Community Psychology*, 40, 62–76. http://dx.doi.org/10.1002/jcop.20503

Hook, J. N., & Davis, D. E. (2012). Integration, multicultural counseling, and social justice. *Journal of Psychology and Theology, 40*, 102–106.

Humes, K. R., Jones, N. A., & Ramirez, R. R. (2011, March). Overview of race and Hispanic origin: 2010. *2010 Census Brief—U.S. Census Bureau*. Retrieved from http://www.census.gov/prod/cen2010/briefs/c2010br-02.pdf

Hunter, M. L. (2005). *Race, gender, and politics of skin tone*. New York, NY: Routledge.

Isasi-Díaz, A. M. (1989). Mujeristas: A name of our own. *The Christian Century, 106*, 560–562.

Isasi-Díaz, A. M. (1996). *Mujerista theology: A theology for the twenty-first century*. Maryknoll, NY: Orbis Books.

Isasi-Díaz, A. M. (2008). *Se hace camino al andar*—The road is made by walking: What the future demands of women-centered theologies. *Feminist theology, 16*, 379–382.

Isherwood, L. (2011). An interview with Ada María Isasi-Díaz. *Feminist Theology, 20*, 8–17. http://dx.doi.org/10.1177/0966735011411796

Jost, J. T., & Kay, A. C. (2010). Social justice: History, theory, and research. In S. T. Fiske, D. Gilbert, & G. Lindzey (Eds.), *Handbook of social psychology* (5th ed., Vol. 2, pp. 1122–1165). Hoboken, NJ: Wiley. http://dx.doi.org/10.1002/9780470561119.socpsy002030

Keister, L. A., & Moller, S. (2000). Wealth inequality in the United States. *Annual Review of Sociology, 26*, 63–81. http://dx.doi.org/10.1146/annurev.soc.26.1.63

Kiselica, M. S., & Robinson, M. (2001). Bringing advocacy counseling to life: The history, issues, and human dramas of social justice work in counseling. *Journal of Counseling & Development, 79*, 387–397. http://dx.doi.org/10.1002/j.1556-6676.2001.tb01985.x

Koskan, A. M., Hilfinger Messias, D. K., Friedman, D. B., Brandt, H. M., & Walsemann, K. M. (2013). Program planners' perspectives of promotora roles, recruitment, and selection. *Ethnicity & Health, 18*, 262–279. http://dx.doi.org/10.1080/13557858.2012.730605

Lopez, M. H., Morin, R., & Taylor, P. (2010). *Illegal immigration backlash worries, divides Latinos*. Washington, DC: Pew Hispanic Center. Retrieved from http://pewhispanic.org/files/reports/128.pdf

Martín-Baró, I. (1994). *Writings for a liberation psychology*. Cambridge, MA: Harvard University Press.

Morales, A., & Hanson, W. E. (2005). Language brokering: An integrative review of the literature. *Hispanic Journal of Behavioral Sciences, 27*, 471–503. http://dx.doi.org/10.1177/0739986305281333

Pew Hispanic Center. (2012). *When labels don't fit: Hispanics and their views of identity*. Washington, DC: Author.

Prilleltensky, I. (2008). The role of power in wellness, oppression, and liberation: The promise of psychopolitical validity. *Journal of Community Psychology, 36*, 116–136. http://dx.doi.org/10.1002/jcop.20225

Prilleltensky, I. (2012). Wellness as fairness. *American Journal of Community Psychology*, *49*, 1–21. http://dx.doi.org/10.1007/s10464-011-9448-8

Russo, N. F., & Vaz, K. (2001). Addressing diversity in the decade of behavior: Focus on women of color. *Psychology of Women Quarterly*, *25*, 280–294. http://dx.doi.org/10.1111/1471-6402.00029

Smith, K. M. (2010). Female voice and feminist test: *Testimonio* as a form of resistance in Latin America. *Florida Atlantic Comparative Studies Journal*, *12*, 21–37.

Spinola, M. E. (2013). Malinches and Guadalupanas: Representations of the motherly figure among the street children in Mexico City. *Trabajo Social Global*, *3*, 75–94.

Squires, A., & O'Brien, M. J. (2012). Becoming a *promotora*: A transformative process for female community health workers. *Hispanic Journal of Behavioral Sciences*, *34*, 457–473. http://dx.doi.org/10.1177/0739986312445567

Thoits, P. A. (2010). Stress and health: Major findings and policy implications. *Journal of Health and Social Behavior*, *51*, 41–53. http://dx.doi.org/10.1177/0022146510383499

Torres, T. L. (2013). *The paradox of Latina religious leadership in the Catholic Church: Las Guadalupanas of Kansas City*. New York, NY: Palgrave Macmillan. http://dx.doi.org/10.1057/9781137370327

Torres, C., & Gerassi, J. (1971). *Revolutionary priest: The complete writings & messages of Camilo Torres*. New York, NY: Random House.

U.S. Census Bureau. (2010). *Current population survey: Annual social and economic supplement, 2010*. Retrieved from http://www.census.gov/population/age/data/2010comp.html

Vasquez, M. J. (2012). Psychology and social justice: Why we do what we do. *American Psychologist*, *67*, 337–346. http://dx.doi.org/10.1037/a0029232

Vera, E., & Speight, S. (2003). Multicultural competence, social justice, and counseling psychology: Expanding our roles. *The Counseling Psychologist*, *31*, 253–272. http://dx.doi.org/10.1177/0011000003031003001

Walker, K. (2008). *Chilean women's resistance in the arpillera movement*. Ottignies-Louvain-la-Neuve, Belgium: Council on Hemispheric Affairs. Retrieved from http://www.cetri.be/spip.php?article911&lang=fr

White, M. (2000). *Reflections on narrative practice: Essays and interviews*. Adelaide, Australia: Dulwich Centre.

Xu, Y. (2011). Ethnic variations in the relationship between socioeconomic status and psychological distress among Latino adults. *Race and Social Problems*, *3*, 212–224. http://dx.doi.org/10.1007/s12552-011-9048-0

VI

LOOKING FORWARD

11

THE VALUE OF PROMOTING WOMANIST AND MUJERISTA LEADERS

MELBA J. T. VASQUEZ

Changing demographics are fostering an examination of leadership and diversity. Only recently have scholars begun to address the diversity of leaders in terms of culture, race, ethnicity, gender, and sexual orientation. Consequently, the ability of research and theory to address some of the most important aspects of contemporary leadership has been constrained. Key issues to be addressed, identified by Eagly and Chin (2010), include (a) the limited access of individuals from diverse identity groups to leadership roles; (b) the shaping of leaders' behavior by the intersections of identities as leaders and as members of racial, ethnic, culture, gender, or other identity groups; and (c) the potential of individuals from groups formerly excluded from leadership roles to provide excellent leadership because of their differences from traditional leaders. Understanding key issues involved in leadership diversity promotes understanding for optimizing leadership in society.

http://dx.doi.org/10.1037/14937-012
Womanist and Mujerista Psychologies: Voices of Fire, Acts of Courage, T. Bryant-Davis and L. Comas-Díaz (Editors)

In this chapter, I describe how diversity in leadership is a compelling interest for society, and I present the case for promoting womanist and *mujerista* leaders, on the basis of the belief that they have much to offer society.

DIVERSITY IN LEADERSHIP IS A COMPELLING INTEREST

Despite increasing representation of women and racial and ethnic minorities in leadership, they are still significantly underrepresented. Economists, sociologists, psychologists, and others have explored reasons for the underrepresentation (including gender and race gaps in wages and promotions) and have investigated such issues as human capital variables (e.g., education, training, job experience) and structural factors (e.g., occupational segregation). The near-unanimous conclusions are that such variables account only for a portion of the gaps and that discrimination is a more significant factor (Eagly & Chin, 2010).

Sanchez-Hucles and Davis (2010) posited that the United States is not producing enough leaders to meet the organizational demands. They suggested that women of color are among those from diverse groups who can fill the void, especially because of indications that women are highly suited for more advanced leadership positions (Catalyst, 2005; Eagly & Carli, 2007).

U.S. Supreme Court Justice Sandra Day O'Connor conveyed her belief that diversity in leadership is a compelling interest. During the 2003 Supreme Court decisions (*Gratz v. Bollinger*, 2003; *Grutter v. Bollinger*, 2003) regarding considering race to ensure a critical mass of racial and ethnic minority applicants in higher education, Justice O'Connor declared that it was important and necessary to cultivate a set of leaders with legitimacy in the eyes of the citizenry. A university education is important, she believed, so "that the path to leadership be visibly open to talented individuals of every race and ethnicity" (Jayson & Rodriguez, 2003, p. A1; Lemann, 2003). She believed that universities are partly in the business of training a leadership corps for society and that a society with racial and ethnic tensions can benefit tremendously from having an integrated leadership (Lemann, 2003, p. 4, 14). This perspective affirms with judicial authority the existing national consensus that the presence of diversity in leadership positions in society is compelling.

WHAT MAKES A GOOD LEADER?

Expectations about good leaders are changing, along with demographic changes. Eagly and Chin (2010) made a strong case for the importance of diversity in the workplace, and called for leadership theories that acknowledge and promote the value of diversity. As leadership theories become more inclusive and integrative of a more global complexity and interdependence, more diversity in expectations of what makes a good leader will be accepted. Trimble (2015a) suggested that people bid farewell to the alpha male human leadership style; his research has indicated that more effective leadership qualities are much more diverse.

In a special issue of the *American Psychologist*, Klein and Wang (2010) questioned the way in which Eagly and Chin (2010) implicitly defined diversity in the context of promoting more diverse leadership. Although Klein and Wang expressed appreciation for raising the issues that the glass ceiling still exists and that modern theories of leadership can benefit immensely from increased participation by scholars and practitioners who are not Western, White, upper-class men, they also challenge the focus on what they called *surface-level diversity* or salient, visible characteristics, such as gender, race, and ethnicity. They proposed examination of *deep-level diversity*, which they defined as heterogeneity in underlying psychological characteristics, such as personality, attitudes, and values. They suggested the importance of disentangling the two leadership related variables that surface-level diversity affects, including leadership opportunities and leadership effectiveness. Klein and Wang argued that although surface-level characteristics can lead to problematic discriminatory disparities in leadership opportunities, surface level diversity is not clearly a major factor in determining leadership effectiveness.

Eagly and Chin (2010) argued that gender, race, and ethnicity have a psychological reality at deeper levels than the surface of the human body, resulting in categorizing and stereotyping by the perceiver, as well as central aspects of people's self-definitions. Those self-definitions are influenced by an attempt to live up to the standards congruent with identities, resulting in identities based on group memberships that affect behaviors in organizations and groups, including the exercise of leadership. They also made the point that the experiences that result from their identities, including discrimination, and how they have come to negotiate minority and majority cultures, result in lived experiences that can also influence leaders' effectiveness. They proposed that the common emergence of strengths-based and resiliency models among members of groups who have been excluded from the privileges in society, including from leadership, are important to consider. Indeed, many who have been marginalized combine that experience with their opportunities and privileges to obtain leadership to promote and advocate for improvement in the conditions related to oppression for marginalized groups.

How do individuals develop a consciousness that involves care for others, especially those who are oppressed? To answer this question, Caldwell and Vera (2010) identified those who care about social justice. Through a qualitative, critical incident research design, they identified critical incidents that cultivated a social justice orientation among counseling psychology doctoral students and professionals. Analysis of rank-ordered items indicated that the categories of "exposure to injustice" and "influence of significant persons" were most frequently ranked as the most influential critical incidents in the development of a social justice orientation. Thus, the lived experience of those who have been exposed to injustice as well being exposed to those who teach, model, and mentor those values to others promote the development of a social justice orientation (Vasquez, 2012, 2013).

A series of recent studies (Chin & Trimble, 2014; Thompson, Trimble, Chin, & Stout, 2015; Trimble, 2015b) described the need for a new culturally resonant model of leadership. Sixty-four leadership characteristics were derived from the current literature on leadership, from structured interviews and focus groups obtained from different ethnically diverse samples. Both men and women reject those characteristics generally associated with the so-called "alpha male leadership style." Additionally, male participants found characteristics regarding organizational skills the most necessary, whereas female participants found those regarding personal attributes the most necessary. As discussed in Trimble (2015b), the Rasch leadership item rankings for survey participants found the top 10 ratings to include: honest, integrity, adaptability, self-knowledge, caring, authentic, compassionate, communicator, warmth, motivating. The bottom 10 ratings included competitive, emotionally tough, forceful, submissive, aggressive, conflict inducer, indirect, dominant, celebrity, self-centered. Future studies will include examining the differences between perceptions of necessary leadership characteristics in the context of culture, race, and political ideology. Trimble (2015b) presented evidence that society has changed in regard to the expectations of leadership style. He described President Barack Obama's leadership style as creative, honest, fair, respectful, value-centered, sensitive, achievement-focused, self-confident, engaging, and mindful.

The combination of these research findings and theoretical positions (Caldwell & Vera, 2010; Chin & Trimble, 2014; Eagly & Chin, 2010; Thompson et al., 2015; Trimble, 2015b) led me to consider that the developmental models of womanist and mujerista identities described in this volume may be related to leadership effectiveness. Most studies have found that participants with higher levels of womanist internalization attitudes had higher levels of self-esteem (Alcaron, 1998; Poindexter-Cameron & Robinson, 1997). In the final stage of this developmental model, internalization, the woman fully incorporates into her identity her own positive view of what it means to be a woman, and refuses to be bound by external definitions (Boisnier, 2003).

Although higher levels of self-esteem do not necessary lead to increased leadership effectiveness, I posit that the lived experience of having womanist and mujerista internalized attitudes lead to more effective leadership experiences, particularly in the ability to not only develop, learn, and apply leadership skills but also promote the values from the lived experience and to influence others as well. For example, empirical research on federal appeals court decisions indicate that in sex discrimination and sexual harassment cases, female judges were significantly more likely than male judges to find for the plaintiff (Liptak, 2009; Peresie, 2005). Even more interesting was the finding that the mere presence of a woman or Black person on a three-panel appeal court increased the probability that a White man would find for the plaintiff (Peresie, 2005; Liptak, 2009). The implication is that the presence of a woman of color in most settings not only increases social justice attitudes and behaviors but also may influence awareness of colleagues, including increased understanding and empathy for the perspective represented by that identity. I posit that this would be particularly true for those who have a womanist mujerista identity and especially true if one had reached the developmental level of identity as described by Nygreen, Saba, and Moreno (see Chapter 2, this volume). They state that womanist and mujeristas'

> racially conscious strands of feminism center on the unique experiences and perspectives of women of color, while promoting liberation, self-definition, and self-determination for all women. They all articulate intersectional analyses of oppression, recognizing how socially constructed categories of race, class, gender, sexuality, and nationality overlap and intersect with each other, shaping women's (and men's) experiences and opportunities in ways that position them multiply as both oppressed and privileged. They all assume that institutionalized racism works in gender-specific ways and that institutionalized sexism works in race-specific (and class-specific) ways. They all explore how various levels of oppression interact with and reinforce each other—on the micro level of face-to-face sexism (acts of prejudice, insults, microaggressions, harassment, violence against women); together with the larger institutional structures of gender oppression; and finally in the cultural realm of beliefs, assumptions, and ideologies that promote or legitimize women's subordinate social status. (p. 43, this volume)

Marian Anderson was a world-renowned African American opera singer whose career was affected by racism. For example, in 1939, the Daughters of the American Revolution refused to allow her to sing in their Constitution Hall in Washington, DC, which is considered to have been part of the reason that Eleanor Roosevelt invited her to sing at the Lincoln Memorial at a critically acclaimed open air concert on Easter Sunday, 1939. Anderson, a resilient leader in the struggle for Black artists to overcome racial prejudice in the United States, is quoted to have said, "Leadership should be born out of the understanding of the needs of those who would be affected by it" (as cited in Lewis, 2005).

Perhaps the experiences and processes implied in these descriptions of identity approach the deeper level diversity described by Klein and Wang (2010) and by Eagly and Chin (2010) in explaining how the lived experiences of diversity contributes to more effective leadership. The presence of diverse leaders in society is significant for numerous reasons, as described previously. Exposure to injustice is a critical incident identified by Caldwell and Vera (2010) as leading to caring about social justice, along with the influence of significant persons. Women of color leaders who have the lived experiences resulting in mujerista or womanist identities can promote positive changes in institutional and organizational life, and they may bring unique skills, values, and perspectives to their leadership activities. They may have the capacity to be constructive social justice change agents in their communities.

A CASE IN POINT

U.S. Supreme Court Justice Sonia Sotomayor was the first Latina appointed to that role. Justice Sotomayor was in Austin, Texas, in February 2013. In one of her interviews, she made a very touching comment that people perceive poor neighborhoods as riddled with crime. She indicated that in fact, the majority of poor people are hard-working, contributing members of society who reflect dignity, goodness, and compassion for others. To have a Supreme Court Justice who knows this reality is so important! Having people with this kind of background in positions of leadership is significant and critical, especially in key decision-making positions that have ultimate power to influence others.

It is unfortunate (in my opinion) that in the Supreme Court decision *Schuette v. BAMN* (2014; brought by the coalition to defend affirmative action), the majority reversed a lower court's decision to set aside Michigan voters' denial of affirmative action. Although the decision did not question the principle that consideration of race is permissible in certain cases, it did validate the belief that voters in states may choose to prohibit the consideration of racial preferences. Sotomayor articulated the minority report with clarity and elegance. Her articulation, in fact, is relevant to the content of this chapter—that is, the importance of remaining open to approaches to ensure that persons are treated with fairness and equal dignity, and have access to the credentials that lead to increased diversity in leadership in society. She referred to the importance of "race-sensitive admissions policies." She states, in part, that

> While our Constitution does not guarantee minority groups victory in the political process, it does guarantee them meaningful and equal access

> to that process. It guarantees that the majority may not win by stacking the political process against minority groups permanently, forcing the minority alone to surmount unique obstacles in pursuit of its goals—here, educational diversity that cannot reasonably be accomplished through race-neutral measures. . . . I have faith that our citizenry will continue to learn from this Nation's regrettable history; that it will strive to move beyond those injustices toward a future of equality. And I, too, believe in the importance of public discourse on matters of public policy. . . . I firmly believe that our role as judges includes policing the process of self-government and stepping in when necessary to secure the constitutional guarantee of equal protection. Because I would do so here, I respectfully dissent. (*Schuette v. BAMN*, 2014, Sotomayor, dissenting, p. 6)

Justice Sotomayor reminded the Court that for much of its history, the United States has denied to many of its citizens the right to participate meaningfully and equally in its politics, and provides evidence of that (*Schuette v. BAMN*, 2014). She further articulated a principle that she describes as elementary and essential to the equal protection jurisprudence; that is, that governmental action cannot deprive minority groups of equal protection when it alters the political process in a manner that uniquely burdens racial minorities' ability to achieve their goals. She articulated the belief that race-sensitive admissions policies further a compelling state interest in achieving a diverse student body precisely because they increase minority enrollment, which necessarily benefits minority groups. Sotomayor stated: "Constitutionally permissible race-sensitive admissions policies can both serve the compelling interest of obtaining the educational benefits that flow from a diverse student body, and inure to the benefit of racial minorities." (*Schuette v. BAMN*, 2014, Sotomayor, dissenting, p. 16).

Sotomayor most clearly articulated her belief that race matters because of the long history of racial minorities' being denied access to the political process, and because of persistent racial inequality in society that cannot be ignored, and that has produced stark socioeconomic disparities. She concluded that the way to stop discrimination on the basis of race is to speak openly and candidly on the subject of race, and to apply the constitution with eyes open to the unfortunate effects of centuries of racial discrimination (*Schuette v. BAMN*, 2014, Sotomayor, dissenting, p. 46).

What leads to such an articulate, wise justice of color who understands the experience of people of color, and who has the courage to dissent, versus another justice of color who seems to reject support of all the legal, constitutional opportunities ironically provided him in his accomplishments? My hypothesis is that Sotomayor would be categorized as mujerista and that the process of becoming mujerista has resulted in a sensibility and approach to power, knowledge, and relationships rooted in convictions for community uplift. Clearly, women of color and members of other diverse groups who obtain leadership have potential opportunities to take courageous, advocacy positions that make a difference in society in the contexts in which they provide leadership.

On a much lesser scale, I have had such opportunities. To share my personal experience, when I served as the first Latina and first woman of color president of the American Psychological Association (APA) for 2011, I was able to designate social justice as a major theme for the APA Annual Convention in August 2011 in Washington, DC. Some of the presidential projects/initiatives included appointment of task forces to examine psychology's perspective on grand challenges in society, including reducing and preventing discrimination, educational disparities and immigration. The results included the following reports, all available on the APA website:

- *Crossroads: The Psychology of Immigration in the New Century* (APA, 2012a);
- *Pathways to a Better America: Preventing Discrimination and Promoting Diversity* (APA, 2012b); and
- *Ethnic and Racial Disparities in Education: Psychology's Contributions to Understanding and Reducing Disparities* (APA, 2012c).

These reports were written by several very hard-working expert researchers, reviewed by advisors, vetted by members of APA's boards and committees, and received as official APA reports by the 170+ Council of Representatives, APA's governing policymaking body. Because of the strength and salience of these evidence-based resources, the APA Presidential Task Force on Immigration has already held congressional briefings in Washington, DC, with the help and support of APA government relations staff, on the very important and timely topic of immigration. These are the visible outcomes; serving on the board of directors enables for many more behind-the-scenes influences.

As I consider my own development as a mujerista, I know that my working class background has sensitized me to appreciate the importance of dignity and integrity in people who often had little material wealth but who had so much to offer humanity through acts of kindness and compassion. And I grew up in an era in which I saw that programs (e.g., resulting from Lyndon Johnson's War on Poverty), when carefully designed and managed, can make a positive difference in people's lives. I have observed and experienced oppression in various ways, at times on a daily basis, and early in my life, I became clear that my life would be focused on being involved in an attempt to give voice to the values I cherish. I am fortunate that my profession of psychology has provided the opportunity to be productive in my consulting, psychotherapy, scholarship, and leadership activities.

THE CHALLENGES

Representation of diversity in leadership of various aspects of society is slowly increasing, but still has challenges (Vasquez & Daniel, 2010). Hymowitz and Schellhardt (1986) described some of those challenges symbolically by applying the term *glass ceiling*, a concept popularized in the 1980s to describe a barrier so subtle that it is transparent, yet so strong that it prevents women and minorities from moving up in the management hierarchy. Eagly and Carli (2007) used the term *labyrinth* to describe the uneven path of upward progression for women in organizations involving challenges, indirect forays, and ventures into foreign territory. Others describe increased barriers posed by the sexism and racism that women of color encounter and use symbolic terms *concrete wall* or *sticky floor* (Bell & Nkomo, 2001; Betters-Reed & Moore, 1995; Sanchez-Hucles & Davis, 2010). Research has demonstrated that differences in educational levels, training, job experience, and occupational segregation account for only a portion of the gender and race gaps in wages and promotion and that discrimination is a contributing factor (Eagly & Chin, 2010). Despite convincing evidence of the effectiveness of female leaders, they face several barriers and challenges.

Research has confirmed that discrimination by the majority population is largely responsible for the underrepresentation of women and women of color in leadership positions. Discrimination, bias, and negative stereotyping on the part of those in power, as well as structural, systemic discrimination are the root causes of differential treatment as reflected in policies and practices in the social system. The evidence indicates that people (both men and women) report preference for male bosses; it is more difficult for women to be promoted into leadership roles than it is for men; it is more difficult for women to be perceived as effective leaders than it is for men; and leadership challenges are higher for women of color than for White women and men (Eagly & Carli, 2007; Holvino & Blake-Beard, 2004).

THE STRATEGIES FOR SUCCESS

To increase the representation of womanist feminist leaders in society, a variety of both organizational and personal strategies are recommended. Vasquez and Daniel (2010) identified and recommended organizational strategies for empowerment. Many of these strategies would have the benefit of promoting womanist mujerista identities as well! People who receive mentoring, for example, report having more satisfaction, career mobility and opportunity, recognition, and a higher promotion rate than nonmentored individuals (Jeruchim & Shapiro, 1992). Other strategies include expression of nonambivalent belief in capabilities of a mentee or supervisee, constructive criticism, conceptualizing intelligence and abilities as expandable qualities, leadership training, and promoting an environment in which diversity is respected. People who have been negatively stereotyped, in particular, require positive, optimistic mentor–mentee or supervisor–employee relationships (Steele, 2010).

Personal strategies to develop a strong womanist mujerista identity might include risk taking; persistence; acquiring credentials, skills, and abilities; learning from mistakes without allowing them to define oneself; supporting others who make mistakes; transforming pain, rejection, and loneliness into constructive energy and action; finding and providing mentorship; and practicing self-care, including having healthy relationships. Collective identities that emphasize family loyalty lead women of color to fall back on families to provide support (Cheung & Halpern, 2010). Lending a hand of support to others on an individual, community and societal level is an empowering strategy as well!

MORE RESEARCH IS NEEDED

Many have described the importance of incorporating dimensions of diversity in leadership theories and research (Eagly & Chin, 2010; Sanchez-Hucles & Davis, 2010). Despite the similarities in the histories, experiences, and values of members of racial/ethnic groups, they still have much diversity within them. An important goal is thus to increase research on women of color leaders, including whether successful women of color leaders might have more of a tendency to score high on womanist and mujerista measures. This also includes research on the complexity associated with the intersection of the multiple identities that result from identification with more than one salient identity group. Socialization in more than one identity group changes a wide range of psychological processes, such as personality, cognition, perception, attributions, social interaction and identity development (Sanchez-Hucles & Davis, 2010).

CONCLUSION

Women, including women of color, have made tremendous strides in acquiring career achievement and leadership in the past three decades. However, various challenges still exist. Research has confirmed theoretical perspectives as to why women and women of color in particular are underrepresented in leadership positions, including discrimination, bias, negative stereotyping and structural, systemic discrimination reflected in policies and practices in the social system. These processes account for continued low representation of women, people of color, and especially, women of color in leadership positions (APA, 2012b).

Thus, a current challenge and goal is to increase the numbers and effectiveness of women from diverse backgrounds, with multiple identities, as leaders and to encourage their desire, skills, experience, and vision to be change agents in their communities. The contributions of womanist and mujerista leaders can lead to positive changes in a variety of settings, and opportunities for leadership experiences and leadership training can increase the diversity, number, and effectiveness of women of color as leaders. Justice O'Connor conveyed her belief with judicial authority that a society with can benefit tremendously from having an integrated leadership (Lemann, 2003, pp. 4–14). The presence of diversity in leadership positions in society is critical and compelling.

Research indicates differences in leadership style, but not in leadership effectiveness, between men and women; evidence demonstrates that female leaders are effective as leaders (Eagly & Carli, 2007) and that typical differences in the leadership styles of women and men are quite small when they occupy the same managerial role (Eagly & Chin, 2010). Although a minimal amount of research has been conducted with women of color, identity variables can affect a leader's style, behavior, emergence, and effectiveness in many complex ways (Ayman & Korabik, 2010).

Various organizational strategies can increase the sense of capability, motivations, and leadership goals of women of color, and personal strategies can contribute to ongoing empowerment (Vasquez & Daniel, 2010). The development of womanist and mujerista identities may serve as a part of the empowerment process as well.

REFERENCES

Alcaron, M. C. B. (1998). The relationship between womanist identity attitudes, cultural identity, and acculturation to Asian-American women's self-esteem. *Dissertation Abstracts International*, *58B*, 3954. (UMI NO. AAM9738286).

American Psychological Association. (2012a). *Crossroads: The psychology of immigration in the new century*. Washington, DC: Author. Retrieved from http://www.apa.org/topics/immigration/report.aspx

American Psychological Association. (2012b). *Dual pathways to a better America: Preventing discrimination and promoting diversity*. Washington, DC: Author. Retrieved from http://www.apa.org/pubs/info/reports/promoting-diversity.aspx

American Psychological Association. (2012c). *Ethnic and racial disparities in education: psychology's contributions to understanding and reducing disparities*. Washington, DC: Author. Retrieved from http://www.apa.org/ed/resources/racial-disparities.aspx

Ayman, R., & Korabik, K. (2010). Leadership: Why gender and culture matter. *American Psychologist, 65*, 157–170. http://dx.doi.org/10.1037/a0018806

Bell, E., & Nkomo, S. (2001). *Our separate ways: Black and White women and the struggles for professional identity*. Boston, MA: Harvard Business School Press.

Betters-Reed, B. L., & Moore, L. L. (1995). Shifting the management development paradigm for women. *Journal of Management Development, 14*, 24–38. http://dx.doi.org/10.1108/02621719510078876

Boisnier, A. D. (2003). Race and women's identity development: Distinguishing between feminism and womanism among Black and White women. *Sex Roles, 49*, 211–218. http://dx.doi.org/10.1023/A:1024696022407

Caldwell, J. C., & Vera, E. (2010). Critical incidents in counseling psychology: Professionals and trainees' social justice orientation development. *Training and Education in Professional Psychology, 4*, 163–176. http://dx.doi.org/10.1037/a0019093

Catalyst. (2005). *Women "take care," men "take charge": Stereotyping of U.S. business leaders exposed*. Retrieved from http://www.catalyst.org/knowledge/women-take-care-men-take-charge-stereotyping-us-business-leaders-exposed

Cheung, F. M., & Halpern, D. F. (2010). Women at the top: Powerful leaders define success as work + family in a culture of gender. *American Psychologist, 65*, 182–193. http://dx.doi.org/10.1037/a0017309

Chin, J. L., & Trimble, J. (2014). *Diversity and leadership*. Thousand Oaks, CA: Sage.

Eagly, A. H., & Carli, L. L. (2007). *Through the labyrinth: The truth about how women become leaders*. Boston, MA: Harvard Business School Press.

Eagly, A. H., & Chin, J. L. (2010). Diversity and leadership in a changing world. *American Psychologist, 65*, 216–224. http://dx.doi.org/10.1037/a0018957

Gratz v. Bollinger, 539 U.S. 244 (2003).

Grutter v. Bollinger, 539 U.S. 306 (2003).

Holvino, E., & Blake-Beard, S. (2004). Women discussing their differences: A promising trend. *The Diversity Factor, 12*, 1–7.

Hymowitz, C., & Schellhardt, T. C. (1986, March 24). The glass ceiling: Why women can't seem to break the invisible barrier that blocks them from the top jobs. *Wall Street Journal*, pp. 1, 4.

Jayson, S. & Rodriguez, E. (2003, June 24). Affirmation action in colleges upheld: UT official hails ruling, saying "Hopwood is dead." *Austin American Statesman*, pp. A1, A5.

Jeruchim, J., & Shapiro, P. G. (1992). *Women, mentors, and success*. New York, NY: Fawcett Columbine.

Klein, K. M., & Wang, M. (2010). Deep-level diversity and leadership. *American Psychologist, 65*, 932–934. http://dx.doi.org/10.1037/a0021355

Lemann, N. (2003, June 29). Beyond Bakke: A decision that universities can relate to. *The New York Times*, p. 14.

Lewis, J. (2005). *Leadership quotes of the week: Marian Anderson on leadership and understanding*. Retrieved from http://www.brainyquote.com/quotes/quotes/m/marianande109742.html

Liptak, A. (2009, May 31). The waves minority judges always make. *The New York Times*, pp. OP1, OP4.

Peresie, J. L. (2005). Female judges matter: Gender and collegial decision-making in the federal appellate courts. *The Yale Law Journal, 114*, 1761–1788. Retrieved from http://www.yalelawjournal.org/note/female-judges-matter-gender-and-collegial-decisionmaking-in-the-federal-appellate-courts

Poindexter-Cameron, J. M., & Robinson, T. L. (1997). Relationships among racial identity attitudes, womanist identity attitudes, and self-esteem in African American college women. *Journal of College Student Development, 38*, 281–293.

Sanchez-Hucles, J. V., & Davis, D. D. (2010). Women and women of color in leadership: Complexity, identity, and intersectionality. *American Psychologist, 65*, 171–181. http://dx.doi.org/10.1037/a0017459

Schuette v. BAMN, 572 U.S. __ (2014). (Sotomayor, J., dissenting).

Steele, C. M. (2010). *Whistling Vivaldi and other clues to how stereotypes affect us*. New York, NY: Norton.

Thompson, J., Trimble, J. E., Chin, J. C., & Stout, K. (2015, May). *Identifying and developing more culturally sensitive diverse leadership measurement prototypes*. Poster session presented at the annual convention of the American Psychological Society, New York, NY.

Trimble, J. E. (2015a, April 11). *Culture and leadership* [Ted Talk]. Retrieved from https://www.youtube.com/watch?v=fuHj3jsBdKE

Trimble, J. E. (2015b, August). *Identifying and developing more culturally sensitive and diverse leadership styles*. Paper presented as part of a symposium on race/ethnic relations and the Obama presidency: Perspectives of leaders in the field, at the 123rd Annual Convention of the American Psychological Association, Toronto, Ontario, Canada.

Vasquez, M. J. T. (2012). Psychology and social justice: Why we do what we do. *American Psychologist, 67*, 337–346. http://dx.doi.org/10.1037/a0029232

Vasquez, M. J. T. (2013). Women of color leaders: Benefits for all. In L. Comas-Díaz & B. Greene (Eds.), *Psychological health of women of color: Intersections, challenges, and opportunities* (pp. 373–408). Santa Barbara, CA: ABC-CLIO.

Vasquez, M. J. T., & Daniel, J. H. (2010). Women of color as mentors. In C. A. Rayburn, F. L. Denmark, M. E. Reuder, & A. M. Austria (Eds.), *A Handbook for women mentors: Transcending barriers of stereotype, race and ethnicity* (pp. 173–188). New York, NY: Praeger.

12

CONCLUSION: TOWARD GLOBAL WOMANIST AND MUJERISTA PSYCHOLOGIES

LILLIAN COMAS-DÍAZ AND THEMA BRYANT-DAVIS

> To survive in the Borderlands, you must live *sin fronteras*, be a crossroads. (Anzaldúa, 1987, p. 194)
>
> For I am my mother's daughter, and the drums of Africa still beat in my heart.
>
> —Mary McLeod Bethune

This anthology introduced the womanist and *mujerista* psychologies. Womanist and mujerista psychologists challenge structures that oppress women of color; affirm their lived realities; and create knowledge to heal, empower, and liberate. Womanist and mujerista psychologies are conceptual and spiritual sisters. Indeed, the term *mujerismo* is translated as "Latina womanism." Born out of the need to represent women of color's specific feminism, these psychologies have evolved to address the intersecting oppressions of women from marginalized groups. The differences between these worldviews and dominant feminism can be illustrated with the phrases "Womanism is to feminism as purple is to lavender" and "Mujerismo is to feminism as salsa is to ketchup." In this manner, womanist and mujerista psychologies echo multicultural feminism, women of color feminism, decolonial feminism, and third world U.S. feminism. What distinguishes womanism and mujerismo from other feminisms of color is not a difference in substance but in emphasis, as Nygreen, Saba, and Moreno (Chapter 2, this volume) observed. Likewise,

http://dx.doi.org/10.1037/14937-013
Womanist and Mujerista Psychologies: Voices of Fire, Acts of Courage, T. Bryant-Davis and L. Comas-Díaz (Editors)

the distinctions between womanist and mujerista psychologies are not in content but are in the accent they place on issues. For instance, although womanist psychologists promote a new consciousness among African American women, mujerista psychologists help Latinas to develop a new *mestiza* and *mulata* syncretistic consciousness.

In this concluding chapter, we discuss womanist and mujerista psychologies' trajectory. We speak in a womanist–mujerista language, one that is scholarly, personal, spiritual, communal, and sociopolitical. In this vein, we use voices of fire to articulate the promotion of women's agency and healing. Then, we give testimony to the promotion of women of color's liberation. Afterward, we describe the womanist/mujerista liberatory and social justice action as acts of courage. Subsequently, we envision the emergence of a transnational and global womanist/mujerista psychology. We end the chapter in spirit—we conclude with a womanist/mujerista prayer and a psychopolitical manifesto.

VOICES OF FIRE: NAMING AND HEALING

> Because we have been historically barred from the writing profession (it is assumed) that we have nothing of interest, much less of value to contribute.
>
> —Ana Castillo

Womanist and mujerista worldviews inspire, inform, and foster wholeness, as well as healing and emancipation. Womanist and mujerista psychologies are based on women of color's strengths, connections, and spirituality. Therefore, the contributors in this anthology raised their voices in a choir of healing, transformation, and liberation. They infused psychospirituality, collectivism, communalism, and sociospiritual activism into their psychological work. As psychospiritual movements womanism and mujerismo compose a healing social justice sonnet made out of multiple spiritualities, religions, and traditions. These are movements because they are purposeful, dynamic, and collaborative; their political agenda is the psychological and spiritual well-being of African American women and Latinas. Womanists and mujeristas are dissident daughters of theology of liberation and liberation psychology. The contributors in this volume illustrate how a unique type of multicultural feminist spirituality heals, empowers, and promotes a spiritual social activism. In fact, they showed how as spiritual archeologists, womanists and mujeristas name themselves, reclaim their spiritual gifts, and strengthen their historical continuity. In doing so, womanist and mujeristas use spirituality as a vehicle for transformation. Therefore, womanist and mujerista psychologists help women to rescue their ancestral knowledge and wisdom. Through this process they commit to self-reflexivity, *conscientización* (Freire, 1970), critical analyses, and collective emancipation. Moreover, womanist and mujerista psychologists speak in creative, inclusive, syncretistic, and passionate voices. As Nygreen et al. (Chapter 2) suggest, womanist and mujerista worldviews inspire, inform, and guide for humanization, wholeness, and healing.

To achieve their goals, womanist and mujeristas psychologists developed interdisciplinary theory, inquiry, and praxis. They built a transformative knowledge to empower, heal, and emancipate women of color. In other words, womanist and mujerista psychotherapists help their clients to engage in a critical analysis of what is personal and what is sociopolitical. Within this perspective, a womanist/mujerista healing involves a soul-making process, infused by a knowledge grounded in ethics. In this fashion, womanist and mujerista psychologists work within a holistic healing orientation to accompany their clients, witness testimonies, speak words of truth, and foster spiritual development. They attest to the power of self-naming and healing properties as psychopolitical aspects of the development of a womanist identity. Moreover, these psychologists use *testimonio* as an eloquent example of a womanist mujerista healing, inquiry, and social activism.

In the name of spirit, womanist and mujerista psychologists help women of color to retrieve their souls. Within this context, *soul retrieval* refers to the holistic healing of soul wounds and the promotion of liberation. Indeed, healing and liberation are two streams that flow throughout the chapters in this volume. Additionally, the chapters offer examples of a psychospiritual healing, restoration, and renewal. Moreover, they embrace a collective healing orientation and, thus, honor the wellness of the community.

In addition to theory and practice, womanist and mujerista psychologists use research methods to explore women of color's integration of mind, body, spirit, and community. Notwithstanding these inquiry approaches, the expansion of womanist and mujerista psychologies' investigative methods needs more development. Drawing on this assertion, womanist and mujerista psychologists need to integrate quantitative research into approaches congruent with women of color's worldviews. In other words, these research methods require to bridge psychology, spirituality, and social justice (Chapter 8). That is, psychologists need to focus on techniques for generating knowledge addressing social justice concerns, including sensitivity to power dynamics, at every stage of the inquiry process. As they promote healing and development, womanist and mujerista psychologists follow their words of fire with acts of courage.

ACTS OF COURAGE: LIBERATION AND SOCIAL ACTION

Womanist and mujerista psychologists subscribe to a racialized, gendered psychology of liberation. They help marginalized women to engage in conscientización (Freire, 1970) to become aware of their external and internal oppressions. Womanist and mujerista psychologists take a stance against racism, sexism, classism, and their intersection and, thus, commit to struggle against all kinds of oppression. In this process, they understand that liberation is incomplete until they work toward the liberation of everyone. As a result, womanist and mujerista psychologists engage in social spiritual justice action grounded in a deep culturally contextualized caring for the self, community, and humanity. Moreover, womanist and mujerista psychologists' social justice action reflects their commitment to eradicate racism, sexism, and oppression. In this fashion, they endorse activism.

Activism is a call to arms for womanist and mujeristas. Indeed, social justice action is a psychospiritual and ethical mandate for womanist mujerista psychologists. These psychologists embrace an inclusive spiritual activism of being in the world (Rodriguez, 2002). As such, the womanist and mujerista social action takes diverse forms, ranging from mothering, preaching, political participation, teaching, and writing, to creativity and generativity.

VISIONS: CREATIVITY AND GENERATIVITY

Womanist and mujerista psychologists help women of color to develop and enhance their visions. They foster women's dreams, aspiration, intuition, and creativity. Creativity among womanists and mujeristas bears spiritual, healing, and social activism functions. Indeed, womanist and mujerista psychologists understand that creativity elevates the spirit and enables women to redeem themselves, thrive, and soar. Certainly, creativity among women of color is a vehicle for awareness, resistance, empowerment, and healing (Chapter 7). Following these notions, creativity acts as an antidote against despair, anomie, and oppression. Moreover, *artivism* is a Latina feminist construct that designates the use of art for social justice action (Sandoval & Latorre, 2008). Diverse forms of creativity, including artivism, function as an activism that counters the negative images of African American women and Latinas. In this fashion, a womanist and mujerista creativity fosters collective liberation.

As an act of courage, generativity is a significant component of womanist and mujerista psychologies. In fact, tending and taking care of others is a womanist and mujerista principle (Cozart & Gordon, 2006). Following this line of reasoning, womanists and mujeristas are invested in the well-being of their children, families, communities, and humanity. As womanists exercise generativity, mujeristas work toward the well-being of the Latina/o community and the world. Moreover, as an illustration of generativity, womanist and mujerista leaders develop a type of prophetic vision, one that enables them to represent their communities in a powerful and successful manner (Chapter 11).

Under the aegis of generativity, many women of color are socialized in terms of race and gender identities from an early age at home, community, and society. In this fashion, they grow up learning from mothers, grandmothers, aunts, female relatives and role models, and other female figures, how to survive as a female of color in a racist and sexist society. Womanist and mujerista psychologists commit to generativity as they help women of color transcend the survivalist mode. Notably, they pledge to assist women's development of a healthy identity, cultural strengths, and spirituality. Moreover, they mentor clients into committing to social justice action. Within their generativity, psychological practitioners engage in teaching womanist and mujerista psychologies. Indeed, the common elements of womanist and mujerista pedagogics include critical analysis, anti-oppression stance, global solidarity, and political action. According to Harris (2013), teaching womanism is a revolutionary act that focuses on a race, gender, and class critical analysis of inequalities. Moreover, she added that a womanist pedagogy requires practitioners to work toward human transformation and a social justice ethically. Even more important, teaching womanist and mujerista psychologies involves the humanistic value of working towards the liberation of all people worldwide (Beauboeuf-Lafontant, 2002).

A WOMANIST/MUJERISTA GLOBAL PSYCHOLOGY

Womanist and mujerista psychologists are spiritual activists who endorse solidarity with oppressed individuals around the world. In this context, they acknowledge that we are all connected. For this reason, they commit to decolonization, social justice, and international human rights. Indeed, womanist and mujerista psychologists prefer to focus on global solidarity rather than on an exclusive feminist sisterhood. Therefore, international women's issues are of major concern to them. This awareness helps womanist and mujerista psychologists to speak against inequality, injustice, and violence against women around the world. Inspired by the womanist/mujerista mandate of caring (Cozart & Gordon, 2006), these feminists "hear" the cries of women in domestic violence, and those of girls and women raped and abused in war zones. They mourn for victims of gendercide, honor killings, dowry burnings, acid attacks, and other horrific attacks on women and girls. Moreover, womanist and mujerista psychologists witness the plights of refugee and trafficked girls and women. As a result, these psychologists extend their social justice activism into the international arena. In this way, they recognize that the lives of women are interrelated in a worldwide panorama. As a concrete example, what happens to an undocumented Latina affects the upper-middle-class White American woman who hires the undocumented woman's sister as a maid. Therefore, relative to mainstream feminism, womanist and mujerista psychologists use an inclusive lens to provide a transnational analysis of gender within the intersectionality of multiple oppressions. Furthermore, womanist and mujerista psychologists foster feminism beyond borders and without borders. To this end, they contribute to the development of transnational and international feminism.

Although womanists and mujeristas achieved prominence in the United States, these ideas have existed as unnamed forms for thousands of years throughout the world (Castillo, 2010; Maparyan, 2012). In the following sections, we present descriptions of the emergence of feminism in Africa and Latin America. We believe this historical trajectory may foresee the development of womanism and mujerismo in the international scenario.

A Psychological Exploration of African Womanism/Feminism

To create global change, international womanism is needed. From Uganda to the United States, greater collaboration is needed so that positive work can be done locally, nationally, and globally to dismantle oppression (Mbire-Barungi, 1999). As there is diversity of cultures across the continent of Africa, there is diversity in the perspectives of African womanism(s) and feminism(s) (Steyn, 1998). Although there has to be caution in not overgeneralizing or erasing cultural and ethnic considerations, womanists can agree on some key priorities globally, and we need to commit to working on them (Mbire-Barungi, 1999).

African women are very aware of the realities of gender inequality across the continent, and they have been engaged in a struggle to correct these injustices through grassroots activism, the dissemination of information, and policy creation (Coquery-Vidrovitch & Raps, 1997). The core ideas of womanism and feminism are not new in Africa. Even before the specific English words *feminism* and *womanism* were uttered in Africa, African women had a long history of fighting patriarchy (Salami, 2013). Historically, African womanists included women who fought alongside men in wars, as well as women political leaders, advocates, mothers, teachers, and other activists. In contemporary times, the influence of African womanist thought can be seen in multiple issues, such as addressing the high rates of intimate partner abuse, poverty, HIV/AIDS, female circumcision, sexual assault, and human trafficking.

In the early 20th century, womanist groups existed across Africa even when they were not using the term *womanist*, such as the Bantu Women's Club and the Egyptian Feminist Group.

The goal of the United Nations Decade for Women was the promotion of equal rights and opportunities for women around the world (Mioko & Jennison, 1985). Three large international meetings were held to strategize solutions for issues such as pay equity, violence against women, landholding, and basic human rights. Today African womanist scholars, activists, artists, politicians, and psychologists have formed and sustained a number of organizations, including the African Feminist Forum and the African Gender Institute.

One of many outlets for psychological womanist transformation in African societies is the school system. In South Africa, Skelton and Francis (2008) argued that the school is a site where positive gender relations should be promoted and modeled. African feminism in education systems in Botswana highlight the ways transformational learning requires the recognition that gender roles and gender expectations influence the way people process knowledge; essentially, marginalizing voices and experiences reduces the opportunity for new insights. Okhamafe (1989) argued that African feminism is needed to confront not only the influence of oppressive forces and socioeconomic realities but also the psychological realities of intimacy, loneliness, and the role of marriage (Ntseane, 2011).

Seven primary agenda points have been consistently attributed to African feminists or womanists, although they have many other perspectives and focus areas: (a) dismantle the psychological and political system of patriarchy; (b) undo the gender-specific burdens of race-based oppression in the form of colonialism, imperialism, and racialized trauma; (c) adapt cultural traditions that are disadvantageous to women—such as patriarchal polygamy, genital cutting, widow abuse, and barriers to women's property rights—in ways that honor culture and preserve women's rights; (d) develop Africa financially and politically, recognizing that poverty multiplies negative consequences for women; (e) dismantle mindsets that seek to control and suppress women's sexuality including the sexuality of African lesbians; (f) build collaborations for a global feminism/womanism, particularly with Latina and Asian feminists/womanists; and (g) infuse love in all that is done, including in the expressive arts and in the pursuit of justice for the purposes of radical transformation, decolonization of minds, depatriarchalizing of minds, and the creation of new healing traditions. All of these priorities are directed at achieving spiritual, social, economic, racial, gender, and psychological equality. Salami (2011) presented many of these points in psychological terms.

A Psychological Exploration of Latina Feminism/ Mujerismo in Latin America

Feminism in Latin America is a unique endeavor, as it differs from the feminism in the United States and Europe in that it opposes the severely oppressive political and socioeconomic realities pervasive in a class-oriented society (Carr, 1990). Specifically, Latin American feminists strive for political participation, social class equality, human rights, and reproductive justice health. An iconic example is *Las Madres de la Plaza de Mayo*, the Argentine human rights women's group who emerged to protest the disappearance of people (*desaparecidos*) during Argentina's Dirty War (Comas-Díaz, 2008).

As discussed in this volume's introductory chapter, some Latin American feminists criticized the term *mujerismo*, labeling it divisive. In this way, early Latin American feminism neglected the intersectionality of multiple oppressions among women, leading to the invisibility of marginalized groups of women. Because socioeconomic class, race, and gender are intimately related in Latin America (i.e., poverty is associated with being dark and/or indigenous), original Latin American feminism did not include LatiNegras (Afro Latinas; Comas-Díaz, 2003) or indigenous women. However, the face of Latin America feminism is currently changing. While Afro Latinas create their own brand of feminism of color, indigenous (Mapuche, Mayan, Quechua, Quiche, and others) women fight for their political and human rights, giving birth to an indigenous feminism (Charleswell, 2014). Additionally, Uruguayan feminists fight against cyber machismo, and Salvadoran feminists oppose laws that jail women who have had a miscarriage (Rogers, 2015). Moreover, groups of Peruvian feminists endorse a *Pachamama* (Inca goddess) syncretistic ecofeminism and transfeminism. Furthermore, Chilean feminists formed *Con-spirando* (to conspire), a post-Christian goddess-oriented feminist group (Vuola, 2002), to integrate feminism, spirituality and politics.

Womanist and mujerista psychologies offer a feminist shelter to groups of marginalized women in Latin America. To illustrate, contemporary Latin American feminists are joining U.S. Latina feminists to infuse transnational *conocimiento* into global feminism. For instance, Maria Lugones (2015), a self-named mixed-race indigenous feminist Argentine woman, advanced the concept of coloniality of gender (Lugones, 2008) to explain how the colonial/modern system ranks women as inferior to men, leading to the disruption of solidarity between women and men.

Womanista

Out of the aforementioned international developments, a global feminism of color could emerge. For instance, when womanist and mujerista psychologists nurture the development of a coalitional consciousness, they pledge to be accountable to themselves, their communities, and to the world. *Womanista* (a combination of womanist and mujerista) could serve as a banner to guide the emergence of an international feminist of color psychology. A womanista psychology could address the personal and collective plight of oppressed women around the world. A challenge of a womanista global psychology, however, is to provide enough flexibility to accommodate the diversity and complexity of oppressed individuals throughout the world.

SPIRIT: PRAYER AND PSYCHOPOLITICAL MANIFESTO

As we conclude this volume, we are compelled to go beyond theoretical, practical, and research implications. To honor womanist and mujerista values, we cannot end without offering a prayer and a political manifesto in recognition of the spiritual and political roots of both psychologies. Given our roots in psychology, the prayer is for the liberation of minds and the manifesto is psycho–spiritual–political in nature.

Prayer

Great Spirit, who transcends time and is present in this very moment
Holy Spirit, who is reflected in the beauty, wisdom, and strength of women of African descent and Latinas
Mother Father Creator, whose love flows to all across race, gender, economic, and sexuality lines
We bring before you our mothers, our sisters, our daughters, and ourselves
We bring before you our fathers, our brothers, and our sons
We pray that we would be transformed by the renewing of our minds
We pray that insecurity, fear, shame, doubt, and anger will not consume us
We pray that emotionally, mentally, and spiritually we would be able to resist everything that seeks to dishonor us
We pray that we would oppose division and live in unity one with another
We pray that within our families and communities addictions are broken and that destructive thinking and habits are unable to dictate our lives
We pray that there will be an outbreak of thriving, growth, and empowerment that defies the negative predictions that are made about our people
We pray that like the great women who came before us, you will awaken us so we may live with courage
We pray that your Divine Love will cancel out injustice, oppression, and self-sabotage
We pray that you will speak to us and through us so that our radiance would not be diminished
We pray that we would be mentally free to know, love, and accept ourselves and our daughters and sons
We pray that you would work through us to create safe spaces for us to rest, heal, reflect, remember, envision, and soar
May our hope be restored. May our fire continue to burn. May our minds, bodies, and spirits know wellness.
Let it be so and so it is. Amen. Asha. We agree.

Psychopolitical Manifesto

We call for an end to the political disenfranchisement, labor exploitation, miseducation, and physical and mental health disparities of women of African descent and Latinas in the United States and globally.

We call for the end of violence against women, namely, sexual violence, intimate partner abuse, child abuse, community violence, stalking, harassment, human trafficking, and modern-day slavery.

We call for the end of the trauma of oppression, including but not limited to classism, racism, sexism, able-bodyism, heterosexism, and ageism.

We cancel the social acceptance of misnaming and mistreating African and Latina women as subservient sexual and labor objects.

We reclaim our right to name ourselves, define ourselves, and speak for ourselves.

We call for the end of color-blind, gender-blind therapy that ignores our sociocultural context.

We call for psychological consultants to stop assuming to know us better than we know ourselves.

We call for the end of psychological research that ignores or pathologizes us, refusing to acknowledge our strengths and resources.

We call for the end of invisibility and tokenism in the leadership of psychological organizations that marginalize women of African descent and Latinas.

We demand psychological training programs that prioritize training in cultural respect, including attention to race, gender, socioeconomic status, sexuality, disability, migration status, age, and religious/spiritual orientation.

We require psychologists to become familiar with the contribution, sacrifice, struggles, and victories of women of African descent and Latinas.

We mandate that attention be given to the psychological, social, emotional, financial, physical, and spiritual costs of societal oppression, with all of its intersecting forms, and that program development, research, and funding priority be given to the redress of these costs.

We decree that psychologists who are unwilling to look at themselves, including their identity, biases, power, privilege, and socialization processes are ill-equipped to effectively serve women of African descent and Latinas.

We declare that women of African descent and Latinas have cultural healing resources and systems of support that need to be acknowledged, respected, and integrated into any plan for their care, healing, and growth.

We declare that women of African descent and Latinas have wisdom, strength, need, humanity, spirit, and artistic capabilities that should be attended to and cultivated.

We declare that women of African descent and Latinas are worthy and deserving of life-affirming, dignity-affirming care, and undiluted empowerment.

We invite women of African descent and Latinas to unmask from internalized oppression, refuse the costume given to us by racist patriarchy, return to sender the stereotypes that have been fed to us since childhood, dismantle the socialization messages that require our silence and objectification, disrupt the script that requires that we remain in the margins of our own stories.

We invite women of African descent and Latinas to embrace only those things, habits, and people that promote your peace and well-being and to pursue your wellness.

We invite women of African descent and Latinas to reclaim their voice, spirit, art, minds, bodies, hearts, dreams, visions, families, communities, and political power.

We invite women of African descent and Latinas to make time to roar and to make time to rest.

Let justice come. Let equality come. Let wellness come.

REFERENCES

Anzaldúa, G. (1987). *Borderlands/La Frontera: The new Mestiza*. San Francisco, CA: Spinster/Aunt Lute Publishers.

Beauboeuf-Lafontant, T. (2002). A womanist experience of caring: Understanding the pedagogy of exemplary Black women teachers. *The Urban Review, 34*, 71–86. http://dx.doi.org/10.1023/A:1014497228517

Carr, I. C. (1990). Women's voices grow stronger: Politics and feminism in Latin America. *NWSA Journal, 2*, 450–463.

Castillo, R. A. (2010). The emergence of Indigenous feminism in Latin America. *Chicago Journals, 35*, 539–545.

Charleswell, C. (2014, October 17). *Latina feminism: National and transnational perspectives*. Retrieved from http://www.hamptoninstitution.org/latina-feminism.html#.VbpwPRzUPRg

Comas-Díaz, L. (2003). LatiNegros: Afro Latinos' quest for identity. In M. Root & M. Kelley (Eds.), *Multiracial child resource book* (pp. 168–177). Seattle, WA: Mavin Foundation.

Comas-Díaz, L. (2008). *Spirita*: Reclaiming womanist sacredness in feminism. *Psychology of Women Quarterly, 32*, 13–21. http://dx.doi.org/10.1111/j.1471-6402.2007.00403.x

Coquery-Vidrovitch, C., & Raps, B. G. (1997). *African women: A modern history*. Boulder, CO: Westview Press.

Cozart, A. C., & Gordon, J. (2006). Using womanist caring as a framework to teach social foundations. *The High School Journal, 90*, 9–15. http://dx.doi.org/10.1353/hsj.2006.0010

Freire, P. (1970). *Pedagogy of the oppressed*. New York, NY: Seabury Press.

Harris, M. L. (2013). *Teaching womanism is a revolutionary act*. Retrieved from http://www.ecclesio.com/2013/02/teaching-womanism-is-a-revolutionary-act-by-melanie-l-harris/

Lugones, M. (2008). The coloniality of gender. *Worlds & Knowledge Otherwise*, 1–17. Retrieved from https://globalstudies.trinity.duke.edu/wp-content/themes/cgsh/materials/WKO/v2d2_Lugones.pdf

Lugones, M. (2015, April 11). *Mestizaje and communality*. Keynote address at The Feminist Architecture of Gloria Anzaldúa: New Translation, Crossings, and Pedagogies in Anzaldúan Thought. Institute for Humanities Research, University of California, Santa Cruz.

Maparyan, L. (2012). *The womanist idea*. New York, NY: Routledge.

Mbire-Barungi, B. (1999). Ugandan feminism: Political rhetoric or reality? *Women's Studies International Forum, 22*, 435–439. http://dx.doi.org/10.1016/S0277-5395(99)00037-0

Mioko, F., & Jennison, R. (1985). The UN Decade for Women and Japan: Tools for change. *Women's Studies International Forum, 8*, 121–123. http://dx.doi.org/10.1016/0277-5395(85)90057-3

Ntseane, P. G. (2011). Culturally sensitive transformational learning: Incorporating the Afrocentric paradigm and African feminism. *Adult Education Quarterly, 61*, 307–323. http://dx.doi.org/10.1177/0741713610389781

Okhamafe, E. I. (1989). African feminism(s) and the question of marital and non-marital loneliness and intimacy. *SAGE: A Scholarly Journal on Black Women, 6*, 33–39.

Rodriguez, J. (2002). Latina activists: Toward an inclusive spirituality of being in the world. In M. P. Aquino, D. L. Machado, & J. Rodriguez (Eds.), *A reader in Latina feminist theology* (pp. 114–130). Austin: University of Texas Press.

Rogers, T. (2015). *Meet the young feminists who make it happen in Latin America and the Caribbean*. Retrieved from http://fusion.net/story/56314/this-is-what-it-means-to-be-a-young-feminist-in-a-machista-society/

Salami, M. (2011). Seven key issues in African feminist thought. Ms. *Afropolitan*. Retrieved from http://www.msafropolitan.com/2012/08/7-key-issues-in-african-feminist-thought.html

Salami, M. (2013). A brief history of African feminism. Ms. *Afropolitan*. Retrieved from http://www.msafropolitan.com/2013/07/a-brief-history-of-african-feminism.html

Sandoval, C., & Latorre, G. (2008). Chicana/o artivism: Judy Baca's digital work with youth of color. In A. Everett (Ed.), *Learning race and ethnicity: Youth and digital media* (pp. 81–108). Cambridge, MA: MIT Press.

Skelton, C., & Francis, B. (2008). *Feminism and "the schooling scandal."* London, England: Routledge.

Steyn, M. (1998). A new agenda: Restructuring feminism in South Africa. *Women's Studies International Forum*, *21*, 41–52. http://dx.doi.org/10.1016/S0277-5395(97)00086-1

Vuola, E. (2002). *Limits of liberation: Feminist theology and the ethics of poverty and reproduction*. New York, NY: Sheffield Academic Press.

INDEX

ABOUT THE EDITORS

Thema Bryant-Davis, PhD, is an associate professor of psychology at Pepperdine University. She was the 2015 recipient of the California Psychological Association Distinguished Scientist Award. She is also a past president of the Society for the Psychology of Women and a former American Psychological Association (APA) representative to the United Nations. She received the Early Career Distinguished Contributions to Psychology in the Public Service award. Dr. Bryant-Davis is the director of the Culture and Trauma Research Lab at Pepperdine University and a past associate editor of the journal *Psychological Trauma*. Her work has been published in numerous peer-reviewed journals, and she is the author of *Thriving in the Wake of Trauma: A Multicultural Guide* and coeditor of *Surviving Sexual Violence: A Handbook of Recovery and Empowerment* and *Foundations of Resilience: Religion and Spirituality in Diverse Women's Lives*. A licensed clinical psychologist, Dr. Bryant-Davis earned her doctorate from Duke University and completed her postdoctoral training at Harvard Medical Center. Her research focus areas include trauma psychology, ethnic minority women, oppression, coping, and spirituality. She is a contributing author to APA's resolution against racism, xenophobia, and intolerance. *ESSENCE* magazine named her among women who are shaping the world.

Lillian Comas-Díaz, PhD, focuses her academic, professional, and personal work on multiculturalism, feminism, spirituality, and mental health. She developed a Latino community mental health program in Connecticut, was a faculty member at the Yale University Psychiatry Department, became the director of the Yale University Hispanic Clinic, directed APA's Office of Ethnic Minority Affairs, and cofounded the Transcultural Mental Health Institute. Currently, Dr. Comas-Díaz is a psychologist in private practice and a clinical professor at George Washington University's Department of Psychiatry and Behavioral Sciences. With more than 150 publications, her recent books include *Multicultural Care: A Clinician's Guide to Cultural Competence*; *Psychological Health of Women of Color: Intersections, Challenges and Opportunities* (with B. Greene); *Women Psychotherapists' Reflections on Female Friendships* (with M. Weiner); and *Women Psychotherapists: Journeys in Healing* (with M. Weiner).